CITY LIMITS: CRIME, CONSUMER CULTURE AND THE URBAN EXPERIENCE

Keith J Hayward

Lecturer, School of Social Policy,
Sociology and Social Research,
University of Kent, Canterbury

glasshouse press

London • Sydney • Portland, Oregon

First published in Great Britain 2004 by
The GlassHouse Press, The Glass House,
Wharton Street, London WC1X 9PX, United Kingdom
Telephone: + 44 (0)20 7278 8000   Facsimile: + 44 (0)20 7278 8080
Email: info@cavendishpublishing.com
Website: www.cavendishpublishing.com

Published in the United States by Cavendish Publishing
c/o International Specialized Book Services,
5824 NE Hassalo Street, Portland,
Oregon 97213-3644, USA

Published in Australia by The GlassHouse Press,
45 Beach Street, Coogee, NSW 2034, Australia
Telephone: + 61 (2)9664 0909   Facsimile: +61 (2)9664 5420
Email: info@cavendishpublishing.com.au
Website: www.cavendishpublishing.com.au

British Library Cataloguing in Publication Data
Hayward, Keith J
City limits: crime, consumer culture and the urban experience
1 Crime 2 Consumption (Economics) – sociological aspects
I Title
364.2'5

Library of Congress Cataloguing in Publication Data
Data available

ISBN 1-90438-503-6

1 3 5 7 9 10 8 6 4 2

Printed and bound in Great Britain

To my parents – Maureen and Peter Hayward
– with much love and thanks

Acknowledgments

Some books, it is said, 'write themselves' – the present volume is not one of them. Right from the outset this book has been a struggle; a long, drawn out personal and theoretical journey that, more than once, looked like it might never end. Consequently, it is with palpable relief that I pen these final few words of acknowledgment and thanks to the many people who have helped me arrive – not a moment too soon – at this position of closure. Any errors or infelicities, of course, are mine alone.

To start with, I must record my tremendous thanks to my friend and publisher Beverley Brown. A detailed account of the various ways in which Beverley helped with this project would require a separate volume. Suffice it to say that without her exhaustive comments and insights, *City Limits* would not have been finished. Like Beverley, Wayne Morrison was also in at the inception of the project all those years ago. His stimulating ideas and indefatigable nature never fail to amaze me. Jock Young was a source of much inspiration – I'm grateful to him for his support and friendship. Likewise, being exposed to Jeff Ferrell's world of anarchic creativity proved both challenging and thought-provoking. By staying true to his personal mantra, 'Live like it matters', Jeff's life and criminology stand as a refreshing antidote to what passes for much criminological 'knowledge' today. On the subject of mottos, in the highly unlikely event that Mike Presdee were ever to have a family crest, it would surely bear the Latin inscription *Non illigitamus carborundum*. Thanks Mike and Gill for all the dinners, drinks and late night chats. I am also deeply grateful to Mark Fenwick for providing me with some direction way back when I should have been writing about urban regeneration but was instead self-indulgently exploring the poetics of Baudelaire. He helped me plot (something akin to) a course through those difficult 'early years' of academic life when everything seems so daunting.

Many other academic friends also influenced (or corrupted – depending on your perspective) the following pages: Colin Sumner gave theoretical criminology historical colour and sociological context long before cultural criminology had gathered any theoretical traction; Richard Jones and Wendy Chan provided wise counsel from afar – my thanks to them; John Muncie gave me my first real writing break – so he's as much to blame as anyone. Thanks also to Ken Tunnell and Mark Hamm for playing it like they mean it; to my former colleagues, Elizabeth Stokes, John Strawson, Stephanie Eaton and Jane Pickford, at the School of Law, University of East London; and to UCLA professors Rick Abel and Eric Monkonnen, who provided me with assistance and advice during my research trip to Los Angeles in 1998.

I would also like to express my thanks to the majority of my colleagues in the School of Social Policy, Sociology and Social Research at the University of Kent. You don't need to have read any Georg Simmel to know that it can be difficult finding your feet in a new city – even one as friendly and village-like as Canterbury! In this sense I am especially grateful to Iain Wilkinson, Frank Furedi and Azrini Wahidin. Their friendship allowed me to overcome the withdrawal symptoms I felt on leaving behind the edgy urban underworlds of London's Shoreditch, Whitechapel and Bethnal Green – after all, it was on the streets of these neighbourhoods that many of the ideas for this book first surfaced.

On the subject of urban influences, my time spent in Columbus, Ohio, San Francisco and various other US cities also played an important part in shaping my thinking about city life. Looking back, it was here that I was first exposed to what one might describe as a form of proto cultural criminology (not that such a term would ever have been used). Working in pool halls and record shops, driving tour buses and hanging out with musicians taught me a great deal about how crime and culture readily collapse into each other. Thanks, then, to the likes of Mike Hummel, Dan Dow, Colin Harris, Jordan Shlain and, most of all, Dave Diemer ('The Captain') for broadening my horizons.

Numerous other friends also helped in many unseen ways; thanks to Frank Palser for his friendship and for the subsidised rent during the impoverished studentship years; Chris Cathey and Andy Burnham for providing regular breaks from writing; Famke and the family van Heel for good companionship; Kester Aspden for his humour and his sense of the bizarre – criminology's loss is church history's gain! Thanks also to my 'legal team', James Henderson, Adam Atkinson and Harry Steinberg, for happy times in disparate locations. In another place, far away from academia, Owen Neal and Dave Pritchard always showed an interest in what I was doing – my thanks to them. Les Bilsberry was a superb art teacher, and whilst I'm not weighed down by fond memories of my school days, I recognise that my interest in art had much to do with him. Thanks also to my editor Jon Lloyd and the nice people at Glass House Press.

Finally, I must thank my parents for their support, and for affording me the time and space to arrive – albeit somewhat circuitously – at this point.

Keith Hayward
March 2004

Illustration Acknowledgments

Grateful acknowledgment is made to the following persons and organisations for granting permission to reproduce the following material in this work:

The Nelson-Atkins Museum of Art, Kansas City, Missouri, for allowing the reproduction of Claude Monet's *Boulevard des Capucines*.

The National Gallery of Art, Washington DC, for allowing reproduction of *The Lone Tenement* by George Bellows.

The Ludwig Meidner-Archiv, Jeudisches Museum der Stadt Frankfurt am Main, for allowing the reproduction of Ludwig Meidner's *I and the City*.

The Museo Thyssen-Bornemisza, Madrid, for allowing the reproduction of George Grosz's *The Big City*.

The Indianapolis Museum of Art, William Ray Adams Fund, for allowing the reproduction of Edward Hopper's *The Hotel Lobby*.

Martin Creed for allowing the reproduction of Work No 203: *EVERYTHING IS GOING TO BE ALRIGHT* by Martin Creed.

Peter Davies, The Saatchi Gallery, London, and the Gagosian Gallery for allowing the reproduction of *The Hip One Hundred*.

Richard Prince and The Barbara Gladstone Gallery for allowing the reproduction of *Tell Me Everything*.

Sean Landers and the Andrea Rosen Gallery, New York, for allowing the reproduction of *Self-Something*.

Tom Sachs and the Tom Sachs Studio for allowing the reproduction of *Prada Toilet*.

The Home Office Stationary Office for permission to reproduce Figures 4.4 and 4.5 from Sheena Wilson's article 'Vandalism and "defensible space" on London housing estates', in Clarke, RVG and Mayhew, P (1980) *Designing Out Crime*, London: HMSO.

Thanks to Kenwood Electronics for allowing us to reproduce their advertisement for their car stereo, Model KDC 8021.

Every effort has been made to trace all the copyright holders, but if any have been inadvertently overlooked, the publishers will be pleased to make the necessary arrangements at the first opportunity.

Contents

Acknowledgments | v
Illustration Acknowledgments | vii
List of Plates | xi

Introduction | 1

1   **Imagining the Urban Experience** | 17

2   **City Life at Modernity's Edge: A *Tour d'Horizon*** | 47

3   **The Forgotten City and the Lost Offender** | 87

4   **Fear and Desire in Los Angeles** | 113

5   **Crime, Consumer Culture and the Urban Experience** | 147

Conclusion | 197

Bibliography | 201

Index | 235

List of Plates

Plate 1 Claude Monet, *Boulevard des Capucines* (1873–74)

Plate 2 George Bellows, *The Lone Tenement* (1909)

Plate 3 Ludwig Meidner, *I and the City* (1913)

Plate 4 George Grosz, *The Big City* (1917)

Plate 5 Edward Hopper, *Hotel Lobby* (1943)

Plate 6 Martin Creed (1999), Work No 203: *EVERYTHING IS GOING TO BE ALRIGHT* by Martin Creed

Plate 7 Peter Davies, *The Hip One Hundred* (1998)

Plate 8 Richard Prince, *Tell Me Everything* (1987)

Plate 9 Sean Landers, *Self-Something* (1994)

Plate 10 Tom Sachs, *Prada Toilet* (1997)

Plate 11 *New York in the Desert*, New York, New York Casino, Las Vegas, Nevada

Plate 12 Figures 4.4 and 4.5, Sheena Wilson 'Vandalism and "defensible space" on London housing estates'

Plate 13 *Ecology of Fear* by Mike Davis

Plate 14 *Parafunctional Space 1*

Plate 15 *Parafunctional Space 2*

Plate 16 Advertisement for Kenwood car stereos (2001)

Plate 17 Defaced billboard, corner of Cambridge Heath Road and Whitechapel Road, East London

The markets suck us (willingly) out of our cosy, dull niches and turn us into unencumbered actors, mobile in a system, but setting us free they leave us exposed. We feel vulnerable. (Mary Douglas 1992: 15)

Late modernity is a world of increased difficulty and diversity ... To know that there are indeed other ways of doing things which in their own world are considered just as everyday as one's own takes away security. The plethora of worlds presented to the citizen of late modernity seeks to make every citizen into his or her own phenomenologist! (Jock Young 1999: 98)

In the popular imagination, images of crime and the city are closely connected, yet the exact nature of this relationship remains enigmatic. In the 18th century the perception was of innocent rural migrants preyed upon by urban deceit; in the 19th century the picture was class-based and distinguished between the reformable and the unreformable ('deserving' and 'undeserving') urban poor; by the early decades of the 20th century, especially in the United States, the theme of migration resurfaced, but this time with the immigrant cast as the potential criminal. It is to the credit of 20th century socio-criminological theories of crime that this popular image was turned around to become a claim about the particular kind of city environment that new immigrants inhabited. This book continues the long criminological tradition of unravelling the complexities of the 'crime-city nexus', with the specific aim of identifying the myriad forms of relationships that exist between the contemporary 'urban experience', certain forms of criminal behaviour, and the particular social forces and cultural dynamics that one associates with *late modern consumer culture*.

As an object of study, the city is a composite of a physical domain of bricks and mortar, the broader macro cultural and structural forces that determine our relationship to and role within the city and, importantly (and too often neglected in criminological accounts of the city), the everyday round of urban life – the practicalities, prosaic routines, anxieties and changeable moods that punctuate our existence and serve to make up our biographical lives within the city. The primary assertion here is that, in each of these distinct yet interrelated spheres, late modern consumer culture is bringing about significant change and that, moreover, these transformations, whether manifest or surreptitious, can be seen in several important respects as contributing to the contemporary urban crime problem.

If we are successfully to investigate the impact consumerism is having both on the physical and structural nature of urban space and also at the level of individual subjective emotions – the hidden patterns of behaviour and the new and distinct forms of subjectivity precipitated and engendered by a fast-paced consumer society – we must first address the question of how the city or, more accurately, the 'urban experience' can be effectively conceptualised. Every city has its own character, its own feel and its own ambience. Some are elegant, some unsightly, some intimidating, and some mundane. Some are planned and imbued with imposed ideologies, while others are more organic and owe their spatial configuration to natural topography. All, however, irrespective of political ideology or national and cultural peculiarities, have at least one thing in common: from out of the cultural collision caused by any substantial concentration of people, industry and capital, emerges a congress of feelings, impressions and emotions that collectively constitute the urban experience.

In his highly inventive work, *The Practice of Everyday Life*, Michel de Certeau (1984) proposes a tentative framework for thinking about the experiential dimension of urban life. He suggests that if one adopts a type of *distant view* of the city – an abstract 'gaze' that 'lifts one out of the city's grasp' and transforms one into an isolated observer, a 'voyeur' (*ibid*: 92)[1] – it becomes possible, indeed beneficial, to think of the city in terms of a *duality*. On the one hand, there is the 'Concept-city' – a product of what de Certeau calls 'utopian and urbanistic discourse'. This is the city as seen by planners, developers, statisticians and, all too often, criminologists. Here the pluralistic fabric and contradictions inherent in urban life – the other side of the duality – are distilled to leave only quantitative data, demographics and rational discourse. On the other hand, de Certeau suggests that no city can be thought of in such purely conceptual terms. Importantly, de Certeau argues that one also needs to consider the *experiential dimension* of urban existence:

> The problem, de Certeau finds, is that the life of the city, the constellation of lives that make a city what it is, the actual experience of the city, in other words, is not contained in the concept of the city. Lives cannot be mapped in this way – cannot be read – or even truly rendered readable by maps (though of course it is only through maps that they can be read): something always slips away. (Buchanan 2000: 110)

Any understanding (or 'mapping') of urban space must therefore place great store in the multi-layered interactivity that takes place at 'street level', the cultural and social dimensions of everyday city-life that enable the formation of a very different interpretative framework: 'Beneath the discourses that ideologize the city, the ruses and combinations of powers that have no readable identity proliferate; without points where one can take hold of them, without rational transparency, they are impossible to administer' (de Certeau 1984: 95). De Certeau was surely correct to suggest that the contemporary city can only really be understood in terms of this duality – not least because that is how it is produced – for the urban experience is a composite of both the formal, rational organising principles of the conceptual 'planned' city, and the subjective and mythical dimensions of what one might call the 'experiential city'.[2]

This duality is also sharply reflected in many of the cultural practices and social dynamics associated with late modern consumerism – indeed, one of the central themes of this work is that consumer culture is best conceptualised in just such dichotomous terms (see Edwards 2000). However, to understand the inherently

---

1 Miles (1997: 19) asserts that de Certeau's 'gaze' on/at the city suggests a similarity with Michel Foucault's formulation in *The Birth of the Clinic* (1973) of the 'medical gaze', which many other writers, for better or for worse, have associated with Foucault's later concept of 'surveillance'.

2 I am indebted to James Donald's lucid essay 'Metropolis: the city as text' (1992) for framing de Certeau's ideas in this manner. For more on the notion of (the city as) 'duality', see Merleau-Ponty's (1962) analytic distinction between 'geometric space' and (the more phenomenologically grounded) 'anthropological space'; and Jonathan Raban's (1974) dual construct of the 'hard city' of buildings and statistics, and the 'soft city' of 'experience, of illusion, myth, aspiration [and] nightmare'.

contradictory nature of 'consumer culture', one must first be clear about what exactly this term means.

If one wishes to understand contemporary society (and particularly urban society), it is essential to understand the role of consumer culture (for a general overview of the literature in this area, see Lury 1996; Slater 1997; Miles 1998a). For many social theorists (eg, Baudrillard 1970, 1981; Bauman 1992, 1998; Campbell 1989; Featherstone 1994), the culture of consumption is now the most distinctive feature of advanced Western societies.[3] Two major consequences flow from this situation. The first thing to recognise is the extent to which consumerism has permeated all levels of society. The vast majority of people in the industrialised West now live in a world in which their everyday existence is, to a greater or lesser degree, dominated by the pervasive triad of advertising/marketing, the stylisation of social life, and mass consumption. As Philip Sampson has commented: 'Once established, such a culture of consumption is quite undiscriminating and everything becomes a consumer item, including meaning, truth and knowledge' (Sampson quoted in Lyon 1994a: 61). Importantly, in characterising contemporary society as a consumer culture, I am not referring to particular patterns of needs and objects – a particular consumption culture – but rather to a *culture of consumption* (see Fromm 1976; Lasch 1979).[4] *To talk this way is to regard the dominant values of society as deriving from the activity of consumption.*[5]

At this point it is important to address the latent question that constantly overshadows discussions of late (or post) modern consumerism: specifically, how is all this different from classic Marxist accounts of capitalist commodification and the increasing subjection of all aspects of life to mediation through the cash nexus? For example, long before terms such as 'late' or 'post' modernity were being popularised, Raymond Williams (1974, 1981) – echoing the classical tradition of the Frankfurt School (notably Horkheimer and Adorno 1973) – was urging orthodox Marxists toward the study of culture and, in particular, the way that society's needs were increasingly being drawn into the market-place. One important answer can be found in the recent work of Ian Taylor. In a characteristically succinct passage that speaks volumes about the increasing pervasiveness of consumer culture, Taylor asserts that the key difference lies in the fact that 'the "market" is now a *fundamental* motor force in contemporary social and political discourse and practice, in a way that it was not in the 1970s. The market is *hegemonic* in the realm of discourse, and in very many practices (including some domains of that most resistant area of all, the public sector)' (1999: 54). Furthermore, Taylor also makes it clear that currently there is no viable 'oppositional culture' strong enough to challenge the inexorable rise of 'market culture' (compare Ferrell 2001 on various emerging forms of oppositional culture).

---

3 Obviously, the work of the Frankfurt School should also be seen as part of this tradition.

4 Although the present book does not expressly engage with the work of Herbert Marcuse, Eric Fromm and Christopher Lasch, it does acknowledge the range and depth of these works and the centrality of their ideas to subsequent writings on consumer culture.

5 On the subtle distinctions between the terms 'consumerism', 'consumer culture', 'consumer society' and 'consumption', see Edwards (2000: Chapter 1).

I should perhaps make clear at this juncture my own particular position regarding Marxism in what is after all a critique of 'market culture'. The first thing to state is that the present work is not intended as an anti-Marxist statement. By the same token, neither is it rooted in any sense of structured political ideology or analysis of economics. Rather, the locus of dispute is between a type of Marxism that is capable of taking on board the fundamental shift to the 'consumer society' (and thus is able to work through the full implications of this situation) and one that either cannot or chooses not to. In this sense, this book can be seen as following the discursive line of inquiry set down by Zygmunt Bauman, Frederic Jameson and David Harvey (see Chapter 2). In particular, the way each of these theorists locates the important cultural and economic transformations of recent years – I am referring here, of course, to the transformation from production-based society to one increasingly predicated on consumption and its associated values – within the framework of contemporary 'postmodern' debates.[6]

The second important thing to stress (again diverging from classic Marxist accounts) regarding the cultural significance of market culture is the continued move towards consumption as a *mode of expression*. Again, at one level, this may not seem intrinsically new; after all, conspicuous consumption has long-established antecedents (see Mukerji 1983 on 15th and 16th century Europe; McKendrick *et al* 1982 on 18th century England; and Veblen 1925 – the first to use the concept – on the 19th century American industrial and commercial bourgeoisie; see also Williams 1982; Campbell 1989; Bocock 1993: Chapter 1; and Glennie 1995 for a concise overview).[7] However, what is unique about the last few decades of the 20th century is the way that creation and expression of identity via the display and celebration of consumer goods (see Ewen 1988; Campbell 1995: 114–17; Lury 1996) has triumphed over and above other more traditional modes of self-expression (on this specific point see Bauman 1998). Anderson and Wadkins explain:

> In a culture of consumption, the collective focus is on self definition through the purchase of goods. Status differentials are based less on one's role in the productive sphere than on one's ability to consume. Social relations are mediated through objects. ... As group affiliation at work is replaced by individual achievement, and the role of the family as a source of ascribed status is lessened, individuals attempt to differentiate themselves through their 'lifestyles', a term which largely connotes consumption patterns. (1992: 149–50)

6 Very few commentators, it seems, are completely comfortable with the concept of 'postmodernity', which has been plagued by ambiguity, imprecision and debate. Such arguments look set to persist, but what should not be obscured by this theoretical imbroglio is the fundamental fact that society continues to undergo a period of pronounced cultural change, and that whether or not it heralds the onset of an entirely new domain, it does, in my opinion, mark a break (if not a paradigm shift) with what has gone before. Of the various semantics used to characterise the significant economic, social and cultural transformations of the last few decades (ie, postmodernity, late modernity, late capitalism, post-Fordism, risk society, post-industrialism, etc), my personal preference is for the term late modernity (see Giddens 1991; and Garland and Sparks 2000: 198–200 in relation to criminology; see Chapter 2 for more on my particular position regarding these changes).

7 'Consumer culture' does not refer solely to expensive luxury or, more accurately, status goods. As Nava (1992) has pointed out, consumer culture also has much to do with the unprecedented cheapness of all sorts of commodities, even seemingly banal or oblique products.

This relationship between consumer goods and the construction of self in late modernity is of great importance. So encompassing is the ethos of consumerism within (late) capitalist society that, for many individuals, self-identity and self-realisation can now only be accomplished through material means – money (in the form of commodities) as 'self-laundering'? Thus, identity, as Christopher Lasch (1979) brilliantly pointed out, takes on the form of a 'consumption-oriented narcissism'. Twenty-five years after Lasch's seminal monograph, the full force of his message is only now being felt. In the school playground, the pub or restaurant, the nightclub and on the street corner, products and material possessions are now the primary indices of identity for virtually all strata of society, establishing status but, more importantly, imbuing individuals with a (narcissistic) sense of who they are. This is what it means to live in a consumer culture. More problematically, much street crime – from shoplifting to street robbery – should therefore be seen for exactly what it is: neither as a desperate act of poverty nor as a defiant gesture against the system, but nonetheless as a transgressive act that, at one level, enables a relative (or perceived) material deficit to be bridged and, at another level, represents a form of identity construction – if it's true of shopping then it's also true of shoplifting! Consequently, street criminals in many instances can be seen simply as consuming machines, 'urban entrepreneurs' whose primary aim is the accrual of the latest mobile phone or designer accessory[8] – items that in today's consumer society are no longer simply desirable but are importantly perceived (especially by young people) as essential to individual identity, shifting as that may be from moment to moment. However, before exploring any further the specific relationships that now exist between consumer culture and urban crime, we must return to the question of the inherently contradictory and dichotomous nature of late modern consumerism.

First, and most obviously, there is the question of whether the prevailing systems of consumption represent a positive or negative societal development. On one side of the debate there are those commentators who suggest that consumerism offers up potential social and economic benefits by engendering a sense of enhanced creativity, hedonism and 'self-actualisation'. They point to the pleasurable and emotional dimensions of expressing identity, autonomy and self-interest via the consumption and exhibition of goods and services (see Nava 1992 on 'shopping as salvation'). For example, for Colin Campbell (1989), consumerism in Western society is simply an extension of (modernist) Protestant Romanticism – the belief that individuals are rarely satisfied with reality and instead constantly strive towards an intangible 'other' self. Consequently, advertising (in all its related forms) should be understood simply as a function of this general feature of the culture. An even more 'postmodern' reading of consumerism is provided by Mike Featherstone (1994), who, like Campbell, also sees the consumer as somewhat of a romantic figure – 'a postmodern *flâneur*' if you will – relishing the diversity of commodities and the abundance of new sites and avenues of consumption (only now they have become the observer of their *own* performance!). Featherstone claims that what is new and vital in today's consumer society 'is that the practices of dandyism (art) are no longer confined to the artistic or elite enclaves, but are increasingly widespread.

---

8 On this point, it is interesting to note that, in street parlance, mugging is often referred to as 'taxing'.

This is the project of turning one's life into a work of art' (1994: 75). The key notion here seems to be that consumerism is now inextricably linked to an expanding culture of aesthetics wherein to look good is to be good – or, as the mass media insist on telling us, 'image is everything'. For slightly different reasons, other commentators also point to consumerism as a potentially liberating phenomenon (see Miller 1995). De Certeau (1984), for example, has suggested that resistance and oppositional practices have a vital role to play in the consumption process. Consider the influence that consumer lobby groups (or indeed the public more generally) had in bringing about recent changes in manufacturers' production and purchasing processes. One thinks immediately of the recent *volte-face* by major British supermarkets in response to widespread public opposition to genetically modified foods, the rise of organic and ecologically sustainable products and, most recently, the new 'ethical eating movement'. (Of course, from a Foucauldian perspective, this resistance itself might simply be seen as just another part of the very mechanisms of power: see Zizek on Butler's account of Foucault in Butler *et al* 2000.)

Sharply contradicting this position is the more established classical view that casts consumerism in a more negative role. Here it is suggested that the prevailing ethos of consumerism will result only in the continued rise of individualism and the 'death of the social'. There is no room here for the idea that the so-called 'postmodern consumer' might somehow represent the 'hero of the age' (compare with even the supposed 'consumer led' economic recovery post 9/11), capable of 'transcending structural and class hierarchies' and 'renegotiating urban relations'. In fact, such thinking is dismissed as little more than theoretical abstraction. Instead, the point is stressed that many of the practices and processes associated with late modern consumer culture, by their very nature, must exclude as many individuals as they include (possibly even more), thus creating an environment in which the distinction between the 'haves' and the 'have nots' becomes ever-sharper (see Bauman 1987: 149–69, 1998; Clarke and Bradford 1998). Furthermore, it is argued that theories of consumption that overplay the self-valorising potential of consumer culture are deeply troubling in the sense that they focus myopically on the consumption practices of the so-called 'new middle-classes' or 'new petit bourgeoisie' (middle income earners who perpetuate shared values based around standard of living, expressive 'lifestyles' and, importantly, consumption patterns),[9] and thus tend to ignore other major demographic groups such as senior citizens and the unwaged (compare Taylor *et al* 1996; and Miller 1995: 34–39).

It is this latter perspective that holds most sway in social theoretical circles where it is argued that, in the majority of circumstances, the perceived benefits of consumerism are far out-weighed by the cultivation of a more damaging and profound set of sensibilities. This is not to suggest that consumer culture is inherently bad in any simplistic sense. On the contrary, certain aspects of consumerism (in particular, the ability to chose from a globalised market-place) can be both rich and invigorating. However, as the French philosopher Jean Baudrillard (1981) has noted, as the difference between commodities and signs becomes increasingly meaningless and, as one might say, the distinction between the real and

---

9   See relatedly, Savage *et al* (1992); Mafessoli (1996); Wynne and O'Connor (1998).

the fake becomes evermore redundant, ours will become a world of endless reproduction – a place not simply where everything becomes relative, but where relativism itself becomes just another part of the outmoded way of thinking.[10]

Out of this fundamental opposition emerges a second, less obvious duality, one that in many moments is closely commensurate with de Certeau's evocation of the 'dual city' – the 'Concept-city' of 'rational discourse' associated with the structural, spatial and institutional aspects of urbanisation on the one hand, and the 'experiential' city (the 'subjective and imaginative dimension of urban existence') on the other. One important way of understanding this is to pose the duality as a contrast between the new and distinct forms of subjectivity engendered by consumerism *at the level of individual consciousness*, and the imposition at the *societal level* of 'rationalising practices' and other intense forms of social control that, as will unfold in later chapters, are the direct corollary of an unmediated consumer society (see Presdee 2000; Hayward 2002). This is a cultural paradox of some significance. Consumerism instills the mistaken belief that identity and self-worth can be constructed through the display and celebration of consumer products, and the perception that, whenever possible, consumption must take the form of an expressive, exciting, even hedonistic experience – sensibilities that no doubt de Certeau would have seen as contributing to the 'experiential' aspect of street/urban life. However, at the same time, for consumer capitalism to operate effectively, it must employ as its handmaiden a pervasive set of regulatory practices such as security, auto surveillance and other rational (and increasingly actuarial) logics – methods that, by definition, are forced to adopt the 'distant (and disassociated) gaze' that, for de Certeau, exemplify the so-called 'Concept-city'.

From a criminological perspective, conceptualising consumer culture in these inherently contradictory terms serves two purposes. First, it corresponds with current thinking concerned with the increasingly polarised nature of chaotic post-industrial Western economies – the type of thinking that underscores the mass of commentaries on 'social exclusion', 'the underclass' and 'the new urban poor'.[11] Secondly, it trains attention on the enhanced consumer expectation and new forms of desire that together constitute a profound, and arguably unprecedented, recipe for dissatisfaction, anxiety and, importantly, acute social strain. Jock Young recognises the growing importance of this second element – the emotive and subjective aspects of consumer culture – when he states: 'The shift from the stolid mass consumption and leisure of Fordism to the

---

10 Consider, eg, the current situation regarding the marketing and packaging of commodities, and the way that many goods are subject to stylisation and aggrandisement to such an extent that the inherent pleasure of consumption is transferred from consuming the product to 'consuming the sign' (in the case of many foodstuffs one might even suggest that you now 'eat the advert'!: see Boyle 2003: Chapter 4). In today's consumer society the sign is no longer simply a promise or an expectation relating to the future, rather it is the immediacy ('the now') of the advert, wrapping, image or sign that is of fundamental importance. Bauman recognises something similar when he states that 'Goods acquire their lustre and attractiveness in the course of being chosen; take their choice away, and their allure vanishes without a trace. An object "freely chosen" has the power to bestow the distinction on its chooser which objects "just allotted" obviously do not possess' (1998: 58–59). For more on the increasing redundancy of the truth–falsehood distinction within contemporary society, see Lyotard's (1984) classic account of the displacement of 'classical' knowledge by 'information' knowledge.

11 Eg, Murray (1984, 1990); Dahrendorf (1985, 1987); Davis (1986); Wilson (1987, 1993); Fields (1989); McDonald (1997); and New Labour's Social Exclusion Unit (1999).

diversity of choice and a culture of individualism involving a stress on immediacy, hedonism and self-actualization has profound effects on late modern sensibilities' (1999: 10).

Yet these changing sensibilities, these new (and often destructive) emotional states, feelings and desires engendered by Western consumer society are seldom considered, especially within criminological circles. This is a considerable oversight, for the lessons and messages of consumerism have been closely studied and crisply retained – most obviously by young people, so often the target for pronounced so-called 'lifestyle' advertising. This is not to suggest that criminology has never engaged with questions about the putative nature of market culture and, in particular, how it shapes and influences the actions and sensibilities of young people.[12] The work of the broadly Marxist-inspired Birmingham School in the United Kingdom, for example, took great pains to illustrate the extent to which much working-class youth delinquency was the product of symbolic rebellion against the dominant values of society and the contradictions of capitalism (Hall and Jefferson 1976; Hall *et al* 1978). The situation today, however, is a good deal more intense and indeterminate than the one that confronted the members of the Birmingham School in the 1970s, not least because the desire to consume is so universal and pervasive, confronting us at every turn, bombarding us with an unprecedented array of aspirational messages. Moreover, prospects have changed. Class delineations are less highly stratified. People now respond less and less to the inequalities of capitalism by turning inward and creating subcultures of resistance based on a heightened sense of (working) class consciousness and a deep mistrust of all things different or unknown (see Willis 1977). Rather, the market has redirected our gaze outward. As Mary Douglas has commented, capitalism wrests 'us (willingly) out of our cosy, dull niches and turn[s] us into unencumbered actors, mobile in a system, but setting us free they leave us exposed. We feel vulnerable' (1992: 15). With its emphasis on diversity, novelty, play and self-expression, the market attempts to shift parameters of expectation. Consequently, consumer culture and aspirational culture are now locked in a deadly embrace, each begetting the other. In an important and too often overlooked work on the changing nature of everyday culture, Paul Willis articulates this point in clear terms, and by doing so, greatly develops his earlier classic study of working class sensibilities:

> The market is the source of a permanent and contradictory revolution in everyday culture which sweeps away old limits and dependencies. The markets' restless search to find and make new appetites raises, wholesale, the popular currency of symbolic aspiration. The currency may be debased and inflationary, but aspirations now circulate, just as do commodities. That circulation irrevocably makes or finds its own worlds ... Commerce and consumerism have helped to release a profane explosion of everyday symbolic activity. The genie of common culture is out of the bottle – let out by commercial carelessness. *Not stuffing it back in, but seeing what wishes may be granted, should be the stuff of our imagination.* (1990: 26–27, emphasis added)

---

12 The work of the Dutch criminologist Willem Bonger provides us with an early example of criminology's engagement with the subject of consumerism (although Bonger preferred the term 'covetousness'). Consider this quote, evocative of the era: 'As long as humanity has been divided into rich and poor ... the desires of the masses have been awakened by the display of wealth; only to be repressed again by the moral teaching impressed upon them, that this was a sinful thing' (1936: 93).

Directing theoretical imaginations toward the study of everyday (urban) culture is one of the implicit aims of this work. To this end, this book should be seen as emerging out of and contributing to the growing field of study collectively referred to as 'cultural criminology' (see Ferrell and Sanders 1995; Ferrell 1997, 1999, 2001; Presdee 2000; Hayward and Young 2004; Ferrell *et al* 2004). Although the rubrics and methods of the 'cultural approach' are still in the process of being formulated, one significant starting point is the Birmingham School's idea that criminological inquiry should set out to reinterpret criminal behaviour (in terms of meaning) as a technique for resolving certain psychic conflicts – conflicts that in many instances are indelibly linked with various features of contemporary life/culture (especially the work of Tony Jefferson).

Already, something crucial has been added to the mix by the new wave of cultural criminologists: any understanding of deviance must begin with the individual, with the passions and the exciting and violent feelings which crime induces in both offenders and victims. Crime therefore should be understood as the 'existential pursuit of passion and excitement' – a desperate attempt to escape the humdrum realities and banalities of 'regular' life. Utilising an eclectic mix of intellectual influences, this new body of thought-provoking work sets out to develop an explicitly 'postmodern' theory of crime based in many cases around *the phenomenology of the criminal act* (Katz 1988; Lyng 1990; O'Malley and Mugford 1994; Morrison 1995; Duncan 1996; Henry and Milovanovic 1996; Stanley 1996; Van Hoorebeeck 1997). Within this work, a 'phenomenology of transgression' is fused with a sociological analysis of late modern culture in what O'Malley and Mugford (1994) refer to as an 'historically contextualized phenomenology'. Importantly, the term 'phenomenology' is employed in this work not in any formal or methodological sense, but in a more generalised manner as a means of evoking the dynamic nature of experience generally and the experiential (if not existential) dynamic that underpins transgression more specifically.[13] Whilst it is undoubtedly the case that many of these themes can be found elsewhere in the criminological tradition (most notably in the writings of David Matza and Howard Becker), I contend that this new body of work offers something new, not least because of its engagement with debates on the transition into postmodernity.

---

13 Phenomenology's focus on the shared production of social meaning and its attention to the interactive processes involved have been widely taken up in the social sciences (following the publication of Alfred Schutz's work, *The Phenomenology of the Social World* (1967); first published in Germany in 1932) and in criminology (eg, Sudnow 1965; Cicourel 1968). However, whether, in the context of the social sciences (Schutz aside), the term indicates the full philosophical rigour of Edmund Husserl's anti-Cartesianism or Heidegger's account of Being is doubtful. Certainly, very little, if any, criminology has been grounded in the more structured phenomenological writings of Husserl, Jaspers, Merleau-Ponty and, more recently, Levinas. Rather, as Downes and Rock have pointed out: '[w]hat passes for phenomenological sociology is a most partial interpretation of the opportunities offered by the [more formalised phenomenological] school ... Our description of phenomenology is simplified and limited. It is confined to a few arguments which are at the centre of the imported version accepted by criminology. The imported version is an incomplete reflection of the wider span of phenomenology but its framework is orthodox enough. It is designed to explore the practical knowledge which people have of their social world, knowledge which is afforded a paramount significance. Society is not taken to be something apart from practical consciousness. Rather, it is represented as an object or process which exists in, wells up from, and *is* the workings of common sense' (1982: 165–66).

Despite the considerable emphasis placed on the emotional and interpretative qualities of crime, cultural criminology also (very importantly) has the added advantage – because of its inherent engagement with culture (in all its range of meanings) – of 'opening up' questions of aetiology to include *the wider social and cultural contexts in which all individual experience takes place*. In this reconstruction of aetiology, cultural criminology arguably returns to the original concerns of mainstream criminology. However, for me, it returns with fresh eyes, offering new and exciting ways in which to reinvigorate the study of crime and deviance. As Ferrell and Sanders have commented, 'bending or breaking the boundaries of criminology ... does not undermine contemporary criminology as much as it expands and enlivens it' (1995: 17). Might cultural criminology then represent a possible way forward for criminology to reconcile many of its polarised theoretical positions? Specifically, could it help bridge the current divides between theories of crime that emphasise structural, 'situational' and environmental factors, and those that instead prioritise the actions and motivations of the 'individual' – two areas previously thought of as mutually exclusive, irretrievably antithetical?

At first sight, this line of thinking appears to fit with broader shifts that have taken place within the social sciences over the last three decades, which attempted to draw together dialectically 'social structure' and 'human agency'.[14] Clearly, this body of work remains important and insightful (in particular, Giddens's 'structuration theory', in which he attempts to combine structural and action-based approaches into a single theoretical construct that strongly considers the temporal and spatial dimensions of human existence). However, my work is not intended as an explicit continuation of this tradition. Rather, it has a slightly different, more circumspect aim: to encourage disciplinary reflection on,[15] and to unearth new insights into, what at first sight appear to be diverse and unbridgeable theoretical positions specifically within criminology.

There is, in my opinion, one particular area where this approach might prove very useful: I refer to criminology's enduring relationship with the concept of *urban crime/space*. I should state at this point that although one of the goals of this work is to augment mainstream criminological explanations of urban crime by drawing on certain elements of contemporary 'cultural criminology', what follows should not be read purely as a criticism of more established criminological theories. On the contrary, I believe much of this work to be of great insight and importance. Rather, the contention here is that, given the unique social and economic conditions associated with late modernity – I refer here (though not exclusively) to the conditions associated with 'consumer society' – the need to develop certain theoretical links between the existential concerns and individual anxieties of everyday life,[16] and the key macro structural and (increasingly important) cultural

---

14 Eg, in sociology see Berger and Luckmann (1979), Bhaskar (1979), Bronfenbrenner (1979), Dawe (1979), Knorr-Cetina and Cicourel (1981), Giddens (1979, 1984), Bourdieu (1977, 1990), Bourdieu and Wacquant (1992), Layder (1981); in human geography Gregory and Urry (1985), Thrift (1996); and in historical sociology, Abrahams (1982).

15 On criminology's profound reluctance to engage in disciplinary reflection, see Cohen 1988; Nelken 1994; and especially Alison Young 1996.

16 For a detailed exposition of the various modes of consciousness and 'finite provinces of meaning' that constitute the experience – or more accurately 'the foundations of knowledge' – of everyday life, see Berger and Luckmann (1979: 31–61).

determinants that shape our lives and dictate our social roles, is now greater than ever, not least because (as mentioned above) many of the features of late modern consumer culture are bringing about significant changes in *both* these key areas.

First, consumer culture and its associated practices are, in a great many instances, contributing to the *substantial spatial and situational reconfiguration of the post-industrial city* (Harvey 1990: Chapter 4; Jencks 1977; Sorkin 1992a; Gartman 1998; Hannigan 1998: Chapters 3–5). More specifically, one of the primary outcomes of the rise and increased dominance of the consumer society is the redrawing of the contours of the urban landscape along the lines outlined by Zygmunt Bauman (1987: 149–69; 1998), Mike Davis (1990, 1998) and, more recently (and more importantly from a purely criminological perspective), in Jock Young's compelling *The Exclusive Society* (1999: Chapters 1 and 2). Certainly, two of the themes identified by Young as instrumental in the onset of the 'exclusive society' of late modernity – namely the rise of individualism (ie, the creation of what Young describes as individual 'zones of personal exclusiveness': Young 1999: 47–55)[17] and pervasive chronic relative deprivation – are also central components of this book. The connection between such ongoing developments and urban space is of crucial importance, not least because it is likely to precipitate the further profusion of 'criminogenic spaces' (see Garland 1997) as society continues to polarise into safe zones (ie, regulated, privatised consumer spaces) and dangerous urban no-go areas (ie, underfunded enclaves of exclusion and repression).

Secondly, consumerism is also having considerable impact at the level of *individual subjective emotions*. Emotions do not occur within a vacuum;[18] rather, they are both generated and affected by social conditions and cultural codes – in this case consumption codes (see Richards *et al* 2000; Edwards 2000: Chapter 3). Emotions are, as the criminologist Wayne Morrison suggests, 'stimulated by cultural interpretation, and enjoyed or down-played in social interaction' (1995: Chapter 13). One of the ways in which the forms of subjectivity created by consumer culture are being enjoyed and 'down-played' – or perhaps, more accurately, *downloaded* – in social interaction is through crime. (The term 'downloaded' is useful here in that it helps to explain how certain emotions and social messages can be received and assimilated by the individual despite often being inherently contradictory or paradoxical in nature. For example, the emotions engendered by advertising very often both incite *and* deny, compel *and* preclude.) Indeed, it is one of the central assertions of this work that consumerism cultivates tendencies (especially among the young) that can, in certain circumstances, ultimately find expression in specific forms of expressive criminal behaviour. The importance of these new forms of consciousness for criminological theory will be discussed in detail at various intervals throughout the book and, alongside other themes identified as being

---

17 It is important to be precise about what Young means when he talks about the 'rise of individualism within late modernity', as the concept of individualism has always been seen as one of the hallmarks of modernity within classical sociology. Basically, Young's reading of 'late modern individualism' is different from previous forms in that he is referring to the breakup of strong models of identity and subjectivity which previously had defined individualism.

18 For a thoughtful introduction to the social theory of emotions, see Simon Williams (2001); also Denzin (1984); Kemper 1990; Barbalet (1998). For a criminology-specific example, see Fenwick (1996).

constitutive of the contemporary urban experience, will be formulated into a tentative conceptual framework for thinking about a number of urban crimes under conditions of late modernity. However, rather than develop this complex aetiological point in any great detail in the Introduction, I wish instead to focus on a more general question about the nature of social 'strain' under late modern conditions.

One of the unique features of a consumer culture is the way it propagates within individuals the constant demand for more – more products, more stimulation, more experiences – yet while the late modern subject might initially find solace through participation in the multiplicity of consumption practices associated with the consumer society, these are 'escape routes' (compare Cohen and Taylor 1976) that are ultimately futile. Taken as promises, the fantasies and aspirations propagated within the individual by a consumer culture can never be fully realised. Thus, feelings of frustration, social strain and futility abound, a point Celia Lury expresses clearly:

> Consumption expresses the romantic longing to become an *other*, however, whatever one becomes is not what one wants to be. This is because the actual consumption or use of goods becomes a disillusioning experience. The actuality of consumption fails to live up to the dream of fantasy thus we continue to consume endlessly. In the material world, it seems that one's desires can never be exhausted. (1996: 73)

Such sentiments obviously echo the classical 'strain theory' of Robert Merton (1938). However, as Wayne Morrison has pointed out, 'Instead ...of the cultural message being the accumulation of money, *the message now is taking control of our destiny*. Modernity gives us a series of expectations as to self-realization and personal growth ... *but actual human beings have not fully escaped being defined by their location in situations of enablement and restraint*' (1995: 301, emphasis added). This is an important point for it challenges us to reconsider those early strain models in light of pronounced cultural and economic transformations and fluctuations. We must develop more sophisticated analyses of the emotional states, the feelings and the contingencies associated with the concept of strain. In particular, we need to look at the way the self is being assailed by the various and competing cultural messages ushered in by the onset of late modernity. Only when this task has been completed can we begin to understand the processes and motivations that contribute to much contemporary criminality. In a passage that I consider to be of great importance, Morrison begins to explain this line of thought:

> To become self-defining is the fate that the social structure of late-modernity imposes upon its socially created individuality. The individual is called into action; actions which are meant to express his/her self and enable the individual's destiny to be created out of the contingencies of his/her past ... And while resources differ, all are subjected to variations of a similar pressure as modernity moves into postmodernism, namely that of the overburdening of the self as the self becomes the ultimate source of security. The tasks asked of the late-modern person require high degrees of social and technical skills. To control the self and guide it through the disequilibrium of the journeys of late modernity is the task imposed upon the late-modern person, but what if the life experiences of the individual have not fitted him/her with this power? ... much crime is an attempt of the self to create sacred moments of control, to find ways in which the self can exercise control and power in situations where power and control are all too clearly lodged outside the self. (1995: iv)

Such thinking is also highly prominent in the work of Anthony Giddens (1991), who suggests that late modernity has brought about new forms of self 'reflection' and changes in the way people relate to themselves in everyday life (to be more precise, reflection/reflexivity refers to self-observation and the application to the self of the same criteria one applies to others, or, more loosely, awareness of the effects of one's actions on the world). He claims that within the open social terrain of late modernity, new modes of subjectivity are created in which the 'self' is thus seen as a 'reflexive project', for which the individual is now solely responsible.

As these passages imply, we now inhabit a world in transition. In recent decades we have witnessed the demise of the modernist project of 'reason and progress', and with it the erosion of a set of 'established' modernist assumptions, norms and sensibilities. The world orientated to work and production, especially as manifested in the manufacture of 'solid' tangible goods, has given way to a world of 'intangibles'. We now reside in a far more 'precarious' world characterised by a 'chaotic reward system' and 'a sense of unfairness and a feeling of the arbitrary' (Young 1999: 9). Consequently, if we are to be successful in tackling the contemporary crime problem, it is essential that we acknowledge what Jock Young, drawing on Giddens, describes as the 'ontological insecurity' that is now such a striking feature of modern life (Young 1999: 97–104). In short, we must engage with the contingencies and dilemmas (the dilemmas of the contingent?) brought about by the late modern condition. Here everything is subject to change and reconstitution. Even previously stable and seemingly inexorable social components – gender, sexuality, the individual subject, the family unit, the human body, etc – have in recent times been rendered mutable. While such a set of social circumstances may in the long term offer society a whole new range of opportunities and possibilities, in the short term they also throw up understandable feelings of melancholia and uncertainty. Large numbers of people are now being forced to reconsider their past, present and future as they face up to the fact that many of the teleological presuppositions they clung to for so long have collapsed and cannot be reconstructed.

However, we fail to embrace this 'new world' and our reluctance and scepticism are palpable. We cling instead to the vestiges of the modernist programme. Morrison is acutely aware of the inchoate position in which we find ourselves. While other writers project a fully-formed 'postmodern subject', Morrison is more circumspect, choosing instead to describe the forms of existence that are common to individuals trapped in a partly modern, partly postmodern landscape. For him, the question is straightforward: how can we each reconcile ourselves to newness and change when, all around us, modernity reverberates solemnly in the background? In short, Morrison is attempting to articulate the *dilemmas of transition*:

It is no longer possible to make sense of the world in its totality, we are adrift in a sea of communication – reality is debauched by signs, it becomes a perversion of reality. Where are we now? What is the meaning of our present times? How can we actually tell? We move inside a spectacular distortion of facts and representations – the triumph of simulation. How can talk of socialisation make sense? What are we going to socialise the next generation into if there is no stable structure for them to find their place? (Morrison 1995: 309)

Such feelings are especially pronounced among young people (Taylor 1999: Chapter 3; Cohen and Ainley 2000: 229–32; Hayward 2002). Consequently, given such a 'culture of uncertainty', is it any wonder that young offenders undertake the vast majority of crime? Is it really surprising that crime becomes a way of navigating a path through such uncertain times? This book takes this line of thinking forward by focusing on the particular relationships that currently exist between crime, consumer culture and the urban experience.

Although crime and criminology are the central locus and destination of this text, the book starts elsewhere. In Chapter 1, focus falls on the various ways in which urban social theorists and other commentators on the city have attempted to conceptualise the subtle yet discernible ways our experience of urban space has been framed by the emergence of the modern industrialised city in the mid-19th century. In the spirit of multidisciplinarity (a key component of cultural criminology), the chapter also discusses changing representations of the city in modern art and architecture. If this opening chapter is about modernity, Chapter 2 engages with the 'postmodern', as we strive to assimilate the many socio-economic transformations and cultural processes that confront us in the 21st century city – not least late modern consumption and the changing spatial logic of the urban landscape. The prevailing systems of consumption, it is argued, are bringing about macroscopic and microscopic transformations and fluctuations not only in the physical and structural configuration of urban environments, but also importantly at the level of individual subjective experience. One interesting question (not resolved!) that cross-cuts the two chapters is whether these huge changes simply represent a further extension of modernist consumption practices, or are instead bound up in a distinctly postmodern transition.

All the time in the background is the presence of de Certeau. Deliberately, the tenor of these first two chapters reflects his contention that urban experience is best conceptualised as a *duality*. Modern urban planning initiatives and architectural movements provide a clear illustration of the formal, rational organising principles inherent in de Certeau's 'Concept-city' (the design, character and state of the built environment all have a dramatic effect on our physical relationship with the city), while the changing nature of the subjective urban consciousness more readily corresponds with the experiential dimension of city life 'at street level'.

Having established how social theory has attempted to conceptualise the urban experience, I then turn in Chapter 3 to the particular relationship between *criminological theory* and the city, examining the work of early 'social ecologists' like Quételet and Guerry, the Chicago School, environmental criminology, administrative criminology and – the main focus of the chapter – new left realism. Far from being a simple review of the literature, this chapter seeks to remind criminology what was valuable in its original concerns with the city, mining rich theoretical and experiential traditions that have since been covered over by mainstream criminology's current obsession with theories of (rational) opportunity and control. A key feature of this latter-day shift in criminology has been the marginalisation of social theory as a means of understanding criminality in all its diverse forms (see Fenwick 1996; Van Hoorebeeck 1997: 508).

In examining new left realism, the stance taken here is sympathetic but critical. (Let me make it clear that I distinguish new left realism from Jock Young's more recent work, which moves closer to the new cultural criminology.) What links the present work to left realism is a sense that space and consumerism are central to understanding the complexities of contemporary urban crime – but not if still viewed through the myopic lens of ultimately economistic structural analyses that fail to consider the experiential, cultural dimension of late modern life. It is argued that cultural criminology provides the necessary corrective.

One of the most striking writers on the ills of the contemporary urban condition is Mike Davis, whose *City of Quartz* (1990) dazzled the academic world (criminology aside!) with its postmodern parables of metropolitan meltdown, social polarisation and the militarisation of vast swathes of public space in 'Fortress LA'. Offered from a Marxist (or at least Marxisant!) position, his account is a political critique of self-interest and corporate greed in late-millennial Los Angeles. Davis's work is the subject of Chapter 4. Whether LA offers a blueprint for the future – indeed, whether he has even correctly depicted Los Angeles – has generated much controversy, as the chapter documents. Moving on from these debates, the core interest of Davis's work remains the way in which he (sometimes almost incidentally) opens up the importance of emotions and the link to consumerism and urban space. In Davis's reading, the importance of the fear of crime lies in the way that it is redrawing the contours of the urban landscape and the built environment, yet in my version, safety is only part of the story. The chapter describes the growth of an entire industry of 'security as prestige', with the 'feel-safe' factor constituting a new form of urban conspicuous consumption and lifestyle desire. In this ongoing mutation of urban experience, society's current fascination with security and auto-surveillance has become yet another incitement to consume. In a second inspiration from Davis, the chapter elaborates his overly crude vision of a polarised city – a hyperbolic version of Manuel Castells's (1994) 'dual city' – to reflect on the physicality of boundaries and the feelings and emotions within the zone(s) of 'exclusionary space'.

What Chapter 4 starts, Chapter 5 continues in another register. Now, the exploration of fear and desire in Los Angeles is a prelude to a more developed analysis of the roles played by emotions and feelings – not least the new forms of desire and longing that are such a pronounced feature of consumer culture and late modern life – in the aetiology and commission of urban crime. Concretising these thematics through urban space as a 'lived experience', this chapter seeks to develop a tentative conceptual framework for thinking about certain urban crimes under conditions of late modernity. The overall goal is to set out the theoretical foundations on which criminology can construct a bridge between existential/psychic concerns, anxieties of everyday city life, and the macro cultural and situational forces that shape our role and status within society and impact on our willingness or reluctance to engage in criminal activity.

The chapter sets up a play between two contrasting writers whose work, strangely, also evokes the themes of 'fear and desire' and their interlocking character in the contemporary urban setting. 'Desire' first, with Jack Katz's *The Seductions of Crime: Moral and Sensual Attractions in Doing Evil* (1988). Here the focus is on the emotionality that, according to Katz, constitutes crime's 'seductive character', especially those 'expressive crimes' that suspend reality and create a 'limit experience' on the metaphorical edge. Fear enters the frame through Jock

Young's *The Exclusive Society* (1999) and his account of 'ontological insecurity'. I will argue that it is against this backdrop of social anxiety that certain forms of criminal practice become highly attractive as a means of 'exerting control' and 'constructing identity' in increasingly socially precarious lifeworlds. This is more than a matter of different emotionalities in confluence. Rather, Young's work points to what is missing in Katz's focus on individual experience: namely, its failure to consider the broader structural, material and historical contexts within which individual experience occurs (see more recently Young 2003). Notably – and central to the argument of the present book – there is no sense of a historically contingent consumer culture in which the pursuit of excitement through transgression is cultivated via the 'insatiability of desire' and 'the pursuit of the new', short termism, 'impulsivity' and the desire for immediate gratification. As with ontological insecurity, so too excitement offers a way of seizing control of one's destiny – of 'living' (or at least experiencing) 'a controlled loss of control' in the face of an over-controlled, yet at the same time highly unstable, world. In examining the very different responses of the state and the market to this situation, the chapter focuses on the parasitical spiralling of rationality and resistance, joyriders viewing speed cameras as a challenge, the imperative of a radio ban for hard-core 'gangsta' rap music. The chapter ends with a 'grounding' in the gritty particulars of urban space – the inner city housing estate, the town centre and the new urban consumer zones – both present and the future.

Chapter 1
Imagining the Urban Experience

With or without dignity, sumptuous or slovenly, in plush or in tatters, more and more brutal, more rapid, more noisy, the modern world marches on. (Henri Lefebvre 1995: 1)

Centuries of centuries and only in the present do things happen; countless men in the air, on the face of the earth, and on the sea, and all that really is happening is happening to me. (Jorge Luis Borges 1970: 45)

Introduction

Much of what constitutes modern social life today is the product of the city and of the 'urban experience'. This chapter considers the changing nature of that urban experience during the problematic and contentious period of accelerated social change and structural reorganisation that is now referred to – often in very loose and abstracted epochal terms – as modernity. While the term 'modernity' generally refers to 'the modes of social life and organization which emerged in Europe from about the sixteenth and seventeenth century onwards and which subsequently became world-wide in their influence' (Giddens 1990: 1), our concern here is with the more developed forms of modernity, modernisation and (later) modernism that emerged in the 19th century. This period is significant, for it marked the emergence of the concept of *modernité* as a significant analytical tool for understanding society and its associated institutions. At the same time 'modernity' signals an awakening self-consciousness about what it was that was distinct about this era. Lastly, as David Clarke has pointed out, 'it is in the nineteenth century that the immense and varied changes wrought by modernity seem to centre inexorably on the city' (1997: 222).[1]

Prior to the 19th century, the vast majority of human beings lived, worked, played and died in rural communities. However, the massive economic and demographic changes that occurred from the mid-18th century onwards ensured that by 1900 (at least in the West) the traditional rural mode of existence had been supplanted by urbanism as the 'dominant way of life', to use Louis Wirth's memorable phrase. By the mid-19th century, millions had gravitated, willingly or not, to the city from the country, and these new urbanites were immediately confronted by a whole new set of rules, values and mores, a great many of which were totally alien to their traditional agrarian sensibilities.[2] They also had to come to

---

1 Our excavations of the urban experience are not, of course, limited to the 19th century and the emergence of the dominant urban – some might say modern, for the urban and the modern are indissolubly intertwined – consciousness. In Chapter 2, the focus shifts to the various ways in which our experience of urban space is being shaped today by the significant transformations and fluctuations associated with the 'late modern' condition. In this sense these first two chapters should be seen as two halves of the same story.

2 For a detailed breakdown of the demographic transition from a rural to an urban populace, see Weber (1970 [1899]); Abu-Lughod (1991).

terms with the unparalleled spectacle, vibrancy and opportunity of modern urban life in a metropolitan landscape alive with the sounds and rhythms of modernisation. As the allegorical poet Guillaume Appollinaire put it, the modern city danced day and night to 'the music of the madness of machines'.[3] Moreover, the pronounced modulations in the speed, dynamism and temporality of urban life – the by-products of unmediated 19th century capitalism – not only exacerbated the rupture with the past, but also added to the daunting and confusing nature of modern urban life. In Henri Lefebvre's words, this period of rampant modernisation marked the beginning of an 'alternative reality', when *discontinuity* began to permeate society ('The essential thing ... is that discontinuity and the *consciousness of discontinuity* have effectively entered into modernity, with all the problems that implies for becoming': Lefebvre 1995: 180, emphasis added).[4] To function within such a new and formidable environment meant having to reconcile oneself to (and indeed delight in) the 'shock of the new' (Hughes 1991). How, then, did these rural émigrés come to terms with life in the modern city? And what effect did living in a place where 'all that is solid melts into air' have on individual subjectivity?

Before exploring such questions, it is necessary, given the nature of this chapter, to say something briefly about the concept of 'experience'. Whilst experience clearly manifests itself within the individual in the form of private and unique mental states, it is important to recognise that it is also largely the product of a social construction (as Berger and Luckmann (1979) have long since argued). A sociological approach to the question of the origin and effects of our everyday urban experience is therefore perfectly legitimate. That said, I do not wish to suggest that there is now, or indeed ever has been, a universal or generic urban experience. In terms of the way we perceive urban life, every individual has always had (and will continue to have) a very distinct and singular existential relationship with the city. However, it is difficult not to acknowledge that there are certain fundamental elements and features of city life that greatly impact on the way in which we all think about and experience the city.[5] To put it another way, although we each have a very particular relationship with the city, it is a relationship inevitably affected by certain shared experiences that are a direct consequence of, and indeed a constitutive component of, city life. Consequently, any transformation or vicissitude in these core elements of urban life will doubtless have some effect on the individual consciousness, perception and personal biography of the modern urban dweller, resulting ultimately in a subtle transmutation of the individual subjective urban experience. For our purposes, then, it is instructive to think of urban experience as a multi-faceted, multi-nodal construct that includes both an interior and an exterior dimension.

---

3 From Appollinaire's poem, *La Chanson du Mal-Aimé*.

4 It should be stressed that there is no simple correlation between feelings of discontinuity and 19th century modernity, for as Jameson (1991: 154) has pointed out, a sense of discontinuity is also one of the main characteristics of the postmodern condition (see Chapter 2).

5 See Lynch (1960: 7) on what he describes as 'public images': 'the common mental pictures carried by large numbers of a city's inhabitants: areas of agreement which might be expected to appear in the interaction of a single physical reality, a common culture, and a basic physiological nature'.

What follows is an exploratory theoretical investigation into the changing nature of that urban experience. (Crime and criminality *per se* are not central to the analysis at this point.) To this end, several key areas have been selected to illustrate the transition from the project of modernity and its inherent utopian aspirations to the putative conditions associated with late modern society. These areas include (but are not limited to) urban sociology, social theory – in particular, the various ways in which key urban theorists have attempted to conceptualise/capture the subtle, yet discernible, way our experience of urban space has altered since the mid-19th century and continues to be affected today as we strive to assimilate the many changes that confront us – urban studies, urban consumption, and various artistic and cultural interpretations of the city. Lastly, I should make it clear that the various themes discussed in this chapter should in no way be read as a teleological history of the city in modernity or, for that matter, as a positivistic set of factors for categorising urban experience. Instead, they should be seen as threads woven together within the same tapestry, each explaining or enhancing the other and, consequently, all contributing in differing ways to the same overall picture – the ever-changing nature of urban experience.

The street as experience, the city as dyad

Nowhere are the ambiguities and tensions of modernity more deeply inscribed and more readily apparent than at street level. Then, as now (and very often in the same space or moment), the street acts as a mirror, reflecting back modernity's inherent contradictions – its civilising and rationalising imperatives as well as its exotic and (often) repressed 'otherness', its possibilities and failures, its pleasures and its pains. It is on the city street, as John Jervis suggests, that we experience 'a tension between the purported smoothly-functioning rationality of city life and our everyday experience of what life in the city really entails. The city of project and consumerism is a city in which fragmentation, change and disorder are as apparent as their opposites, providing the dynamism that makes city life so challenging' (1998: 68). Our exploration of the urban experience begins, then, with two very different attempts to understand the mid-19th century metropolis from the nook and cranny perspective of the city street. Taken together they provide a clear illustration of the dyadic and sharply contradictory nature of the city, as (the emergent) modern urban consciousness and the grand narratives of modernity rise and fall together.

Our starting point is Paris, 'the capital of the 19th century' and the very epitome of the 'disturbing newness' associated with this period of mass modernisation. In contrast to the established public order of more traditional times, it was a place characterised by vast massed crowds, chance interactions, dazzling sensory spectacles, novel fashions and mass public culture and entertainment (see Olson 1986: Chapter 4). It was here, in the teeming streets and glittering arcades of Paris, that the term *modernité* first found favour as a way of understanding the bizarre novelties and sensations associated with urban life. But how could this bombardment of the senses, this street level theatre of dynamism and restlessness, be effectively conveyed or articulated? For writers and commentators of the period, such as Balzac and Dumas, one way of making sense of this 'new world' was through an engagement with the sometimes 'heroic', sometimes 'spectral' (but always nonchalant) figure of the 19th century '*flâneur*'. Simply stated, the *flâneur* was a loiterer, an idle 'stroller' or *promeneur*, a detached observer concerned with the sights, sounds and contingencies of mid-19th century Parisian street life.[6] As a social type, the *flâneur* is perhaps best described as an up-market drifter ('He is a gentlemen ... yet he is subtly *déclassé*, and above all he stands wholly outside of production': Wilson, quoted in Clarke 1997: 63). Quintessentially urban, the *flâneur* relished the anonymity of the crowd, for it provided a sense of freedom from family, friends and other traditional conventions, enabling him (for the *flâneur* was invariably a masculine construct: Wolff 1985; Pollock 1988; see below) to traverse the streets of Paris observing everything from rag-pickers and prostitutes to aesthetes and bohemians (see Buck-Morss 1986).[7] From this (wholly masculine) position of anonymity and indeterminacy, the *flâneur* was able to observe and experience the evanescent, transitory practices of 19th century capitalist society.

For the poet and essayist Charles Baudelaire, the *flâneur* was the perfect articulation of urban *modernité*. Unlike previous writers on the city (most notably his compatriot Jean-Jacques Rousseau, with his 18th century protestations about urbanism, artifice and the horrors of *le tourbillion social*), Baudelaire was concerned not with denouncing the city as a moral development in civilisation, but rather with describing the nuances and subtleties of modern life and their discrete effects on the consciousness of modern men and women. He shared with the *flâneur* a 'childlike' fascination with the spectacle of the city and, in particular, the new transitory ever-changing urban world of café society, heroic dandyism, high fashion, the petit bourgeois pleasures of La Grande Jatte and the mercantile expansion of the Second Empire of Napoleon III (Baudelaire 1964: 1–12). Importantly, it was not that Baudelaire simply saw the *flâneur* an interesting social type. Rather, his interest was held by how the *flâneur* could operate as a tone and position of observation – in other words, the scope or 'gaze' of the *flâneur*. By simultaneously adopting the dual role of a curious 'voyeur and critic' (Collier 1985: 34), the *flâneur* was the perfect vehicle to encapsulate the experiences of the modern city. This is where the notion of a specifically urban consciousness begins (and, importantly, its identification with the modern). In Baudelaire's writing we see the emergence of 'modern individuals' as 'urban individuals', finally 'aware of themselves as moderns', identifying 'the intimate unity of the modern self and the modern environment' (Berman 1982: 132). However, in relying so heavily on the *flâneur*, Baudelaire only ever offers a descriptive, or more accurately an *impressionistic*, account of the urban experience (and a particularly masculine one at that) – what de Certeau would later describe as the 'poetic experience of space' (the 'subjective and experiential dimension of urban existence', the multi-layered social interactivity that takes place at street level). For all the variety it encompassed, for all the preoccupation with the discontinuity between rural and urban, past and present, traditional and modern, the worldly gaze of the urban observer (whether cynical, fanciful or melancholic) remained

---

6   To be precise, the figure of the *flâneur* was most prominent in the period immediately after the Revolution of 1830 up until the emergence of the first department stores in the late 1850s.

7   See relatedly, Jane Rendell's piece on 'male ramblers' in early 19th century London: 'The rambler represents a new kind of urban identity which emerges in this period – the young, single, heterosexual and upper-class man of leisure, fashion and sport' (1998: 76).

equally both detached and unmoved by the immense, highly visible social, spatial and class discontinuities emerging in the process of capitalist industrialisation. For this arch describer of the urban, there is little to say about the way the metropolis became synonymous with notions of crime, degeneracy, dangerousness and social polarisation, far less to understand it. For this, we need to embark on an altogether different stroll through the city.

Inevitably, the infrastructure and urban design of a great many cities simply could not cope with population influxes of such magnitude, and the lack of appropriate housing and extreme poverty among the industrial poor quickly resulted in overcrowding, disease and the continued deterioration of already squalid conditions. Manchester, in the North of England, was just such a city, and for Frederick Engels it was the perfect test case to substantiate his thesis about the corrupting influence of capitalist relations. Engels saw 'the transformations brought about by the Industrial Revolution as a gigantic process of concentration and polarization, whose tendency is to create a growing proletariat, an increasingly small bourgeoisie of increasingly large capitalists, both in an increasingly urbanized society' (Hobsbawm 1969: 10). Importantly, Engels also drew attention to the role played by social conditions, poverty and frustration at class inequalities in the commission of urban crime:

> The contempt for the existing social order is most conspicuous in its extreme form – that of offences against the law. If the influences demoralizing to the working man act more powerfully, more concentratedly than usual, he becomes an offender as certainly as water abandons the vaporous state at eighty degrees, Réaumur. (Engels 1969 [1844]: 159)

Without equal as a socio-political critique of the exploitation of casual workers engaged in 19th century industrial employment, *The Condition of the Working Class in England* was also extremely influential in the particular way it approached the whole question of the urban.[8]

In this unforgettable text, Engels not only achieved his primary aim of linking urban immiseration (including crime) directly to capitalist expansion (in its mass industrial stage);[9] he also established the value of seeking out the individual experiences of the working class city-dweller. He achieved this feat by taking to the streets and embarking on a series of walking tours of some of England's most insalubrious neighbourhoods. Like the *flâneur*, Engels wanted to experience the city first hand, but unlike his French 'counterpart', he was not interested in reading the city in terms of 'aesthetic splendour' or 'poetic experience'. His aim was more fundamental and uncomplicated: to unearth empirical evidence to substantiate his polemic against capitalist exploitation. Thus, Engels relied heavily on oral testimony, local reportage and direct observation to drive his account of the city, and in doing so (unwittingly) laid the foundations for a new and immediate form of

---

8   See Graeme Davison (1983) on Engels's influence on the development of urban sociology.

9   For David Harvey, the urbanisation of consciousness cannot be understood independently of the urbanisation of capital. In his companion books *Consciousness and the Urban Experience* (1985a) and *The Urbanisation of Capital* (1985b), Harvey employs a developed Marxist perspective to promote his key proposition that 'a city is an agglomeration of productive forces built by labour employed within a temporal process of circulation of capital' (1985a: 250).

proto ethnography – *the city was now also the site of first-hand observation for the empirical social sciences*. And while the *flâneur*'s implicit aim was to capture the 'disturbing newness' of the city and its effects (both negative *and* positive) in constituting the emerging urban consciousness, Engels prioritised the more hidden side of the city, its unimaginable poverty and foulness. For Engels the city slum and the industrial factory were 'something repulsive, something against which human nature rebels' (Engels, quoted in Wilson 2001: 72). It was this more disturbing aspect of urban life that quickly (and understandably) came to dominate subsequent social accounts of the modern city. The strong emphasis on description and detail remained, only now it was the unadulterated horror and squalor of street life that took centre stage. This was the start of a new culture of observation, a culture that would in turn carry with it a series of implicit and explicit – but always purposive and influential – rationalising rubrics.

Reading, recording and rationalising city life

By the time of Engels's writings, 'lawlessness' and the perceived 'depravity' of the 'degenerate poor' had become pressing concerns for the Victorian middle and ruling classes. Urban crime in particular was a major focus of concern, especially when one factored in the growing political unrest that was bubbling under the surface in many British cities (Stedman-Jones 1971; Pearson 1975: Chapter 6). In a bid to comprehend the full scale of the problem and identify the root cause of urban 'lawlessness', social researchers and reformers increasingly immersed themselves, in a manner reminiscent of Engels, within the poverty-stricken neighbourhoods (or 'rookeries' as they became known due to their intense overcrowding and single point of entry and egress) and criminal subcultures of the 19th century city slum.[10] Consider this description of a secreted rookery – typical of the period – by Andrew Mearns, a philanthropic clergyman of a type one closely associates with the Victorian period:

> Few who read these pages have any conception of what these pestilential human rookeries are, where tens of thousands are crowded together amidst horrors which call to mind what we have heard of the middle passage of the slave ship. To get to them you have to penetrate courts reeking with poisonous and malodorous gases arising from accumulations of sewage and refuse scattered in all directions and often flowing beneath your feet; courts, many of them which the sun never penetrates, which are never visited by a drop of cleansing water ... You have to grope your way along dark and filthy passages swarming with vermin. Then, if you are not driven back by intolerable stench, you may gain admittance to the dens in which tens of thousands of beings who belong, as much as you, to the race for whom Christ died, herd together. (Mearns, quoted in Hall 1996: 16)

This was an account of a form of urban experience that had not been seen before. Of these early ethnographic studies, arguably the most influential was the work

---

10 As a result of this movement, some stunning 'proto-ethnographic' studies were produced, most notably the work of Frégier and Buret in Paris; and in London, Thomas Beames's *The Rookeries of London* and later the work of Charles Booth and Andrew Mearns.

undertaken by Henry Mayhew. Like many Victorian reformers and philanthropists, Mayhew was a man of no small plans. His stated aim was to compile 'a cyclopaedia of the industry, the want, and the vice of the great Metropolis ... the first attempt to publish the history of a people' (Mayhew, quoted in Pearson 1975: 156). While he may have fallen some way short of this ambitious goal, Mayhew will long be remembered for his thoroughgoing investigations of the life, conditions and criminal proclivities of the 'dangerous classes' in infamous East London rookeries such as Shoreditch, St Giles and St Luke's. Proceeding from the assumption that insalubrious environmental conditions and high poverty levels actually bred deviance and degeneracy,[11] Mayhew entered into the largely unexplored territories of 'outcast' London, compiling data and conducting hundreds of interviews with everyone from 'Hindoo [sic] beggars' to 'Horse and dog stealers'.

Given the period, one should not lose sight of the fact that Mayhew's survey was deeply sensitive to the plight of London's poor.[12] Indeed, like Engels before him, Mayhew was also keen to privilege the notion of oral testimony and personal experience in the commission of urban crime (he is often quoted as saying that he wished 'to publish the history of a people from the lips of the people themselves – giving a literal description of their labour, their earnings, their trials and their sufferings, in their own "unvarnished" language': Mayhew 1968 [1862]: back cover). However, there is a second side to Mayhew's methodology, a side that tells us much about the way the notion of urban experience began to change around this point. Noticeable alongside the (quasi) naturalistic accounts of London street life are a vast array of tables, graphs, illustrations and composite indices.[13] These classificatory grids represent an important shift towards *the quantitative and empirical categorisation of social action*. Thus viewed, the unpredictability of the urban setting is made predictable, readable and categorisable. No longer was it simply a question of trying to come to terms with the 'disturbing newness' of city life, or indeed of

---

11 Mayhew and many of his fellow ethnographer-reformers often reinterpreted the popular scientific theories of the day to serve their own ends, the most notable example being the way they drew upon an adulterated version of (the then popular theory of) Lamarckism to underscore their 'degeneracy theory'. Simply stated, Lamarckism was a late 18th century evolutionary theory based on the inheritance of acquired characteristics (ie, species first adapt to a particular environment and then pass on these adaptations via genetic transference). Initially, Lamarck's ideas were seen as fundamentally progressive, not least because the environment was seen as an agent for betterment. However, in the hands of 19th century degeneracy theorists, the opposite belief emerged: that bad environments – the so-called 'criminal milieu' or 'dangerous habitat' – would bring about negative adaptations. Moreover, these deviations from (what was often described with typical Victorian sententiousness as) the 'civilised norm' would then be passed on to children along with other social concerns of the period such as madness or syphilis.

12 This section should not be read as an outright criticism of this body of work. On the contrary, in many ways these early ethnographic studies represented what for the time at least was a fairly advanced sociological explanation of crime. Moralising as these studies may be, they offered a far more sophisticated and progressive hypothesis than the atavistic pathological assumptions that were soon to be proffered by the Italian deterministic tradition.

13 Eg, Mayhew painstakingly documented the various criminal strata he encountered on the streets, categorising offenders with evocative monikers (drawn from the criminal lexicon of the time) such as 'Stook-Buzzers' (handkerchief thieves), 'Bluey-Hunters' (thieves who stole lead from roofs), and 'Star-Gazers' (window pane thieves) (see particularly Mayhew 1968 [1862]: vol iv, pp 23–27).

unearthing the forgotten or hidden parts of the city, it was now about making order out of chaos, classifying and imposing a sense of rationality on the city.[14] As Elizabeth Wilson has commented in her wonderful book on the culture of cities, in the modernist city nothing could be hidden, 'Utopia was to be barren of secrets and of anything resembling an alternative world' (2001: 150).

While rudimentary, oral ethnography within the 'modern city' would continue apace – most notably with Andrew Mearns's evocative pamphlet *The Bitter Cry of Outcast London* (1883) – increasingly, ethnographic practices came to be employed alongside ever-more sophisticated statistical surveys, thus the move away from colourful, almost literary, accounts of the urban poor, toward a more structured quantitative empirical approach to data collection within the city. This tendency is best exemplified in the work of the Liverpool shipowner, Charles Booth, who, compelled by the work of Mayhew and Mearns, rigorously and meticulously set about researching the full extent of poverty and hardship in London's working class neighbourhoods – only this time the emphasis was solely on systematic recording and statistical analysis (Booth published many of his early papers in the Journal of the Royal Statistical Society: Booth 1887, 1888). Exhibiting the classificatory zeal synonymous with the period, Booth succeeded in quantifying – with a degree of accuracy hitherto unprecedented – the full extent of poverty, homelessness and unemployment in the capital.[15] Consequently, Booth's classificatory investigation is generally accepted as the first truly modern empirical sociological survey of an urban locale (Hall 1996: 28–31). In Booth's work we see the beginning of the link between statistical analysis and large-scale projects of civic reform and governmental rationalisation, such as the Housing of the Working Classes Act 1890 (see also Booth 1901). The door to the 'Concept-city' was pushed firmly open.

Mayhew and his fellow ethnographic-reformers derived their knowledge of the urban experience from the street, from an understanding of the micro nuances of street life/association – both its severe limitations and its many possibilities (not least its ability to function as an agent of social cohesion). They witnessed firsthand the visceral and emotional charge of the metropolis,[16] as well as the wretched pestilent conditions of the 'city of dreadful night'. What started out as a quest to

---

14 Having identified what he believed to be the causative factors behind the problem of crime in Victorian London, Mayhew was quick to proffer his solution: the promotion of 'disciplined habits' with a strong emphasis on 'the work ethic'. His prescription for young delinquents, of whom he wrote so tirelessly, was that they should be schooled in only 'virtuous and industrious habits' (Mayhew 1968 [1862]: 275). For more on the social, moral and political beliefs of the early ethnographers, see Radzinowicz and Hood (1990: Chapter 3).

15 His findings led him to conclude that London's 'abject poor' could be divided into four subgroups ranging from those in low-paid casual employment to groups he described variously as 'savage', 'criminal' and 'almost incapable of improvement' (Booth 1892). (Charles Booth is not to be confused with William Booth, the founder in East London of the Salvation Army.)

16 The perception of the metropolis as a multi-layered, multi-dimensional entity is also much in evidence in the literary arts of the period. In the work of Dickens, Dostoyevsky and (to a lesser extent) Zola, we see a similar attempt 'to capture within a realistic mode the totality of city life' (Keating 1984: 133; see also Pike 1981). This notion of the city not simply as a corruptive force, but also as a transformative agent is also present in later works that locate the city at the centre of the narrative (most obviously Joyce's *Ulysses*, dos Passos's *Manhattan Transfer* and Döblen's *Berlin Alexanderplatz*).

understand, quickly and understandably became an exercise in ameliorative change. The city was rendered knowable and urban experience distilled down to a series of empirical categories and rigid typologies. Of course, this is only one story in many about the objectification and rationalisation of modern city life, yet it remains a useful trope in that it tells us much about how the 19th century city was unearthed and came to be perceived in wider society. However, if we are to gain a more rounded picture of the rationalisation of the modern urban experience, we must embark on an altogether different theoretical journey – a circuitous route that takes us back to our starting point, the streets and arcades of Paris, and another meeting with the spectral figure of the 19th century *flâneur*.

From *flâneur* to consumer: the metropolis as 'the primal landscape of consumption'

> The intoxification to which the *flâneur* surrenders is the intoxification of the commodity around which surges the stream of customers. (Benjamin 1973: 55)

As an emblematic figure of 19th century modernity, the *flâneur* is perhaps unique in the number of insights it offers us into the metropolitan experience. This becomes particularly apparent when one considers the more sophisticated and extrapolative historical and analytical investigations into *flâneurie* (and the Parisian arcades) undertaken some 70 years after Baudelaire's writings by the German philosopher, critic and some-time Marxist, Walter Benjamin. Benjamin's imaginative engagement with this particular period of capitalist development is interesting in that it provides us with an alternative reading of modernity, an account that also prioritises the *experiential dimension* of city life (in de Certeau's terms, the way city life 'at ground level' impacts on subjective forms of emotionality). Although concerned primarily with the commodity and the commoditisation of human life, this is no economistic reading of urban capitalism. Benjamin instead viewed the city as a 'sensual' spectacle (or, as he put it, a 'phantasmagoria', the dream world of urban capitalism) and set about unearthing the 'material traces' of the fabric of the 19th century metropolis, with the intention of uncovering the immediate, emotional and mystical facets of modern city life. The story that unfolds will be an unfamiliar one within mainstream criminological discourse.

While Benjamin's work is often seen as opaque and lacking in focus – something that, not surprisingly, has left his writings open to contradictory and controversial interpretations within the fields of cultural history, critical literature, sociology and philosophy (see Arendt 1973; McCole 1993: 10–21) – for our purposes it is possible to discern two fairly focused themes that emerge from Benjamin's *oeuvre*. These themes are enlightening not only because they help us further excavate the urban experience of the modern age, but also because they glimpse the future and tell us much about the urban condition today.[17]

The first theme is Benjamin's emphasis on the spatial and metaphysical ambiguities brought about by 19th century urbanisation. Benjamin offers a

---

17 See Zukin (1995: 253–57); Featherstone (1998); Wilson (2001: Chapter 7).

powerful, yet highly nuanced, characterisation of the experiences, frustrations and failed possibilities associated with modernity. The focal point for this concern, and many other aspects of his work, was the Parisian arcade (Buck-Morss 1989): glass-covered, gas-lit passageways in which seemingly everything was on sale ('Food, drink, roulette and vaudeville shows were abundantly on offer, and, in the first-floor galleries, sexual pleasures could be bought': Donald 1992: 440).[18] It was here, he argued, that the link between 'phantasmagoria' (understood in Benjamin's terms as a form of 'sensual immediacy'), new forms of technology and the commodity fetish was at its strongest.[19] He was fascinated by the 'mythical' qualities of the arcades, viewing them as both 'threatening' and 'alluring' – *places in which the emotions were stimulated and where the social constraints of public and private life were challenged.*

In his fragmentary work *The Arcades Project* (*Passagenarbeit*), Benjamin (1999) described the ornate shop fronts as 'dream houses' where the rich came to conspicuously consume and where the poor came simply to marvel at the dazzling cornucopia of commodities and artefacts on show under the glass and iron canopies. Benjamin claimed that within the arcades a specific *inversion of space* took place between what was interior and what was exterior, the effect of this inversion being a type of 'porosity' in which the traditional inside/outside distinction is undermined/made permeable. Although the arcades were enclosed, the glass construction of the shop windows exposed their interior. Consequently, because they were in essence corridors, effectively they had no specific exterior. For Benjamin, this raised complex spatial questions. Hence the 'disquieting ambiguity' caused by *the blurring of the public and private realms*: 'The passage[way] did not possess a fixed meaning, did not define a place, but was parasitic upon other places to which it led and the purposes for which it was used ... As an already ambiguous interior, the arcade provided the further equivocation of a private space that was public' (Caygill 1998: 132–33). With this notion of 'porosity' Benjamin presages much postmodern discourse. Consider, for example, how his work in this area (since its re-discovery in the 1970s) has been used to make sense of the shopping experience and spatial dynamics within the contemporary shopping mall (compare Featherstone 1998: 910–12).

It is also interesting to compare Benjamin's ideas on the spatial and metaphysical ambiguities of modernity with some of the themes contained within Frederic Jameson's (1991) influential *Postmodernism: or the Cultural Logic of Late Capitalism* – for many, the defining text in the postmodern vanguard. Clearly, Benjamin's notion of 'porosity' (the blurring of the inside-outside distinction) within urban space prefigures Jameson's reworking of the concept of space in his notorious description of the Bonaventure Hotel, Los Angeles (see Chapter 2 for a detailed discussion of Jameson's work in this area). However, less obvious is the way that this theme of the erosion of the distinction between interior/exterior and natural/artificial also

---

18 For a pictorial and architectural history of early 19th century shopping arcades, see Geist (1983).

19 See Gilloch (1996: 118–19) for an insight into Benjamin's particular approach to commodity fetishism.

marks, for Jameson, the changing nature of artistic/cultural expressivity in the move from modernism to postmodernism.[20]

For Benjamin, the spatial anomalies brought about by urbanisation opened up a series of exciting possibilities for developing innovative forms of human experience based upon new social relations and a new relationship with nature. However, the futility of such progressive ideas quickly became apparent to him as he documented how such brief moments of public-private porosity (at least within the 19th century arcade) were vanquished by the inexorable rise of capitalism, commodity fetishism, and the ultimate transformation of the arcades into department stores and places of residence ('whether as places of selling, dwelling or mere passage, the arcades lost the speculative challenge they originally posed to the opposition of public and private and the artificial and the natural': Caygill 1998: 133). This brings us neatly to the second substantive theme in Benjamin's work – the emergence of the modern consumer, a process brought about *inter alia* by the transformation of the arcades into functional capitalist emporia (see Miller 1981), the rise of commodification and the subsequent triumph of the consumer (consumption) over the *flâneur* (*flâneurie*).

In his famously incomplete reading of the rise and fall of the arcades, Benjamin recounts how the mythical and sensual qualities of the arcades ultimately lost out to the more rationalised and organised spectacle of the new department stores that sprang up in the wake of Haussmann's redevelopment of Paris in the 1850s (see below). While this might appear to be a transition of little consequence, it actually tells us much about how the culture of consumption became an intrinsic feature of the contemporary urban experience. On the face of it, the new department stores were closely related to the arcades and shared many features in common – not least the reliance upon grandiose commodity displays and ostentatious decoration. However, the department store had a very different remit: to 'democratise desire', stimulate demand and expand the urban retail trade (Chaney 1983; and see Porter-Benson 1986 for a related account of the development of department stores in the US). As Sharon Zukin has commented, the 'department stores placed before the public, in a great big "bazaar", goods that previously had been confined to small, specialised, elegant boutiques for a custom and luxury trade. The new availability of consumer goods to customers' sight, touch and smell democratised desire and made the exotic familiar' (1998: 827). Here, for the first time, we see the emergence of rationalised forms of *mass urban consumption* (Williams 1982). Similarly, from this point forward, we also see the start of the enduring influence of mass consumption (and its associated practices) on the built environment and the design and form of urban space: 'The depiction of the new *galeries* and department stores of Paris

---

20 For example, Jameson (1991: 11) uses Edvard Munch's painting *The Scream* as 'a dramatic shorthand parable' of the transformation to postmodernism. For Jameson, *The Scream* is not only 'a canonical expression of the great modernist thematics of alienation, anomie, solitude, social fragmentation, and isolation' but it also amounts to a 'virtual deconstruction of the very aesthetic of expression itself, which seems to have dominated much of what we call high modernism but to have vanished away ... in the world of the postmodern': 'The very concept of expression presupposes indeed some separation within the subject, and along with that a whole metaphysics of the inside and outside, of the wordless pain within the monad [the individual in the painting] and the moment in which, often cathartically, that "emotion" is then projected out and externalized, as gesture or cry, as desperate communication and the outward dramatization of inward feeling' (*ibid*).

during the Second Empire are a vivid reminder of the interplay between retailing, consumption and urban social life; they were the harbingers of the contemporary retail forms which have become a defining feature of urban form' (Miles and Paddison 1998: 821; see also Chapter 2).

In the same process, the *flâneur* was transformed into the modern 'consumer' (Benjamin 1973: 55; Bauman 1993: 173–74). As Clarke has observed in his enlightening reassessment of the practice of consumption within the modern/postmodern city:

> The gaze of the *flâneur* ... was in effect captured – or more precisely, *bought* – by the spectacular display offered by the commodified spaces of the city ... There was money to be made in the *flâneur's/flâneuse's* gaze, and it is this commodified specularity that came to provide the model that would henceforth irradiate social space in its entirety. (1997: 230)

The *flâneur* had become trapped in a mesh of increasingly pervasive rationalised consumption strategies. Not only was his primary habitat – the indeterminate, interstitial spaces of the city – under threat from the rapid expansion of mass consumption and its associated activities, but, more importantly, his role as observer-commentator of urban phantasmagoria was now virtually obsolete, as more and more people (from all walks of life) could experience for themselves the fantasy world of commodity capitalism. This 'opening out' of the commercial world was also abetted by the growth of newspapers and the possibilities this afforded for mass advertising (Leiss *et al* 1986; Richards 1991; see relatedly, Anderson 1991), and the spectacle of the great exhibitions of Paris and London (see also Frisby 2001: 104–16 on the German exhibitions of the 1890s):

> During the Second Empire of Napoleon III, this urban phantasmagoria burst out of the confines of the original arcades and spread throughout Paris ... This ostentation reached its peak in the world expositions that, in the wake of London's Crystal Palace in 1851, were held in Paris in 1855, 1867, 1889 and 1900 ... In these international fairs Benjamin saw the origins of a 'pleasure industry' and advertising techniques in which spectacle and fantasy were skillfully calibrated to the tastes and dreams of a mass audience. (Donald 1992: 440)

The *flâneur's* gaze had been transformed into the shopper's gaze, yet one should be wary, as Mike Featherstone points out, of slipping into a simple 'rhetoric of decline' and joining 'the stream of intellectual critics of mass culture from the mid-19th century onwards who had a fear that the rise of the masses would mean a lowering of standards and the engulfment of individuality' (1998: 917). The reality is more complex. Rather than simply lamenting the decline and pacification of the *flâneur* from 'outsider' aesthete to conformist consumer – a stance that Benjamin himself would surely not have countenanced – it is beneficial also to consider other important socio-spatial changes that took place as a result of this emerging period of mass urban consumption (see, for example, Horkheimer and Adorno 1973 on the emergence of 'mass society'). One such key transformation occurred in the way the modern city reformulated the gendered dimension of public space.

The growth of the department store took place alongside a series of other key social developments such as increased wages, the extension of credit facilities, the proliferation of recognisable brand names, the expansion of railway networks and, most importantly of course, the continued spread of urbanisation. Taken together, these developments facilitated the further propagation of commercial and retail practices, ultimately creating the mass market – not just in France but elsewhere in Europe and, of course, in the US. One of the main consequences of this situation was the effect this had on women's roles in society, in particular, the way it transformed the sex-segregated, male-dominated, 19th century ideological division between the public and private realm.

The new department store owners and other retailers were quick to realise the potential benefits of female customers (especially those drawn from the expanding middle classes) and set about creating more affordable, safer and alluring retail spaces in which they might shop (see Glennie 1995: 185–90; Auslander 1996). The result was that the female shopping/leisure experience took on a very different meaning from that of more traditional times:

> The transformation of buying into shopping (in the modern sense) and the subsequent 'leisurization' of shopping itself, offered middle-class women new opportunities within the public sphere. A growing number of women found in shopping a legitimate reason to escape the domestic sphere. Men already had their own pubs and clubs, their sports, etc. Moreover, they dominated the urban streets during the nineteenth century. With the coming of the department stores, middle-class women now also obtained a public space in which they could meet each other and experience a certain, albeit limited, kind of public freedom of movement. (Laermans 1993: 87)

This, of course, is not to suggest that women were invisible in public life prior to the mid-19th century, far from it.[21] Rather, it is to assert that, following the emergence of mass commodity capitalism, they were afforded far greater access both to safer public spaces (including everything from in-store women's meeting rooms to 'ladies-only' dining rooms) and to more formalised employment roles within the burgeoning retail sector, albeit of a low-paid and unregulated nature. However, this open access to public space proved something of a poisoned chalice:

> [t]he coming of the department stores gave women a public place of their own. In the department stores, they were treated courteously and could meet each other without the traditional fear of being harassed by violent men ... But at the very same time they reproduced certain stereotypes of women as 'good mothers' and 'good housekeepers' ... Their constant offering of bargains, their temporary price cuts and their sales campaigns alluded to a presupposed sense for economy and domestic responsibility among their female public. Moreover, the ads and displays made clear that the store managers frequently invoked 'the mothering complex' ... These allusions, of course, assumed the traditional link of femininity with motherhood and responsibility for education ... Women were redefined as professional shoppers or consumers and their performance of their traditional roles was thoroughly 'commodified' or redefined in terms of commodities. (Laermans 1993: 95)

Despite acknowledging that, certain caveats withstanding, the activity of consumption can be a very liberating and progressive experience – especially when

---

21 In recent years, and in sharp contrast to the established view that women in the mid-19th century did not engage in the activities of *flâneurie* and that their role in public life was negligible (Wolff 1985; Pollock 1988), there has emerged a new body of literature that suggests the situation was not so clear-cut. In the work of Nava (1997) and, most notably, Wilson (2001) we are presented with accounts of women frequenting establishments as diverse as museums, galleries, restaurants, tea rooms, hotels, even saloons and public bars. Wilson also points to the possibility of the 19th century female writer as *flâneuse*: 'To read the journalism of the mid-to-late-nineteenth century is to be struck by their presence rather than their absence' (*ibid*: 84).

considered within the context of the socially divided 19th century city – ultimately, as this albeit solitary example illustrates, the emergence of a protean mass urban consumption culture brought with it a series of highly moralising and regulatory practices that were deeply embedded with systematic and rationalising objectives.[22] To put it bluntly, *opening the door to the modern consumer had exposed the city to the operant rationality of mass consumption,* a process that, in turn, was predicated on the rigid 'ordering' of urban space. Such a situation inevitably influenced the future design and physical layout of a great many cities (see below), but less obvious is the contiguous effect of these ordered processes on the then still nascent urban consciousness. The emergent mass markets served to exacerbate the 'mechanisation of modern life', leading ultimately to what Ewen and Ewen have described as 'the commercialization of the self' (quoted in Laermans 1993: 99). It is to this new aspect of the urban sense of self – this new 'technocracy of the eye' (1993: 82) – that we now turn in a bid to further elucidate some of the other new and distinct ways of thinking and behaving that were precipitated by life in the modern capitalist metropolis.

The city as state of mind: Georg Simmel's 'the metropolis and mental life'

The most substantive theoretical interpretation of the emotions and feelings associated with the rise of the mass market and capitalist commodity fetishism, alienation, drastically changing social roles and the increased tempo of modern life on the *consciousness* of the urban dweller, was unquestionably provided by the German social theorist Georg Simmel. The work of Simmel takes us far beyond simple description of the processes and subtleties of modern life and into the more systematic realms of sociological inquiry. One might say that in the Simmelian *oeuvre* we begin to see the formulation of the urban experience as a theoretical entity. That said, Simmel does not limit himself solely to the rational discourses associated with the structural or institutional aspects of urbanisation (de Certeau's discourse of the 'Concept-city'); rather:

> ... he was interested in de Certeau's other space: the representational space within which a mass of transitory, fleeting and fortuitous interactions take place, and the ways in which these are translated into inner, emotional life. Rather like Baudelaire before him or Benjamin after, he presents the metropolis as the location of the everyday experiences of modernity, as a complex, interwoven web or labyrinth of social relations. Like Baudelaire, he therefore uses an impressionistic method to record the psychological impact of modern life. (Donald 1992: 446)

Working at the start of the 20th century, Simmel's sociology of modernity was concerned with how the individual personality adapted to and 'protected' itself from the 'profound disruption, fluctuations and discontinuities of the external metropolitan milieu'. Like Freud, Simmel saw the psyche as being a product of inner dualities and conflicts. Individual social action is thus a consequence and a reflection of these fundamental tensions ('the conflict between society and

---

22 On this point, see Horkheimer and Adorno's account of this period of urban expansion in *The Dialectic of Enlightenment* (1973), in which the authors use the terms 'mass society' and 'administered society' almost interchangeably.

individual is continued in the individual himself as the conflict among his component parts': Simmel quoted in Smith 1980: 90). At the core of the personality is the individual's 'spiritual existence' or 'creative spirit' and it is the primary goal of every urbanite to strive to enhance this inner creativity. However, this goal is challenged by the 'psychic overload' of city life:

> The psychological foundation, upon which the metropolitan individuality is erected, is the intensification of emotional life due to the swift and continuous shift of external and internal stimuli ... To the extent that the metropolis creates these psychological conditions – with every crossing of the street, with the tempo and multiplicity of economic, occupational and social life – it creates in the sensory foundations of mental life, and in the degree of awareness necessitated by our organization as creatures dependent on differences, a deep contrast with the slower, more habitual, more smoothly flowing rhythm of the sensory-mental phase of small town and rural existence. (Simmel 1995 [1903]: 31–32)

For Simmel, the infinite sensations and situations, the endless shocks, surprises and distractions of city life had the effect of bringing about what one might describe as a psychological metastasis within the modern urbanite. This took the form of a shift from a *subjective culture* (shaped by interior consciousness) to an *objective culture* precipitated by over-exposure to external stimuli (ie, the 'psychic overload' associated with the mental, almost cinematic, images that abound within the metropolis – not the least important of which being the circulation of commodities and other objective forms of urban capitalism). 'The external world becomes part of our internal world ... The fleeting, fragmentary and contradictory moments of our external life are all incorporated into our inner life' (Frisby 1985: 62). In turn, this shift brings about what Simmel describes as 'neurasthenia' or a pathological 'increase in nervous life'. The 'restlessness' and 'helpless urgency' provoked by the bustle and excitement of modern life, combined with the bombardment of the senses by external stimuli, left the urbanite in a state of accentuated nervousness. To negate these nervous energies, the individual is forced to develop a calculating exactitude or 'intellectuality' – 'the reduction of qualitative values to quantitative ones'. In other words, the modern city-dweller created a sense of emotional 'distance' from both the visceral emotions of the city and the multiplicity of urban social relationships, evolving into a cold, detached 'intellectualistic' individual, something akin to the Weberian model of instrumental rationality (see Smith 1980: 108–12). Importantly, the calculating rationality of metropolitan interaction was further exacerbated by the reduction of social relationships to simple monetary exchange.[23]

---

23 For Simmel, this 'mathematisation' of urban social life was a direct consequence of the expanding money economy ('... this psychological intellectualistic attitude and the money economy are in such close integration that no one is able to say whether it was the former that effected the latter or vice versa': Simmel 1995 [1903]: 33). Simmel stated that relationships based around calculus and money exchange can only ever be impersonal, 'non-committed' relationships. The growth of the (mature capitalist) money economy not only facilitated personal anonymity but also ensured that strong traditional relationships based around family, custom and locality are superseded by personal associations related instead to acquisitive values that require considerably less emotional attachment (ie, specialised occupational roles and group affiliations). Put simply, *money exchange objectifies human social interaction* (see Smith 1980: 101–08).

This strategy of self (psychic) preservation eventually led to the emergence of what Simmel called the 'blasé attitude', as the psychological apparatus of the modern city-dweller finally became immune – or more accurately 'indifferent'[24] – to the sights and spectacles of city life. By screening out all but a manageable amount of external stimuli, the individual is now in a position to tolerate and finally assimilate the city's excesses. While these elements of Simmel's work have received much attention, it is often the case that his account of city life in modernity is accepted too readily and thus remains, in my opinion, somewhat undeveloped. For instance, seldom considered is the question of whether or not the 'blasé attitude' and 'indifference' described above were actually totally effective barriers against the onrushing impressions of city life. Certainly, as Simmel made clear in his earlier work *The Philosophy of Money* (1978 [1900]), the situation was considerably more complex. Could it be the case that Simmel's 'blasé attitude', as David Frisby has suggested in the following important passage, has a further dimension to it?:

> If the blasé figure is the one 'unreservedly associated with the metropolis' and the mature money economy, then this figure is surely *not* one devoted to calculation – which requires being attuned to value differences – but rather to the fortuitous stimulations that the sites of modernity offer. As a modern response to the calculability of everything, the blasé attitude accords with a situation in which 'something definite' at the centre of our existence is missing. The conscious distance and indifference which metropolitan dwellers develop as defence mechanisms, and which give the impression of coolness and reserve, *are only part of their response to the capitalist metropolis*. There exists, too, a 'secret restlessness', a 'helpless urgency that lies *below* the threshold of consciousness', *which propels us towards ever-new stimulations*. (2001: 11, emphasis added; see also Frisby 1985: 98)

Thus, Simmel claimed the modern individual also strove for:

> ... momentary satisfaction in ever-new stimulations, sensations and external activities ... We become entangled in the insatiability and helplessness that manifests itself as the tumult of the metropolis, as the mania for travelling, as the wild pursuit of competition, and as the typical modern disloyalty with regard to taste, style, opinions and personal relations. (Simmel 1900, quoted in Frisby 2001: 251)

In other words, a secondary consequence of the urban blasé attitude is the *desire to differentiate*. The prevalence in society of the blasé attitude made it more and more difficult for individuals to develop and express their subjective personalities – arguably, such individualisation itself being a product of the drive for difference. Consequently, many members of urban society began to (further) differentiate themselves from others by exaggerated displays and heightened shows of individuality:

---

24 As with other 'pathologies', it is possible for 'indifference' to take on more 'extreme manifestations', as Frisby has suggested: 'Indifference, for instance, can be amplified into active distrust, reserve or even hostility, thereby creating less fluid and more inflexible demarcations in metropolitan interaction between social circles' (2001: 151). This point is particularly interesting when considered in relation to a much lesser-discussed aspect of Simmel's work, namely, his interest in spatial boundaries, a point returned to in Chapter 4.

The metropolitan personality yearns to be recognized as somehow unique in a world of objective processes and things grown to such proportions as to dwarf the individual's unsatisfied yearning for personal 'significance'. Feeling trivial and impotent in the face of 'objective culture' ... the individual rebels by flamboyantly displaying the subjective self. (Smith 1980: 110–11)

Importantly, this search for new 'stimulations' and 'sensations' took place, in the majority of cases, *within* the modern highly rationalised world. Rather than seek out *alternative, contradictory* (or even rebellious) external stimuli, the modern urbanite actually pursued stimulations 'that were themselves constitutive of the rational economic system of life' (Frisby 2001: 11). That this was the case is hardly surprising. The various modes of rationalised urban consumption introduced in the mid- to late 19th century had, by this point (the first decade of the 20th century), become a central and influential feature of urban society. As a consequence, many of the key aspects of urban life – or, in Simmelian terms, primary external stimuli – such as 'circulation in the metropolis, travel, taste and style' had already become commodified. The modern urbanite was now caught up in perhaps the key constitutive principle of modernity – *the drive for order via the processes of capital accumulation*.

In this sense, then, Simmel anticipated the emergence of consumption as a key source of widescale social expression. Because of such sentiments, Simmel's work has received a new lease of life in recent years as many commentators have interpreted Simmel's writings on the fragmentary nature of modern life as in many ways prefiguring some of the central tenets of postmodernity (see Featherstone 1991; Bauman 1992; Frisby 1992).[25] One commentator has even described Simmel's work as 'a sort of proto-postmodernism' (Kasinitz 1995: 19). By contrast, in Frederic Jameson's terms, this conception of the subject, with its outside and inside, would be classically modern. In a bid to maintain neutrality regarding this modernity/postmodernity distinction, suffice it to say that Simmel's ideas resurface at various intervals throughout this work, the general intention being to try to extend his theoretical framework for use in our present times. Simmel's work also serves another purpose here. In representing city life as a series of experiential foundations based on a subjective world in chaos, Simmel can also be seen as the philosophical progenitor of a succession of artistic and cultural intermediaries who themselves were captured by the dynamic effects of the city. It is to some select examples of this work that I now turn in a bid to further elucidate the modern urban experience.

---

25 While Simmel's work resonates strongly with many cultural and social analyses undertaken by contemporary theorists, it is important to recognise the fact that Simmel's thinking is (unsurprisingly) more commensurate with orthodox Marxist accounts of the extension of commodity relations under conditions of high capitalism than with the ideas of contemporary postmodern commentators such as Baudrillard, in that it remains firmly tethered to ideas of 'objectification' rather than notions of 'signification'. With this important reservation, it can be said, however, that, by highlighting the symbolic significance of money and the cultural importance of consumption, Simmel can be seen as the intellectual progenitor of research into 'postmodern' consumer culture and the 'world of signs' (see Chapter 2).

Visions from the street: the modern urban experience as artistic motif

> Like Simmel's individuals the artists too were under pressure ... deeply disturbed by a burgeoning external culture which was often as oppressive as it was stimulating. (Jeffrey 1977: 1)

> ... expressionism in fact is essentially nothing other than a revolt, a cry of despair of the present day personality, enslaved and condemned to powerlessness. It is, above all, in the first instance, a *cultural* movement, in the second, an *artistic* movement. (Kracauer 1918, quoted in Frisby 2001: 256)

The close of the 19th century and early part of the 20th century saw the social sciences make great strides in the interpretation and analysis of the discontinuities brought about by capitalist modernisation: most obviously the work of Durkheim on the dissolution of traditional values and their replacement with new forms of social integration based around the industrial system; Weber on the extension of rationalisation and the calculating bureaucratic mentality into more and more avenues of social life; and Marx on the corrupting and alienating forces of industrial capitalism. Yet, with the obvious exception of Simmel, it was rare for studies of this period to focus attention solely on the modern metropolis, and rarer still for them to consider the experiential dimension of city life. Consequently, we must look elsewhere if we are to further unearth the effects of these discontinuities on the *subjective emotions* of the modern urbanite.[26] To this end, I have decided to step outside of the formalised social sciences. Following the theoretical lead of David Harvey and Frederic Jameson, my excavation of the modern urban experience will now proceed by focusing on the ways in which many of the cultural producers of the period attempted to represent in artistic form the disparate psychic sensations and pronounced social inequalities associated with late 19th century and early 20th century metropolitan existence. Such an approach is entirely consistent with earlier sections on Baudelaire and Benjamin in which literary themes formed a major element of the narrative.

Inevitably, this approach has its limitations – not least the fact that artists do not purport to be social theorists. Moreover, employing art as an adjunct to (or an embellishment of) theory is almost unprecedented in mainstream criminology.[27]

---

26 One could, of course, turn to the lesser-discussed work of Ferdinand Tönnies, or even Werner Sombart, but even here the emphasis was more on the negative aspects of the city (Tönnies famously loathed cities) rather than the changing psychological moods and emotional states precipitated by metropolitan life.

27 One recent exception is Jonathan Wender's thoughtful paper, 'The eye of the painter and the eye of the police: what criminology and law enforcement can learn from Manet'. Wender uses a 'phenomenological aesthetics of the ordinary' (as interpreted through the work of the French Impressionist painter Edouard Manet) to identify the 'underlying foundations of police–citizen encounters, other than by means of their usual analytic delimitation by mainstream criminology' (2001: 4–5). It is perhaps worth pointing out to those who would cast doubt on the application of such (ostensibly) theoretical work to 'real world' situations, that Wender is in fact a serving police officer with over 13 years' experience. Other examples of the use of art as an aid to criminological theory include Sumner (1994); Claire Valier's use of painted images of punishment in her thoughtful essay 'Looking daggers: a psychoanalytical reading of the scene of punishment' (2000); and the opening of Michel Foucault's *The Order of Things* (1970), in which Velázquez's painting *Las Meninas* is used as a representation of representation in the Classical age.

However, by using art in this way, we are offered something new, something immediate and, above all, something beyond the realm of traditional criminological discourse.[28] The images selected in this section represent a series of interpretations of modern city life that go far beyond abstract empiricism or distant and heavily reinterpreted ethnographic accounts of everyday life. Instead, they provide us with a cultural snapshot of urban subjectivity at a time of unprecedented temporal change and urban tumult. In this sense, each of these images can be seen as an attempt to capture a specific moment, a fleeting portrait of a rapidly changing environment. When, in these works, the artist takes us out into the street and the chaos of the crowd, he has but one aim: *to make sense of the challenges posed by the urban experience*. As David Harvey has commented, 'if the "eternal and immutable" could no longer be automatically presupposed, then the modern artist had a creative role to play in defining the essence of humanity' (1990: 18–19).

The city emerged as a legitimate object of artistic attention during the second half of the 19th century. This is not to suggest that the city never featured in earlier artistic movements, only that previous attempts to represent it in art (most notably, the historical representations of the city in early religious and (later) Renaissance art, the 'realistic' city vistas popular in 17th century Dutch painting, and the minute cityscape reproductions of the Italian 18th century *vedutista* school) were more concerned with the city either as a totality (ie, a 'city state'), or as a metaphysical backdrop or exemplar linked to religious or classical idioms. What was different about mid-19th century city art was that it strove to capture the *intimate experience and vibrancy* of urban life. It should be stated, however, that this shift in focus was not an immediate one. Even with the added impetus in the 1860s of Baudelaire's *cri de coeur* to artists and writers to draw inspiration from the cityscape and, in particular, the 'newness' (in terms of the aesthetic spectacle) of the metropolis, it took several decades for the modern city to emerge as a focal point of cultural and artistic attention. By the end of the 19th century, however, artists on both sides of the Atlantic had firmly established the metropolis as a primary motif in Western art.

It is generally accepted that the first representations of the modern metropolis in Western art were undertaken by the Impressionists during the 1870s (Shapiro 1984: 97; Whitford 1985: 45). At this point, in the work of Degas, Manet, Renoir and Monet, we see a gradual gravitation towards the urban milieu (Plate 1), and a tentative, albeit temporary, estrangement from established Impressionist subject matter such as still life, landscapes and the rural idiom. Often these artists were themselves *flâneurs*, and thus relished the chance to capture 'the newness' and romance of the city in their work, what Baudelaire had described in his seminal essay 'The painter of modern life' (1964, first published in 1863) as the 'transient, the fleeting, the contingent' as characteristic of modernity. However, while these and other artists (see the later renderings of post-Impressionists like Pissarro and Marquet) were successful in representing the restless character of the lower middle classes, their artistic gaze rarely extended

---

28 Merleau-Ponty would see the use of art in this manner as a useful way of 'relearning to look at the world' (Merleau-Ponty 1962, quoted in Wender 2001: 5).

to include the industrial poor, the unemployed or the more insalubrious sections of urban society. As Collier suggests, for artists like Monet, it was 'the constantly shifting appearance of the city' that was of interest rather than 'the experience of living in it' (1985: 47). Such selectivity, however, would not continue. Elsewhere, artists were no longer prepared to draw a veil over the darker, corrupting aspects of the metropolis.

Contemporaneously, the city also emerged as an object of attention in the art and popular culture of the US. Towards the end of the century, the pronounced uncertainty in the early realism of Winslow Homer and Thomas Eakins heralded a departure for American art from its traditional fascination with the natural-frontier idiom, and by 1900 many artists had began to forsake the pastoral imagery of America's great wildernesses for the bustle and vibrancy of the urban environment (Baigell 1971). The city of choice for this new breed of more politically charged artists, such as realists John Sloan, Robert Henri, George Luks, and George Bellows, was New York, at the time the very epitome of metropolitan modernity. These 'realists' set about capturing the less seemly side of the city, with the intention of unearthing and portraying the unvarnished realities of urban life amongst the industrial poor (Plate 2). It is interesting to note that at the same time these early urban representational painters were venturing into the back streets of New York in an attempt to 'record life' in the city, the first Chicago School researchers were also embarking on their own investigations into life in the tenements and run-down neighbourhoods of Chicago (see Chapter 3). Although not in any way connected, both groups shared a fundamental concern with what lay behind the immediate façade of routine and regularity. In the case of the Chicagoans, of course, the goal was to try to understand how these commonplace functions of urban life affected or contributed to levels of crime and deviance.

A very different and, for our purposes, more enlightening artistic reaction to urbanism was taking place in Germany at the start of the 20th century. The phenomenal growth of German cities following reunification in 1871 was met with great scepticism by many commentators apprehensive about the harmful consequences of modernisation. Similarly, the pervasive effects of urbanisation were not readily accepted by a fragmented nation steeped in Völkisch traditions and regional mores. Such misgivings as regards the metropolis were much in evidence in the highly metaphorical German Expressionist art of the 1910s, in particular the work of Ludwig Meidner and Ernst Ludwig Kirchner. Meidner was fascinated by the urban motif, and his subjective art reflects what was for him the hostile and confusing nature of the urban experience. In Meidner's 'apocalyptic self-portrait', *I and the City* (1913) (Plate 3), we see, almost for the first time in modern art, the city represented as a soulless, almost violent entity. Gone was the light and distance of earlier Impressionist cityscapes, and in its place a darker, more visceral interpretation of the city. Kirchner also painted Berlin in a similarly dramatic and disturbing fashion. Drawing upon the allegorical paintings of Edvard Munch and the Belgian psychological painter James Ensor, Kirchner repeatedly attempted to represent the alienation and futility of city life in his emotional and anxiety-ridden paintings. Although only 40 years had passed between the early portrayals of the metropolis in the work of the Impressionists and the harrowing, almost neurotic compositions of the German Expressionists, it was abundantly clear that by 1914 a dramatic transformation in cultural attitudes regarding the metropolis had taken place.

Paradoxically, many of the elements of modern urban life that Kirchner and Meidner believed would eventually consume and dehumanise the individual – crowds, mass consumption, technology, mechanisation – were the very same features of the modern city that inspired abstract painting of the 1910s and 1920s. Abstract artists rose to the challenge of metropolitan modernisation, 'reconstituting painting' in the hope that, by employing new forms of representation, they would 'disclose the truth of appearance more fully than anything before' (Jeffrey 1977: 3). A prime example of this development is the work of Robert Delaunay, whose oversized paintings of Paris, and especially the Eiffel Tower, are often used as the symbol *par excellence* of the 20th century metropolis. However, such unconditional devotion to modernisation and technological progress was, by the 1920s, the exception rather than the rule.[29] Many artists were focusing instead on the alienation and dehumanisation of urban life. For example, in the cityscapes of CRW Nevinson (especially *The Soul of a Soulless City*, 1919–20), Abraham Walkowitz and, most memorably, Joseph Stella, we can clearly see the artists' palpable concern with the mechanistic, 'regimented' qualities of the metropolis and how modern buildings and infrastructure were perceived to be suffocating and subjugating human existence (see Mellor and Jeffrey 1977; Shapiro 1984: 108).

Disenchantment with the inherent alienation of modern urban experience was at its most pronounced in the work of German artists like George Grosz, Otto Dix, Karl Hubbuch and Max Beckmann. For the painter and Communist George Grosz, the city was a site of both enthrallment and corruption, and his urban cityscapes – most memorably *The Big City* (1917) (Plate 4) – reflected this tangible ambiguity:

> At first the scene [*The Big City*] pulsates with the excitement of hurrying crowds, speeding vehicles, huge buildings and flashing neon signs. A closer look reveals something closer to pandemonium. Figures collide, a tram seems out of control, a hearse is pitched over, everything is in uproar as though the asylums had opened their doors and the streets were suddenly full of lunatics running riot. (Collier 1985: 60)

No such uncertainty was present in the work of Otto Dix, a painter who viewed the city simply as an edifice to capitalist inequality, and whose realist paintings were a scathing condemnation of urban life in 1920s Berlin. Likewise, his contemporary Beckmann also viewed the city as an epicentre of exploitation, deprivation and improbity, his paintings and lithographs of Berlin abounding with images of prostitutes, disfigured war veterans, cripples and beggars. In the work of these artists we see the metropolis exposed 'as the place of crime, perversion, mechanization, and economic and sexual exploitation ... The inhabitants of these

---

29 One area of modern art where technology and the modern industrial city were celebrated was in the Italian Futurist movement of the 1910s and 1920s (eg, the work of Umberto Boccioni, Carlo Carrà and Gino Severini).

scenes are mass-men, decadents, or freaks, and they are offered no hope of redemption' (Shapiro 1984: 115–16).[30]

Ultimately, perhaps the most memorable, and for our purposes instructive, portraits of the psychological character of the lonely, isolated modern urbanite came out of the US in the work of the American social realist, Edward Hopper (eg, *New York Corner*, *Hotel Room*, *Automat*, *New York Office* and, most famously, *Nighthawks*). In a series of unforgettable paintings Hopper continued the realist tradition of glorifying the prosaic nature of urban existence (including, at times, consumption), only this time, beneath the realistic tableaux, something else was apparent, something less tangible. While, on the face of it, the intrinsic theme in these works is a tension born of emptiness, in truth they take us far beyond the simple tropes of alienation, isolation and *anomie* so apparent in earlier Expressionist art. In Hopper's urban paintings (and in the works of contemporaries such as Philip Evergood, Raphael Soyer and Ben Shahn) something else is present. Imbued in his characters is a strong sense of acceptance, or, more accurately, a pronounced fatalism. Time has passed and the modern urbanite has now come to expect and accept the detachment and anonymity associated with the urban experience (Plate 5). By this point, technology and rationality have exerted a firm grip on the modern subject, and in Hopper's works this is immediately apparent. *These are images of subjugation and resignation.*

It is interesting at this point to revisit the ideas of Walter Benjamin (remember, Hopper and Benjamin were close contemporaries). In *One Way Street* (Benjamin 1979) – a work that attempts to identify common elements of urban experience in various cities – Benjamin argues that the modern urban experience should be understood in the broad terms of 'the intermediate concept of the experience of resistance'. By this he means that, in the pre-modern era, human action, movement, etc, was hindered by simple, identifiable and inexorable forces: 'the boundless resistance of the natural world.' By contrast, the 'modern urban experience is characterized by resistance *without a substantial entity that can be identified as its cause.* The experience of resistance does not rest on there being something – a substance – which resists us, but is a symptom of an intangible obstacle to our movement'

---

30 Such tendencies are also much in evidence in early mass cinema. From the inception of the medium, film-makers were intrigued by the metropolis and its effect on the individual. Early filmic representations of the city quickly established a pattern that was rarely deviated from – the city as an alienating force. See, eg, early German films such as Grune's sinister *Die Strasse* (1923) and Mayer's *Berlin: die Symphonie einer Grosssadt* (1927), a sprawling documentary that 'in portraying the density and vitality of big-city existence ... managed to convey an impression of aimlessness and of the sacrifice of individual freedom to an unrelenting city machine' (Sutcliffe 1984a: 154). The most celebrated example of early cinema's deep mistrust of the city is Fritz Lang's *Metropolis* (1926). The technically sophisticated sets, cinematography and visual construction employed by Lang in his adaptation of Thea von Harbou's novel evoke many of the apprehensions and fears concerning the rampant technological innovation, mechanisation and industrialisation underway in Germany during the 1920s. The central protagonist of *Metropolis* is the regulated city: its Babylonian towers and intimidating edifices loom large over a downtrodden populace, while massive subterranean machinery subjugates human emotions and feelings. These themes are at their most evident in the film's dramatic climax, '[i]n which the human form does *not* win out over the city's inhumanity, but quite the contrary; the city, as "machine to be shown", wins out over the human body as the tired, naked helpless figure of Brigitte Helm as Maria is *turned into a machine* in the pivotal laboratory sequence' (Minden 1985: 200, emphasis in original).

(Caygill 1998: 130, emphasis added). Ultimately this is capitalism, but what typifies its working is the inaccessibility of the causal process, lassitude and a nebulous sense of hindrance. This is the exact same struggle that is writ large in Hopper's paintings – a struggle against intangible, amorphous and, at this point, unknowable modernising forces.[31]

Artists thus, initially captured by the dynamism of the city, became (variously) appalled by its dehumanising tendencies. However, Hopper yields the definitive moment. His paintings reflect a common sense of acceptance or, more accurately, resignation in the face of the overwhelming forces of modernisation, a state of mind that I will link in subsequent chapters to particular forms of criminal behaviour under current social conditions. However, in the meantime, I wish to move away from subjective interpretations of urban life to the more physical domain of bricks, mortar, steel and glass, for it is here, amid the towering concrete silos and serried ranks of modernist buildings, that we find the clearest expression of modernity's operant rationality, and the most intimate and overt attempt to homogenise urban experience.

Building utopia: modernist architecture and the dream of urbanity

For to plan a large contemporary city is to engage in a tremendous battle, and how can you fight a battle if you do not know what you are fighting for? (Le Corbusier 1986 [1925])

The built environment is fundamental to our experience of city life. Each of us internalises our own individual relationship with the buildings and structures we inhabit and frequent – our homes, our workplaces, the places in which we socialise and the routes we take as we negotiate the city (what Kevin Lynch has called the 'paths', 'edges' and 'nodes' of urban fabric: Lynch 1960) – and thus our experience of the city cannot fail to be composed of a highly personal, subjective dialogue with architecture. In the words of David Harvey: 'If we experience architecture as communication, if, as Barthes insists, "the city is a discourse and this discourse is truly a language", then we ought to pay close attention to what is being said, particularly since we typically absorb such messages in the midst of all the other manifold distractions of urban life' (1990: 67). However, at the same time there is a series of public images and experiences that we all share and that sharply reflect some of the core values and ideals that gave shape and meaning to the modern industrial city. Nowhere are these ideals and values more apparent than in the history of urban design since the mid-19th century. As Jervis states, 'the modern city, with its sleek buildings, its streamlined streets, can be presented as a hymn to rationality, a key exemplar of the project of modernity. The modernization of the city has been an attempt to impose a rational form on an inchoate mass, and thereby

---

31 One could also make the claim that Hopper and Benjamin seemed to share a fundamental interest in the spatial aspects of urban experience. As Germain Viatte (1989: 64) has argued, Hopper's work often 'deploys a constant to and fro between exterior and interior, between the limitless space that has always fascinated American artists and the shrinking world that encloses the isolated individual'. Urban life being seen not just in terms of subjugation, but also as a *bounded* experience.

produce a city that would be intelligible, legible' (1998: 67). This, then, is a story about an attempt to build an urban utopia.

Given that, in everyday language, the use of the word 'model' as an adjective implies striving towards an ideal, perhaps it would have been provident from the outset to have named the field of study known as urban planning with the alternative appellation, 'urban modelling', for rarely, if ever, have the theoretical underpinnings of a discipline been so heavily influenced by a core group of protagonists whose shared and abiding characteristic was their lofty, unfettered idealism (see Fishman 1982; C Boyer 1986; and the wonderful, culturally rich collection *Ideal Cities* by Ruth Eaton 2002). (We are reminded here, of course, of one half of de Certeau's depiction of the (modernist) framework for thinking about urban life – the 'Concept-city' of 'utopian and urbanistic discourse'.)

The notion of designing urban space is clearly not a new phenomenon,[32] yet it is conventional to begin the contemporary story in mid-19th century Paris with Baron Georges Haussmann's 'creative destruction' of Second Empire Paris. Charged by Napoleon III with the task of transforming Paris into a thoroughly modern and monumental capital city, Haussmann embarked on a course of redevelopment of unprecedented size and scope (Giedion 1978: 529–65). Although ostensibly an ameliorative project including slum clearance, the overall plan was also infused with both a fundamental concern with social control and the hope that life in the city might become rationalised via the process of urban modernisation. In this sense, Haussmann's redevelopment of Paris can be seen as representative of city planning in modernity more generally.

Demonstrating a penchant for wholesale restructure, Haussmann demolished whole swathes of the old Parisian *quartiers* during the reconstruction, and within 17 years he had carried out the Emperor's plans and transformed Paris into the 'capital of the nineteenth century' (Olsen 1986: Chapter 4). However, behind the imposing new façades, hardship and poverty continued for a great many Parisians. Haussmann had no interest in relocating the former inhabitants of the inner-city neighbourhoods he had obliterated and the homeless hordes were left with no option but to remain within the city. As a consequence, the problems of crime, degeneracy and epidemic among the Parisian poor never really dissipated, and soon, behind the rows of regimented and ordered street fronts, disorder once again ineluctably flourished, only this time, the freedom of movement afforded by the new boulevards served to expose even more graphically the class divisions and inequality of life in modern Paris – a dichotomy that confronted Baudelaire on virtually every street corner but which, ultimately, he failed to understand.

In summary, from the point of view of dealing with the urban poor, the first major city-planning initiative of the modern age had been a failure. Rather than dealing head on with the litany of urban problems that abounded in the modern industrialised metropolis, Haussmann had simply tried to eliminate them. This would not be the last time such a charge would be levelled at modern city-planners.

---

32 For a history of early systematic town planning, see Morris (1979).

The mass overcrowding that characterised the industrialised city at the turn of the century and, in particular, the inherent problems of London's inner-city slums (see Roberts 1971) brought about a more progressive attempt to reconfigure the modern city. As has been well-documented, the population of the great cities exploded during the 19th century,[33] resulting in the creation of the most abhorrent living conditions imaginable in the traditional lower working class areas of many great cities. Despite the intrepid research of Mearns, Mayhew, Frégier and Booth, bringing the deplorable conditions endemic in late 19th century London and Paris to the attention of the bourgeoisie, political and governmental response was muted, and the dreadful plight of the working classes was largely ignored. With no end in sight to the problems of urban overcrowding and poverty, the growing consensus among reformers and social scientists by 1900 was that the metropolis itself might be the root cause of social ills, potential political revolt, and even possible biological contagion. Furthermore, the belief that overcrowding within the city was a seedbed for degeneracy and depravity was borne out by increased levels of disorder, thuggery, and socialist agitation in many cities across Europe. It was the last development, the increased threat of Bolshevism and political insurrection, that ultimately forced the establishment to tackle the problems of the inner city with policy intervention. The result in the UK and the US was the related planning concepts of the mass-transit suburb and the Garden City.

While the first planned railway suburbs were constructed in the US, it was in Great Britain that the mass-transit suburb would flourish as a planning concept. London County Council had previously experimented with new suburbs on a small scale at White Hart Lane (1904–13) and Norbury (1906–10), but it was in the post-World War II era that the mass-transit suburb would take off. Between the Wars, approximately one and a quarter million new homes were built in Greater London alone (Johnson 1964), a large proportion of which were situated within mass housing estates on the suburban ring. The key figure here is Raymond Unwin, whose plan for a series of 'peripheral satellites' was implemented by the London County Council. Huge housing estates providing cheap and sanitary accommodation were constructed in London at sites such as Waitling, Downham, and at Becontree.[34] While these uninspiring estates served their purpose and placated the working class by providing 'visible proof of the irrelevance of revolution' (Parliamentary Secretary to the Local Government Board, quoted in Hall 1996: 71), their ultimate legacy was the uniform mass suburb as a central tool of the modern planners' trade. These homogeneous estates mirrored the rationalised forms of mass production and thus further trapped the individual in an existence of alienated production, standardised consumption and urban *anomie*.

The other panacea for the ills of the 19th century slum was the Garden City movement. Ebenezer Howard, the founder of the movement, had grown

---

33 See Chandler and Fox (1974); Mitchell (1975); Wohl (1977); Evenson (1984); Matzerath (1984).

34 The lack of imagination and rejection of diversity that characterises these huge estates designed by architects whose remit was to house an increasingly dissatisfied working class is typified by the Becontree Estate in East London: a homogeneous sprawl of uniform houses, never fully integrated into the transport network, that offers residents very little in the way of cultural diversity.

disillusioned with city life and attempted a 'marriage of town and country' in a new type of settlement founded on 'community action' and 'co-operation', and designed around that most enduring of modernist motifs, the concentric circle model. Howard put forward his plan for a union of co-operative commonwealths in *Tomorrow: A Peaceful Path To Real Reform* (1898), a book of undeniable vision that, as the title suggests, had as its premise a fundamental interest in reforming not only the problems of the overcrowded city, but the social structure as a whole. For Howard, it was not enough just to placate the proletariat: instead he fostered the quixotic belief that the working classes could be offered a better future via the radical reconfiguration of urban settlements along communal lines. However, the reformist goals of the Garden City model were crucially undermined by Howard's political naiveté. Capitalism was now so developed that it was impossible to allow wholesale implementation of Howard's plans, and thus (with the exception of Letchworth, Hampstead and Welwyn Garden City) the only garden cities actually constructed were diluted prototypes undertaken not by Howard, but by lesser urban designers. Although Howard's ideas would have lasting resonance in planning history,[35] his Garden City was doomed to failure. Modern life had moved on, and Howard's faith in communal values and the rural idiom had been supplanted by the erroneous perception inherent within modernist culture that technology, and in particular architectural engineering advancements, could create perfectly ordered individuals and thus a perfectly ordered society.

The buildings of the future had been a reality in the US for some time. Louis Henry Sullivan, Dankmar Adler and other members of the Chicago School of Architecture had, since the 1890s, been making use of new construction techniques, such as the load-bearing steel frame, reinforced concrete and sheet glass, in the development of that most synonymous emblem of modernism – the skyscraper. Although it would take 50 years for skyscrapers to become commonplace features in European cities, the belief that modern architectural developments used in tandem with radical urban-planning concepts might enable urban designers to create truly modern and progressive cities immediately gained support. In Italy, in 1914, Sant'Elia and Chiattone produced the *Futurist Manifesto of Architecture*, a document that expressed a passionate fascination with machinery and the conviction that 'technology could reform culture' (see da Costa Meyer 1995). However, for the most part, the Futurists' urban predictions remained consigned to the drawing board and it was left to others to take up the challenge offered by the new construction techniques.

In the meantime, the pre-eminent position of the metropolis in modern society came under assault from a strong anti-urban movement. The tendency towards *de-urbanism* within planning, based around the theories of Kropotkin, Geddes and Howard, independently gained support both in Russia (where it was envisaged that town and country would ultimately become indistinguishable) and in the US, most notably with Frank Lloyd Wright's Broadacre City model. However, visions of a

---

35 The Garden City concept would be developed with some success in the US and Europe, and also greatly influence the 'de-urbanist' school of planning in the 1920s (especially in Russia, eg, Sokol Garden City). Later, Howard's ideas resurfaced, albeit in adulterated form, in the 'New Town' programme in Britain during the 1940s and 1950s.

hybrid of the urban and the pastoral were woefully misjudged and the metropolis ineluctably triumphed over proposed de-urbanist alternatives. Indeed, increased employment opportunities in urban areas ensured that between 1900 and 1920, metropolitan populations in the West continued to expand rapidly. Consequently, industrialised cities, already spatially segmented along class, race, sex and ethnic grounds, continued to develop in a very unregulated and unplanned manner. It was against this backdrop that the International School of architecture and urban design emerged to postulate its own inimitable prescription for the ills of urbanity and the modern metropolis.

In stark contrast to anti-urbanist thinking, the International School believed it possible to create a unitary, egalitarian urbanity through modernisation and modernist urban design. The School's advocates and practitioners unflinchingly subscribed to the Saint Simonian belief that 'ultra-modernity' in harness with large-scale urban planning could create the perfectly ordered society. Despite (or perhaps because of) such flawed logic, the International School of the 1920s and 1930s marks the apogee of ill-fated 20th century attempts to create an urban utopia. In reality, the International School produced very little; however, its legacy was an enduring one, and ill-conceived notions such as the *machine à habiter* and the related belief in 'super-urbanisation' would ultimately wreak havoc in the lives of city-dwellers the world over in the post-World War II era.

Influenced by Italian Futurism, the rectilinear geometry and technocratic pastorals of the International School reflected a style that was intended to be universal, classless and absolute. Here was the ultimate attempt to reject cultural heterogeneity and rationalise the urban experience. The School had devotees in Europe (most notably Mies van der Rohe and Gropius in Germany, JJP Oud in Holland, and Luçat in France), the US (Hood, Howe and Lescaze, and Neutra) and elsewhere (Nicolaiev and Fissenko in the Soviet Union; and Yamada in Japan) (Riley 1992), but it is most closely associated with the ideas of the Francophile Swiss Calvinist Charles-Édouard Jeanneret, or Le Corbusier as he preferred to be called. Le Corbusier was an exceptionally gifted architect who, had he restricted himself to small projects such as his brilliant *Villa Savoye* (1929–31) and the Chapel at Ronchamp (1950–55), would doubtless have assured himself a less controversial, but still seminal, position in the history of architecture. However, as his *nom de guerre* intimates (Le Corbusier loosely translates as 'the crow-like one'), the self-styled 'Supreme Architect' preferred to take a 'birds-eye' view of the urban environment – the paradigmatic viewpoint of the 'Concept-city' – and, consequently, he became obsessed with designing an entire city.

Le Corbusier's social utopianism was based on the concept that 'new ways of building required new ways of living' and he promoted the International Style with the slogan 'Architecture or Revolution', boldly asserting that the unremitting functionalism of his buildings – and indeed the city as a whole – would inevitably make for a more rational way of life, thus reducing the threat of urban political insurrection (Le Corbusier 1928a, 1928b, 1935). Permeating his work was the minimalist belief that buildings and homes should be free of decoration and extraneous ornament:

We have become willing ... to live in *arbitrary* surroundings ... fashion has grafted itself onto our sickness: the fashion of complicated forms ... These undisciplined good intentions produce the kinds of streets you see all around you in Buenos Aires or, for that matter, in European cities – those atrocious displays of platitudes, laziness, and academic pretension. (Le Corbusier, quoted in Guiton 1982: 35–36)

He similarly despised the randomness of chance interaction, a phenomenon that for the likes of Simmel and Baudelaire epitomised life in the modern metropolis, and for de Certeau characterised the street level of urban experience. Consequently, he urged his architectural acolytes 'to kill the street'. The promenade, piazza and market were anathema to Le Corbusier: 'Cafes and places of recreation will no longer be the fungus that eats up the pavements of Paris', he declared in a typical outburst of unashamed absolutism. Le Corbusier believed that, for cities to succeed, planners must 'decongest the centres of our cities by increasing their density' (cited in Hall 1996: 207). This paradox could be resolved only by demolishing the existing city centre and replacing it with a network of skyscrapers that would enable people to 'live in the air'. Given Le Corbusier's mindset, we should be eternally thankful that in the majority of cases his urban designs were never fully implemented.[36] However, despite being phenomenally unsuccessful at transforming his utopian cityscapes into built reality, Le Corbusier remains perhaps the central figure in the history of 20th century urban planning, for, despite widescale criticism of his architectural rationale, his misguided planning ethos went on to dominate urban design in cities around the globe for almost 50 years.

While modernism in architecture and urban design was understandably placed on hold during World War II, it was to resurface with a vengeance in the 1950s and 1960s in the shape of the Le Corbusier-inspired tower block and the high-rise mass estate. Indeed, a great many post-war governments adopted the multi-storey model as the most expedient way in which to rebuild war-torn, bomb-damaged cities. Unfortunately the blind faith placed in these watered-down versions of the *machine à habiter* was misjudged. One does not need to be a student of town planning to realise the abject failure (in most cases) of the high-rise mass-housing estate. A walk through any of these vertiginous estates today highlights all too acutely the shortcomings of the Le Corbusian prescription for our inner cities. Indeed, the 'Supreme Architect's' legacy is glaringly evident in crumbling estates the world over, from The Gorbals to La Grande Borne, from the Punjab's Chandigarh to Pruitt-Igoe – precisely what was dynamited in St Louis in 1972 (see Chapter 2; Hall 1996: 235–40).

The history of urban planning in modernity is indeed an unfortunate one. Instead of sticking to the fundamental task of designing urban spaces that might go some way to alleviating the social problems and embedded conflict of interests that

---

36 The notable exception was Le Corbusier's *Unité d'habitation* (1946–52) in Marseilles. Built as a prototype for a much larger project (never completed), the *Unité* was 18 storeys high and designed to accommodate 1,600 residents. The design included many of the architectural features that Le Corbusier believed would facilitate a 'new kind of living' within his *machine à habiter*. Built on concrete *pilotis* (stilts), and incorporating the Corbusian trademark *brise-soleil*, the *Unité* had its own shopping mall and concrete roof garden, but the design proved to be socially problematic. The Marseillais residents despised the functional interiors, eschewed the in-house facilities, and instead steadfastly upheld the habits and mores of provincial French living.

are symptomatic of the modern industrialised city, planners too often blindly followed that most dominant tendency synonymous with intellectual modernism – unfettered utopianism. Despite making some substantial inroads in overcrowding and sanitation, many other social problems, from urban crime to community isolation, have persisted. Indeed, rather than dissipating, these problems have spread outward to the suburban tractlands and beyond. The fact that we no longer believe that society's ills can be cured by large-scale public urban planning speaks volumes about the maladroit efforts of city-planners in the modern age and, perhaps more worryingly, opens the door to the free market – most obviously through the emergence of the so-called 'private-sector-led model of urban renewal' (see Zukin 1998: 830–35).

But what was the reason for such abject failure? Perhaps the answer can be found in the *Congrès Internationaux d'Architecture Moderne* – one of the pivotal texts of modernist architecture. As Holston (1986) has pointed out, the *Congrès Internationaux* outlined five principles of modernist city-design – housing, work, recreation, traffic and (later) the administrative function – each one oriented to functionalism and steeped in the belief that 'rational man' will enjoy living in a 'rational building'. In this account, the diverse concerns, complex dynamics and social heterogeneity that constitute the very fabric of urban life have, in accordance with the Le Corbusian doctrine, been conveniently banished from the equation. Instead, we have an architecture of imposition, implemented by architects who believed that the alienation and *anomie* characteristic of the 19th century metropolis could be eradicated by new buildings and urban designs that would create order and balance, and thus reduce the urban experience to a series of homogeneous temporal and spatial spheres delineated by class concerns and gender and employment roles. Today, thousands of sub-Corbusian estates exist in a state of decrepitude requiring almost constant repair and reinvestment. Geographically and economically isolated, these estates stand as perfect examples of what happens when urban environments are designed by architects who choose to privilege the concerns of aesthetic functionalism as a programme of 'rational' eradication of the complex social and cultural dynamics of the street and the multi-layered interactivity of urban life.

Conclusion

The city and the urban experience have always been at the heart of the story of modernity and this chapter has sought to display this implicit theme through an ensemble of accounts from social and cultural theory. Central to this account is the city as the locus of all that is new and challenging, a world of disruption and discontinuity with all that went before. At one level, this has been an excavation of the city from the experiential level, from the streets, as it were, from Benjamin's beguiling arcades to Hopper's dissociated urbanites; however, set against the backdrop of pronounced demographic, economic and social change occurring during the 19th and early 20th centuries, at another level the picture that emerged was one of an urban environment gridded by inexorable regulatory and rationalising discourses that were such a constitutive element of the classical project of modernity. Yet this is by no means the end of the story. Our task now is to bring the situation up to date as the modern world continues to march ever-onwards.

Chapter 2
City Life at Modernity's Edge:
A *Tour d'Horizon*

Our world, for good or ill, has begun to operate on principles different from those that have dominated much of the [20th] century and we tend to see ourselves as part of a culture that we may not altogether understand but which we recognize as being 'after' what we have known. (Stevick 1985: 135)

Determination is dead, indeterminism reigns. (Baudrillard 1988: 127)

Times are tough when things have got no meaning. (Oasis, *Stand by Me*, 1997)

Introduction

Few would dispute the fact that over the last three decades huge cultural, aesthetic, economic, social and technological changes have taken place. The question that has preoccupied academics in seemingly endless exchanges has been how best to characterise these various transformations and fluctuations. For sociologists especially, the issue has been one of epochs and eras. On one side is the view that this round of change is evidence of the demise of the modernist project (variously defined) and society's ultimate transition into conditions of 'postmodernity' (eg, Baudrillard 1981; Huyssen 1990; Jameson 1984, 1991; Lyotard 1984).[1] The opposing perspective, generally associated with theorists such as Giddens (1984, 1990), Beck (1992) and Berman (1982), is more circumspect, suggesting instead that the changing nature of society does not involve anything as significant as a paradigm shift and thus that current social and economic transformations should be situated in the realm of 'late modernity' or 'late capitalism'. The debate can be conceptualised around the knotty question of whether the 'postmodern' represents a qualitative break with or merely a quantitative intensification of what has gone before. Are we experiencing the inauguration of a new historical era/epoch, or simply an extension – perhaps more accurately an augmentation (maturation?) – of existing tendencies? Complexity is added to the picture by the realisation that 'modernity' has all along been considerably more heterogeneous than its self-descriptions (Frisby 1985, 2001), a situation that casts considerable doubt on these established, yet rather schematic, and ultimately 'binary' distinctions.

One of our main goals, then, must surely be to try to unravel the semantic and descriptive categories that surround these epochal debates. In particular, we must reconsider this 'will to binarise' and how it has the unfortunate effect of *framing* discussions of the 'contemporary' so that they are forced to fit neatly into this 'modern'/'postmodern' definitional divide. Much circulates around a grouping of

---

1   For more on the distinction between modernity, modernism and postmodernity, see Bauman (1991: 4). For a general review of the impact of postmodernity on the social sciences, see Rosenau (1992); Seidman and Wagner (1992). For criminology specifically, see Schwartz and Friedrichs (1994).

distinctive features. On the one hand, their individual importance is *inflated* by taking them as definitive of the either/or pair of modern or postmodern – almost as if each element is being forced to bear the weight of this huge distinction. On the other hand, there is a tendency to *downrate* their significance by ignoring the explanatory discourses and linking dynamics that surround these changes, leaving us with little more than a kind of semantic scrapbook or hyper-list, an interesting, if conceptually limited, theoretical mapping exercise. (Of course, at this point, one could argue that this very line of inquiry might itself be cast as a sort of contest between postmodern and modern ideas of theory: 'superficial' versus 'deeper', more analytical modes of understanding; successful groupings of indicators versus grounded aetiological explanations.) Ultimately, the effect of this double movement is to suppress the investigatory pursuit of these contrasts and changes because everything gets short-circuited back into the binary classification exercise.

We should instead seek out less pejorative forms of analyses (of these changes) that are not fettered by such binary reductionism. The position put forward here is that, irrespective of whether or not we are currently living through a period of wholesale structural or epochal change – late modernity or postmodernity – we are experiencing significant, if not extraordinary, modifications to many of the taken-for-granted assumptions and modes of organisation associated with the era of classic modernity, and that these changes need to be investigated. This more 'agnostic' position enables us to talk of our inhabiting (or perhaps more accurately, of travelling through) a continuous yet discontinuous moment, what one might usefully describe here as an inchoate period of (yet to be fully realised) societal and epochal hybridity. Hence, it is not my intention to describe anything so bold as a distinctly 'postmodern experience', nor for that matter to rely on the discourses associated with late modernity. Rather, it is my contention that the contemporary world is in fact a composite of *both* modern and 'postmodern' features. The point therefore is to identify not just the changes underway in society but also the important continuities, for our current times are clearly constituted from both. Perhaps the following passage by the criminologist Wayne Morrison best captures my position:

> Instead of a radical break it is more apt to define postmodernism as the intensification and multiplication of trends and features of modernism occurring simultaneously within modernity while denoting the problematising and ambivalence of modernity ... We live within modernity but at a distance from the assumptions which gave it security, which made modernity appear 'natural'. It is therefore possible to talk of ourselves as living in late-modernity, or the post-modern condition, or postmodernism, but not to talk of our inhabiting post-modernity. (Morrison 1995: v)

What, then, of the city in this era of 'epochal hybridity'? Cities have always been at the cutting edge of societal change and upheaval, a point made in detail in the previous chapter. This situation clearly continues today, with cities from Las Vegas to London, Kuala Lumpa to Kingston, Jamaica being held up as multiple loci or compound aggregates of the various changes and transformations associated with the discourses of post and late modernity. Consider, for example, Ed Soja (1989) on the 'postmodern geographies' of Los Angeles; Saskia Sassen (1991, 1994) on 'global cities' such as Hong Kong and Sydney; Manuel Castells on 'information cities' like Tokyo and Frankfurt (1989, 1996); the mass of writings on the changing economic dynamics of the 'post-Fordist' city (eg, D Harvey 1987, 1990; Esser and Hirsch 1994); post-industrial urban social exclusion (eg, Wilson 1987) – both geographic (eg, Sibley 1995; Garreau 1991) and physical (eg, Davis 1990: Chapter 4; Christopherson 1994; Blakely and Snyder 1997) – and the various forms it takes in cities as diverse as Paris (Wacquant 1996), Capetown (Dixon 2001), Philadelphia (Nightingale 1993) and Vancouver (Lees 1998); the shifting nature of urban ethnicities (Back 1996; Bourgois 1995; Davis 2000) and gender relations (Massey 1991; Wilson 2001); and the transformative role of a whole host of 'new urban culture(s)' (eg, Zukin 1991, 1995 on the new 'liminality' associated with New York's de-industrialised, gentrified spaces; O'Connor and Wynne 1993 and Mellor 1997 on the re-branding of Manchester; and Corcoran 1998 on the fashionable 're-imagining' of Dublin). The important thing to recognise here is that, within many of these accounts, the city itself becomes the contested terrain on which intellectual debates about the 'postmodern' continue to rage. Some commentators have even gone as far as to postulate the idea of a fully-formed 'postmodern city' (see Watson and Gibson 1995; Hill 1995; compare Robins 1991: 7–10). Kevin Robins summarises much of the thinking behind this recent tendency:

> The postmodern city is projected as the antithesis of modernist abstraction and anomie: it is about the renaissance of urban culture and sensibilities. In this city, architecture and planning are informed by a new respect for place and tradition. If modernism was driven by universalizing forces, then postmodernism is about a return to difference and particularity. The historical development of capitalist societies and cities is seen in terms of a kind of duel between the universal and the particular. (1991: 1–2)

As the quote suggests – not least through the use of the term 'duel' – such accounts simply mirror the binarism associated with the narratives of epochal polarisation, this time as glimpsed through the beguiling lens of the city. Once again, what is needed is the construction of a more agnostic approach that shies away from making any major pronouncements about the constituent features of postmodern cities/spaces – after all, as illustrated in the discussion of Benjamin and Simmel in Chapter 1, the discourse surrounding the postmodern city is often presaged in accounts of the urban experience within the modern city. In other words, we should recognise that the changes underway in our cities today are as much about continuity and modification as rupture or schism. The geographer Ed Soja makes this point clearly:

> [t]here is not only change but continuity as well, a persistence of past trends and established forms of (modern) urbanism amidst an increasing intrusion of postmodernization. In the postmodern city the modern city has not disappeared. Its presence may be diminished, but it continues to articulate with both older and newer forms of urbanization and to maintain its own dynamic of change, making the normal adjustments and reformations of the modern city and the distinctive processes of postmodern restructuring difficult to disentangle. (1995: 126)

One such 'continuous' theme is consumption, a practice that is at the very heart of every city, irrespective of temporal epoch. Yet, despite a long and convoluted history (Bauman 1983; Bocock 1993: Chapter 1; Glennie 1995), the practices associated with urban consumption often tend to be ignored, or at best are subsumed by more theoretical interpretations of the city or the wider debates surrounding temporal periodisation (see Glennie 1998: 945–47). Stephen Miles explains:

> The historical dimensions of urban consumption are all too often either entirely neglected or glossed over by contributors to the field ... In particular, many theorists have taken to describing contemporary expressions of the 'postmodern city' without reference to any historical precedent [which] has resulted in an inaccurate understanding of the role of consumption in the development of city life. (1998b: 1002)

As a result of this tendency, important questions about the evolving nature of urban consumption/consumerism remain underplayed.[2] Without remotely attempting to portray the long and varied history of consumption and the city, this chapter will try to illustrate how consumer culture is functioning as an agent of economic and social change, both in terms of the physical layout of the city and at the more experiential level. Indeed, urban consumer culture serves as the linking dynamic for many of the arguments postulated not just in this chapter but also throughout the book.

Prioritising consumer culture to such an extent inevitably gives rise to a whole series of questions. How are we to understand the many 'contradictions of consumer culture' (Edwards 2000)? If modernity was/is ostensibly based around diverse rationalising processes, what new forms are these ordering structures likely to take in a world based predominantly around the practice of consumption? Could it possibly be that these so-called rational social forms are now having the opposite effect and actually contributing to the disintegration and fragmentation of established forms of urban praxis? Moreover, and more provocatively, are we already experiencing the ascendance of new 'irrational' modes of understanding and ways of 'making sense of the world' that ultimately might challenge consumption as a mode of expression? Comprehensive answers to all these questions may prove elusive, yet we should not be discouraged from undertaking the simpler, preliminary task of identifying the diverse and pervasive ways in which consumer culture is engendering change, both in terms of the physical and spatial layout of the city and at the less tangible level of our everyday round. It is the assertion of this work that only when we fully understand these changes and their consequences will we be in a position to confront the contemporary urban crime problem from a more realistic perspective.

'Postmodernity', consumption and the city: capitalism in transition?

Whilst mainstream criminology has shown a marked reluctance to engage with debates surrounding 'postmodernity', other branches of the social sciences (most notably cultural and critical studies, sociology, and urban geography) have not. For example, in *The Condition of Postmodernity* (1990), the Marxist geographer David Harvey – coming down heavily on one side of the binary epochal divide – claims that our changing times represent nothing less than a new phase in the capitalist world system. He substantiates this position with some dazzling illustrations of the

---

2 These readings of urban consumption also tend to downplay the familiar problems associated with comparative analysis (see Skocpol and Somers 1980). Put simply, research in this area often imposes a model of consumption drawn from one country onto another without taking into account national or cultural differences.

way in which society, especially the city, is being affected by what he describes as 'a sea change' in 'cultural and political-economic practice'. However, before exploring the implications of such claims for the urban form, it is important to fully understand Harvey's particular interpretation of the *economic* foundations of 'postmodernity'.

For Harvey, the 'postmodern condition' can only really be understood when set against the backdrop of economic change. Drawing on the broadly Marxist-inspired economics of the 'regulation school',[3] Harvey bases his narrative of change on the demise of the 'Fordist' regime of production and accumulation and the emergence of a new stage of the capitalist economy called 'post-Fordism' (see Amin 1994 for an overview). Immediately we find ourselves in 'binary mode', this time in the sense of having the economics of modernity set squarely against an economics of postmodernity. Of course, these categories are far less mutually exclusive than Harvey's account would have us believe, and his interpretation of events has been challenged on a number of grounds. I will return to these criticisms later, but in the meantime let us be clear about the assumed wisdom surrounding Fordism/post-Fordism and exactly what Harvey means when he talks about a new capitalist system.

Broadly speaking, Fordism refers to the stage of industrial capitalism based on the highly mechanised and rationalised production principles pioneered by Frederick Taylor and Henry Ford. As a system of production based around assembly line techniques and high industrial productivity, Fordism was first established in the US at the beginning of the 20th century where it matured and spread to Europe, reaching its peak (according to most accounts) during the post-World War II period. Importantly, Fordism does not simply refer to techniques of production, but rather to the particular economic ordering in which a mutually dependent relationship is maintained between capitalist mass-production and mass (standardised) consumption by (relatively) high wages, widely available credit facilities and a dominant ideology that stresses continuous personal consumption. Fordism thus marked a key moment in economic and social history because it heralded the arrival of *the mass consumption stage* in modern society. No longer was personal consumption the preserve of the affluent few (as in Veblen's account); it was now open to the many, based importantly on the (carefully calibrated) expansion of working class purchasing power (Goldthorpe *et al* 1968). Thus, economists talk of the emergence of a 'demand-led' economy.

It should be stressed, however, that, as a strictly market-based economic strategy, Fordism was severely limited in terms of social organisation. It required high levels of government investment and regulation at both state and local levels to maintain full employment and a sense of shared prosperity. Even beyond a reproducible set of economic arrangements, Fordism was also about establishing order, even homogeneity, through the creation of uniform social rights and shared public values. To function effectively, Fordism required the support of a far-reaching welfare state capable of providing standardised services, everything from housing and education to health and social care. How this system of provision and

---

3   Eg, Aglietta (1979); Lipietz (1982, 1987); R Boyer (1986).

governance was *controlled and regulated*, therefore, is of central importance to understanding how capitalism functioned during this period – hence the term 'regulation school'. In sum, while it is generally accepted that Fordism 'came to maturity' in the period between 1945 and 1973, it did so only so far as it was buttressed by Western governments' strict adherence to Keynesian monetary and fiscal policies that kept public spending high in a bid to maintain and regulate aggregate demand.

From a criminal justice perspective – something often overlooked in social theoretical accounts of the Fordist period (see the interesting article 'Post-Fordism and criminality' by John Lea 1997) – it was assumed that this more (ostensibly) cohesive and equal society would in turn facilitate the creation of a more democratic criminal justice system: 'A new popular consensus around crime control could parallel that around universalist social welfare rights. The consolidation of shared values through mass consumption, mass education and social mobility would, in turn, standardize sensitivities to violence, concepts of harm and victimization, around those deployed by criminal law and criminal justice agencies' (1997: 43). Such assumptions, however, were to prove overwhelmingly naive. The complexities of the situation – not least the particular dynamics associated with a burgeoning consumer culture (see below) – had been grossly underestimated, and the alleged cohesiveness and social harmony of the post-war period were soon sorely exposed.

By the 1970s, the winds of economic change were blowing (see Gamble and Walton 1976): not in respect of the dominant economic and financial order – capitalism was clearly too strong to be realistically challenged as the major organising principle in industrialised societies – but through a series of transformations in the way capitalism went about securing and accumulating profit. In Harvey's view (following that of 'the regulationists'), the most important of these changes was the satiation of the mass markets for consumption goods. Tastes had changed, and the previously stable demand for highly standardised products associated with classical Fordist modes of production was in decline. Brand-consciousness had been raised by the growth of advertising, and as a result consumers were demanding more diverse product forms and new modes of consumption. At the same time, Western nations were rocked by a series of significant economic and financial variations, not least serious problems in the labour market during the late 1960s and early 1970s, including protracted industrial disputes over issues relating to pay, working hours, employment rights and contracts (Harvey 1990: Chapters 8–10).[4] This situation was further exacerbated by the unwavering support of major governments for Keynesian demand management strategies – a politico-economic path that led in turn to rampant inflation, 'stagflation' and ultimately an end to post-war economic growth. By the mid-1970s,

---

4 It has been suggested that this particular crisis was also due to the fact that, by 1970, work tasks and labour could be sub-divided no further (a process embodied in the widescale implementation of notorious 'time and motion' studies). In other words, specialisation in the labour process had peaked, thus productivity growth slowed and profits diminished (Lipietz 1987).

governments and producers alike needed something new to kick-start a capitalist system that was seriously malfunctioning.

The deep cracks that appeared in the Fordist compromise during the mid-1970s inevitably forced many manufacturers to seek alternative methods of capital accumulation. The result was the emergence of what Harvey describes as 'a series of novel experiments in the realms of industrial organization', experiments that, he claims, add up to nothing less than 'the early stirrings of the passage to an entirely new regime of accumulation' (1990: 145). These experiments represented a major digression from the economic wisdom that underpinned Fordism and thus were seen by many as strong evidence of a transition to so-called post-Fordism. As outlined above, from the 'regulationist' perspective, the key concern is how capitalism as an economic system continues to reproduce itself, or, more accurately, how it 'regulates its internal contradictions' (especially those between production and consumption). In this case, the regulationists argue, it was achieved through the restructuring of production techniques and labour markets, alongside a series of related changes in the system of social and political regulation. Let us consider each of these developments in turn. In terms of the restructuring of production methods, Harvey sums up the new post-Fordist approach as 'flexible accumulation', claiming that it is a process:

> [m]arked by a direct confrontation with the rigidities of Fordism. It rests on flexibility with respect to labour processes, labour markets, products, and patterns of consumption. It is characterized by the emergence of entirely new sectors of production, new ways of providing financial services, new markets and above all, greatly intensified rates of commercial, technological and organizational innovation. It has entertained rapid shifts in the patterning of uneven development, both between sectors and between geographical regions, giving rise, for example, to a vast surge in so-called 'service-sector' employment as well as entirely new industrial ensembles in hitherto underdeveloped regions. (1990: 147)

Post-Fordist flexible accumulation, then, according to Harvey and the regulationists, is driven by the need to respond rapidly to the more fluid demand patterns that emerged as a consequence of the satiation of mass markets. Thus, we see a move away from vertically-integrated extractive-manufacturing industries toward more readily adaptable and 'disintegrated' corporate structures, alongside an acceleration in the pace of product innovation, which in turn precipitates the creation of 'anti-Fordist', highly-specialised, small-scale market niches.[5] From the perspective of the labour market, post-Fordism is also characterised by the break up of Fordist employment patterns. This has typically taken the form of the replacement of secure, unionised labour with unstable, de-unionised and increasingly out-sourced 'flexible' forms of employment. Inevitably, these changes have been felt most deeply in former industrial and manufacturing heartlands, where work – often above all else – was the key marker of cultural and personal identity. (Of note at this point is the extent to which many criminologists – eg, Taylor *et al* 1996; Taylor 1999; Currie 1996, 1997; Hall 1997 – see this last, distinctly 'post industrial' development as,

---

5 For an excellent illustration of flexible production methods in practice, see Lash and Urry (1994: 113–23) and Storper (1994) on the rise of the culture industries (film, publishing, music, TV, etc) since the 1970s.

perhaps, the key causal factor in the rise of crime post 1970.) Finally, and very importantly, the 'Fordist crisis' was mirrored by a related crisis in governance and societal regulation as the Keynesian welfare state began to unravel. The subsequent demise of public services – not least the apparent inefficiency of the criminal justice system – ensured that any universal sense of collective solidarity was lost. In its place, according to the regulation school, emerged a new 'mode of regulation' based around, *inter alia*, the deregulation and privatisation of public services, changing patterns of local and global financing, greater public–private relationships and the fostering of an 'entrepreneurial culture' within the public sector.

Arguably, the central theme of Harvey's account[6] – and here again he is representative of a number of other theorists – is the way the economic changes associated with post-Fordism find expression in a set of ('postmodern') practices, processes, sensibilities and tendencies that have become inscribed at the *cultural level*: namely, pastiche, ahistoricism, the importance of spectacle and simulation, and the various ways in which time and space are being 'compressed' and 'fragmented' by fluctuations in production and exchange mechanisms brought about by the changing nature of late 20th century capitalism. By 'time-space compression' Harvey is referring both to the shrinking of space along lines associated with notions of the 'global village' and to the erosion of 'time horizons' to such an extent that 'the present is all there is'. An obvious example of this so-called 'simultaneity' would be the way in which the Internet and other computer-mediated technologies dramatically speed up global-local communications/transactions (see Harvey 1990: Chapters 16 and 17; Castells 1989, 1996 on the 'space of flows' within the globalised information economy and how this process erodes the meaning of space and place; and Jameson's 1991 notion of 'schizophrenia', below).[7] Such insights are, of course, of great importance in terms of understanding the changing nature of the contemporary urban experience, and are thus discussed in this context in the next section; however, in the meantime, I wish to focus on the way Harvey locates the city as the crucible of postmodernity.

Harvey's ideas about 'time-space compression', 'flexible specialisation', the dissolution of knowledge, 'placelessness', the valorisation of consumption and many other facets of his 'postmodern condition' find their most compelling outlet in the city. The postmodern city, he argues, revels in the 'chaotic flux' of temporal fragmentation; it parodies history (not least through simulations of traditional styles), modernist notions of progress and other grand narratives, and champions

---

6 Although it does not appear on the book's cover, Harvey's *The Condition of Postmodernity* actually includes the sub-heading: 'An Inquiry Into the Origins of Cultural Change.'

7 As evidence of this point, consider the distinction between work patterns in the industrial age versus those of today. Under industrial capitalism, work was largely about collective action at a fixed location. Consequently, most individuals' working regimes were spatially and temporally regimented. Today, however, as a result of a combination of flexitime, 'annual hours' systems and the mass use of e-mail, fax, answer machines and digital communications, many of us now have the power to reschedule our lives. However, while 'technology has the potential to free the modern office worker from the shackles of time', typically the result is the increased demand for *instantaneous action*: 'New technology can sometimes create a time pressure of its own, as it gives us a sense of always being available to respond immediately ... we can be on the job twenty-four hours a day. The division between work time and leisure time becomes less clear' (Newman and Lonsdale 1996: 25–27).

irony as an important cultural aesthetic (irony being seen as a useful tool in the undermining process). He discusses at length how city life and urban culture are being transformed by postmodern themes within architecture and urban design (Harvey 1990: Chapter 4), as well as the various ways in which urban consumption patterns are being affected by a highly sophisticated postmodern consumer culture based on the new playful cultural aesthetic ('The bombardment of stimuli, simply on the commodity front, creates problems of sensory overload that makes Simmel's dissection of the problems of modernist urban living at the turn of the century seem to pale into insignificance by comparison': 1990: 286). This shift in aesthetic and cultural practice can be conceptualised as a move away from the fascination with the 'new' – characteristic of an epoch, the modern – toward a more playful celebration of the 'now'. 'The relatively stable aesthetic of Fordist modernism has given way to all the ferment, instability, and fleeting qualities of a postmodernist aesthetic that celebrates difference, ephemerality, spectacle, fashion and the commodification of cultural forms' (1990: 156), he declares in a statement that illustrates the extent to which his economic ideas find expression in an expansive cultural analysis. It is this type of commentary that has underscored a mass of subsequent writings on the so-called 'postmodern city'. The following passage by Dilys Hill typifies the absolutism of much of this literature – no hesitation about epochal binarism here:

> The postmodern is the metropolitan. The city is the site of that consumerist, imaged world of the Disney utopia of cultural relativities which have displaced the order of authority and tradition. The deindustrialization of cities has turned them into centres of consumption, of malls and museums. At the same time the suburban shopping mall and motorway negate the notion of city as definable space: we inhabit a 'placeless' world of interchangeability ... The contemporary restructuring of urban space, with its flexible specialization of production, dissolution of hierarchies and capital mobility, has transformed the urban landscape. City centres become refurbished downtowns of corporate and cultural headquarters while industry and major retailing migrate to the suburbs. (1995: 242)

So goes the standard narrative associated with accounts of the 'postmodern city'. Yet to what extent is this representation an altogether accurate one? Can urban space really be understood in terms of the 'postmodern'? Or is the reality of the contemporary city too complex to be located within this type of schematic binary distinction? Certainly, for many critics, the chain of events underpinning the notion of the postmodern city is a problematic one – not least, they question the all-too-straightforward economic transition from a Fordist mode of accumulation to a post-Fordist one.

To start with, critics point to the very loose historiography that surrounds the transition from Fordism to post-Fordism. For example, Ferruccio Gambino (1996) argues that the regulationists' account of the transition into post-Fordism is deeply flawed, both in the way it links Fordism with purported notions of prosperity and social cohesiveness (see also Gartman 1986) and, importantly, in its temporal reading of Fordism as a system of production. He points to the fact that Fordism in the classical sense (ie, 'an authoritarian system of series production based on the assembly line, with wages and conditions of work which the workforce is not in a position to negotiate by trade union means') was in fact extremely short-lived, lasting in this form only until 1941, when, after a series of often violent confrontations, 'Fordism was eliminated' following the establishment of organised trade unions. Gambino's argument here is that, by ignoring the important distinction between 'pre-trade union Fordism' and 'unionised Fordism', the regulationists glossed over the complexities and nuances of social movements and human interactions, thus reducing the 'working class in the United States to a mere *Fordist object*' (Gambino 1996).

Similarly problematic is the post-Fordist reading of the emergence of product distinctiveness and model differentiation. As we have seen, in the regulationists' account, the move away from mass standardisation of goods was a response to a string of crises in Fordist production in the late 1960s and 1970s brought about by the satiation of mass markets. Out of this situation, they argue, emerged more flexible production techniques, which in turn created 'a new consumption system' predicated on highly differentiated products and services and specialised niche markets. However, this account has also been criticised for its selective history, with many commentators pointing out numerous, much earlier examples of product differentiation and flexible specialisation.[8] It has been argued, for example, that Ford's main rival General Motors pioneered product diversification as early as the late 1920s, marketing 'a graded hierarchy of cars, ranging from the low-priced Chevrolet to the luxury Cadillac'. According to David Gartman, by the 1930s, '[C]onsumers could pick a car that matched their income and lifestyle, achieving a sense of individuality in their purchases. Many of the distinctions between GM's makes were purely superficial, decorative geegaws attached to the cars' surfaces to give them a different visual reading' (1998: 128). Similar claims have been made about the rise of highly segmented markets in the fashion industry during the 1930s, as customers sought out more individualised clothing lines that catered for changing personal tastes and the growing desire to transcend demarcated class lines (Ewen and Ewen 1982; see also Chapter 1 on the emergence of the department store). In an interesting article, Gartman develops this line of critique by locating it within the familiar debates associated with classical 1970s Althusserian Marxism. Crudely stated, Gartman challenges the idea that there exists a 'neat and synchronous chronology' between Fordism/modernism and post-Fordism/postmodernism. While at one level he 'applauds the efforts' of Harvey and Jameson (see below) in outlining the cultural transmission from modernism to postmodernism, at another level he restates the familiar argument that 'capitalism and culture do not progress in some unilateral lock step dictated by economics' (1998: 126). Instead, he asserts that cultural changes ultimately brought about the economic transformations of post-Fordism and not vice versa. However, rather than get caught up in these highly complex Althusserian questions about the 'relative autonomy' of culture and economics, I wish to concentrate instead on the particular questions surrounding the regulationists' economic account of the transition into post-Fordism.

---

8 See Gambino (1996) for early examples of flexible specialisation in both the American and Japanese motor industries.

The challenge over historiography also extends to many other areas. For example, strict Marxists subscribe to a very different, more fundamental account of economic change during the second half of the 20th century, locating the true causation elsewhere. The criminologist John Lea explains this alternative position in a detailed and comprehensive passage that is worth quoting in full, not least because, as he points out, it goes to the very heart of Marxist political economy:

> An alternative view would find the original cause of post-war expansion in the destruction of capital during the Second World War combined with a temporary post-war stability of the international monetary system. The expansion of consumption into new mass-produced commodities is seen as a *consequence*, rather than a cause, of profitable production. *The current crisis is not a matter of the exhaustion of markets as such, but of the over-accumulation of capital.* From this perspective what is central to the present transition is capital's determination to replace the Keynesian welfare state with a regime of low wages, impotent unions and highly flexible labour with a strong emphasis on women and ethnic minorities. Simultaneously, much Fordist production is being 'decentralised' to low wage, politically authoritarian Third World areas. 'Post-Fordism' can be another name for the fact that in order to restore the conditions for profitable accumulation, capital must intensify its attack on the working class ... *From this perspective, diversification of production and consumption is entirely secondary.* It is not the 'discovery' of new niche markets that replace an exhausted Fordist mass consumption, but the restoration of profitability through the 'discovery' of a low wage flexible diversified working class. Much of the so-called postmodern diversity of lifestyles is [simply] a *cynical inversion of this growing social polarisation*. (1997: 49, emphasis added)

Indeed, the whole way in which the discourse of post-Fordism uses the economic register has been found to be very limited (see Fine and Leopold 1993 for a definitive statement). For example, it has been asserted that Harvey overly prioritises matters relating to production while largely ignoring the fact that consumption is an *economic* as well as a cultural activity.[9] As Ben Fine (1995: 136–37) has commented, the focus on production techniques and processes unintentionally re-establishes the 'assumed primacy of production' that, ironically, Harvey and the regulationists had 'intended to critique'. Indeed, from a political economy perspective, the 'exhaustion of mass markets for consumption' hypothesis depends upon some loose and 'generalised notion of variety and satiation', which is problematic to say the least:

> Neither the empirical evidence for these [post-Fordist] propositions, nor an explanation for them, has ever been satisfactorily offered. Instead, the idea of what must constitute consumption passively follows upon the analytical requirements of the theory of production, and the determinants of differentiation within consumption are left as self-evident ... In displacing a stereotyped notion of the past as Fordist by the post-Fordist production of the future, a political economy is employed which is as determinist as the

---

9   Similarly, Daniel Miller's depiction of Harvey: 'Consumption is either disregarded or reduced to postmodern style as a kind of ideological reflection of changes in production (as in Harvey)' (1995: 6) – perhaps unsurprising given Miller's uncompromising views on 'consumption as the vanguard of history'. Nor can orthodox economics necessarily boast of refined analysis of consumption; as Fine (1995: 127–33) has commented, both political and orthodox economists have long since operated with abstract and theoretically impoverished models of consumption (see also Chapter 5).

theories of mass production that are heavily criticised as dogmatic ... Thus, the political
economy of post-Fordism is driven by an *unexplored* consumption which is satisfied by
flec-spec production. (1995: 136–37)

Such criticisms have gathered a good deal of theoretical traction, challenging both
simple assumptions about postmodernity and the idea that we are witnessing a
new phase in the capitalist world system. Yet we should not let these arguments
blind us to the undeniable fact that our world has begun to operate on a number of
principles different from those which actively dominated much of the 20th century
(certainly this is the case in economics), and that ours is indeed a new world that we
now 'recognize as being "after" what we have known' (Stevick 1985: 135). How
best, then, to identify these new principles? Using Harvey's analysis as an exemplar
of the purported transition into these 'new times', and whilst acknowledging, of
course, the caveats set out above, it is my contention that Harvey's work provides
us with *three* main insights.

First, and very importantly in terms of the present work, is the way Harvey
locates the city as the main seedbed for the propagation of 'postmodern culture'.
Here, of course, he is not alone.[10] Over the last two decades there has been
sustained interest in the various ways in which highly influential *cultural* processes
have transformed cities from centres of production, manufacture and
administration into 'postmodern' sites of consumption, spectacle, leisure and
simulation.[11] As Stacy Warren has commented, the cultural now 'permeate[s] every
aspect of urban life: the political, social, historical and economic' (1996: 547).
However, while these tendencies find their most eloquent expression in Harvey's
work, it is unclear from his analysis just how these cultural processes will ultimately
play out within the nook-and-cranny reality of the city. Will the affirmative version
of postmodernity lead to better public programmes, more harmonious social
relations, and the enhancement and empowerment of diverse social movements?
Are we about to witness the onset of a new urbanity that is both more culturally
sensitive and in tune with our globalised times? Or will the cultural and economic
forms associated with postmodernity lead to even greater social polarisation, spatial
segregation and privatisation of public space (*à la* Davis 1990; Garreau 1991;
Christopherson 1994; Sibley 1995; see Chapter 4)? One thing remains certain: the
contours of the urban landscape may have changed, but the underlying forces
remain the same.[12] Indeed, the very term 'postmodern' is as much about modernity
and all its associated social and economic constraints and cultural biases as it is
about an idealised version of what will replace it. This point is particularly well

---

10 See also Jameson (1984); Eco (1986); Cooke (1988); Stephanson (1988); Warren (1996); Scott
(1997).

11 Eg, Baudrillard (1983); Soja (1989); Zukin (1991, 1995); Sorkin (1992a, 1992b); Hannigan (1995,
1998).

12 In many ways these questions have been rehearsed before in Benjamin's writings on *The
Arcades Project* (see Chapter 1). In that particular case it was the emergence of industrialised
urban culture and the mass consumption stage of the mid-19th century that presented a series
of exciting possibilities for developing innovative forms of human experience based upon new
social relations. However, as Benjamin documents, such progressive ideals were quickly put to
the sword by the inexorable rise of capitalism, commodity fetishism, and the ultimate
transformation of the arcades into department stores and other spaces of mass consumption.

made in the feminist critique of Harvey. Gillian Rose (1991, 1993) and Doreen
Massey (1993), for example, suggest that, because Harvey sees modernity only in
terms of masculinity, his mapping of the 'postmodern' is likely to be similarly
limited (see also Deutsche 1991; Massey 1991; Bridge 1997). Rose, especially, pulls
no punches in her critique of this type of leftist geography, claiming that Harvey
'seems able to make sense of postmodernism only as a feminine Other, and hence
his fear, his fascination and his rejection' (Rose 1991, cited in Jarvis 1998: 47).

The second thing to take from Harvey's account of postmodernity is the
emphasis he places on the most influential of the cultural processes currently
shaping the spatial logic of the contemporary city – the culture of consumption.
(This is not to suggest that the Fordism/Keynesianism model itself was not
consumer-orientated – in the sense of stimulating demand – rather, it is to point out
that, under the newer 'system', the consumer's role is afforded far greater emphasis
(see also Lee 1993). In Daniel Miller's words, 'What we are documenting here is the
shift in power from production to consumption, irrespective of the forms of
distribution and the behaviour of capital and states *per se*': 1995: 7.) Despite the
criticisms voiced by Fine and Miller, there is still the clear sense in Harvey's work
that the 'postmodern city' is unquestionably the *consumers' city*. This transformation
from 'producer society' to 'consumer society' has been the stuff of much
observation (see Clarke and Bradford 1998 for an excellent review of this shift in
relation to the city; and Miles 1998a, 1998b).[13] However, perhaps the most
influential analysis of this transition (at least in social theoretical circles) is the work
of Zygmunt Bauman (1997, 1998), who, while making the point forcibly, also takes
time to emphasise the considerable ambiguity that surrounds the interrelationships
between systems of production and modes of consumption:

> In the industrial phase of modernity one fact was beyond all questioning: that everyone
> must be a producer first, before being anything else. In 'modernity mark two', the
> consumers' modernity, the brute questionable fact is that one needs to be a consumer
> first, before one can think of becoming anything in particular. (1998: 26)

> The difference between then and now is not as radical as abandoning one role and
> replacing it with another. Neither of the two societies could do without at least some of
> its members taking charge of producing things to be consumed, and all members of both

---

13 One could choose any number of examples to illustrate the fundamental point that 'consumer-
driven' markets have eclipsed 'producer-driven' markets. However, in keeping with the
automotive theme, consider the recent 300% increase in monthly sales of the Citroen Berlingo
Multispace following a favourable review by BBC TV presenter, Jeremy Clarkson. Prior to
Clarkson's famously out-of-character endorsement on the car show *Top Gear*, Citroen were
only selling approximately 200 Berlingos a month in the UK. Such examples have resulted in
economists now referring to the car market as a 'highly segmented consumer-driven market'
(see Hamilton 1993). Previously, even as late as the early 1990s, under a producer-driven
market, cars were still occasionally 'produced in obsolescence'. Under this system, cars were
produced in numbers that far exceeded immediate consumer demand, in the knowledge that
these units would continue to sell in small numbers for long periods of time (on this point see
also Harvey (1990: 156) on the erosion of the 'half-life' of typical Fordist commodities under
conditions of 'flexible accumulation'). However, even this example should not be taken as
evidence of a pure form of post-Fordist production. As was the case with product
differentiation, economists have pointed out numerous other earlier examples of 'just in time'
production practices within the automotive industry (see, eg, the literature on the early 'flec
spec' methods associated with 1950–60s 'Toyotism').

societies do, of course, consume. The difference is one of emphasis, but that shift of emphasis does make an enormous difference to virtually every aspect of society, culture and individual life. The differences are so deep and ubiquitous that they fully justify speaking of our society as a society of a separate and distinct kind – a consumer society. (1998: 24)

In Baumanian terms, then, while we still need to 'problematise' postmodernity, the centrality of the consumer in contemporary society is not in question. Such a position is interesting for it suggests that, rather than striving to outline anything as pronounced or fully formed as an ideal model of 'postmodernity', or for that matter a pure form of post-Fordist capitalism, we would do better concentrating on what John Lea calls 'the dynamics of transition' (Lea 1997: 49) – in this case the transformative aspects associated with our unmediated consumer culture. Such an approach would seem entirely logical. If ours is indeed a world in transition, a world of contingencies and dilemmas (the dilemmas of the contingent?), it makes sense that individuals trapped in a partly modern, partly postmodern landscape will seek out processes and modes of experience that help them bridge the gap to these 'new times'. Consumer culture serves just such a purpose, not least because it is both reassuringly familiar and yet full of purported future promise. Such an approach has the added advantage of side-stepping many of the definitional problems associated with the 'will to binarise' outlined earlier. The key thing here is not to talk of consumerism as a prototypical feature of a new 'postmodern condition', but rather to highlight the increased *intensity and pervasiveness* of consumerism and its associated practices. This approach also acknowledges the pivotal role played by Fordism in the development of the mass consumption stage and, moreover, the extent to which Fordist culture opened the door to heightened material expectations and a subsequent set of personal values based around simple notions of relative deprivation (in the sense of Robert Merton's classic formulation). Furthermore, thinking about consumerism in this way also allows us to refine Harvey's analysis so that it more fully considers the complex dialectical role played by culture in shaping economic development, freeing up what Gartman (1998: 135) calls the 'synchronous and uniform conception of social change' that, all too often, underpins the standard postmodern narrative. Ultimately, then, the issue is not one of forces versus relations of production, or economism versus culture (or even 'relative autonomy'); rather, it is the need to address the formidable array of writings that stress – whether at the economic or cultural level – the full implications of the shifts that fully-fledged consumerism has wrought. (For instance, access to credit revenue is now very often as important as earnings themselves; notions of freedom, social value and, very importantly, sense of identity are now firmly coupled with the sphere of consumption: see below.)[14]

Lastly, the significance of Harvey's work lies perhaps not so much in what he says, but in the way he says it – particularly in the manner in which he arrives at his

---

14 Again, at this point, it might seem that my issue is with Marxism as an ideological perspective. However, this is not the case. Quite clearly, this line of thinking can be expressed using Marxist vocabulary, most obviously in the work of Frederic Jameson and his augmentation of Ernest Mandel's theory of capitalist periodisation (see Jameson 1991: 35–36).

conclusions. In *The Condition of Postmodernity*, Harvey seems to be advocating a shift away from the more traditional forms of Marxist political praxis that infused the 'new urban sociology' of the 1970s,[15] towards more interpretive (and aesthetic) modes of critical examination – an approach that closely overlaps with much work currently being undertaken under the emergent banner of 'cultural criminology'. Indeed, in many ways his work comes close to the kind of dual 'mapping' of city-space advocated by de Certeau, in that it fuses together the imaginary nature of city life (Harvey states that a city is a 'like a theatre, a series of stages upon which individuals could work their own distinctive magic while performing a multiplicity of roles': 1990: 5) with the type of urbanistic discourse generally associated with more traditional rational forms of economic geography. (Interestingly, Harvey introduces his central argument in a manner closely reminiscent of de Certeau, by contrasting the experiential and highly personalised account of London life presented in Raban's (1974) *Soft City* with the 'hard city' as depicted in maps, statistics and much empirical sociology.) Such dynamic forms of theoretical expression are also very much in evidence in the work of that other seminal theorist of the postmodern, the American literary theorist and Marxist dialectician, Frederic Jameson. It is to his work that I now turn in an effort to assess how some of the key themes associated with the 'postmodern condition' are impacting at the level of the contemporary subjective urban experience.

Slipping the moorings of time and space: the subject in transition?

> Is Time outside me, I started wondering in high school. When things began to go so fast. Or is Time inside me. If OUTSIDE you have to keep pace with fucking clocks and calendars. No slacking off. If INSIDE, you do what *you* want. Whatever. You create your own time. Like breaking the hands off a clock like I did once so it's just the clock face there looking at you. (Quentin P, the central character in the novel *Zombie* by Joyce Carol Oates (1995))

In his far-reaching text *Postmodernism, or, the Cultural Logic of Late Capitalism* (1991), Jameson delves deeper into the theme of 'time-space compression', claiming that one of the key transmutations currently taking place in contemporary society is the way in which spatial considerations are displacing temporal concerns as the dominant ordering principle in our daily lives (1991: 16).[16] To comprehend the full force of this message, it is necessary first to understand something of earlier historical spatio-temporal frameworks, including, most obviously, the way that time and space were conceptualised and experienced within modernist culture. I apologise in advance for the broad sweep of my narrative here.

---

15 For Harvey (1973, 1978, 1982, 1985a, 1985b), Castells (1976, 1977, 1978), Pickvance (1976) and the other leading lights of the neo-Marxist school of 'new urban sociology', the concept of the city as an autonomous or distinct social form was always spurious. Instead, they believed that a city's form always followed, or rather corresponded to, the prevailing economic order, hence their constructs 'the capitalist city', 'the socialist city' and 'the communist city'.

16 To be more precise, Jameson is suggesting 'the distinction is between two forms of interrelationship between time and space rather than between these two inseparable categories themselves' (Jameson 1991: 154).

Understandings of pre-Enlightenment conceptions of time and space are at best equivocal (even unforgiving modernist anthropology was forced to acknowledge the complexity of certain non-modern space-time systems). Time in this context is understood in terms of a rite(s) of passage enriched by fundamental and universal conceptions of human existence: 'life begins, we age, and then we die' (see Elias 1978; Dollimore 1999). Within these societies, representations of 'place' and 'space' were often tightly bound up with abstract concerns, whether cosmological, animistic, mythical, superstitious or sacred. However, with the unfolding of the Enlightenment and its inexorable drive towards purposive rationality, conceptualisations of time and space inevitably changed:

> The conquest and control of space [in modernity], for example, first requires that it be conceived of as something usable, malleable, and therefore capable of domination through human action. Perspectivism and mathematical mapping did this by conceiving of space as abstract, homogeneous and universal in its qualities ... Builders, engineers, architects and land managers for their part showed how Euclidean representations of objective space could be converted into a spatially ordered physical landscape. Merchants and landowners used such practices for their own class purposes, while the absolutist state (with its concern for taxation of land and the definition of its own domain of domination and social control) likewise relished the capacity to define and produce spaces with fixed spatial co-ordinates. (Harvey 1990: 254)

Despite such fundamental transformations in the ordering principles of society, people's experience of time and space would have been constrained by a combination of the rigidities of primitive transport modalities and lifestyle routines linked to finite places bound up by 'an intricate territory of interdependence, obligation, surveillance and control' (1990: 241). It was not until the political, technical and economic transformations associated with the Industrial Revolution that the next 'radical readjustment in the sense of time and space' occurred. Nineteenth century mass modernisation brought about an unprecedented acceleration in technological change and scientific innovation (as discussed in Chapter 1). Such developments marked a radical break with traditional lifeworlds, leading to what theorists typically describe as the shrinking or 'compression' of both time and space. At the physical level, '[s]paces that had been separated by hours of labor or travel raced by in almost simultaneous coexistence, emphasizing a quick, superficial perception' (Gartman 1998: 123), while along the dimension of time, change took the form of a challenge to the established narrative of life:

> The continuous skein of time in premodern societies, guarded by nature and religion, was torn asunder by the new technologies of production and consumption, rendering it chaotic and contingent. Time was no longer governed by the rhythms of human tradition but was reduced to a rationalized, objective thing, under the control of the alien technologies of stopwatch and assembly line. (1998: 123)

The commodifying effects of the various processes associated with capitalist 'clock-time' on human subjectivity have been the stuff of much classic observation.[17] For

---

17 See Thompson (1967) and Giddens (1991) for a general review; or Giddens (1981) and Urry (1991) on the more specific point about modern capitalist 'labour time' constituting and mediating identity; see above for a discussion in relation to the practices associated with Fordism.

our purposes, the key thing to recognise is that the formalised ordering of social and economic practices associated with capitalist utilitarianism ensured that modernity was an epoch *more heavily vested in temporality* – and especially 'external temporality'. In other words, modernity was predicated on an explicit sense of temporal history that operated in parallel at *both* the 'social' and the 'individual' (or 'biographical') level. First, at the social level, modernity can be characterised by a strong sense of 'periodisation'. For example, Lyotard's (1984) account of grand narratives as characteristic of modernity sees sequential temporal periodisation linked to the concepts of change, development and rational progress, creating a strongly historicist temporal sequence (indeed, the metropolis itself was often viewed in this way, with many cultural producers, from Fritz Lang to Piet Mondrian, linking the modern city with their concept of the future). Secondly, at the individual level, each life was seen as having its own biography – or 'unique linear story' – that would unfold given the fullness of time (compare Rabinbach 1992). As Jameson suggests, in modernity, personal identity was forged through a 'temporal unification of the past and the future with the present before me' (1991: 26).

In contrast, Jameson asserts that postmodernism is more heavily vested in a sense of 'space' – or more accurately, the production of a concept of space that operates not only at a physical level but also as 'a new kind of mental entity' (1991: 165). This notion of space stands as perhaps Jameson's central illustration of the emergence of postmodernism. The clearest illustration of Jameson's claim that the concept of space has been reworked can be found in his famous description of the Bonaventure Hotel in downtown Los Angeles. For Jameson, the Bonaventure is an exemplar of postmodern urban space: an alluring yet – to us still modern subjects – incomprehensible place where the individual is bombarded by superficial reflections, bewildered by pastiche, and confused by its symmetrical spatiality to such an extent that it becomes difficult to locate oneself within its imposing structure. What physical characteristics serve to create such a situation? First, the overall vernacular of the Bonaventure Hotel is mimetic, in that it borrows its architectural form from the surrounding environment. This key theme of non-differentiation of building from environment contrasts sharply with one of the central ideas of architectural modernism (see Chapter 1), most obviously in the way it eschews any statement about social betterment or the rational advancement of society through brute power or rationalisation. Secondly, the Bonaventure is linked to the outside world via what one might describe as a series of stealth entrances (again this is in contrast to the modernist architectural aesthetic which favoured a single, monumental, clearly demarcated entrance from street to hotel interior), with each entrance admitting the resident/visitor into the hotel at various levels, but always introducing them into an ongoing crowd/shopping scene (what Jameson describes as 'a new and historically original hypercrowd'). The result is a new form of public–private aperture: 'In this sense, then, ideally the "minicity" of Portman's Bonaventure ought not to have entrances at all, since the entryway is always the seam that links the building to the rest of the city that surrounds it: for it does not wish to be part of the city but rather its equivalent and replacement or substitute' (1991: 40). Such a line of thinking is reminiscent of Walter Benjamin's ideas on private–public 'porosity', but indicates a situation that is much more intense.[18] Thirdly, various other architectural features are also identified by Jameson as contributing to the emergence of a 'radically different spatial experience' (eg, escalators and elevators that no longer function as simple people movers but are instead designed as 'gigantic kinetic sculptures'; networks of walkways and 'elevator gondolas' which ensure the process of idle strolling is replaced by 'a transportation machine' that navigates the individual through a world of signs and homogenised experiences; and the use of revolving floors and super-fast inside-outside lifts to further blur individual physical trajectories).

Importantly, Jameson extends his analysis beyond the architectural/physical realm. Space is used in a more metaphorical sense, and the themes of 'flatness', 'superficiality' and 'depthlessness' elucidated in his account of the Bonaventure Hotel are opened out and discussed in relation to other areas of cultural production and ultimately temporality – in the sense of undermining 'historical depth'. According to Jameson, this process is a central feature of a new stage of 'multinational' or 'global' consumer capitalism (1991: 35–36), its aim to erode the distinctiveness of place and thus flatten out (perceptions of) time. Our world comes to resemble life inside a Las Vegas casino: timeless, season-less, exploitative, and totally indistinct from what is going on in hundreds of other casinos all over the city.

Through a detailed investigation of postmodern culture, Jameson develops his argument by suggesting that our sense of temporality and history – both at the level of the public sphere and at the level of the individual personality – has been eroded by the processes of capitalism (in its late 20th century Western form) to such an extent that society is no longer capable of effectively 'engaging with its past'. Jameson describes this distinctly postmodern process as the ongoing 'crisis in historicity' – a development that challenges established longitudinal (modernist) conceptions of time. We now inhabit a world of *simultaneity* (an 'eternal present'), a place in which history and cultural antecedents are unashamedly cannibalised, ransacked and subjugated in a bid to *constantly stimulate the present*.[19] A key contributory factor in this process is the ever more pervasive practice of *pastiche* (a mode of cultural production that undermines historicity by juxtaposing symbols, styles and images from different cultures and temporal contexts in the form of cultural 'quotations'). As far as Jameson is concerned, our sense of chronological order (including our faith in progress) has dissipated and, as a result, very few current cultural experiences and expressions are now truly new; rather, they tend to rely upon and borrow imagery, motifs and temporal signs from the past, mixing them up to create a cocktail of free-floating, quasi-historical retrospective

18 On this point see also Jameson's comments on the way that the Bonaventure's glass construction 'achieves a peculiar and placeless disassociation of the Bonaventure from its neighbourhood' (1991: 420).

19 In the decade or so since Jameson first articulated this particular point, it is interesting to reflect on the extent to which the cross-hatching of time has migrated from high art to popular culture. Consider mainstream cinema: in recent years there has been a whole spate of films that have played on the idea of fusing the past, present and strangely illusory futures, including but not limited to *Memento* (2000), *Vanilla Sky* (2001), *Run Lola Run* (1998), *Donnie Darko* (2001), *My Own Private Idaho* (1992), *Waking Life* (2001), *Minority Report* (2002), *Solaris* (2002), and (most sophisticatedly) David Lynch's *Mullholland Drive* (2001) and David Cronenberg's *Spider* (2002).

representations. When employed at the level of the built environment, the contributory effect of these developments on postmodern spatiality and temporality is obvious (see 'Conclusion' of this chapter).

The importance of all this theorising – and something often neglected in accounts of Jameson's work – is that ultimately he poses a series of vital questions about how these changes will affect human subjectivity. First, with regard to the way in which we function within the physical environment:

> I am proposing the notion that we are here in the presence of something like a mutation in built space itself. My implication is that we ourselves, the human subjects who happen into this new space, have not kept pace with that evolution; there has been a mutation in the object unaccompanied as yet by any equivalent mutation in the subject. We do not yet possess the perceptual equipment to match this new hyperspace, as I will call it, in part because our perceptual habits were formed in that older kind of space I have called the space of high modernism. (1991: 39)

This theme of the 'modern' subject adrift in postmodern or late modern spatial forms is vitally important in terms of the overall hypothesis of the present work. Consider, for example, how it resonates with the Wayne Morrison quote that featured in the introduction to this chapter: 'We live within modernity but at a distance from the assumptions which gave it security, which made modernity appear "natural".' Secondly, Jameson extends this line of thought to include transformations taking place at a more general societal level:

> It may now be suggested that this alarming disjunction point between the body and its built environment – which is to the initial bewilderment of the older modernism as the velocities of the spacecraft to those of the automobile – can itself stand as the symbol and analogon of that even sharper dilemma which is the incapacity of our minds, at least at present, to map the great global multinational and decentered communicational network in which we find ourselves caught as individual subjects. (1991: 44)

Ultimately Jameson is arguing that the changes identified above contribute to the death of any sense of a unified coherent subject. Just as there is no longer a collective social history, so too the individual loses a sense of self as the subject of narrative – this is what it means to be postmodern. Once again, Jameson uses artistic and cultural references to illustrate his point. In this case, he contrasts the key themes of modernist art and literature – namely, the classic modernist notion of the alienated subject (as typified by such works as Munch's *The Scream*) – with select observations of contemporary postmodern artworks (eg, the Language Poets of San Francisco, the video installations of Nam June Paik and the music of John Cage). His aim here is to chart the demise of the 'personal' or 'unique' style of the modernist author (as a metaphor for the loss of centrality of the individual) in favour of the pronounced 'fragmentation' and 'waning of affect' of image, object and individual. This process, he continues, leads in turn to the increasing 'superficiality' of postmodern culture, which is itself still parasitic on the subject of modernity.[20]

---

20 That said, Jameson (much later) also suggests that the term 'fragmentation remains too weak and too primitive a term' to define postmodernism: postmodernism is now 'no longer a matter of the break up of some pre-existing older organic totality, but rather the emergence of the multiple in new and unexpected ways, unrelated strings of events, types of discourse, modes of classification, and compartments of reality' (Jameson 1991: 371–72).

In sum, Jameson is suggesting that we are witnessing the emergence of something that approximates a 'postmodern subject': someone who, because of the *privileging of the present* associated with today's postmodern spaces/cultures, is now unable to unify the past, present and future of their own 'biographical experience of psychic life' (1991: 26). He further contends that the implosion of the past and future into an incessant and uninterrupted present is bringing about variations of behaviour, motivation and personality that he describes as constituting *a fragmentation of the individual psyche* – or what he terms 'schizophrenia'. Jameson's interpretation of the emergence of schizophrenia as a general rather than a clinical condition draws on the psychoanalytical writings of Jacques Lacan and his account of the schizophrenic 'subject' as unable to locate himself or herself in relation to either speech, language, memory or experience, or indeed in any temporal sequence of past, present and future. As a consequence, the individual is forced to live in a world of the 'perpetual present' (*simultaneity*) where life is experienced through the recognition and assimilation of unstructured free-floating signifiers remote from any specific signifieds.[21] In short, schizophrenia (in its non-clinical sense) is now the 'normal' mode of being for the postmodern subject.

In his work on postmodern space and schizophrenia, Jameson is articulating the end of the 'old closed, centred subject of inner-directed individualism' and the formation of its replacement: the 'new non-subject of the fragmented or schizophrenic self' (1991: 345). Such a construct fits perfectly with our earlier notion of a world in transition, the world of contingencies and dilemmas that 'we recognize as being "after" what we have known'. Whereas in the previous chapter we saw the emergence of an urban experience based around the shift in consciousness precipitated by the move from rural to urban modes of existence – feelings of alienation, restlessness and increased 'nervosity'; the formation of the blasé calculating attitude; and the rationalisation and mathematisation of social life – in this chapter we have charted how a new kind of spatio-temporal experience/imagination is developing, one that is trying desperately to come to terms with the intense fragmentation of self, space and time propagated under 'postmodern' conditions.

In these, and other ways, Jameson is trying to imagine what a postmodern subject might yet look like – even, as he acknowledges, from a position of transition. It is this transitional element that is key, for while few would argue that the categorisation of experience in terms of classic alienation and 'existential authenticity' is now something that belongs to an obsolescent register associated with the epoch of high

---

21 On this point in relation to spatiality, see Featherstone (1998: 919–23) on the 'electronic *flâneur*' and the points of contact between the urban and the expanding consortia of digital information systems that now abound. 'The urban *flâneur* typically sauntered around, letting the impressions of the city soak into his subconscious. The electronic *flâneur* is capable of great mobility; his [sic] pace is not limited to the human body's capacity for locomotion – rather, with the electronic media of a networked world, instantaneous connections are possible which render physical spatial differences irrelevant' (1998: 921; for more on this line of thinking, see Chapter 5). Stenger (1991), meanwhile, has described 'bulletin board culture', and especially the opportunities it provides for users to adopt multiple personalities, as 'springtime for schizophrenia'.

modernity,[22] it is patently too early to talk of the existence of a truly 'postmodern subject' – many other vestiges of the modern subject have yet to be expunged. This being the case, our goal should be to try to describe a *subject in transition* – a strange hybrid of the modern and the postmodern. As stated earlier, such a task is already underway in the criminology of Wayne Morrison and his various accounts of the forms of existence that are common to individuals floating in a partly modern, partly postmodern landscape. For Morrison, the dilemmas that currently confront us – at both the individual and societal level – are the *dilemmas of transition*. Moreover, and more importantly for our purposes, he argues, much contemporary criminality should be understood as a result of our distinct failure (as yet) to reconcile ourselves to the fundamental changes currently being wrought by rampant consumerism, multinational capitalism, globalised (especially computer-mediated) technologies, the mapping of social relationships not just to local but to national and international class realities, simultaneity, depthlessness and time-space compression. Consequently, while Jameson's account represents perhaps the best approximation of what a 'postmodern subject' might well resemble, it is to Morrison's more circumspect (and less metaphorical) characterisation of a 'subject in transition' that I now turn in a bid to further sketch an outline of the contemporary urban experience.

From the 'shock of the new' to the world of the now: consumer culture and the late modern urban condition

For three months during the spring of 1999, a neon sign bearing the words 'EVERYTHING IS GOING TO BE ALRIGHT' lit up the night sky across Clapton, East London. Nearby residents grew so fond of it they lobbied their local authority to make the sign a permanent fixture. The sign was in fact Work No 203, part of a series of minimalist installations by the young British artist Martin Creed (see Plate 6). Creed's work is important because it encapsulates many of the key themes associated with the modern British art movement, not least the strong desire to make us think differently about our everyday lives – not in a detached, esoteric or intellectual way, but in a very real, immediate and accessible sense through the lens of the 'now'. Modern art is always important because it represents and reflects the very essence of our cultural times (just think of the way Hopper's paintings evocatively captured the feelings of acceptance and fatalism that were such a prominent feature of early 20th century modernisation: see Chapter 1). What, then, does a neon fire sign on top of a former East London orphan asylum tell us about the cultural climate of our world in transition?

---

22 The corrosion of modernist categories of experience such as alienation within contemporary culture is perhaps never better summed up than in the following passage by Harvey: 'We can no longer conceive of the individual as alienated in the classical Marxian sense, because to be alienated presupposes a coherent rather than a fragmented sense of self from which to be alienated ... Modernism was very much about the pursuit of better futures, even if perpetual frustration of the aim was conducive to paranoia. But postmodernism typically strips away that possibility by concentrating upon the schizophrenic circumstances induced by fragmentation and all those instabilities (including those of language) that prevent us even picturing coherently, let alone devising strategies to produce, some radically different future' (1990: 52–53).

Traditionally (if I can use that word in this context), the primary focus of modern art has been the 'shock of the new' (Hughes 1991) – a sort of coming to terms with new technology, new ways of living, new modes of subjectivity. At one level, this clearly remains the case today, with much contemporary art simply reflecting many of the features of our mainstream culture – materiality, heterogeneity, depthlessness and the demise of pre-existing reality (very occasionally even society's problems!). However, at another level, something else is happening. Whereas modern artists used to be overtly preoccupied with, and indeed intensely anxious about, the various discontinuities that emerged between 'the new' and what came before it, in the art of today there is a palpable sense that everything has now caught up with the new and, as a consequence, very little is experienced as truly novel or unknown (Jameson's 'absence of newness').[23] Instead, artists strive for *immediacy*, to be 'in the moment', if you like, to express the rawness of 'now-ness'. As the leading commentator on modern British art, Matthew Collings, succinctly puts it: 'Modern art's new sights are part of glamour, part of fashion and they fit with the spirit of the now' (1999: 13). The key thing here is that the 'now' no longer has to be the 'new'. Such an assertion fits perfectly with Jameson's claim that we currently inhabit a world of simultaneity (an 'eternal present'), a place where history and cultural antecedents are used simply as tools (or tricks) to stimulate the present. In many cases the result is a new type of visual imagery: one in which nothing and something square up to each other in a strange bout of parody and symbolic juxtaposition. Let us consider some prominent features of this new visual imagery by way of an introduction to more social theoretical debates about our changing cultural times.

First, there is the theme of repetition/reappropriation. Collings explains: 'Repetition is part of art but since the 1980s it has become speeded up. Styles are now repeated immediately and not decades after they first appeared, because style itself doesn't mean anything and it is untied from its moorings. In fact style is not style but a new thing you can mop on or off, like hip-hop' (1999: 227). In the case of Martin Creed's work, what is being repeated is the nothingness associated with 1960s' Minimalism (mixed with other earlier ideas from the Fluxus and Conceptualist movements). Other prominent examples include the way that Glen Brown, Gavin Turk and the Chapman brothers recycle and reappropriate historical art iconography and subject it to an ironic re-telling.

Fairly obviously, the use of earlier artistic movements and images in this way contributes to a second feature of this new visual imagery, the 'play of signs' that point to each other rather than to any tangible reality or sense of the future, for example, the way that controversial artists Gilbert and George mix Old Testament verse with images of excrement, or the way that Martin Kippenberger juxtaposed the everyday objects of ordinary life with nonsense aphorisms. A more interesting aspect of this approach is the idea that the signifier itself can somehow take on a heightened symbolism. Obvious examples would include Tracey Emin's wonderful

---

23 Such sentiments are eloquently expressed by those doyens of American independent lo-fi music, Superchunk, who declare in their song, *Kool*: 'There's nothing new, there's nothing new, everything's borrowed, everything's used.'

appliqué work; 1997 Turner Prize winner Gillian Wearing's much-copied 'Signs that say what you want them to say and not signs that say what someone else wants them to say'; Bank's stuttering politico sign-paintings; conceptual artist Lawrence Weiner's 20-foot high painting of the word 'REDUCED' in silver letters on the wall of the Bilbao Guggenheim (apparently an allegorical statement on corporate involvement in the art world); and of course Martin Creed's urban installations (see also Work No 220, *Don't Worry*, another neon sign, this time atop a run-down church in Bow, East London).

Lastly, perhaps the most striking feature of modern art today is the way it effortlessly crosses back and forth into mainstream contemporary culture. Thanks to a combination of the above themes, its undeniable immediacy and its rather contrived attempts at 'shock and awe', it has become the perfect vehicle for mass 'consumption' and dissemination.[24] No longer the preserve of the intellectual elite, modern art is now all about accessibility, almost as if much of today's art is created as a corporate brand, primed and ready for exploitation.[25] At the immediate level, this takes the form of the increasingly popular 'celebrity artist' endorsement/association, such as Tracey Emin's advertisement for Blue Sapphire Gin, Gillian Wearing's 'association' with various advertising agencies, the use of Damien Hirst's spot paintings in the advertising and marketing of Go Airlines, or the Chapman brothers' foray into designer neck ties. Moreover, there already exists a host of artists, such as Peter Davies (Plate 7), Richard Prince (Plate 8), Sean Landers (Plate 9) and the 2002 Turner nominee, Fiona Banner, whose work consists largely of painted words – jokes, lists, or blocks of text (literally signs!) – rather than pictures, images, abstractions or metaphor. It is a short step from such clever and engaging works to the commercial billboard or the advertiser's strapline. Creed's neon signs, for example, could easily be mistaken for a new marketing technique known as 'brandalism', a process by which advertisers use subversive means such as graffiti and illegal 'fly posters' to serve corporate ends (see Alvelos 2004 and Chapter 5). Perhaps the ultimate example of this play of signs in modern art is the work of Tom Sachs. Sachs 'loves the symbolism' of labels and brand names so much he creates sculptures from ultra-chic designer packaging, including a Chanel chainsaw, a Hermès hand grenade and a Prada toilet (see Plate 10). By using reified designer names typically associated with qualities unrelated to their utilitarian functions (cars that promote a sense of 'freedom', or perfumes with 'romance and love': on this point see the huge body of work by Russell Belk) and then re-associating these symbols with other more oblique objects, Sachs succeeds in inverting the sign, yet, at the same time, his work is not in any way a critique of our spontaneous consumer culture – far from it. Rather, it is a celebration: art as part of consumer culture, just as consumer culture is now art for many people.

---

24 It is estimated that over 300,000 people visited *Sensation*, a 'controversial' 1997 exhibition of young British artists at the Royal Academy.

25 In 2001, contemporary art website www.eyestorm.com claimed that traffic to its 'mail order art site' had 'more than doubled in the past month to 90,000 new hits'. The co-founder of the site, David Grob, makes no secret of the fact that his ambition is for Eyestorm 'to become to art what Nike is to sportswear' (quoted in Eshun 2001).

Such thinking is much in evidence in the work of Jean Baudrillard, a philosopher who has much to say about the urban experience, past, present and future. Described as the 'high priest' of postmodernist thought and often dismissed as a 'semantic conjurer', Baudrillard's theoretical importance is too often obfuscated (sometimes intentionally) by some of his more contentious comments. This is unfortunate, as Baudrillard's work, from his early Marxist writings on the consumer society and the proliferation of signs (1968, 1970, 1975, 1981) to his more recent metaphysical interpretations (1983, 1988, 1994), clearly illustrates the way in which the subjective urban experience was, like modern art, affected over the latter decades of the 20th century by the increasing importance placed on consumerist values within society. Baudrillard argues that society is now constituted around reflexive 'signs' and 'codes' that have no referent to any 'reality' but their own. He asserts that we (in the West) now inhabit a world of 'hyperreality', simulation – the 'play of signs'. Kellner explains: 'In this new situation a person's labour power, body, sexuality, unconscious, and so on are not primary productive forces, but are to be seen as "operational variables", "the code's chess pieces", which are to be mobilized in social institutions and practices' (1989: 62).[26] For Baudrillard, then, ours is a void-like world of empty signs and unfilled desires.

Clearly drawing on Baudrillard, Wayne Morrison suggests that one way of guiding the self through the 'disequilibrium of the journeys of late modernity' is to embrace, rather than to repel, the void – to meet the world of 'cultural mélange' head on. Consequently, in Morrison's account of late modern urban social dynamics we see a subtle, yet discernible, shift in emphasis taking place, from 'subject' to 'fractured sense of identity'. Because the embattled 'subject in transition' (partly modern, partly postmodern) is pre-programmed with an innate desire to achieve authenticity (see Boyle 2003), fulfilment and meaning – the subjective hangover from an over-indulgence in modernist messages – the late modern subject is forced to seek some sense of direction (a difficult task in a directionless world?). In short, a touchstone of social identity must be found. The fact that the resulting identity is simply a fleeting construction, changeable from one moment to the next, matters nothing. In a world of depthlessness, superficiality and simulation, it is not the end product itself that is important, but rather the ability to formulate the cultural messages of our late modern world into a refuge against the intangible. But what are the materials out of which this refuge is to be constructed? The answer, of course, is our pluralised consumer culture, a social system in which goods and services are employed as a means of identity fortification, as investments in image and status based on cultural signification (Ewen 1988; Lury 1996). Morrison explains:

> The late modern or post modern is characterized by the cultivation of consumption consumer lifestyles, which were established under capitalism, and which render the self as a matter of signification, as a matter of the style of presentation. The public self is an array of masks ranked by the prestige and exchange value of their appearance(s),

---

26 For Baudrillard, this world of pure simulation ultimately serves only to further enhance social control. Baudrillard points to the fact that the tentacles (in codified form) of hyperreality, stylisation and free-floating signs have extended to virtually all avenues of contemporary society, from politics to pornography, from cosmetic surgery to 'postmodern' art.

located in a internationalized media-orientated mass culture in which the meaning of personal civility, personal pleasure and desire, is principally understood by values flowing from the technologies of representation (advertising, films, television, magazines). (1995: 308)

As Morrison suggests, such a situation is not altogether new. Remember, it was 19th century production-oriented capitalism that first stressed the ideology of continuous personal consumption. Similarly, products have been differentiated by image for over 50 years following the satiation of homogeneous Fordist mass markets. However, what is important, as Baudrillard makes clear in the following passage, is that in contemporary society the situation is made more acute by the retreat of alternative meaning systems and markers of identity:

Undoubtedly objects have always constituted a system of recognition (reparage), but in conjunction, and often in addition to other systems (gestural, ritual, ceremonial, language, birth status, code of moral values, etc). What is specific to our society is that other systems of recognition (recognisance) are progressively withdrawing, primarily to the advantage of the code of 'social standing'. (Baudrillard, quoted in Morrison 1995: 314)

Many commentators see nothing wrong with such new modes of consumption (eg, Featherstone 1987, 1994; Campbell 1989; D Miller 1995). They celebrate the democratic potential of consumer culture to 'unpick class hierarchies' and 'undermine fixed status groups'. Echoing the central tenets of liberal capitalism, these commentators play up the self-valorising potential of consumer culture as an expression of individual freedom and autonomy, even going so far as to suggest that freedom of consumer choice/expression and the rise of so-called 'consumer sovereignty' will ultimately result in a more dynamic, creative and equable society. It is my opinion that such accounts are fundamentally flawed, both at the individual level and at the social level.

First, at the *individual level*, the operant principles of late modern consumer culture now function in a way that represents (for a great many) the complete opposite of freedom. To be clear about this point we need to set aside the well-documented 'manipulation of the consumer' debate that has so preoccupied cultural studies and its precursors in structuralist analysis for over two decades. By now it should be clear to all that the vast majority of consumers are not stupid, and typically are all too well aware of the manipulative strategies to which they are being subjected (after all, the 'machinery' of advertising and marketing has long been exposed and, as Baudrillard intimates above, consumers' ability to recognise code as code is now incorporated into the advertising process).[27] Instead, we need to focus attention on a more straightforward question: will an increase in material possessions result in greater happiness? This, after all, is the fundamental existential paradox (or 'riddle') of consumerism.

Being aware of manipulation is one thing; dealing with the anxieties, frustrations and neuroses over personal style – whether in terms of clothes, looks or lifestyle – now associated with consumerism is quite another. For instance,

---

27 Consider as an example of this point the following strapline from a poster for the Freeport Designer Outlet Village in Braintree, Essex: 'Ours is a shallow, meaningless consumer society where our possessions define us – *enjoy.*'

recent psychological research in this area suggests that the pleasurable aspects of consumption are becoming increasingly short lived (see Chapter 5). In other words, while we are constantly urged to define ourselves by what we buy and display, almost in the same moment, we are confounded by the diminishing returns gained from the quicksilver world of consumerism. The charade of self-improvement that comes from purchasing a new pair of shoes or the latest digital gadget is thus only ever a temporary fix.[28] This situation is greatly intensified, of course, by the extent to which consumer culture now propagates within individuals the constant demand for more – more products, more excitement, more stimulation, more experiences. Colin Campbell (1989) articulates this as 'the pursuit of the new'; however, given Jameson's characterisation of contemporary experience as becoming 'a series of pure and unrelated presents' – a series of 'nows' – perhaps 'the pursuit of the "now"' is a more appropriate term, not least because it suggests the idea of *excitement*. Semantics aside, the important thing to bear in mind is that consumption, or, more accurately, the anticipation and experience of consumption, generates an undeniable sense of pleasure. It also simultaneously develops various related forms of subjectivity peculiar to the late modern condition based around impulsivity (of desire and its satisfaction), spontaneity, 'forward flight' and *simultaneity* (see Chapter 5 for a more developed analysis of this point). This concomitant search for instantaneous experience, coupled with the breakdown of classical modernist temporality, has real consequences, not least in terms of attitudes towards social norms.[29] As Morrison puts it:

> The time-horizon has been shortened; instant, rather than delayed gratification has resulted in the pursuit of short-term goals at the expense of building up long-term projects. This short-term time horizon is said to result in a willingness to disregard the normative structures which are supportive of longer-term methodologies and projects. (1995: 309–10)

---

28 Anyone involved in the high street fashion industry will recognise immediately why I have chosen to use the term 'charade of self-improvement' to describe the idea of creating identity via the display of consumer goods (see Edwards 2000: Chapter 7). While to the consumer, fashion appears to be connected to self-expression and the process of marking oneself out as an individual, in reality fashion is all about belonging. It is about fitting in rather than standing out. Furthermore, thanks to recent developments, it is now possible to use other people's identity to help create your own. In recent years we have seen the forging of strong links between the 'celebrity identity' and the customer – links that now go far beyond the long-established contractual celebrity endorsement. This is about lifestyle, the recreation of the *celebrity sensibility* and all that now stands for in today's society. Eg, when Kylie Minogue admitted borrowing a make-up artist's MAC lip gloss recently, sales went up over 150%; similarly, the producers of hit TV show *Sex and the City* took to warning designers in advance if the show's star, Sarah Jessica Parker, planned to wear their products in the show, thus enabling retail outlets to increase their orders. Inevitably, this process will become increasingly rationalised as manufacturers seek to take advantage of what renowned style journalist Polly Vernon humorously describes as 'If-I-don't-get-that-now-I'm-gonna-die' moments. Companies are already experimenting with digital technology that will soon enable the home-viewer to order a product featured in a movie or TV show by remote control. We are only months away from a system that will allow us to purchase Tom Cruise's *Mission Impossible II* sunglasses, or James Bond's Omega watch from the comfort of our armchair. The implications for product placement 'tie-ins' are immense (see Swann 2000).

29 One could point to the growing clinical interest in so-called 'shopping disorders' as evidence of this point.

A number of contemporary cultural developments contribute in no small way to this tendency to privilege the immediate and the short term. Central among them is the intense speed at which the material commercial world now operates. Thanks to a combination of 'just-in-time' delivery techniques, the expansion of credit facilities (Ritzer 1995; Spiers 1995; Singletary and Crenshaw 1996) and so-called 'digitised sales loops', the consumer can now purchase goods on-line in milliseconds (see also Paul Virilio's work on 'accelerated/speed culture', eg, 1986, 1991).[30] Similarly, fashion cycles are now far shorter and quicker than ever before. The columnist and 'trend spotter' Charlotte Williamson ruefully explains:

> What's hot and what's not changes in a nanosecond and we know about the Next Big Thing before it happens. Thanks to the hype we had *Harry Potter* fatigue before the film even came out; likewise, The Strokes' backlash started way before the band had released its first album. Of course, it doesn't help that nowadays the world is effortlessly accessible. With a bit of Google-ing we can find out what shoes are big in Tokyo, or the hot new band in Miami. And just in case we've missed a beat, fashion designers have an eye on every major street in every major capital. A gradual filtering of ideas? Forget it. In our throw away society, where the straight-off-the-catwalk-on-to-the-public philosophy of Topshop and Hennes means an entire look lasts less than a month, there's a constant desire for the new ... So novelty is the only thing that stays desirable. (2002: 17)

A business built on the very modern 'cult of the new season' (a process that involves a constant built-in obsolescence) is thus undone when the 'new' moves into hyper-speed – a poetic irony perhaps?

Such a situation is not limited to the fashion world. Increasingly, at a more general level, we are being encouraged to eschew long-term conservatism – in the sense of saving and waiting – and instead pursue a course toward individual gratification, plotted by materialistic desires and located as sources of pleasure and identity (McCracken 1988). (Even high street banks, traditionally the exemplar of prudence and moderation, now encourage instant gratification. A recent advertisement for the National Westminster Bank included the image of a sports car with the strap-line, 'Don't wait. Get it now!'.) Whether the teleology of grand narratives or the world of shopping, we see the unravelling of time as directional and developmental.

Secondly, at the more *social level*, affirmative accounts of consumer culture also have a tendency to focus exclusively on the consumption practices of the so-called 'new middle classes' or 'new petit bourgeoisie', middle income earners who perpetuate shared values based around standard of living, expressive 'lifestyles' and, importantly, consumption modalities.[31] Consequently, while Mafessoli and

---

30 In a world increasingly reliant upon the Internet, the 'sales loop' is getting ever tighter, creating what has been described as 'the ultimate in instant gratification' (Kessler 1997: 86). On-line sales can now be completed in milliseconds, and every month new software packages are being developed that can speed up the order-taking process, forward information to customers on new products and sales, and even co-ordinate sales representative visits. The recent advertising campaign for Internet provider Blueyonder.com clearly tapped into this sensibility: 'Let's get one thing straight. I don't like the little blue bar [the 'loading' bar at the bottom of the computer screen]. In fact, little blue bar – I hate you! I want my downloads and I want them now ... then and only then can I relax.'

31 See Lash and Urry (1987); Savage *et al* (1992); Mafessoli (1996); cf Wynne and O'Connor (1998).

Featherstone talk of such things as 'fluid socialization', so-called 'consumer tribalism' and the notion of adopted 'temporary identities', little coverage is afforded other major demographic groups such as senior citizens, single mothers and the unwaged (compare Taylor *et al* 1996; D Miller 1995: 34–39) – a point Miles is keen to stress:

> [t]he tendency ... is to discuss consumption in an overgeneralised fashion, with little attempt to contextualise the socioeconomic experience of class in the construction of social life ... It is all well and good discussing the consumption patterns of cultural intermediaries, but what implications do the construction of middle-class ghettos of consumption have for those sectors of the population who cannot call upon the sorts of cultural and economic resources discussed by Featherstone and Wynne and O'Connor? (1998b: 1003)

One representation of late modern society that does recognise that consumer culture, by its very nature, must exclude as many people (maybe even more) as it includes is Zygmunt Bauman's (1987) conceptualisation of the 'seduced' and the 'repressed'. Like Baudrillard, Bauman has profound concerns over the way consumer society is transforming the city. However, Bauman eschews Baudrillard's more esoteric musings and concentrates instead on the more systemic role played by urban consumption in terms of the structural, spatial and social reconfiguration of the contemporary city (1991, 1997) – the terms 'seduced' and 'repressed' acting as shorthand categorisations of a new dialectic of socio-spatial control within the consumer society (1987: 149–69). The primary group – the 'seduced' – are integrated into society by their desires and perceived needs: they are 'the people to whom public relations techniques and advertising, replacing police and ideology, are addressed ... the people on whom the reproduction of capital primarily depends' (1987: 180). For these core members of society, coercion and repression – in their classic modernist forms (eg, authority, policing and normative regulation) – are far less important:

> The seduced of society ... need no longer fear the stick of repression, insofar as they willingly accept the carrot of seduction. The threat of repression remains, however, to shore up the decentralized, deregulated, privatized form of auto-surveillance that has been delegated to society's seduced by the formerly centralized power of the state. (Clarke and Bradford 1998: 876; see also Garland 2001 more generally)

Instead, this group is integrated into society by their seduction into a world of market circulation and self-perpetuating hyper-consumerism. For Clarke and Bradford (closely drawing on Bauman) this is a world in which social integration is 'guided by needs' rather than 'constrained by norms' (1998: 875) – a point with which Morrison would doubtless agree.

Opposed to the 'seduced' (although not in any overt political sense) stand the 'repressed': an increasingly marginalised group whose consumption patterns do not sufficiently integrate them into the consumer society (even though, as Bauman suggests, they may 'stupidly think otherwise'). These are the people who have failed to bridge the cultural/financial gap that dictates entry into the consumer society, and consequently they still require high levels of normative regulation and active repression via the traditional elements of social control. A crucial aspect in this transition has been the emergence of post-Fordist economics (see above). John Lea explains how we now have:

... a post-Fordist type of social structure characterized by the growth of high paid employment in financial services, the decline of 'Fordist' manufacturing employment and stable middle income communities and the growth of the informal sector of flexible, low wage, unorganized labour in construction and increasingly privatized city services, sweated labour trades such as clothing, restaurants etc. Working class organization is weakened as industrial unions decline with the emigration of Fordism, and public sector unions ... decline with the privatization of city services and the welfare state. Meanwhile, the pool of permanently unemployed expand in the form of an 'underclass' which no longer fulfills the functions of a 'reserve army of labour' in competition with the employed but inhabit the informal sector and increasingly its criminal parts. (1995: 5)

Thus we see the formation of a sector of society that, as far as the successful reproduction of capital is concerned, is now obsolete – or, more accurately, 'not-yet-eliminated' ('The consumer society no longer grants a place to those it marginalizes, rendering their very identity as members of society problematic and questionable': Clarke and Bradford 1998: 76). One might say that a 'separate world', populated by the 'new poor', is emerging as an inevitable by-product of the late 20th century market economy.[32] This is a world often overlooked by commentators such as Featherstone and Campbell when discussing consumer culture but, as Bauman points out, 'Without the second of the two nations ['the repressed'], the picture of the post-modern world is fatally incomplete' (1987: 169).

From a criminological perspective, such a situation raises two very important points. First, and most obviously, one of the great strengths of Bauman's analysis of the consumer society is the way he begins to theorise the link between consumer culture and issues of social and spatial polarisation/segregation. We now have a situation wherein the consumption and living spaces of the 'haves' are being segregated and insulated from the abandoned zones of the 'have nots', ensuring that repression – in one form or another – is back in vogue: 'We now have two worlds, at opposite poles, which are increasingly out of touch with each other – much as the no-go areas of contemporary cities are carefully fenced off and bypassed by the traffic lines used for the mobility of the well-off residents' (Bauman 1997, quoted in Clarke and Bradford 1998: 876). These are the spaces/zones that feature in Mike Davis's account of 'the New Bantustans' of Los Angeles, Loic Wacquant's ethnography of 'hyperghettoization' (2001), David Sibley's 'geographies of exclusion' (1995), Manuel Castells' 'dual cities' (1994) and the decaying inner-city enclaves of Wilson's 'Ghetto Underclass' (1987, 1993). It is interesting to reflect on just how much the demarcations and social divisions associated with Bauman's categorisations of the 'seduced' and 'repressed' resonate with the work of Jock Young (1999, 2003) on the growing 'binary distinction' between the 'largely satisfied majority' and the 'excluded and despondent minority', and the way this in turn leads to 'moral exclusion' and the subsequent creation of yet another (demonised) 'other' (see also Galbraith 1992). In sum, in a bid to reject those for whom the market fails, it appears that the 'haves' are starting to fortify the ramparts. The effect of such a situation on many individuals'

---

32 See Murray (1984, 1990); Wilson (1987); Fields (1989); McDonald (1997); and New Labour's Social Exclusion Unit (1999).

experience of urban space (both public and private) is likely to be dramatic, and thus is a subject I return to in length in Chapter 4.

A second and more complicated point concerns the interrelationship between the social control element of Bauman's 'seduced'/'repressed' analysis and consumer culture and its associated forms of concomitant subjectivity based around desire, simultaneity, new modes of individualism and impulsivity (as outlined earlier). To understand this point, it is important first to recognise the part played by commodity culture in the historical development of 20th century governance and social regulation.

In recent years, much has been made of the shift from a system of governance based around 'disciplinary forms' (ie, from a productivist perspective, the inculcation of the general norms and beliefs associated with Fordism among entire populations: see Foucault 1977 for the classic account of 'disciplinary power') to one based more on 'risk management' and the monitoring and governing of people at aggregate level.[33] Central to these accounts is the belief that risk-based forms of calculation and social control are inherently more effective and cost-efficient than those based around the disciplines, primarily because of their 'low-profile, low intervention mode of operation'. This assumption has led many commentators to declare that risk-based power systems are now the primary ordering principle in contemporary society. For the Australian criminologist, Pat O'Malley, this narrative is problematic (1993: 162–66). Not only does he cast doubt on the purported efficiency of risk-based power, but he also challenges the supposed primacy of so-called 'risk society', as Ulrich Beck has named it.[34] O'Malley suggests that while there is no doubt that post-disciplinary, risk-based technologies (such as private insurance and other actuarial practices) are alive and well, they are not sufficiently comprehensive to add up to a complete replacement of the 'disciplinary society'; rather, they should be viewed as a temporary eclipse: 'While risk based technologies play a key role in this new order, the heyday of "risk-society", identified here with the hegemony of Keynesianism, emerges in this account as no more than an interlude, an effect of the impact of historical crises in the transition to consumerism' (1993: 166). For O'Malley at least there is another side to the story:

---

33 See Simon (1987, 1988); Ewald (1990, 1991); Miller and Rose (1990); Castel (1991); Gordon (1991).

34 Beck's construct of 'risk society' is based on the idea that modernity invented the concept of an open future, or at least one that could be controlled by human agency – notably through innovations such as the law of contract, which in essence was an attempt to control contingency via legal means. (What were the grand narratives themselves, if not an attempt to control progress by linking it to a teleological programme?) However, as modernity unfolded, and we became increasingly aware of the interconnectedness of the social and environmental world, such ideas were threatened – not so much by the fear of uncontrollable contingencies, but by the realisation that *our very attempts to control risk often serve only to produce even greater risks*. A prominent recent example of this phenomenon would be the UK government's attempt to deal with the BSE crisis. Following the BSE outbreak, the government enforced a series of centralising and standardising practices within British abattoirs. Such rigorous standards ensured that numerous local slaughterhouses were forced to close. Thus, when foot and mouth disease appeared shortly afterwards, the disease spread quickly because farmers had been forced to transport their animals longer distances as a result of the closure of local abattoirs.

[t]he hegemony of discipline has been challenged and toppled not by the emergence of a still more efficient power ['risk society'], but by a culture formed in resistance to discipline and its cultural milieu. The rise of a culture of consumption has challenged discipline, by generating and sustaining robust refusals which discipline could not crush, and perhaps more vitally, by undermining the political and cultural validity of its assumptions and the strategies it reflects. (1993: 181)

Central to this alternative reading is what O'Malley describes as 'the culture of excitement' – something he sees (*pace* Daniel Bell, Colin Campbell and Norbert Elias) as stemming largely from 'the Romantic resistance to the bloodless rationality of the Enlightenment and of the self-denying productivism of modern capitalism' (1993: 167). The importance of the Romantics, however, should not be overstated; rather, 'their role in history was [more] to assist in the translation of these ideas into a central place in the culture of modernity'. More important, he argues, was the development and intensification of 20th century commodity culture, in particular, the way it served to 'amplify' this 'culture of excitement', a culture that, since the Enlightenment, had been suppressed and consigned either to the emotive, sensual works of the 18th century Romantics, or the carefully controlled spaces associated with historic forms of 'carnival' (see Bakhtin 1968). For O'Malley, even the 19th century classic expansion of commodification was already dependent on a culture of excitement:

... the development of commodification, driven by relentless pressure to find opportunities for profit, meshed well with the cultural emphasis on excitement. To the extent that excitement feeds on the novel, even requiring novelty for its replenishment, then the cult of excitement offers the foundation conditions for an almost inexhaustible market for commodities. Conversely, the process of commodification (for example through advertising), locks into this process. It sensitizes consumers to the array of opportunities for excitement and thus further consumption, but most crucially establishes over and over again the importance of excitement as a cultural value in itself ... The reproduction of the commodity market thus has come to rely on, and in turn to reproduce, the culture of excitement. (O'Malley 1993: 168)

It was this process in tandem with other important 20th century developments – the growth of urbanisation and the separation of labour and leisure – that ultimately brought about the downfall of disciplinary forms of governance:

Discipline, it begins to appear, has been cast adrift by commodity culture's erosion of the *laissez-faire* Protestant Ethic in which discipline had its roots. Out of its time, it became vulnerable in all fields to a politics of failure, and the source of this is a strategic discipline – which may arbitrarily be termed neo-liberalism – more consonant with governing a culture of consumption. (1993: 170)

In other words, the emergence of risk society is but the point of struggle that saw the demise of 'productivist *laissez-faire* strategies' and thus permitted/enabled the subsequent rise of discourses associated with 'neo-liberalism' (which of course is itself orientated around consumption and the subsequent rise – from a productivist perspective – of so-called 'enterprise culture'). The result is a form of governance and regulation far more divisive than one based around the strategic discourses associated with 'risk society'. It is at this point that O'Malley's analysis closely overlaps with that of Bauman: 'The bifurcated technologies of neo-liberalism create a stark contrast *between government of those within and those outside the charmed circle of the market, creating potentially explosive problems of social comparison'* (1993: 181, emphasis added). The reason why O'Malley's account is more instructive than Bauman's, at least for the purposes of the present work, is because of the stress he places on excitement and associated emotions in the transition to the 'bifurcated' consumer society. This notion of excitement (along with other related emotional states and feelings – excitement, desire, fantasy) as reinterpreted and engendered through modern consumer culture will constitute a major theme in the remaining chapters of this book. In particular, the importance of such new forms of consciousness for criminological theory will be discussed at length and, along with other themes identified in this chapter as being constitutive of the contemporary urban experience, formulated into a conceptual framework for thinking about certain urban crimes under conditions of late modernity. However, in the meantime, in a bid to further elucidate the changing nature of the urban experience, I now wish to turn to developments in the physical environment of our cities, in particular, the changing nature of contemporary architectural practice and urban design and how this is further contributing (in no small way) to the emergence of the forms of late modern subjectivity outlined above.

Paradise now: architectural postmodernism from the consumer vernacular to the urbanoid environment

> Less is a bore. (Robert Venturi, postmodern architect)

There remains at least one area of cultural practice where the notion of the 'postmodern' is not surrounded by theoretical imbroglio.[35] In the field of architecture, the rupture with modernism and the embracing of a new and distinct postmodern sensibility has been both decisive and pronounced. Most famously, some even cite a moment in architectural history – the 'highly symbolic' demolition of the prize-winning Pruitt-Igoe housing blocks in St Louis, Missouri (built by Minoru Yamasaki in the 1950s) at 3.32 pm, 15 July 1972 – as the exact moment at which postmodernism 'happened' (Jencks 1977; Lyotard 1984). For this reason, I have chosen to focus on postmodern architecture – considered by many to be the quintessential urban art form – to further illustrate the changing nature of urban space and thus the urban experience. By way of introduction two themes stand out.

First, the term 'postmodernism' in architecture refers to an art of 'rejection'. As McLeod has commented, the emphasis of postmodern architecture has been on 'the

---

35 Obviously, examples of the postmodern aesthetic abound in many other areas of the arts. In literature, the works of Borges, Calvino, Vonnegut, Auster, Pynchon, Rushdie and Eco best exemplify the characteristics of postmodern fiction (see Hassan 1971; Wilde 1981; McHale 1987; Jarvis 1998: Chapters 6–9); in art 'the postmodern' is difficult to pin down chronologically (see Alloway *et al* 1981; Paoletti 1985 for early attempts); however, recent works by the likes of Paul McArthy, Sarah Lucas, Liz Payton, Glenn Brown and – OK – Damien Hirst best illustrate some of its most contemporary (and contentious) manifestations; in film, everything from *Bladerunner* to *Blue Velvet*, from *Repo Man* to *Reservoir Dogs* has been daubed (often erroneously) with the tag of postmodernism (see Harvey 1990: Chapter 18; Corrigan 1991; Denzin 1991; Jarvis 1998: Chapters 10–13); lastly, although less clearly defined than in other arts, composers like John Cage, Steve Reich, Laurie Anderson and Philip Glass provide examples of musical postmodernism (see Nyman 1974; Battock 1981).

repudiation of existing [modernist] styles and beliefs rather than on the construction of a cohesive, theoretical, and formal program' (1985: 19). The story begins in the US in the mid-1960s when certain architects began to argue against the core ideology of the European architecture of the Modern Movement and its implicit belief in rational design for a rational society – Le Corbusier's 'modern machine for living' (see Chapter 1). Such a reaction was unsurprising given what McLeod describes as modern architecture's evident and much-denounced failure (hence the symbolic importance of blowing up the Pruitt-Igoe housing block):

> [t]he tragedies of World War II, the tyrannies of Stalinist Russia, and the advance of multinational capital had largely shattered such utopian faith. Mass housing had created social problems, not solved them. The failures of advocacy planning and self-help projects in the 1960s only contributed further to the sense of political impotence. Few architects were able to sustain a belief in their craft as a powerful social force. (1985: 30)

The result was the abandonment both of the universal styles, technocratic design and geometrical formalism associated with the International School, and the ethos of widescale social reform that so underpinned the modernist movement (and coupled architecture with urban planning), hence an initial shift away from universal large-scale metropolitan planning initiatives towards a field of architectural practice that expressed instead the 'aesthetics of diversity' and the idea of the so-called 'collage city' (see Harvey 1990: 66–75; Krier 1987).

Secondly, from a purely aesthetic perspective, postmodern architecture held firmly to the idea of 'architecture as art'. The doyen of the 'new breed' of postmodern architects, Frank Gehry, explains: 'Painting had an immediacy that I craved for in architecture. I explored the process of new construction materials to try giving free spirit to form. In trying to find the essence of my own expression, I fantasized that I was an artist standing before a white canvas deciding what the first move should be' (Gehry, quoted in Jodidio 1995: 36). This mode of thinking created a situation whereby virtually anything formed part of the architect's palette. Consequently, an architectural style emerged that was both eclectic and self-referential (Jencks 1977: 87). For example, the work of Michael Graves draws heavily on architectural quotations from various international styles, including a collage of Italianate and Mediterranean forms; the 'deconstructivist' designs of Frank Gehry reflect the urban streetscapes and beach boardwalks of Los Angeles in their use of corrugated iron, chain-fencing, wooden logs and asphalt; while the buildings of Eric Owen Moss (described by modernist-turned-postmodernist architect Philip Johnson as 'a jeweler of junk') include broken industrial components, girders and chains to evoke memories of the fading industrial landscape.[36]

What became the manifesto for architectural postmodernism was unofficially set down in *Learning from Las Vegas: The Forgotten Symbolism of Architectural Form* (Venturi *et al* 1972). The authors of this inventive and provocative work not only launched a full-scale assault on the central tenets of architectural modernism – the

---

36 Other examples of architectural postmodernism include the work of Charles Moore, Allan Greenberg, RoTo and Franklin Israel.

correlation of form and function – but also expressed hopes that 'postmodern' urban design might in the future become an inclusive 'architecture of the people'. No longer was architecture to be the preserve of the intellectual avant-garde; instead, it had to become easier to read, decipher and understand. Thus, following the credo set out in *Learning from Las Vegas*, postmodern architects attempted to reflect and indeed celebrate (what they saw as) the existing chaotic heterogeneity of the contemporary urban environment and the wider pluralistic society. Naturally, such an approach threw up a tension: how were postmodern architects to reconcile the theme of 'going with the flow of the city' with the idea that architects must seek 'the essence of their own expression' in front of a blank canvas? The solution was the creation of an *aesthetics of inclusion*. Venturi and his collaborators urged their followers to draw inspiration from everyday cultural references, everything from popular classical motifs (such as Greek colonnades) and historical tropes (like Tudor beams) – in Jamesonian terms, the past stimulating the present – to the neon glow of the Las Vegas strip and the materialistic values of the consumer society. The result was a multi-faceted design ethos that was highly decorative, self-referential, contradictory, 'playful' and at times excessive (see also Venturi 1977; Jencks 1977, 1980; and Moore and Allen 1976).

This 'uncritical espousal of the commercial vernacular' (Huyssen 1990: 240) unsurprisingly proved highly controversial. For many critics, both then and now, such revelling in 'gross' popular culture was both gratuitous and vulgar. For others, however, such criticism was 'patently absurd'. They argued instead that we should rejoice in the way Warhol's 'Pop Art' (postmodern architecture's great influence) and Venturi *et al*'s new postmodern aesthetic 'exploded the reified dogmas of modernism' (1990: 240). Venturi, of course, was unapologetic, declaring in an article appropriately entitled 'Mickey Mouse teaches the architects' that 'Disney World is nearer to what people want than what architects have ever given them' (Venturi, quoted in Harvey 1990: 60; compare with Fjellman 1992: 317). Jencks concurred, arguing that because the market is society's most powerful and pervasive language, architects should feel no remorse whatsoever about designing consumption-orientated buildings.

At the conceptual level, the debate has continued to circulate in more or less these terms. What, then, of meaning within these mimetic landscapes? Is postmodern architecture really nothing more than an art of stimulation, self-reference and playful deception, an ephemeral landscape of empty signs? Or are there deeper cultural sensibilities inscribed in this world of play, parody and pastiche? Then again, why does culture have to be 'deep' in the world of postmodern surfaces? Certainly, unbridled appreciation of the 'consumer vernacular' brings into play many of the concerns expressed earlier by Baudrillard about the 'play of signs' and consumerism (see above). Postmodern architecture clearly exemplifies these phenomena. In celebrating futuristic landscapes, faux historical recreational resorts, computer-programmed animated neon and the spectacle of skyline advertising, Venturi and his collaborators are, in effect, championing market aesthetics as a legitimate architectural influence in the process of making the sign the ultimate commodity. Such debates are by now familiar – perhaps too familiar?

Postmodernism meanwhile had migrated off the drawing board, out of the architecture brochures and coffee table books. It took hold elsewhere in a surprisingly 'real' set of environments and unpredicted applications. By the late 1970s and early 1980s, the effects of recession, rapid de-industrialisation, corporate flight and the subsequent problems of unemployment, homelessness and urban crime ravaged a great many cities throughout Europe and North America. In a bid to turn the flagging fortunes of these cities around, many regional policy-makers and city governments embarked on ambitious downtown and inner-city regeneration projects.[37] The vast majority of these projects followed what Sharon Zukin describes as the 'private-sector-led model of urban renewal' (1998: 830–35), a model that placed consumption at the very centre of the design remit. Naturally, the consuming spaces and recreational places that were created often relied heavily upon features promoted by postmodern architects (Harvey 1990: Chapter 4; Sorkin 1992a; Gartman 1998: 133–35; Hannigan 1998: Chapters 3–5).[38] Mammoth shopping malls, galleries, up-market restaurants[39] and entertainment complexes, as well as heritage, leisure and cultural sites,[40] were all 'wrapped in a style of decoration and diversity' (Gartman 1998: 134), a style echoing the ideas expressed in *Learning from Las Vegas*. Even office buildings and corporate headquarters located within regenerated and gentrified areas were frequently given a postmodern architectural makeover in a bid to 'lighten' their image – 'after all, people did not want to look at an ugly modernist box that screamed efficiency and rationalization when coming downtown to shop, play or live' (1998: 134).

Stylistically and economically, this form of mainstream (dumbed down?) postmodern architecture was very appealing in that it could easily be exported and 'plugged into' the built environment of virtually any city. With its pseudo-classicism, playful consumer vernacular and themed quasi-public spaces, postmodern urban design could replicate itself practically anywhere, so long as it sufficiently incorporated a degree of local specificity into its design (Abel 1986). Certainly its ubiquitous style and standardised form appealed both to politicians

---

37 Consider, eg, the inner-city redevelopment in cities like Cleveland, Baltimore, San Francisco and Detroit in the US, Bristol, Cardiff, Liverpool and London's Docklands in the UK, and Barcelona, Lille and Hamburg in Europe.

38 Zukin notes that it was around this time ('after 1980') that 'a cultural and geographic shift' took place 'from suburban shopping malls to urban, mixed-use complexes including offices, shopping and entertainment' (1998: 830; see also Kowinski 1985; Shields 1989; Gardner and Sheppard 1989; Crawford 1992; Goss 1993). Similarly, Featherstone points out that this was the time when in some cases the city centre and shopping centre began to converge: 'Some of the larger ones such as the West Edmonton Mall are veritable towns, if not cities in extent. In some instances, glass roofs have been placed over city centres as in the case of Rovaniema, the capital of Finnish Lapland. To walk through the centre of Singapore represents a movement through a series of air-conditioned shopping centres' (1998: 917).

39 Restaurants were a favourite commission of postmodern architects during the 1980s, primarily because of their often experimental design remit. Consider, eg, Gehry's restaurant designs and Morphosis's Kate Mantilini Restaurant in Beverly Hills (1986), and 72 Market Street Restaurant in Venice Beach (1982–85). Furthermore, by the mid-1990s, many of the central features of these postmodern designs – the minimalist chic of stripped floors and chrome and glass interiors – had been exported in watered-down form to thousands of trendy eateries in city centres the world over.

40 On the growth of so-called 'spaces of nostalgia' and historical theme parks within the city, see Boyer (1992).

keen to revive urban space by combining entertainment, tourism and real estate initiatives into a single redevelopment project (eg, Liverpool's dockland redevelopment), and to multinational corporations who viewed these urban spaces as major sources of revenue stream in the new post-Fordist economy.[41] As such, many of the central features of mainstream postmodern architecture – including everything from the intentional distortion of time associated with the 'Vegas casino aesthetic' to the confusing spatiality of postmodern bastions like the Bonaventure Hotel (see above) – have come to be regarded as commensurate with the new highly contrived urban entertainment centres and redevelopment projects that sprang up in city after city during the 1980s and 1990s. With historical motif, ironic play, architectural quotations from various international styles, creative geometry and expansive design ideals, the followers of Venturi and Jencks set about transforming run-down inner cities into consumer playgrounds for the urban middle class. These urban regeneration schemes also marked the return of urban planning on a mass scale – something that postmodern architects had previously opted to reject, yet this time around, public initiatives were coupled with private commissions and partnerships. Furthermore, it is now often the case that the initial catalyst for regeneration is not local council or national government initiatives but simply the relocation of a sufficient number of the *nouveau* bourgeoisie (like-minded individuals who share a similar 'cultural' outlook, consumption patterns and lifestyle demographics) into a specific neighbourhood (Mullins 1991; Filion 1991). Style magazine waffle and estate agent hyperbole ensure that others quickly follow (see Zukin 1995). In short, the landscape of spectacle, semiotics, pleasure and cultural diversity so lauded by the high priests of architectural postmodernism during the late 1960s and early 1970s had, by the mid-1980s, become little more than a regeneration industry.

If this unexpected outcome seems to echo the fate of modernism – Le Corbusier's utopian dreams ending up as the design for the post-war estates and high-rise complexes – for the urban sociologist John Hannigan, the comparison can only be unfavourable to postmodernism:

> Modernism may have been a project gone wrong but it was honestly conceived out of a desire to improve deteriorating cities through social engineering. Postmodern architecture and design, by contrast, lacks this altruistic impulse. Rather than a liberating force which opens up the city to a more pluralistic cultural experience, it more often seems to represent another means for sugarcoating the intrusion of multinational capital into contemporary landscapes. (Hannigan 1995: 171)

The willing conduit of globalised capitalism, postmodernism is meretricious for Hannigan not only because of its inherent inauthenticity, but also because this in turn opens the door to manipulative social strategies (see also Ferrell 2001: Chapters 1 and 2). Architectural developments such as San Francisco's Fisherman's Wharf,

---

41 The recent plans to redevelop Croydon town centre (Park Place) in South London by private property development company Minerva plc are of interest here. According to the plan, the project's aims are twofold: first, the development of new premises for Nestlé and Allders plc (Croydon's largest retailer); and secondly, the creation of 110 new shop units and 12 restaurants. Concerns over the future of public space and the provision of other public amenities barely feature in Minerva's glossy brochure.

Canada's West Edmonton Mall (complete with street scenes from around the globe: see Hopkins 1990), Gateshead's MetroCentre (Chaney 1990), Ocean Dome indoor beach near Myazaki, Japan (with its 13,500 tons of water and space for 10,000 people: see Boyle 2003) or New York's South Street Seaport (with its simulated sounds and smells of the waterfront) are seen simply as signifiers of places without any real substance or reality, environments of 'spectacle ... surface glitter and transitory, participatory pleasure', in the words of David Harvey (1990: 91). Such locations are little more than a cleverly masked form of social control (compare S Cohen 1979; Shearing and Stenning 1985; Davis 1992b; Scheerer and Hess 1997). In the relationship between consumer and consuming space the dazzled spectator is but a dupe. This is reminiscent of Marcuse's early work on pacification of the proletariat, or indeed Bauman's argument that 'the seduced of society need no longer fear the stick of repression/exclusion insofar as they willingly accept the carrot of seduction'.

In the excellent *Fantasy City: Pleasure and Profit in the Postmodern Metropolis* (1998), Hannigan describes the phenomenal rise of what he terms 'urban entertainment developments' (UEDs) and, in particular, how they are contributing both to a 'new phase of entertaining consumption' and, more worryingly, 'new expressions of forms of social control'.[42] UEDs represent a world of casinos, megaplex cinemas, hotel complexes, themed restaurants, branded virtual-reality arcades, interactive theme parks, 'mega malls' and entertainment complexes, all wrapped up in the decorative, playful style closely associated with architectural postmodernism. So far, Hannigan claims 'we've only glimpsed the leading edge of this "Fantasy City" but there is every indication that by the next millennium this will have become a global trend' (1998: 1). Hannigan backs up this statement with numerous examples of the growth of UEDs in North America, the Asia-Pacific Rim, Europe (Centro in Oberhausen, Port Vell in Barcelona and Kinepolis in Brussels), and even China, where 41 theme parks were developed in the 1990s.

Hannigan links UEDS to what Paul Goldberger (1996) terms 'urbanoid environments', inauthentic spaces of illusion and control:

As such, they [urbanoid environments] contribute to the rise of the 'private city' in which the disorganized reality of older streets and cities is replaced by a measured, controlled and organized kind of urban experience which is intimately linked to a fusion of consumerism, entertainment and popular culture. Such quasi-urban environments ... seek to provide all the energy, variety, visual stimulation and cultural opportunities of the real thing, while, at the same time, shutting out the problems that have come to accompany urban life, notably poverty and crime. In doing so the new developments

---

42 According to Hannigan, the postmodern *Fantasy City* has six defining features: (i) 'Theme-o-centric'; (ii) aggressively branded; (iii) operates 24 hours a day (as per the Nevada casino model); (iv) modular (ie, comprised of a standard array of components, eg Hard Rock Cafe, Pizza Hut, HMV, IMAX theatre etc); (v) postmodern in design (includes technologies of simulation and spectacle); and (vi) *Fantasy City* is *solipsistic* ('isolated from surrounding neighbourhoods physically, economically and culturally'). Hannigan suggests that the solipsistic nature of *Fantasy City* ensures that what emerges is '[a] metropolis which ignores the reality of homelessness, unemployment, social injustice and crime, while eagerly transforming sites and channels of public expression into 'promotional spaces' (1998: 4): you can write corporate values onto the surface of the city.

end up discouraging the mixing of different classes of people in order to make the city safe for the middle-classes. Goldberger laments this strategy, observing that it blurs the lines between city and suburb, with the former taking on certain characteristics more associated with the latter. (Hannigan 1998: 6)

But this is a more significant move than Hannigan apparently realises. Goldberger's analysis take us beyond the simple concept of the duped and pacified consumer and into an environment where we are actually living within representations of the city, actually inhabiting a world of signifiers of the urban.[43] Architectural postmodernism is no longer simply *referencing* the consumer vernacular: it has now actually morphed into 'Consumerville'. As Mike Davis (1998: 392–98) has suggested, certain city spaces are becoming sites of *hyperreal simulation* (see Plate 11, *New York in the Desert*). For instance, consider the way that the mythical Hollywood has, in recent years, broken free from its physical and geographical moorings to be re-conceptualised elsewhere, this time without the violence, drugs, prostitution and poverty that, by the 1970s, had become its stock in trade: 'As Hollywood's immiseration eroded the historic linkage between signifier and signified, it gradually became possible to imagine the resurrection of HOLLYWOOD! in a more affluent, more secure neighborhood' (1998: 396). Tourists can now 'experience' Hollywood either in Orlando, Florida (at Disney-MGM or Universal Studios – the latter complete with its own 'replica' Hollywood Boulevard and Rodeo Drive), or even more locally, just down the road from the real 'warts and all' Hollywood, at the $100 million CityWalk complex, a four-block-long mall linking Universal Studios with its huge cinema complex. In this 'idealised reality' the shopper can 'enjoy' what Davis describes as 'easy, bite-sized pieces' of Los Angeles, from the Native American theme store Adobe Road to a plastic 'King Kong hanging from a seventy-foot neon totem pole', all lovingly cloaked in what project designer Richard Orne calls 'a patina of use' (cited in Spiller 1993). Here, among the faux street scenes, replica landmarks and pre-aged buildings (including 'gum wrappers embedded in the terrazzo flooring'), tourists experience an imaginary Los Angeles free of all those pernicious social problems that make contemporary urban life so distressing (see also Dickinson 1997 on Old Pasadena). Nor is Britain immune from these seemingly futuristic developments. Increasingly, a creeping homogeneity is threatening the cultural identity of the 'picturesque' English town, creating what journalist John Vidal describes as 'Nowhereville, England' (2003). Using the Shropshire market town of Oswestry as an example of cultural blandness, he states:

Today, it [Oswestry] appears increasingly like 1,000 other prosperous-looking small British towns, boasting much the same smart bollards, mock antique street lighting,

---

43 Against this backdrop, cities are fighting ever harder to re-brand themselves in a bid to attract inward investment. Robins explains: 'If city cultures cannot be re-imagined, then perhaps they could be re-imaged. Modern cities have always, of course, advertised their civic grandeur to the world ... Now, in a world in which inter-urban competitiveness operates on a global scale, cities are propelled into a race to attract increasingly mobile investors, consumers, and spectacles (sports and media events). As cities have become ever more equivalent and urban identities increasingly "thin", however, it has become necessary to employ advertising and marketing agencies to manufacture such divisions ... The particularity and identity of cities is about product differentiation' (1991: 3). This situation is now so out of hand that even a city's skyline can be subject to legal action over copyright (Usborne 1998).

mass-produced paving slabs, anonymous housing estates and ubiquitous chain stores. The high street has the same banks, building societies and charity shops as towns in Devon and Northumberland, the old cattle market is now a car park, the most popular place is a JD Wetherspoon chain pub, and the main road has been diverted to the front door of the largest supermarket. (Vidal 2003)[44]

From the 'designed-in grit' of Universal City's CityWalk to the mass-produced coaching lamps and homogenous 'olde world' street signs of middle England's market towns, this is the landscape of consumption – homogeneous and plastic, but safe and entertaining – in Davis-speak, a 'junk-food' version of the real urban experience. The urban imaginary has arrived.

Conclusion

In this chapter I have attempted to offer some brief insights into how best to conceptualise city life and the urban experience *today*, the aim being to draw on these insights in later chapters to help us further understand the contemporary urban crime problem. After a brief discussion about the changing nature of the times we live in, attention turned to changes in the economic constitution of late modern society. The role of culture in these changes was prioritised, and especially the fundamental shift from a 'producer-driven society' to one predicated on consumption. Our concern then moved on to the changing nature of subjective forms of temporality and spatiality under late modern/postmodern conditions. Central to this account was the death of any sense of a unified coherent subject and the subsequent *privileging of the present* associated with today's 'postmodern' spaces/cultures, 'the world of the now'. It was then postulated that the unique feature of an unmediated consumer culture is the extent to which it propagates within individuals the constant demand for more – more products, more excitement, more stimulation, more experiences. The focus of the penultimate section was the way commodity culture is contributing to a pronounced redrawing of the social and spatial urban landscape. The work of, *inter alia*, Zygmunt Bauman and Pat O'Malley on the 'bifurcation of society' was considered, the latter on the particular relationship between new forms of social control and 'the culture of excitement'. Lastly, we looked at the changing nature of the built environment in our cities, and in particular at how the ideas and design ethos that underpinned postmodern architecture quickly became re-appropriated to serve the needs of the market.

It is hoped that the one theme to emerge above all others from these short synopses is that the urban experience and the urban environment are increasingly constituted around consumer culture and its associated practices. Hence, just because certain sections of the population are, on the face of it, excluded from entering and operating effectively in the consumer palaces and entertainment complexes of the late modern urban landscape, it does not mean that their desires

---

44 Vidal's comments were a response to a recent report by The Council for the Protection of Rural England (2003). The report's author, Flora Gathorne-Hardy, stated: 'The value of diversity cannot be understated. It is our shared record of the past. The variations help us root our lives, giving people a strong sense of place and inspiration for the future' (quoted in Vidal 2003).

or perceived needs will dissipate. On the contrary, in the environment of consumer-orientated desire/incitement, the likelihood is that these desires will become even more insistent, resulting in pronounced frustration, anxiety, and ultimately incivility and crime. Whilst such thinking is clearly concurrent with earlier theories of social strain (eg, Merton 1938), I hope to argue in the remainder of this work that hyper-consumerism (and its associated social tendencies) is contributing to the crime problem in ways that are new and qualitatively different from those expressed in classical accounts of strain theory. More specifically, I shall suggest that late modern consumer culture is engendering – especially within young people – certain concomitant forms of subjectivity that, in many cases, ultimately find expression in criminal behaviour, a line of thought explored in detail in Chapter 5.

Chapter 3
The Forgotten City and the Lost Offender

In the rich literature on the city we look in vain for a theory of urbanism presenting in a systematic fashion the available knowledge concerning the city as a social entity. (Louis Wirth 1995 [1938]: 8)

... where our methods grow more powerful and precise ... we move ever further away from our data and the complex realities they represent. (Jeffrey Fagan 1993: 381)

Introduction

The city has always been a flickering presence within criminology, variously the source of immediacy, concern, visibility and inspiration, yet, despite this interest, the concept of the city has rarely been fully integrated into developed analyses of crime. This tendency is even more pronounced today. The increased prevalence of so-called 'scientific' methodologies within our discipline has ensured that, even though the majority of criminologists tend to study urban crime (in one form or another), seldom does their work overlap with related disciplines such as urban studies or urban geography, or indeed even urban sociology. Even within contemporary criminological theory, the city is all too frequently lost in the moment of abstraction, appearing only as an afterthought, a sort of theoretical shadow or 'sideshow'.[1] Urban crime is thus torn free from its physical context – the city. Street crime, for example, exists not as in any way connected to street life (or, for that matter, the life of the street), but as an autonomous, independent act, divested of all the complexities and inequities that are such a feature of the daily urban round. Consequently, what has been lost to criminology is the great potential for understanding the relationship between urban space and urban crime signalled, for example, by Robert Park *et al*'s (1925) book *The City* – a monument to the city as a living, breathing, socio-cultural entity.

Having spent time in the previous chapters introducing the idea of the urban experience through a range of different disciplines and theoretical positions, I now wish to offer a few select observations about *criminology's* particular 'view of the city'. In this sense the chapter turns on the idea of the 'environment', for it is through environmental (and more recently spatial) discourse that notions of city life – albeit increasingly nominal and abstracted notions – are typically constructed and understood within criminology. I will also argue that there has been a secondary consequence of the way criminology has predicated its understanding of the 'urban' on the various and competing discourses associated with environmentalism – the further removal of the 'offender' from the criminological viewfinder. Consigned now to the 'spatio-temporal round' and the abstracted 'mappable crime

---

1   One interesting recent exception is Vincenzo Ruggiero's book, *Movements in the City: Conflict in the European Metropolis* (2000).

environment', the offender is becoming 'lost' to mainstream criminology in much the same way as the city has been 'forgotten'.

Then ... discovering space and crime

As the history of criminology is told, a key moment – indeed, it is sometimes portrayed as a regrettably lost moment – is identified as early *environmental* approaches to crime. Not specifically focused on the city, yet later to become one of the key aspects of the urban condition, the environment as a way of thinking about space turns out to be immensely mutable, slippery and open-ended, a point of assemblage of what became differentiated, even competing, perspectives and techniques. Like its cognate term 'ecology', the early environmental approach to crime can best be understood through its position at the junction where, from the mid-19th century through the first half of the 20th century, the social sciences sought both to draw on *and* distinguish themselves from the natural sciences. Equally, because of this pivotal position, the term 'environment' has played host to considerable internal strife within criminology. Indeed, as will emerge throughout this chapter, there is no singular meaning or predicted application that can be associated with or deduced from the discourses associated with environmentalism.

Quételet and Guerry: early ecologies of crime and the emergence of 'l'homme moyen'

> We will know in advance how many individuals will dirty their hands with the blood of others, how many will be forgers, how many poisoners, nearly as well as one can enumerate in advance the births and deaths that must take place ... [Here is] a kind of budget for the scaffold, the galleys and the prisons, achieved by the French nation with greater regularity, without doubt, than the financial budget. (Quételet, cited in Beirne 1993)

> Most of the methods we use in criminology to infer relationships are based on mean values of distributions. (Maltz 1994: 434)

What brought together a Belgian astronomer mathematician and a French lawyer with a penchant for *cartes thématiques* was their common dream that collecting and analysing statistics would one day yield a picture of every country's 'national budget of crime'. Set against the backdrop of unprecedented demographic and social changes – not the least important of which being the onset of mass urbanisation – this proto-criminology saw its task as fundamentally predictive, a deeply modernist project that sought to manage the future through knowledge. Indeed, so certain was the Belgian, Adolphe de Quételet, of these new methods that he gave his work the wonderfully sanguine moniker 'Social Physics': through statistical analysis, society's ills could be identified and cured. The idea of a budget of crime, comparable (even superior) to a nation's financial budget, speaks of the intimacy with which the new science was to be associated with the state and the possibility of taking on ever more areas of the social into its sphere of governance. It suggests too – for the science of economics was beginning to emerge from the wider sphere of political economy – that human moral behaviour (André-Michel Guerry was the author of 'Essai sur la Statistique Morale de la France')[2] was a specific sphere with its own 'laws', regularities and norms[3] – and, of course, departures (deviations) from the norm. Pivotally, this was also the point of entry of (what later come to be called) *environmental influences*. Just as the well-governed state must attend to its regional and local specificities, so too variations in crime patterns were calibrated against a vast range of factors, from climate and diet to education, age and sex. (Violent crimes were more common in the summer months, while crimes against property were more frequent during the winter.) Deviations must be explained, and that was the task assigned to the 'environment'.

What made this vision possible were two developments. On the one hand, there was a series of late 18th/early 19th century breakthroughs in mathematics, statistics and the theory of probability, emerging especially in the study of astronomy. Where mathematical techniques already had begun to be applied as social calculus, notably in the area of insurance (see Hacking 1990), these innovations opened up a much wider range of social applications, of which the study of crime was the leading example. On the other hand, a body of observations had begun to be accumulated by the state (state-istics), taking as its first object the question of crime – national crime statistics were inaugurated in a rudimentary form in 1827 with the publication by the French government of the *Compte général de l'administration de la justice criminelle*. The use of criminal statistics in this manner spread rapidly,[4] especially to Britain, where administrators and academics were soon forming statistical societies in a bid to disseminate their findings. Among the first to document real variations in crime rates was the lawyer, Joseph Fletcher (1848), who, developing the statistical template provided by Guerry, proposed a link between education and crime, education being understood as an environmental element. However, from a purely urban perspective, it was the work of Rawson W Rawson that was to prove most significant. Collating early crime statistics, Rawson identified the connection between high population density and crime rates, stating that the 'collection of large masses of the population in crowded cities conduces more than anything else to the creation of those causes, whatever they may be, which stimulate the commission of crime' (Rawson 1839).

As the history of criminology is told today, this distinctly modernist project and its dream of an ordered society go by a variety of epithets: 'environmental', 'ecological',[5] even 'social' and 'proto-sociological'. Yet it is precisely these standard depictions that the American criminologist Piers Beirne challenges in his superb

---

2 For this work, Guerry drew chiefly on the *Annals d'hygiène publique et de la médecine légale* of 1829. The *Annals* provided 'the chief organ for doctors of alienation, suicide and crime' (Hacking 1990: 76).

3 Cf Michel Foucault's 'Governmentality' in Burchell *et al* (1991).

4 Within a few years, numerous other criminal studies based upon Guerry and Quételet's cartographic methods began appearing in continental Europe (eg, Parent-Duchâtelet (1836); Robriquet (1841)).

5 These two terms were not in fact used in the social sciences until the late 19th century (the first use of 'ecology' is generally attributed to Ernst Haeckel (in 1878), the German biologist and philosopher), but the conceptual frame they convey, focusing on the relationship between behaviour and locality, does suit the work of Quételet and Guerry very well.

alternative history of criminology's origins, *Inventing Criminology: Essays on the Rise of 'Homo Criminalis'* (1993). While he bemoans those accounts that dismiss Quételet and Guerry as dilettanti and amateurs in the world of statistical analysis (eg, Vold *et al* 2002: 21–26), or their complete lack of mention in other histories of the discipline (eg, Mannheim 1972), he reserves his most important criticisms for those commentators who fête these early ecologists as proto-sociologists, most famously as set out by Taylor, Walton and Young in *The New Criminology*:

> The first attempts to tackle the problem of crime scientifically were social rather than biological. The transition between classicism and positivism was largely effected by the 'moral statisticians'. (Taylor *et al* 1973: 37)

Instead, in Beirne's alternative version, what is of crucial significance is that Guerry and Quételet were *positivists*. However, it is vital to avoid the naive yet widespread conflation of positivism and biologism. On the contrary, as Beirne emphasises, their importance lies not as valiant precursors of the fight against a yet to be invented biological positivism (a complete red herring), but in their role as statisticians – and far from amateur or dilettante. It is this *mathematisation of crime* that is key to understanding positivism; Guerry and Quételet figure as progenitors of criminology's enduring dependence on (and fascination with) the statistical prediction and production of facts and correspondences through which criminality is yielded up.

This in turn allows one to appreciate what might otherwise seem the rather quirky insistence on Quételet's part that his new analysis was deeply and significantly 'social' and, moreover, that, for the first time, human conduct could be appreciated as a truly social phenomenon. Yet, interestingly, this claim was not at all based on the presence of 'environmental' factors in the analysis. Rather, *it was because of the use of statistics*. The very fact that human conduct 'revealed itself' as patterned was what freed it up to study and understanding as social behaviour, more than a matter of mere chance and coincidence, of the play of human passions and emotions, or the individuality of decision making. How extraordinary to discover that I and 50,000 other Frenchman all went to buy the same shirt in a particular month (remember, this is also the era of the emergence of the concept of 'the market' in its economics sense rather than its local-market sense). Or, sticking to Quételet's own examples, one can almost imagine his wonder as he discusses how such a volatile and seemingly personal and individual event as murder could actually turn out to have standard rates of frequency, to vary relatively little from year to year. In other words, for these early positivists – although this goes quite counter to our early 21st century sensibility – it is precisely what makes human behaviour comparable to the physical world (or, to be more precise, to be amenable to the same sorts of calculations as the planets when used as navigational aids to shipping) that makes us recognisable as *social* beings.

It also accords with a sense that the terms 'environmental' and 'ecological' somehow fall short of being truly 'social', as signifying merely the charting of behaviour in a particular locale, as presenting 'surface' patterns and predictability rather than underlying depth and explanation. To this extent, Quételet and Guerry do indeed capture the key elements of positivism as 'a superficial science', to use David Matza's term (1964: 5), as the science of a Hume or a logical positivist, eschewing deep metaphysics in favour of 'facts' and 'observables' (even if such 'observation' is created by its very techniques, through which the patterns 'emerge into visibility').

However, it is not inappropriate that it was through this technology of practical application – the mathematics of organising everyday life – that Quételet made the extraordinary statistical transfer of application for which he is famous (along with his other well-known statistical device 'the Quételet index', or body mass index (BMI), a statistical tool used in the calculation of obesity). The general problem of navigation tables that had been preoccupying mathematicians throughout the 17th and 18th centuries was how to reconcile all the various observations of the same object, eg, the North Star, taken from different positions. Evidently, maximising the number of locations and observations promoted accuracy, yet all observations were generically error-laden by human fallibility – weather conditions, deficiencies in observation instruments and so on. Using the normal distribution curve and its algebraic equivalents developed in the theory of probability in relation to throws of the dice, a series of innovations allowed the error to be calculable as normal pattern of distribution around a true value or arithmetically a mean. (This is an extremely simplified version!) Hence 'the bell curve became indelibly associated with errors'.[6] The middle part of the curve represents the true value and the edges deviation – or, more precisely, observational error – although in the case of celestial mechanics (and dice throwing), because of the nature of the objects, it was reasonable to take this as an approximation to empirical reality. Quételet's huge move was to show that the same 'error law' applied to the distribution of human characteristics, beginning modestly with physical characteristics such as strength. Because similar curves could be found, they were read in the same way: the mean was taken as closest to the true value, and the further the values deviated from the norm, the more they represented 'error', unwanted deviations, but in the process it became 'forgotten' that these were errors of (deviations in) *observation*. In the next step, the errors of the observer become the deviations of the observed; subjective becomes objective; error of observation becomes deviation in the social world; epistemology becomes ontology – the deviant lives! In drier terms, similarity of distribution was taken to mean that there was a true value among the variables and that this value was exemplified by the mean. Quételet speculated that there might exist ' "*un homme type*", a man who represents his people by height, and in relation to which all other men of the same nation must be considered as offering deviations' (quoted in Maltz 1994: 436). Thus was born the 'average man' or *l'homme moyen*. In one generation, a new course had been plotted: steering a path navigated by 'the starry heavens above' no longer signified the Kantian 'moral law within' but now the laws of statistics and the ideal of the mean average.

L'homme moyen is the heart of Quételet's entire system, the engine that powered the transformation of observations, 'mere' statistics, dead facts, into '*faits sociaux*' ('social facts', Quételet's term).[7] Merely collecting facts is to look backwards;

---

6   The technical arguments and their criminological implications (for Quételet and, even more so, for contemporary criminology) have been explored in the interesting article by Michael Maltz, 'Deviating from the mean: the declining significance of significance' (1994).

7   What untold debts sociology – Durkheim especially – must owe Quételet.

predicting looks forward. The means to calculate the 'true value' of every nation, and even the human race, is to be the new template for those projects of social reform that have so regularly accompanied criminology. 'If the average man were ascertained for one nation, he would represent the type of that nation. If he could be ascertained according to the mass of men, he would represent the type of the human species' (Quételet 1831, quoted in Beirne 1993: 77–78). Indeed, without *l'homme moyen* there could be no national budget of crime, for this is the means to extrapolate from the past to the future, to make crime rates predictable.

Some mutations were to occur to *l'homme moyen*. It was not long before this creature born of statistical techniques – the very 'personification' of statistics – became endowed with a *moral* persona, what Quételet called the 'moral character' of *l'homme moyen*. For did not Aristotle celebrate the ethics of the golden mean, the avoidance of extremes, the regulation of the passions and the possibility of practical reason governing decisions to act? And in the modern age – so much more predictable – so too the habits of foresight could be deemed a requisite of all responsible citizens. Thus, through a slippage around the word *moyen* (mean), *l'homme moyen* became (re)moralised and (re)rationalised:

> The virtues of the average man thus comprised 'rational and temperate habits, more regulated passions, [and] foresight, as manifested by investment in savings banks, assurance societies and the different institutions which encourage foresight'. (Quételet 1842: 78, cited in Beirne 1993: 89)

> With the non-criminality of the average man, Quételet frequently juxtaposed the criminality of vagabonds, vagrants, primitives, gypsies, the 'inferior classes', certain races, with 'inferior moral stock', and 'persons of low moral character'. With the virtues of the average man, he juxtaposed the vices of those deviants who engaged in crime. (Beirne 1987: 1159–60)

It is in the figure of *l'homme moyen*, both as the purely statistical 'reification of the mean' and as a remoralised/rationalised construct, that Quételet's enduring contribution to criminology is to be found. The contribution of positivism is thus not merely criminology's enduring intrication with criminal and other statistics but with the embodied technique that makes them perform and predict: in straightforward terms, the criminal actor itself.

To grasp this fully, it should be clarified that *l'homme moyen* figures twice over, and this constitutes a significant instability or tension in Quételet's work – as indeed in contemporary quantitative criminology more generally. The 'moralised' picture painted by Beirne deals only with the criminal or deviant as 'other', in effect, the object of popular or political discourse made no less concrete by the same annual budget of prison and its adjuncts. The deviant or criminal appears as someone who contradicts the behaviour of this proto-rational actor. Even as a pure 'concretisation of the mean' (to use Maltz's (1994) incisive term), *l'homme moyen* represents – literally by definition – the non-deviant, yet at another level – here crudely and contrary to statistical theory, predefining criminal activity as deviant – this same agent paradoxically appears as the primary object of study. Thus, Quételet also speaks of all 'men' having a certain appetite for crime, and so may seek to study the average of any population, including a law-breaking population – who, in turn, may become characterised as rational or even moral beings.

From practically its first appearance on the intellectual horizons of criminological discourse, the environment (and specifically the urban environment – for, lest we forget, this was the period when the modern metropolis first became synonymous with widespread civic and public concerns about crime and delinquency) was employed in a highly abstracted fashion – in this case as a tool for devising artificially constructed (fixed) interpretations of criminal behaviour.

Once upon a time in the Mid West: the Chicago School

Nowhere in the criminological enterprise is the link between the study of crime and the study of the city more evident than in the work of the Chicago School. Just as Engels and Mayhew sought to understand the 19th century city by entering into its darkest recesses (see Chapter 1), the Chicagoans attempted to unravel the complexities of early 20th century modernity by taking to the streets of their own heaving metropolis. For Robert Park, Ernest Burgess and the other key members of the School, the social effects of rapid industrialisation and population expansion were central to the way they set about theorising the link between crime and the 'environment'. Accordingly, their work encapsulated the dynamism and air of progress that was such a feature of Chicago's brief but frenetic history (see Mayer and Wade 1969).[8]

In 1810, Chicago was an insignificant frontier outpost distinguished only by the presence of a backwater military station, Fort Dearborn, which stood at the meeting point of Lake Michigan and a 'sluggish' and 'singularly unimpressive' river. However, Chicago's inauspicious beginnings belied its important geographical position. The crude settlement was situated in the middle of the great water-highways of the mid-continent and, consequently, Chicago played an important role in the opening up of the West. Its prime position as a prairie seaport and its proximity to major communication and transportation arteries resulted in a staggering gravitation of people, industry and business capital to the city after 1850. Outwardly at least, Chicago was a resounding success. People from all walks of life rushed to share in the city's prosperity. As a result, in just over a century Chicago was transformed from a trading post of some 300 people into one of the world's greatest cities, with a population exceeding 4 million. One of the striking features of this phenomenal expansion was that Chicago became home to a panoply of ethnic groups: not only was the city a point of gravitation for migrating African-Americans keen to escape the poverty and repression of the rural South, but it was also a destination point for large numbers of European immigrants. By 1900, Chicago was an amalgam of disparate social worlds and conflicting identities. In this and many other ways Chicago emerged as perhaps the quintessential metropolis – certainly, few cities were more radically transformed by the processes of 19th century modernisation.

---

8 There are many comprehensive and eloquent 'reviews' of the work of the Chicago School: see Faris (1967); Rucker (1969); Carey (1975); Diner (1980); Bulmer (1984); Pfohl (1985); Smith (1988); and, perhaps less eloquently by myself, Hayward (2001a). For an alternative and occasionally amusing insight into the lives and times of some of the main Chicago School figures, see the interesting article by Lindstrom and Hardert (1988), in which Kimball Young reminisces with great candour about his time at the University.

Most famously, thanks to the pioneering work of William le Baron Jenney and later Dankmar Adler and Louis Sullivan, Chicago was the birthplace of that most distinctive modern urban form, the skyscraper.[9] Space in the city centre was at a premium and therefore the only practical way for Chicago's architects to build was up – and this they did with a passion. Initially skyscrapers prospered because they provided a rational means of escape for business people and the well-to-do from the dirty, squalid world of street-level Chicago; from the teeming slums and streets running with raw sewage and waste from the meat-packing plants. However, for those excluded from these new edifices to industrial wealth and corporate profit, life continued as normal, with poverty and overcrowding remaining endemic amongst Chicago's industrial poor well into the 20th century. It was such diversity of environments that led the Chicagoans to seek connections between criminality and the urbane locale. In this sense they are famous for two ostensibly very contrasting innovations: the celebrated concentric circle map of the city, and the development of a more interactive, street-level approach to the problem of crime that sought to understand the deviant lifestyle from the 'inside'. Let us look briefly at each in turn.

A point of departure for much Chicago sociology was Burgess's (1925) famous five-ring map of the city. Essentially it represented a bold attempt to *plot diversity*. Burgess contended that Chicago had expanded radially outwards from its inner-city core in a series of concentric circles. He identified five main zones, each two miles wide. At the centre was the business district, an area of low population and high property values; this in turn was encircled by the 'zone in transition', a place typically characterised by run-down housing, high-speed immigration and emigration, and high rates of poverty and disease; surrounding that zone, in turn, were zones of working class and middle class housing; and ultimately the affluent suburbs. Of greatest importance to the Chicagoans was the 'zone in transition'. This was the oldest section of the city and was comprised primarily of dilapidated ghetto housing that was unlikely to be renovated because of its proximity to the busy commercial core. The affordability of accommodation in these neighbourhoods ensured that the zone served as a temporary home for thousands of immigrants too poor to afford lodgings elsewhere in Chicago. A pattern quickly emerged whereby immigrant families remained in the zone only for as long as it took them to become sufficiently economically established to move out and 'invade' an area further from the business district.[10] Consequently, this was an area of great flux and restlessness

---

9 It is interesting to reflect on the extent to which the visual and aesthetic impact of Chicago's dizzying towers of glass and steel impacted on Western artistic sensibilities during this period. For many, Chicago's architecture actually created the very lines and geometric splendour that were the primary elements of early artistic and intellectual modernism.

10 Park postulated that human communities were closely attuned to any natural environment in that their spatial organisation and expansion were not the product of chance, but instead were patterned and could be understood in terms analogous to the basic processes that occur within any biological organism. Thus, Park maintained that the city could be thought of as a super-organism (Park 1952: 118); an amalgamation of a series of sub-populations differentiated either by race, ethnicity, income group or spatial factors. Accordingly, each of these groups acted 'naturally' in that they were underpinned by a collective or organic unity. Furthermore, not only did each of these 'natural areas' have an integral role to play in the city as a whole, but each community or business area was interrelated in a series of 'symbiotic relationships'. Close observation of these relationships enabled Park to conclude that, just as is in any natural ecology, the sequence of 'invasion-dominance-succession' was also in operation within the modern city.

– a place where pre-existing communal ties and traditional shared folkways were undermined and impersonal relations prevailed. Such neighbourhoods were described as 'socially disorganised', and it was within these unintegrated urban spaces that the members of the Chicago School sought to unearth the substantive causes of crime and deviance. This celebrated five-zone concentric circle diagram stands as perhaps the ultimate paradigmatic expression of the city in modernity. Burgess's map spawned a fascination with ecological grids, areal models and other subsequent efforts to further establish causal links between the environment and social action. Most famously, the research undertaken by Clifford Shaw and Henry McKay (Shaw and McKay 1932, 1942; Shaw et al 1929) was largely the product of abstracted demographic analyses, the plotting of juvenile delinquency court statistics onto Burgess's concentric circle model.[11]

In sharp contrast to this type of ecological modelling, the Chicagoans also employed a more proactive, phenomenologically and culturally inspired approach to street life. Like the early American realist painters (see Chapter 1), Chicago School researchers focused not just on the novel, stimulating aspects of human urban existence, but also on the day-to-day practicalities – the mundane as well as the innovative social processes that constituted the urban way of life. In a bid to highlight what was behind the immediate façade of urban tumult, the Chicagoans delved ever deeper into 'the private world of the deviant', producing some stunning and timeless studies of previously hidden urban subcultures, from street gangs to taxi-dance hall girls (eg, Thrasher 1927; Zorbaugh 1929; Cressey 1932). Even arch modellers Shaw and McKay sought to augment their statistical research by focusing on the multi-layered cultural and social interactivity that takes place at street level.[12]

This sensitive approach to the study of urban life/delinquency ushered in a new era of social science research practice, systematising ethnographic methods such as participant observation, the first-hand interview and the individual case history. This approach to the study of crime – initially orientated to the city environment – later became known as the 'appreciative' tradition (see Matza 1969: 24–40, 70–73). Matza explains:

> The decision to appreciate is fateful ... It delivers the analyst into the arms of the subject who renders the phenomenon, and commits him [sic], though not without regrets or qualifications, to the subject's definition of the situation. This does not mean the analyst

---

11 Shaw and McKay's findings had immense implications for criminology. Simply stated, they found that delinquency rates were at their highest in run-down inner-city zones and progressively declined the further one moved out into the more prosperous suburbs. Of critical importance, they also identified that this spatial patterning of juvenile crime remained remarkably stable (often over very long periods of time) irrespective of the neighbourhood's racial or national demographic composition. These findings allowed Shaw and McKay to conclude that delinquency was a product of sociological/ecological factors within the zone of transition rather than individual pathology or any inherent ethnic characteristics. This was a momentous breakthrough that did much to dispel earlier criminological theories that had located the root cause of crime within the individual.

12 Shaw and McKay went on to claim that socially disorganised neighbourhoods perpetuated a situation in which delinquent behaviour patterns are 'culturally' transmitted. In other words, criminal conventions and delinquent traditions are 'transmitted down through successive generations of boys much the same way that language and other social forms are transmitted' (Shaw and McKay 1942: 174). This observation, along with Edwin Sutherland's (1942) related theory of differential association, was an important strand in subsequent criminological theories that attempted to account for crime by reference to deviant subcultures.

always concurs with the subject's definition of the situation; rather, that his aim is to comprehend and to illuminate the subject's view and to interpret the world *as it appears to him*. The view of the phenomena yielded by this perspective is *interior*, in contrast to the external view yielded by a more objective perspective. The deviant phenomenon is seen from the inside. (1969: 25)[13]

So, if the early work of the Chicago School placed such emphasis on seeking out an 'interior' view of a social or cultural phenomenon, why, given the School's undeniable influence on the subsequent development of the discipline (compare Turner 1988), was something akin to the category of urban experience never fully integrated into criminological praxis? How did this emphasis on appreciation as orientated to the urban environment become transformed into the rational abstractions and rigid multi-factorial analyses that characterise mainstream criminological investigations into urban crime today?

As mentioned earlier, perhaps the best way to answer such questions is by locating the School's work in the wider context of the city. In this sense, de Certeau's conception of the *dual* city is again useful. At the most immediate level, the (re)configuration of Chicago's built environment is the living embodiment of de Certeau's 'Concept-city' – the extravagant city planning initiatives and the skyscraper (in conjunction with the gridded street network) exemplifying the rationalised strategies and brute power employed by the powerful in an effort to divest the city of contingency and improvisation. However, equally, the story of Chicago is one of *street life*, the city's drive and dynamism a product of the moment-to-moment emotional experiences and human interactions that were such a feature of Chicago's chaotic and restless social worlds. While, initially, the work of the School reflected both these contrasting registers, in the final assessment it was the 'Concept-city' – as embodied in concentric circles and areal plans – that triumphed, ultimately driving out the inspired and culturally sensitive appreciative ideals and practices.

This particular interpretation of the changing preoccupations of the Chicago School is closely mirrored in David Matza's *Becoming Deviant*. In an important passage, Matza claims that, despite the emphasis placed by the School on subjectivity and 'tell it like it is' research practices, much of their work cannot be considered as 'wholly appreciative' (1969: 18).[14] Instead, it increasingly fell under

---

13 In this sense, one could draw some tentative theoretical parallels between this aspect of Chicago School research (ie, their attempt to look at urban life from both inside and outside) and Walter Benjamin's contemporaneous work on the increasing spatial ambiguity between private and public life/space within the modern capitalist city (see Chapter 1). That Benjamin had any direct influence on the Chicagoans, is, however, extremely unlikely.

14 In recent years, criticism of the Chicago School on methodological grounds has increased, particularly the degree to which interactionist observation was actually employed. Platt (1994: 61) has been especially scathing in her criticisms: 'A close reading of the classic monographs suggests that the extent to which they rely on first hand data collected by their authors has been exaggerated. [Concluding, at p 72] ... the work of the [Chicago School] sociologists would appear minor and dependent; carrying on established traditions of concern funded by external agencies with their own agenda, often ... carried out under the supervision of non-sociologists, drawing many of its data from what was already available.' Platt goes on to question the validity of much of the Chicago School's ethnographic research, claiming that many of the case histories in Thomas's *The Unadjusted Girl* (1923) were transcribed from newspaper articles, and that Zorbaugh's *The Gold Coast and The Slum* (1929) contained published reports made to sound like field-notes (see also Valier 2003).

the influence of policy-relevant social reform (often in the shape of city-funded community projects such as youth club provision), a process which in turn placed a strong emphasis on various forms of 'correctionalism' – hardly surprising, since much of its inspiration was drawn from the philanthropic reform tradition associated with the 19th century ethnographers (see Chapter 1). As Matza makes clear in his comments on Nels Anderson's seminal naturalist ('appreciative') study, *The Hobo*:

> [A]nderson's study, like most emanating from the Chicago school, was supported and partly financed by municipal agencies and commissions that were interested in ameliorating the grievous conditions associated with vice, alcohol, wandering, vagrancy and begging. Thus, the mixture of naturalist and correctional sentiments was institutionally based as well as existing as an intellectual tension in the work of the Chicago school. (Matza 1969: 26)

Thus the street is co-opted 'from above' – in the sense of city planners and government agencies. Such emphasis on policy-driven social research opened the door to de Certeau's 'Concept-city' ('mappable from above', positivist, quantitative), 'inviting in' the perspective of the rational policy-orientated ideal – a road that led ultimately to the creation of disciplinary variants such as environmental and administrative criminology (both of which employ policy-relevant statistical analysis as their handmaiden).

Still continuing to tell the tale *à la* de Certeau, but recognising a degree of subtlety, one notes that the process of abstraction also occurred in sociological as well as statistical ways. As Henry and Milovanovic (1996: 22) point out in their analysis of the Chicago School, as time passed, street life became conceptualised in ever more abstract environmental terms via such notions as the 'subculture' of the street gang, the 'identity' of the neighbourhood, the 'social norms' of prostitution, truancy or vagrancy, and the 'order' of structural class relations.[15]

What, then, is wrong with this de Certeau-inspired story? At one level it is true that this tendency to positivise/mathematise issues of environment, to prioritise space over and above phenomenological place and to abandon a (fully) appreciative cultural analysis has remained popular within criminological circles ever since. However, more fundamentally, what is needed now more than ever is to approach the city as an object, to develop again a theory that constitutes the city as a fully social and cultural entity, that seeks to grasp the way cities function as living, contingent and highly nuanced cultural entities – to transmute into a more contemporary form of discourse Park's original inspiration of the city as super-organism:

> The city may ... be regarded as a functional unit in which the relations among the individuals that compose it are determined, not merely by the city's physical structure, nor even by the formal regulations of a local government, but rather more by the direct and indirect interaction of the individuals upon one another. Considered from this point

---

15 This point is further illustrated when one considers Garland's (1988) excellent history of British criminology. In this reading of criminology's development, the urban setting – the predominate context for most of the above crimes – does not feature. Instead, as Garland illustrates, it is replaced by the discourse of the prison, the psychiatric hospital and other social institutions.

of view, the urban community turns out to be something more than mere congeries of peoples and institutions. On the contrary, its component elements, institutions, and persons are so intimately bound up that the whole tends to assume the character of an organism, or to use Herbert Spencer's term a super-organism. (Park 1952: 118)

Now ... contemporary moments in crime and space

So much for the past and criminology's historical treatment of the crime–city nexus; how is the urban environment approached and understood within criminology today? In the second half of this chapter, I will put forward the claim that, while urban crime/criminality continues to preoccupy mainstream criminology, generating many innovative theoretical and empirical studies, all too often the conceptualisation of city life and urban space that underpins these various accounts is a highly limited one. Most significantly, too much criminology presents us with a lopsided interpretation of the crime–city nexus that frequently distills human lived experience, social diversity and the inherently pluralistic fabric of city life, to leave only the discourse of demographics, statistics, environmental multi-factorialism and rationality.

The rediscovery of space in contemporary criminology – environmental and administrative criminology

Interest in the spatial patterning of crime was rekindled in the late 1970s and early 1980s by the so-called 'second wave' of ecological studies.[16] With this body of work, environmental criminology expanded to include not only the traditional focus (à la Shaw and McKay) on the spatial and residential location of *offenders*,[17] but also a sustained interest in the spatial distribution of *offences* – a move often referred to by environmental criminologists as 'the rediscovery of the offence'.[18] Consequently, since approximately 1980, the primary focus of attention for environmental criminology has been the plotting of 'marked geographical skews in the patterning of offence locations' and how 'these can vary significantly by type of offence' (Bottoms 1994: 602). Such research was in turn used to account for so-called 'crime hot spots' – readily identifiable crime clusterings, as shown on the map of any inner-city police station (most famously described by Sherman *et al* 1989; see also Pierce *et al* 1986).[19]

Environmental criminology with its penchant for 'crime mapping' was only the start. Once identified, 'crime hot spots' had to be tackled on the ground. This was

---

16 Eg, Davidson (1981); Herbert (1982); Evans and Herbert (1989).

17 See Baldwin and Bottoms (1976); Bottoms and Xanthos (1981); Bottoms and Wiles (1986); Bottoms *et al* (1992).

18 See Brantingham and Brantingham (1984); Rengert and Wasilchick (1985).

19 Often these explanations rely heavily on so-called 'opportunity' and 'routine activity' theories (see Cohen and Felson 1979). Studies by Brantingham and Brantingham (1991, 1993), Figlio *et al* (1986) and Rengert and Wasilchick (1985) have all substantiated the (stultifyingly obvious) fact that the urban criminal tends to operate (both opportunistically and spontaneously) in and around areas well known to them – or, to use the correct environmental semantics, the 'cognitively well known area'.

the focus of the 'new administrative criminology' undertaken by the British Home Office Research and Planning Unit on behalf of successive Conservative Governments during the 1980s and 1990s.[20] With its emphasis on short-term, micro-level crime prevention strategies rather than expensive macro-level, 'welfarist' socio-political intervention (along the lines associated with the Chicago School), the 'administrative approach' to the problem of crime sat well with the pervading political ethos of the period, and was thus quickly exported to the US and elsewhere as an immediate and comparatively inexpensive way of combating spiralling crime rates.

Together, these approaches became deployed through various strategies associated with what has since become known as 'situational crime prevention' (SCP: defined here as 'the use of measures directed at highly specific forms of crime which involve the management, design or manipulation of the immediate environment in which these crimes occur ... so as to reduce the opportunities for these crimes' (Hough *et al* 1980: 1); as commented on, for example, by Garland 1997).[21] Once a 'crime hot spot' (such as a run-down housing estate, an unsupervised car-park, a troublesome public house or take-away restaurant, bus stop, football stadium, train station, etc) is identified – typically via a combination of crime pattern analysis and local victim surveys – the goal of administrative criminology is to 'block opportunities' for crime so as to bring these 'criminogenic' pockets of urban space (or more evocatively 'wild zones') back in line with 'the objective processes of ordered territorialization' (Stanley 1990).

The prescription for these spaces is straightforward: local authorities, businesses and, indeed, the public at large are encouraged to employ practical deterrents to ensure that buildings, public spaces and, importantly, people do not provide 'soft targets' for the criminal. Great store is therefore placed on increased physical security and, very importantly, high-profile surveillance, both public and private. The preventative value of closed-circuit television (CCTV) in particular is seen as crucial in the 'fight against crime'. Similarly, pragmatic deterrents, such as secure perimeters, barred windows, vandal-proof public facilities, alarms and even better locks and bolts also feature prominently on the crime prevention agenda (see Clarke and Mayhew 1980).

The advantage of this approach, of course, is that it produces *readily quantifiable results*, typically in the form of local police statistics or victim-orientated

---

20 It is important to recognise that administrative criminology (eg, Clarke 1980; Clarke and Mayhew 1980; Clarke and Cornish 1983; Cornish and Clarke 1986a, 1986b; Clarke 1997) and environmental criminology are each distinct branches of criminology. That said, their convergence has often been remarked upon (as argued by Felson 1998: for a general summary of this point, see Young 1994: 91–97; Vold *et al* 2002: 196; Roshier 1989). Certainly they both rely heavily upon the 'accurate statistical analysis of crime'.

21 SCP also relies heavily on the concept of 'defensible space' (Jeffrey 1971; Newman 1972). Originally an architectural development, defensible space drew upon anthropological research concerning 'territorial' theories of human behaviour to suggest that it was possible for architects to design buildings and urban space that could actually prevent vandalism and robbery, and even assaults and rapes (see S Wilson 1980). Despite creating an initial stir on release, *Defensible Space* was not without criticism, most notably the scathing attack by Hillier (1973: see also the article by Britain's foremost environmental criminologist Sir Anthony Bottoms (1974) that cast doubt on the methodology employed by Newman in his research).

'community-based' surveys – interestingly, the type of survey advocated by left realists (see below).[22] These statistics in turn contribute to a wider framework of government networks based around an actuarial and calculative approach to the control and ('risk') management of social problems.[23] Governments increasingly rely upon 'action at a distance' in evaluating not just the efficacy of localised crime prevention/reduction initiatives (both public and private) but also various other aspects of the criminal justice system.[24] Under such a system, urban space – like the school, the courtroom, and the prison – becomes a focus solely of statistical analysis, at once a place of audit and a testing ground for new initiatives and policy implementation. In other words, so-called 'criminogenic space' simply:

> ... constitutes a new site of intervention for government practices, a new practicable object, quite distinct from the individual offenders and legal subjects that previously formed the targets for crime control. Moreover, the criminogenic situation is like 'the economy' or 'the population' in being a domain with its own internal dynamics and processes. (Garland 1997: 187; see also Garland 2001 more generally)

At first sight this reading of urban space appears to overlook the way 'crime hot spots' feature in popular and political discourse, where they are portrayed as local and highly concretised danger zones, reminiscent in a number of ways of Mayhew's 19th century London. However, if one pauses to consider some of the various illustrations that frequently accompany the SCP literature, one cannot help but notice that, in these stylised representations, 'criminogenic spaces' typically appear as strangely undangerous, sanitised, even clinical spaces (see Plate 12). These diagrammatic representations of 'semi-private through-routes', neighbourhood 'sight lines' or 'points of entrance and egress' are remarkable only in their blandness and homogeneity. To the extent that they are marked out, 'situational spaces' exist only as uncomplicated, unconnected, solipsistic islands in the sea of the city. Rarely understood as part of a wider social network, the buildings and streets in these diagrams are occupied only by individuals whose spatial and temporal trajectories are assumed and who have the characteristics of 'situational (wo)man' (both victim and offender) projected onto them. Indeed, confirming Garland's account of the way the new 'space-target' displaces 'the individual offenders and legal subjects that previously formed the targets for crime control', it is not uncommon for the human actor to be removed from the picture altogether, leaving an image of urban space eerily reminiscent of the opening scene of Robert Wise's film *The Andromeda Strain* (1970) or, more recently, Danny Boyle's *28 Days Later* (2002). In this sense,

---

22 Increasingly, when it comes to matters relating to urban space, there is compelling evidence to suggest that the left and right are converging, if not ideologically then at least in terms of 'policy matters'. Certainly, administrative criminology, like left realism, makes a great deal of the victim. Consider, eg, the way the victim is 'responsibilised' in Neighbourhood Watch schemes and other recent SCP-inspired initiatives such as University College London's Jill Dando Crime Foundation. Not only do these developments represent an attempt to increase accurate 'knowledge of crime' – a policy initially pioneered by left realists in an effort to reduce the overall fear of crime – but they also promote the 'good (responsible) citizen' theme, as commented on below by Alison Young (1996).

23 See Ewald 1991; Miller and Rose 1990; Castel 1991; Gordon 1991; Rose and Miller 1992.

24 This development should be seen alongside the ongoing move within criminal justice in the United States towards a 'systems management' approach to crime and sentencing (see Peters 1986; Heydebrand and Seron 1990; Feeley and Simon 1992, 1994).

these illustrations bear a striking resemblance to the architectural plans of the modernist city planners – the lived reality of urban space simply does not feature in the design remit.

Thus, ultimately, for all the initial differences between SCP thinking and environmental criminology with its emphasis on multi-factorialism, both ultimately translate so-called 'crime hot spots' into the same homogeneous modernist space with its very rigid formalised geography of crime (eg, Wikstrom 1991). Such an approach represents nothing less than the deformation of public space, the *hollowing out* of the urban environment. Complex urban social dynamics are not easily integrated into the type of managerialistic postcode-specific framework that underpins the new space of crime intervention/prevention and, as a result, the various micro processes and cultural specificities that manifest themselves at street level are stripped of their inherent diversity and serendipity.

The lost offender: rational choice theory and the criminology of 'normality'

Ever since criminology first discovered the environment, the more attention that is focused on space, the less attention is afforded to the offender. Sometimes this has been obscured because we have misperceived the history of the discipline – as when we mistakenly believe that environmentalism in Quételet and Guerry is about the offender's formative environment as opposed to the differential distribution of crime across space. Sometimes, as with the Chicago School, a fundamental interest in offenders' lives was covered over by the very reforming ethos that sought to help them. Then, moving further away from that welfarist era and 'theories of social deprivation ... towards explanations couched in terms of social control, and its deficits' (Garland 1999: 353), the so-called 'managerial turn' has apparently 'disappeared' the offender altogether. However, even this can be seen as the result of good intentions. When environmental and administrative criminology joined forces, this was partly a pragmatic response to radical criminology's highly vocal denunciation of the pathologising of the offender, along with the critique of correctionalism. (A favourite radical pastime was to deride the positivism that 'paradoxically' combined both – for how could one ever correct those beings inexorably driven to crime?) Seeking to side-step the issue of criminal motivation, administrative and environmental criminologists were thus free to concentrate solely on the circumstances or 'situations' in which crime occurs. Where the slogan 'change society not the individual' had come to seem idealistic, if not downright expensive, prevention still seemed more desirable (and cost-effective) than imprisonment. *The hollowed out urban space has subsequently resulted in the hollowing out of the offender.*

This is not to say that the criminal actor becomes a complete blank (non) entity, for the correlate of SCP and environmental criminology was the emergence in the mid-1980s of 'rational choice theory',[25] the de-pathologising of the criminal actor. Rational choice theory shares with classical social control theory the premise that 'we are all potential criminals' (ie, there is no special deviant/pathological

---

25 See Clarke and Cornish (1985); Cornish and Clarke (1986a, 1986b); Newman *et al* (1997).

criminality). Clarke and Cornish's rational choice mantra is 'never dismiss a criminal act as wanton or senseless or irrational, but rather to seek to understand the purposes of the offender' (adapted from Vold *et al* 2002: 204). However, unlike control theory, it is not the absence of constraints/control that is important, but rather the utilitarian calculation of pleasure and pain, now made interchangeable with the language of cost benefit analysis. The upshot is an eclectic amalgam that draws together the classical utilitarian ideas of both Beccaria and Bentham, more recent 'deterrence' theories (eg, Gibbs 1968; Zimring and Hawkins 1973) and (related) economic theories of crime (eg, Becker 1968; Hirschi 1969), whose *homo economicus* model maintains that individuals choose crime when they believe the benefits of breaking the law outweigh the perceived costs. Reaching its highest form in sophisticated algebraic expressions, rational choice theorists test the potential efficacy of crime prevention initiatives by reducing the mind of the potential offender ('all crime is a function of its perceived pains and pleasures') to the statistical formula:

$$Y_i = \alpha + \beta_1 (X_{Bi}) + \beta_2 (X_{Ci}) + \varepsilon_i,$$

Under the rubric of rational choice, the human purposes and existential meanings of crime are literally banned from the equation. Thus is the intractable question of criminality reduced to a two-inch formula – at least for the purposes of statistical policy analysis.

This characterisation of the offender has not gone unchallenged. Set against rational calculation is a growing number of crimes containing a high emotional or 'expressive' element (see Chapter 5) – what one might usefully describe here as the world of the 'irrational' actor. While useful as a means of reducing 'shallow end' property or acquisitive crime,[26] the situational/rational choice approach may offer little or no real protection against the violent or so-called 'expressive crimes' that cause most public distress and community disharmony (see Trasler 1986; Morrison 1995: Chapter 16; Presdee 2000; de Haan and Vos 2003).[27] Consider, for example, the inherent problems rational choice theorists might encounter when trying to devise initiatives to stem crimes such as drunken assault, gang-related crime, child molestation or rape (compare Bachman *et al* 1992).[28]

---

26 'Shallow end crime' is a term usually employed by criminological realists to refer to the more prosaic property and street crimes that blight the lives of the urbanite (ie, acquisitive property and car crime).

27 When it comes to crimes of a sexual nature, rational choice theory looks strained indeed. Consider, eg, the way that the leading proponent of the situational/rational choice theory, Marcus Felson, can discuss rape only in relation to population density (Felson 1998: 31) – hardly adequate given that, earlier in his influential text *Crime and Everyday Life*, he states that, according to national victim survey statistics, as many as 72% of rape cases go unreported in the US each year. Surely Felson's approach to such behaviour would benefit from a greater understanding of the primary emotive states, motivations and cognitions of the sex offender. For a critique of the philosophy of rational choice theories more generally, see Zey (1992); Zafirovski (1999).

28 In using rape as an example, I wish to acknowledge the feminist objection that rape is not simply a 'crime of passion' or an 'expressive crime', but that it can take many forms (see Naffine 1997).

Given the line of argument set out in subsequent chapters, I should take a moment here to briefly clarify what exactly one means by the term 'expressive crime', as for many it is something of a problematic phrase. The first thing to state is that, whilst expressive crimes are often very much about the suspension of reality and the creation of a 'limit experience on the metaphorical edge', it does not mean they are not rational in the sense of being 'goal orientated'. On the contrary, I agree with the likes of Marcus Felson (1998: 65) that all crimes are, to a certain extent, means/goal orientated. However, where I strongly disagree with Felson concerns the notion that criminal acts can easily be deconstructed and located within a series of bland (blind!) typologies.[29] Such a position ignores the complex dynamics and existential dilemmas that are at the root of all crimes, especially expressive violence and other forms of emotionally-based criminality. In contrast, I support Jack Katz's (1988) call for specificity, the need to focus on the unique subjective experiences and highly textured situations behind all crimes. For example, with regard to alcohol-related violence, the question criminologists should be seeking to answer is not 'How can we control alcohol-related crime by employing *inter alia* such measures as controlling "barhopping", lowering the prices of non-alcoholic drinks, and serving drinks in smaller glasses?' (all suggestions offered by Felson 1998: 171–76), but rather 'What has happened from a cultural perspective to create a situation where, in the UK, over 80% of the 880,000 violent assaults recorded in 1999 (up 30% on 1997) involved the use of alcohol in one form or another?'.[30]

Even from within the camp, cracks in the rational choice model are beginning to show. One recent test of the rational choice perspective by Lyn Exum (2002) is particularly illuminating. In an unusually interesting empirical study of the effects of alcohol and anger on violent decision making, she states that 'the [rational choice] perspective may not be the general explanation for crime it is proclaimed to be' (2002: 933), concluding later:

> [t]he current study suggests that emotional states such as anger may impact the perceived consequences of a violent, criminal act. Future researchers should therefore consider *expanding tests of the rational choice perspective to include the role of the emotions*, an area of study that has been commonly omitted from choice based theories of offending. At the same time ... rational choice should also recognize the potential impact psychopharmacological agents such as alcohol may play in the decision-making processes ... Finally, future research is necessary to examine the rational choice model's assumption of generality. *Perhaps the rational choice model does not explain violent behaviour equally well across different states of mind.* Instead ... perhaps the model may only explain 'cool-headed' behaviour but then *breaks down when individuals are in an emotionally charged state* ... (2002: 961, emphasis added)

However, as one door closes, another opens. The late modern offender has found a further characterisation in contemporary situational criminology. If rational choice theory seems strikingly reminiscent of Quételet's *l'homme moyen*, this figure in fact

---

29 See, eg, the limited, experiment-based psychological research of the likes of James Tedeschi and Richard Felson (1993, 1994); see also Felson, Ribner and Siegel (1984).

30 For a graphic illustration of the role of alcohol in violent crime within an urban context, see Hobbs *et al* (2000: 706–07).

finds its more exact (and de-moralised) expression in the recent criminology of Marcus Felson. In *Crime and Everyday Life* (1998), Felson de-pathologises the offender even further than administrative criminology, 'normalising' the criminogenic situation so that it becomes inextricable from the fabric of everyday life. Here, criminal opportunities arise out of the routines and transactions that characterise the everyday round within liberal democracies at the end of the 20th century. For David Garland (1999), Felson's reworking of SCP closely corresponds to the managerial turn in the 'war against crime', a strategy of crime control that shifts the focus of attention away from 'individuals to aggregates, from specific cases to population flows, and from individualized justice to the management of resources' (Garland 1997: 190). For rational choice theory, there will always be a small number of people willing to commit crime as long as sufficient opportunities exist. By contrast, for Felson, in society today 'we are all criminals'. Further, it is not just the offender who is de-pathologised, but crime itself. As Garland puts it (slightly fudging): 'In the recent past, crime was always a sign or a symptom, indicative of social dislocation or personal maladjustment. Now crime is what it is and nothing more. It is a reality. A normal social fact' (1999: 360). To put it more precisely, it is not simply the occurrence of crime that is a 'normal social fact' but – overturning this basic Durkheimian tenet – it is a high budget of crime (*high* rates of crime) that has today become the norm.

Thus, contemporary criminology finally pushes the offender to the very edges of the criminological viewfinder – abstracted, normalised, disappeared – marginalising aetiological debates still further within the discipline. Felson's emphasis on normalcy is, by definition, blind to the drive to transcend the mundane, the prosaic – the very routines whose ordinariness strangles everyday life. Similarly, we must set against the 'normalness' of crime argument our contemporary world of risks and extremes, of excess and insecurity. At least subjectively, how can the myriad crimes of the late modern 'subject adrift' ever be absorbed into normalcy?

These questions will be developed at length later in the book. For the moment, however, we trace the further disappearance of the offender, but this time at the hands of a politically and ideologically very different body of criminological research.

New left realism: the (urban) victim strikes back

> The victim assures us that there is an end to the loss of faith, that there is a point beyond which nihilism will not go. (A Young 1996: 51)

The emergence of so-called 'realist' criminology in the 1980s represents yet another twist along the environmental axis. While realism brought forth many new ways of approaching the problem of crime, it also heralded a fundamental change in the way many criminologists (re)conceptualised the notion of urban space. Specifically, the strong emphasis placed by realists on understanding crime from the perspective of the victim ensured that, throughout the 1990s, left realism developed a rather lopsided interpretation of the urban (criminogenic?) environment.

Emerging from the strong tradition of 1970s British radical criminology, left realism was an attempt by socialist criminologists to take a more pragmatic and reflexive look at crime.[31] Formulated largely at Middlesex University in the UK during the Labour Party's unelectable years, left realism was a direct response both to the rise of 'the New Right' and the significant political and cultural transformations that took place during the final two decades of the last century – not least the continued domination of capitalism and the subsequent fall of communist Eastern Europe. It would be too crude to say that left realism was simply an attempt to escape from its own past ideological and materialist moorings, but it is not unfair to suggest that it offers a more pragmatic, policy-orientated approach to the problem of crime than much previous radical criminology. Rather than the focus placed by Marxist criminologists – or left idealists, as realists now prefer to call them(selves) – on macro political theory, and in particular the crimes of the powerful, left realism views crime from both ends of the social structure.

When set out in such straightforward terms, left realism appears highly attractive. Certainly, viewing crime as an 'amalgam' of many 'interacting elements' (eg, the victim, the public, the police and other agencies of social control, the legal rules of criminal law, the criminal act, and the offender) enabled left-minded thinkers at last to consider such 'common sense' issues as causality, crime prevention and the public–police relationship; things that previously had been obfuscated within the critical tradition by the over-arching goal of radically transforming society along socialist lines. Furthermore, this more 'reflexive' stance had the added advantage of enabling the leading lights of left realism to distance themselves from the more contentious views held by a number of radical figures regarding such matters as the abolition of the prison system (see Christie 1981; Hulsman 1983) and the removal of restrictions on drug use. In turn, this freed up left realists to challenge the then popular perception that, by concentrating on the crimes of the powerful – intended to contrast, both in terms of harm and visibility to the authorities, with crimes of the powerless – the left had somehow 'failed to take crime seriously' and in doing so lost touch with the reality of so-called 'normal crimes'.[32]

Needless to say, these developments have been severely criticised by others from within the established radical and critical tradition, for whom the development of the realist approach has been a major ideological step backwards, little more than a retreat to traditional values and, worse still, traditionalism as defined by popular consensus and mainstream legal conceptions of crime and punishment. Hence Stan Cohen stated: 'By their overall commitment to "order through law" ... [left realists] have retreated far from the theoretical gains of twenty years ago. Their regression into the assumptions of the standard criminal law model of social control – criminalization and punishment – is premature' (1986: 131). Likewise, for Pat Carlen, this position is clearly going to be less capable of unravelling the ideological

---

31 See Lea and Young (1984); Kinsey *et al* (1986); Young (1989); Young and Matthews (1992).

32 In relation to crime causation, left realists define a 'normal crime' as a crime in which there is a *clearly identifiable victim*. Typically, this is someone from within the working classes, and thus they constitute the vast majority of incidents reported to the police (eg, the residents of estates plagued by burglars or drug-dealers; city-dwellers harassed by rowdy teenagers; women abused by their partners; the victims of child abuse or racially motivated offences: see Lea and Young 1984: 262).

underpinnings of consensualism or interpreting the frequent shifts within that popular consensus (Carlen 1992: 58). While respecting these honourable critiques, my interest is held more by the way that left realism proceeds with a very unbalanced interest in the victim and matters relating to victimisation.

One of the central planks of left realist criminology has been the so-called 'rediscovery of the victim'.[33] However, as Alison Young eloquently points out, training the spotlight of criminological inquiry so intently on the victim is not without its problems (Young and Rush 1994; Young 1996). For instance, within the realist programme there is a disproportionate interest in a particular sort of victim – typically the city-dweller whose quality of life, it is perceived, is detrimentally affected by the numerous incivilities that characterise contemporary urban society. According to Young, such a focus ensures that the victim becomes a 'filter' through which the criminal justice system is distilled, scrutinised and enforced. In other words, it is an idealised version of the victim that 'determines the value of the real' in realist criminology (Young 1996: 51):[34]

> For all its emphasis on the totality of the criminal process, the reader of Realist criminology is insistently reminded that to be true to the reality of crime, it is necessary to posit the experiences of victims as the a priori of the criminological enterprise, albeit an a priori which is recounted by victims and surveyed by criminologists. In short, a claustrophobic structuralism which posits the systematicity of the real criminal process has as its necessary supplement an unbounded subjectivism of the victim. *The victim is present to excess.* (Young and Rush 1994: 157, emphasis added)

Whilst it would doubtless prove instructive to explore the 'unbounded subjectivism of the victim' by unpicking the exact methodology employed in the various empirical victim surveys conducted under the rubric of left realism,[35] I have chosen instead to develop another aspect of Young's critique, specifically her characterisation of the way that, within the left realist framework, criminal

---

33 One of the main goals of left realist criminology has been to achieve a more accurate measurement of the 'hidden level' of crime, thus substantiating their claim that it is the poor and the working class who are the most victimised in society. For left realists, the official crime statistics collated by the Government are inaccurate indices that are not only highly subjective but also corrupted by political and state agency bias. Thus, they pioneered the use of empirical 'victim surveys' (see Sparks *et al* 1977; Hough and Mayhew 1983, 1985; Kinsey 1984; Painter *et al* 1989) and other types of localised crime surveys as a means of extracting more accurate data on both the incidence and the prevalence of victimisation in a given locality (Evans 1992).

34 Eg, Alison Young has been highly critical of the way that realist criminology has hijacked issues relating to female victims (especially victims of sexual offences) and attached them to a non-radical politics.

35 Given that one of the overarching themes of this work is the connection between consumer culture and crime, I should perhaps point out a separate connection between left realism's interest in the victim and consumer culture. I am referring here to the way in which certain techniques from consumer research were incorporated in the early victim surveys. Starting in the 1970s, techniques borrowed from political and consumer opinion polls began to be applied to individuals randomly selected from the electoral register in a bid to discover if they had been victims of crime, whether reported or not. Such victim surveys often involved postal surveys, backed up by face-to-face interviews, thereby offering the means to discover truer crime figures. As indicated by the sources of the research techniques, victims in these surveys are seen both as individual citizens (voters) to be wooed by politicians and as consumers with rights.

victimisation becomes closely bound up with *notions of citizenship* (A Young 1996: 55–57). Developing her insight, I shall argue that there are in fact two variants on this victim–citizen nexus – one expressive and one instrumental. It is my contention that both these forms ultimately affect the way (realist) criminology comes to view the relationship between urban crime and city space.

The first variant is the (allegedly 'democratic') *expressive dimension* of victimisation. This refers to the way in which victimisation is used within realist discourse to *empower* the individual citizen and express a sense of 'community belonging'.[36] Fairly obviously, this position draws on a long tradition within liberalism and social democracy that links civic and public space with notions of 'community'. What left realists add to the mix is the belief that the problem of crime should also be tackled at local or 'community' level, as opposed to regionally or nationally ('the organisation of communities in an attempt to pre-empt crime is of the utmost importance': Lea and Young 1984: 267).[37] Young argues that, in upholding this position, left realism proceeds from the rather dubious premise that crime somehow serves to 'galvanise' a community by engendering shared feelings of victimisation. In other words, in the realist account, the first step must be for individuals to identify with each other as victims (and hence fellow members of the local community); the next step is the transformation of the victim from *passive* victim to *impassive* agent; and thus, with the move from identification to action, the citizenship is completed:

> Passivity, for the victim, is initially unavoidable in that crime, like illness, happens to the individual, with all the force and randomness of circumstance. Agency can be regained, however, if the individual rejects such passivity and takes up a role in the prevention of crime. In this way, citizenship is acquired. As an active social agent, the citizen will fit locks and bolts to doors and windows, avoid dark streets and purchase alarm systems. If everyone is a victim, then everyone has a part to play in the struggle against crime. (Young 1996: 56)

One could describe this first, expressive form of citizenship as neo-Durkheimian in the sense that it recalls Durkheim's theme that crime is functional because social reaction against it unites communities and reinvigorates social solidarity,[38] joining the local space of community to the national space of citizenship.

---

36 One of the main aims of left realism has been to encourage forms of 'community mobilisation' that might ultimately lead to the creation of new types of social relationships and political organisations. Ian Taylor (1982), for instance, used the phrase 'transitional socialist criminology' to describe initiatives aimed at democratising policing procedures and other elements of the criminal justice system at the 'localised level' (see also Taylor 1993, 1997; Taylor *et al* 1996).

37 This, of course, presupposes the idea that the notion of 'community' is still viable, or indeed still wanted. For certain criminologists like Steve Hall, this is no longer a given in post-industrial society: 'The disturbing possibility is that the eternal hope of liberal democracy in fact rests upon an impoverished, one-dimensional conception of humanity; a conception that ignores the destructive side of the social dialectic, preferring instead to see pre-existent human beings charged with the ineradicable philanthropic potential for tolerant, altruistic and co-operative community; we could call this the myth of the *natural* citizen' (1997: 461–62).

38 For an interesting (re)interpretation of this perspective in contemporary fiction, see JG Ballard's novel, *Cocaine Nights* (1997).

The second form of linkage between criminal victimisation and citizenship operates at a more *instrumental level*, this time via a more acute engagement with the concept of *urban space*. This more tangible focus on space and place owes much to the general revival of interest within mainstream criminology in both the spatial patterning of crime and offender residences, and related research into the situational approach to crime prevention/reduction (see above). What left realism chooses to select from this repertoire is, I would assert, a vision of urban space as filtered through the eyes of the victim, in turn linked back to the romance of 'community'. This, I believe, is a point worth developing in some detail, not least because, as I will go on to argue, it contributes to the further marginalisation of the offender within contemporary criminology.

Let us start by reconsidering that familiar stalwart of left realism, the victim survey – a technique almost always employed in urban areas. In the following quote, again by Alison Young, we see how the victim survey has become increasingly influential in terms of dictating notions of space within left realism:

> [t]he crime survey comes into its own, addressed to the specific task of *capturing the disparate spaces of the city*. A survey is concerned with spatialization ... realism creates a *cartography of the modern subject*. The self-government prescribed for the subject-as-victim has a spatial quality, taking place at nodal points in the city: for example, the entrance door to one's house must be strengthened and the windows locked; the dark street must be avoided for the safety of the well-lit pavement; multi-storey car parks must be avoided after dark. Through self-surveillance and self-policing, the victim asserts himself as a citizen of the city. (1996: 58, emphasis added)

As the above quote makes clear, not only does this particular method of interpreting the spatial dimension of crime further contribute to the (aforementioned) transformation of the nature of agency from victim to *citizen*, it also exemplifies the way that urban space is reduced down simply to a projection of the *victim's space*. If the enduring image of the criminogenic environment within modernist criminology was Shaw and McKay's concentric circle map of the city of Chicago, with its painstakingly plotted grid of juvenile delinquency court statistics and offender residences, then it is the localised victim survey that best represents the way criminogenic space is perceived within much criminology today.

The localised crime/victim survey is not the only way in which left realists promote and prioritise the victim's account of urban space. More recently they have also set about empowering the victim by other means, most notably by further empathising with their plight through a more sensitive and focused reading of space and place.[39] This, of course, is a useful development in so far as it offers a more sympathetic and less homogenising reading of urban spatial dynamics than that presented in administrative criminology (see above). For example, in recent years a growing body of research has emerged that has attempted to prioritise the 'expressed feelings, aspirations and worries' of individuals living in high crime

---

39 Of course, all this revival of interest in the spatial dimension of crime also has the added bonus of enabling left realists to make good on their original promise of re-appropriating policies traditionally (and currently – Etzioni 1993, 1997) favoured by conservatives and right-minded administrators.

areas (Girling *et al* 1997: 2; see also Taylor *et al* 1996; Girling *et al* 1996; Girling *et al* 1998).[40] This engagement with a denser reality (through the eyes of the 'typical' urban victim) is not only refreshing but also points a way forward for a deeper understanding of how urban space functions and how it often contributes to the shape and dimension of the crime problem.

However, this prioritisation of the victim's account of space and place remains problematic because of the intense focus on what Girling *et al* describe as the 'ethnography of anxiety' (itself mediated through an engagement with the literature on risk and the fear of crime). For all its richness, the fact still remains that what is being offered here is a rather one-dimensional account interpreted almost exclusively from the victim's perspective ('every time realist criminology uses the word "crime", it is substituted by victimization': A Young 1996: 55). For example, a close analysis of Girling *et al*'s research into life on a troubled Macclesfield housing estate reveals the fact that, apart from an occasional mention in the transcribed 'crime talk' of the local residents, the criminal himself is virtually nowhere to be seen. Once again, in the realist account of crime, the criminal has 'become a shadowy figure, little more than a blurred reflection in the eyes of the victim' (A Young 1996: 56). Still, the 'shadowy figure' of the (urban) criminal is not quite totally erased from the picture – after all, without criminals there would be no crime, and no crime, no victims.

What, then, has been the fate of the offender within realist criminology? As with environmental and administrative criminology, interest in the offender within left realism has become abstracted. In environmental and administrative criminology, the offender interacts with urban space only in so far as his daily 'spatio-temporal round' is of interest to 'routine activity' theorists and 'crime mappers'. In realism, one could argue that the offender's relationship with space is even more tangential – certainly, the complex motivations, cognitions and emotions (whether city-specific or otherwise) that constitute the law-breaker's experience of crime are rarely discussed (compare Box 1987: 29).[41] Nor is any sustained emphasis placed on the pervasive cultural concerns that relate to the key issues of 'self actualisation' and 'identity creation' (see Chapter 5). Instead, left realists have consigned the offender to a ghostly afterlife in the universalising discourses associated with the realist

---

40 Consider, eg, Girling *et al*'s (1997) research into the effectiveness of CCTV cameras on the troubled Victoria Park flats in Macclesfield. Evident throughout this paper is an intrinsic concern with the localised perceptions of space and place, filtered, of course, through the eyes of the victim-citizen. The authors claim: 'The remit of our research ... has been to situate "crime" and its attendant sensibilities within "local structures of feeling" ...', adding later that 'such an "interpretative" evaluation should be an important task in criminology's engagement with a "topic" [CCTV evaluation] which by its very "technological" image "lures" researchers and its users into a discourse of "scientific evaluation"' (1997: 3). This is a positive step forward, for here we see a large-scale, government-funded programme attempting to temper the quantitative ethos that often underpins situational research with a more sensitive analysis that includes spatial and temporal dimensions grounded in local social relations. See also further discussion in Chapter 4.

41 Pat Carlen (despite being more supportive of the realist movement than Alison Young) is also concerned that, by taking the victim's experiences so seriously, realists have largely ignored 'people's experiences of crime as suspects, lawbreakers, defendants and prisoners' (1992: 57).

construct of 'relative deprivation'.[42] Victims, it would seem, have communities and public spaces, offenders only 'mappable environments' or a relative sense of class frustration.

Conclusion

What next, then, for criminology's relationship with the city? A cold reading of much contemporary policy-driven research reveals the latest twist along the environmental axis. Promoted as an introductory guide to the 'new and innovative' science of crime mapping and aimed largely at 'crime analysts and other practitioners interested in visualizing crime data through the medium of maps', the US National Institute of Justice publication *Mapping Crime: Principle and Practice* (Harries 1999) reveals the full extent of our discipline's current fascination with 'scientific' method. Perhaps the most explicit example to date of ecological and environmental abstraction, *Mapping Crime* offers us a somewhat disconcerting glimpse of the future: a world of 'global satellite orientation', 'scatter diagrams', 'crime moments', 'stick streets' and 'choropleth maps'. Undoubtedly Quételet and Guerry would have relished such technology – the global information satellite replacing 'the starry heavens above' as the latest (celestial!) calculative instrument for interpreting 'the deviations of the observed'.

Such abstraction is, of course, acknowledged. Indeed, Harries even poses the question: 'how much abstraction can we tolerate?' The flawed logic of his answer is enlightening. While initially he accepts that 'more abstraction equals less information', he neatly side-steps this problem by claiming later that one can view this trade-off another way:

> More abstraction equals greater simplicity and legibility (more effective visual communication). [While] Less abstraction equals greater complexity, less legibility (less effective visual communication). (1999: 10)

The unfortunate thing for Harries and his fellow 'crime analysts' is that crime, incivility and transgressive behaviour are very complex, multi-faceted, ever-changing socio-cultural phenomena. Consequently, while the techniques outlined in *Mapping Crime* might well prove useful in enhancing 'visual communication' (and

---

42 Following the welter of victim surveys undertaken in the second half of the 1980s, it became apparent that, although crime occurred across all strata of society, it was undeniably more prevalent in the poorer sections of society, especially those areas populated by the lower working classes and marginalised ethnic groups. These findings were remarkable only in their obviousness, but for left realists they still needed to be accounted for. Their recourse was to revisit Stouffer's (1949) original deprivation thesis. The importance of relative deprivation as a causal explanation of crime is twofold. First and foremost, it explains crime across all levels of the social structure: from street mugging to insider dealing (certainly feelings of relative deprivation can be experienced by anyone at any level of society: see Young 1994: 107). Secondly, it provides a way of accounting for the 'aetiological crisis' by suggesting that improvements in absolute deprivation will not necessarily bring about a reduction in crime – just as conditions of absolute deprivation will not always result in high levels of criminality. To put it in Mertonian terms, crime becomes a way of dealing with feelings of inequality that are engendered by a social system that, on the one hand, constantly promotes the social value and expectation of material accoutrements but, on the other, fails to equably allocate the means and resources for obtaining them.

thus help with the effective development of certain crime prevention strategies), they will undoubtedly be of no use whatsoever in helping us to understand the complex and diverse social and cultural motivations and individual experiences behind a great many criminal offences.

In conclusion, this chapter should not be read as an attempt to divorce city life from essential spatio-environmental questions, or, for that matter, those of social structure; rather, its aim has been to highlight the need for criminology to develop certain theoretical links between individual experience and the key environmental, structural and (increasingly important) cultural determinants that shape our lives and determine both our place within and our relationship to society. Given the social context in which we now find ourselves – not least what was identified in the previous chapter as 'the dilemmas of transition' and the notion of the late modern 'subject adrift – this is a vitally important task. As I have tried to illustrate, since its inception criminology has fallen some way short of gaining a full and inclusive understanding of urban crime in modernity; the task it now faces is to try to devise new ways of looking at the problem under the even more inchoate conditions of late modernity. Not least, it must find answers to a whole new set of questions about the thematics of 'postmodern' space and their effects on the 'subject adrift'. In plain terms, we must reconsider the self and its contingent relationship with the increasingly turbulent and disorientating conditions associated with late modern (consumer) society. Only when this task has been completed can we then begin to understand the processes and motivations that contribute to much contemporary criminality.

To this end, the remaining two chapters of this work will follow through on this line of inquiry by attempting to establish some lasting theoretical linkages between what on the face of it appear to be two starkly different approaches to the problem of crime in contemporary society – one that greatly prioritises the city in its reading of late modernity (Mike Davis's work on the changing spatial and physical configuration of the city and how, in his opinion, these changes simply reflect wider structural concerns) and one that chooses largely to ignore it (Jack Katz's phenomenologically-inspired criminology with its emphasis on the role of emotions and experiences in criminal transgression). In both chapters, a cultural criminological approach will be employed in an effort to present a more fully rounded account of (urban) criminality in late modernity.

Chapter 4

Fear and Desire in Los Angeles

A perfectly plausible view is that, in contemporary conditions, consumerism acts in its own right as a significant means of maintaining social order, leaving older forms of surveillance and control to cope with the non-consuming residue. (Lyon 1994b: 61)

Introduction

As Western society embarks on a new millennium, the quasi-apocalyptic vision of late 20th century Los Angeles offered by Mike Davis in the compelling *City of Quartz* (1990), and developed in his more recent monograph *Ecology of Fear* (1998), has been read by many as prophetic of the future of industrialised cities. His central thesis concerns the privatisation of public space in Los Angeles and the use of architecture, urban planning and excessive police force to 'militarise' whole swathes of the city, alienating and criminalising large sections of the ethnic poor in the process. Davis's work is undeniably powerful and emotive, a high-octane account of metropolitan meltdown, self-interest and corporate greed in late modern urban society. For a whole host of sociologists, urban geographers and (to a lesser extent) criminologists,[1] the Davis 'model' points towards a dire urban future of increasing polarisation and social and economic exclusion in the segregated 'dual city', yet, in a countermove, more recently there has emerged a growing backlash against Davis's fast and loose sensationalism.

In working through these arguments, my aim here is to go beyond both Davis's shortcomings and the bitterness of this recent criticism. More specifically, I will put forward the case that, by stressing at least the rhetoric of traditional Marxist concerns over civic strife and class conspiracy in Los Angeles, Davis has missed out on the more mundane and prosaic outcomes. Exclusion is too crudely understood in his account (both in its mechanisms and its tone), while the issue of response is not even dealt with. Most notably, greater understanding is needed of the way privatised, decentralised forms of auto-surveillance and security are being drawn into the world of consumer culture, and how the exclusionary strategies that result from this situation are being interpreted and responded to at street level (something that one might usefully describe as the 'experience of exclusion'). By exploring these lines of inquiry I hope to offer a more developed theoretical snapshot of how changes at the level of the *physical environment* are affecting the contemporary urban experience – an experience, that, as I intend to make clear, is now increasingly constituted around the interaction, indeed conflation, of *fear* (in terms of issues relating to security) and *desire* (in the form of late modern consumer culture).

---

1 Eg, Smith (1992); Christopherson (1994); Morrison (1995: Chapter 11); Soja (1995); Blakely and Snyder (1997); Leo (1997); Graham and Clarke (2001: 171–86).

The dialectics of dystopia: *City of Quartz* and the death of public space

The point of departure for Mike Davis's grand tour of Los Angeles is the crumbling ruins of what he sees as the city's quixotic 'alternative future' at Llano del Rio – a failed 'ragtime' socialist co-operative movement deep in the Mojave Desert. As a communal utopia, Llano del Rio was a short-lived project. Assailed from the outset by a right-wing media, wrangles over water rights and xenophobic neighbours, it withered and died in the searing Mojave heat. However, for Davis, the story of the demise of the 'Socialist City' in the desert is a powerful metaphor for what he believes transpired in Los Angeles more generally in the latter part of the 20th century: the surrender of social ideals, public space and liberal values to the powerful combination of the demands of corporate capitalism, real-estate developers and middle class self-interest. Davis holds up Los Angeles as the archetypal post-industrial capitalist city – a place characterised by social polarisation, out of control 'no go' inner-city enclaves, oppressive policing and bourgeois paranoia. Portrayed by Davis, Los Angeles is a city lost to unmediated capitalism, a place where civic concerns and public-spiritedness come a poor second to the interests of profit and consumption, and where movement-restricting architectural developments and the demise of public space can be seen as the latest reflection of a rampant capitalist political economy.[2]

Yet this does not explain the almost universal acclaim that greeted *City of Quartz: Excavating the Future in Los Angeles* on publication. Viewing the modern city as a product of capitalist class relations was nothing new in itself (see, eg, Harvey 1973, 1982; Castells 1977). Likewise, the argument that the police are simply an instrument of class control had been well made by thinkers on the Left for decades.[3] Rather, what made Davis's account of Los Angeles so remarkable was his apocalyptic reading of a city apparently teetering on the edge of urban class war. His was the 'dialectics of dystopia', and his streetwise postmodern parables about urban life in Southern California immediately resonated with what remained of the liberal audience in the post-Reagan era.[4] Davis's skillfully spun reportage embraced everything from architecture to Adorno, drive-bys to Disney. His style was unique: it bristled with provocative prose and was imbued with a sense of impending metropolitan meltdown. *City of Quartz* also took on a prophetic aura when, on 29 April 1992, Los Angeles erupted in sustained rioting that resulted in over 12,000 arrests, in excess of 4,000 buildings damaged by fire, rioting or looting, and 54 people killed. The riots, many assumed, went a long way towards confirming Davis's pessimistic predictions.

---

2   The demise of public space brings together Marxists and old-style liberal commentators (see, eg, Mumford 1961; or more recently Mazzoleni 1990 on the 'post metropolitan condition'). Particularly enlightening is Richard Sennett's (1971, 1991) work on the link between 'civil society' as a non-state sphere of social-political interaction and the public space(s) in which these activities are performed. See also Urban Geography (1996).

3   See Piliavin and Briar (1964); Bunyan (1976); Hall *et al* (1978); Reiner (1978); P Cohen (1979); Scraton (1985).

4   As geographer Ed Soja has commented: '*City of Quartz* fed into a kind of left-liberal guilt, because Mike was saying a lot of things that people felt but were afraid to say' (Soja, quoted in Schatz 1997; see Davis 1990: 290).

While *City of Quartz* is incredibly broad in scope, confronting topics as diverse as the Los Angeles Catholic Church and the decline of the California steel industry, it is Chapters 4 and 5 concerning the erosion of public space and the militarisation of the police that have stimulated most debate.

Simply stated, Chapter 4, 'Fortress LA', is a tale of embattled public space in a city riddled with a disproportionate 'fear of crime'. Core to this process has been the loss of public-spiritedness among middle class homeowners, NIMBY ('not in my backyard') activists and corporate organisations over the last two decades. This market-led 'destruction of public space' has seen a propertied elite demanding 'social and spatial insulation' from the rank and file, and an unruly and disenfranchised underclass left to fight it out in under-funded and socially excluded crime-ridden ghettoes. Los Angeles, Davis argues, is a city transformed by middle-class paranoia into something reminiscent of a medieval citadel complete with architectural ramparts.

Davis uses the redevelopment of Los Angeles's so-called 'postmodern' downtown area (see Jameson 1984, 1991; see also Chapter 2) as a central metaphor for his argument that fear and greed beget each other.[5] He starts by highlighting how heavily-subsidised city developers responded to the perceived threat of the 1965 Watts Riots and the continued growth of the downtown Black and Hispanic populations by constructing a new high-rise business district – described by Davis with typical acerbity as a 'demonically self-referential hyperstructure, a Miesian skyscape raised to dementia' (Davis 1990: 229) – in the appropriately named Bunker Hill area, demolishing most of the old financial core and decimating established businesses and communities in the process (1990: 228–32). As Davis explains (in a slightly later essay): 'Key to the success of the entire strategy (celebrated as Downtown LA's "renaissance") was the physical segregation of the new core and its land values behind a rampart of regraded palisades, concrete pillars and freeway walls' (Davis 1992a: 4). In Davis-speak, this was corporate Los Angeles manning the ramparts in a bid to protect its economic interests by excluding those individuals and groups no longer necessary for (or dangerous to) the perpetuation of profit in the city's new globalised economy.

Davis documents how the Downtown 'renaissance' entailed a raft of pernicious physical and architectural initiatives, installing segregation in micro ways. These included urban deterrents such as 'bum-proof' bus benches, overhead sprinkler systems, and 'bag-lady-proof' refuse cages; the replacement of pedestrian thoroughfares with elevated walk-ways leading to entrances raised high above street level; the installation of pedways, escalators, and entrances that could be shut down electronically to deny access to those without the requisite security clearance; the installation of an elaborate CCTV network used to screen out 'undesirables'; and the withdrawal of businesses and shops from the sidewalk to the sanctuary of homogenised enclosed shopping malls, each made safe by an army of hourly-paid rent-a-cops. He rages against the resulting 'sadistic street environments' and

---

5 At another level, Davis is also irked by Los Angeles's much-vaunted 'postmodern' architecture. Opprobrium pours from his pen as he mercilessly puts to the sword the 'stealth houses' and 'bourgeois decadent-minimalism' of ultra-chic (left wing!) urban architect Frank Gehry (Davis 1990: 239; see Chapter 2).

dismisses the whole exclusionary urban design ethos as 'the archisemiotics of class war' (a double functionality of design and message) (see Davis 1990: 232–36; and, relatedly, Ellin 1996: 145). For Davis, such measures add up to nothing less than a 'new class war at the level of the built environment' (1990: 228). Downtown Los Angeles has been transformed into a 'Forbidden City' composed of 'hermetically sealed fortresses' and gentrified retail spaces.

He goes on to explain how this concern with spatial separation has been extended to other parts of the city, with the homeless and transient population of 'Skid-Row' another obvious object of exclusion. He documents how City Hall and corporate Los Angeles used an iniquitous combination of architecture, heavy-handed policing and the closure of public utilities to relocate the urban poor away from the gleaming spires of the gentrified financial centre. Indeed, this use of architecture as a means of fortification and 'enclavization' has spread to dozens of ordinary residential neighbourhoods in and around Los Angeles (1990: 244–50). Alongside the apparently growing reluctance among middle class Californians to improve the lot of the socially disadvantaged through increased taxation and public spending, Davis outlines how there has also emerged a fast-growing tendency to physically exclude poorer Los Angelinos from the suburban landscape. He claims that it is now an increasingly familiar sight in the affluent suburbs of Los Angeles to see private roads, restricted entry-points, secure residential complexes and even privatised parks. For Davis, these so-called 'Gated Communities' stand out as the most blatant expression of the social polarisation underway in American society:

> ... new luxury developments outside the city limits have often become fortress cities, complete with encompassing walls, restricted entry points with guard posts, overlapping private and public police services, and even privatized roadways. It is impossible for ordinary citizens to invade the 'cities' of Hidden Hills, Bradbury, Rancho Mirage or Rolling Hills without an invitation from a resident. (1990: 244)

From behind the pastel stucco walls and manicured crab-grass lawns of middle class Los Angeles, fear of crime is causing so-called 'suburban separatists' to coalesce behind conservative Homeowner Associations and private security firms in a concerted effort to protect both their property (or, more accurately, their property values) and what Davis describes as their 'master-race lifestyles'.[6] If one believes Davis, it would appear that affluent middle-America is, as he puts it in a later essay (1992a: 4), 'padding the bunker' against the perceived threats of an ever-expanding criminal class and the sustained influx of immigrant labour.

Davis is also concerned that the continued growth of the private security industry is irrevocably altering the role of conventional urban policing, as the more mundane elements of police work – residential patrols, street surveillance and the guardianship of property – are undertaken by an unregulated army of poorly-paid private security foot soldiers. Public law enforcement, he claims, has 'retrenched behind the supervision of security macro-systems (maintenance of major crime

---

6   As Angus McLaren – the author of *Our Own Master Race: Eugenics in Canada 1885–1945* (1990) – makes clear, the notion of constructing a 'master race' on the West Coast of North America is not a new one. What is new, as Davis points out, is the shift in tactics from ideals about racial purity and immigration legislation to architecture and urban planning.

Plate 1
Claude Monet (1873–74)
Boulevard des Capucines
Oil on canvas, 80.3 x 60.3 cm
The Nelson-Atkins Museum of Art, Kansas City, Missouri (Purchase: acquired
through the Kenneth A and Helen F Spencer Foundation Acquisition Fund) F72-35
Photo credit: Robert Newcombe

Plate 2
George Bellows (1909)
The Lone Tenement
Oil on canvas, 918 x 1.223 cm
Chester Dale Collection, National Gallery of Art, Washington DC

Plate 3
Ludwig Meidner (1913)
I and the City
© Ludwig Meidner-Archiv, Jeudisches Museum der Stadt Frankfurt am Main

Plate 4
George Grosz (1917)
The Big City [Metropolis]
© Museo Thyssen-Bornemisza, Madrid

Plate 5
Edward Hopper (1943)
Hotel Lobby
Oil on canvas, 32¼ x 40¾ inches
Indianapolis Museum of Art, William Ray Adams Memorial Fund

Plate 6
Martin Creed (1999)
Work No 203: EVERYTHING IS GOING TO BE ALRIGHT by Martin Creed
© Martin Creed
Installation at The Portico (formerly the London Orphan Asylum),
Linscott Road, Clapton, London
White Neon; 13 x 0.5 m

Plate 7
Peter Davies (1998)
The Hip One Hundred
Acrylic on canvas, 100 x 240 in
The Saatchi Gallery, London
Photo credit: Richard Paul

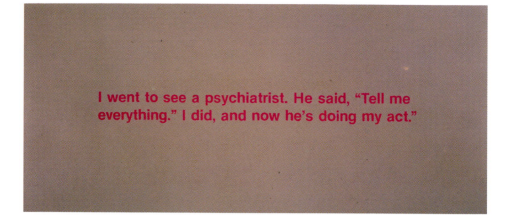

Plate 8
Richard Prince (1987)
Tell Me Everything
Silkscreen, Acrylic on canvas, 56 x 48 in
Courtesy, Barbara Gladstone

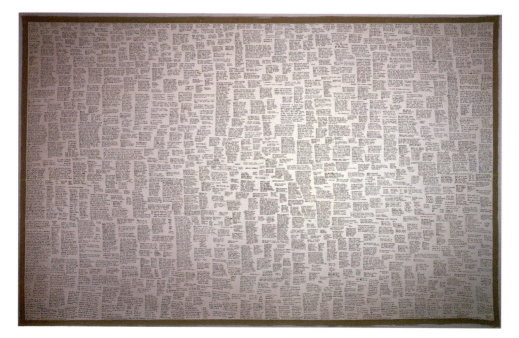

Plate 9
Sean Landers (1994)
Self-Something
Courtesy, Andrea Rosen Gallery,
525 West 24 St, New York, NY 10011

Plate 10
Tom Sachs (1997)
Prada Toilet
Courtesy, Tom Sachs Studio

Plate 11
New York in the Desert
New York, New York Casino, Las Vegas, Nevada
Photo by author (1998)
© Keith Hayward

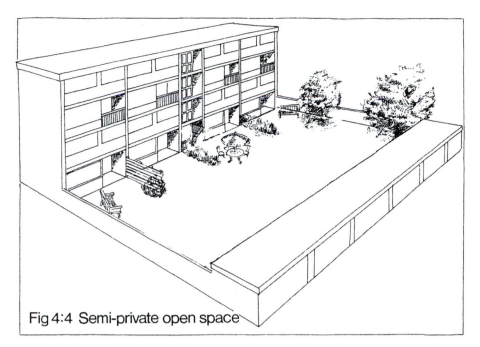

Fig 4:4 Semi-private open space

Fig 4:5 Semi-public open space

Plate 12
Figs 4.4 and 4.5, Sheena Wilson 'Vandalism and 'defensible space' on London housing estates' in *Designing Out Crime* (1980) edited by RVG Clarke and P Mayhew, Home Office Research Unit Publications
Courtesy, Home Office Stationery Office

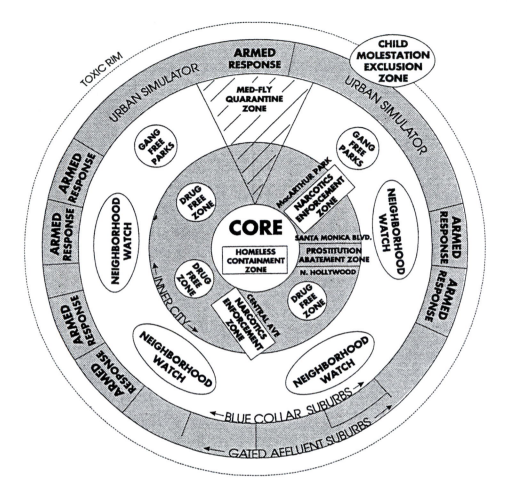

Plate 13
Mike Davis *Ecology of Fear*

Plate 14
Parafunctional Space 1
Photo by author (2004)
© Keith Hayward

Plate 15
Parafunctional Space 2
Photo by author (2004)
© Keith Hayward

we want to be free
to do what we want to do

Model - KDC 8021

KENWOOD

TRANSPORTED BY KENWOOD
call 01635 250 425 or visit www.kenwood-electronics.co.uk

Plate 16
Advertisement for Kenwood car stereos (2001)
Courtesy, Kenwood Electronics

Plate 17
Defaced billboard
Corner of Cambridge Heath Road and Whitechapel Road, East London
Photo by author (2002)
© Keith Hayward

databases, aerial surveillance, jail systems, paramilitary responses to terrorism and street insurgency, and so on)' (1990: 251). Extrapolating to the future, in a section of 'Fortress LA' entitled 'The LAPD as space police', Davis paints a disturbing picture in which increasing reliance upon high-tech, military-style hardware is used in tandem with electronic security tagging (of both people and property), all backed up by ever more sophisticated aerial surveillance and a security-hardened central intelligence database and communication network.[7]

Policing also provides the central thrust of Chapter 5, 'The hammer and the rock' (the 'hammer' referring to Operation HAMMER, the controversial LAPD Chief Daryl Gates's proactive attempt to 'take back the streets' of South Central Los Angeles from drug-dealers and gang members; 'the rock' referring to crack cocaine rocks). Crudely put, Operation HAMMER was zero-tolerance policing on steroids. Whole swathes of South Central were 'swept' by Gates's 'Blue Machine', with anyone remotely resembling a gang member either arrested or interrogated and indexed in an electronic gang roster for cross-referencing purposes at a future juncture. Davis describes the crackdowns as resembling 'Vietnam-era search-and-destroy missions'. Used alike by both senior police officers and city officials, the rhetoric of the Vietnam War was employed to mitigate the often flagrant suspensions of civil liberties in the policing operation, while at the same time currying political favour with paranoid middle class Angelinos.

Against the backdrop of Reagan's 'war on drugs' (see Currie 1993) with its overtly racist underpinnings, Davis paints a picture of draconian, Black- and Hispanic-orientated curfews, coercive drug deals manufactured by police officers in an attempt to entrap high-school students, and other practices that had the combined effect of stigmatising and creating a whole 'gang generation'. The situation for Los Angeles's ethnic youth was made even more oppressive, he argues, by a state criminal justice system that lost all sense of even-handedness in its efforts to curtail the gang problem. Davis highlights numerous cases of what he describes as 'Kafkaesque class justice' in which disproportionately high sentences were meted out to gang members, often for only minor offences. The demonisation of Black and Hispanic youth as a direct result of the 'war on drugs' is further evidenced by California's official prison statistics: 'Black males from Southcentral are now three times more likely to end up in prison than at the University of California' (Davis 1990: 307). The situation will irrevocably worsen as the already overstretched state prison system fills up with even more ethnic youths criminalised as a by-product of America's 'war on drugs' and 'gang-busting' initiatives (see also Davis 1995a).

But for Davis there were other factors at work. Writing at the height of the 'crack epidemic',[8] he makes much of the way the 'political economy of crack' emerged as a major feature of the depressed ghettos and barrios of South Central and East Los

---

7   In *Discipline and Punish*, Foucault (1977) famously argued that the modern criminal justice system of the late 18th and 19th centuries functioned essentially to throw up known, identifiable – and hence manageable – groups of criminals. At first sight it might seem that such high-tech developments represent little more than new spatialised forms of this practice.

8   The crack epidemic is usually acknowledged as taking place between 1985 and 1991 (Currie 1993). See, relatedly, Reinarman and Levine (1989).

Angeles during the 1980s. 'Through "crack" they [street gangs] have discovered a vocation for the ghetto in LA's new "world city" economy' (1990: 309). Urban street gangs and ghetto cliques, starved of traditional avenues for economic advancement, turned to drug sales (and, in a few isolated cases, trafficking, ie, crossing state boundaries) in a bid to achieve status and peer recognition. In a city built on capitalism and conspicuous consumption, the crack cocaine trade quickly emerged as an integral part of the city's economic 'food chain'. With few blue-collar – let alone white-collar – jobs available, and society polarised around wealth and status, 'cocaine capitalism', if one believes Davis, is likely to become an increasingly familiar facet of the urban landscape – an overt reflection of the inner logic of capitalist society.

Davis is in no doubt about how this situation came about, handing out the blame in a typically scathing denunciation:

> Without the mobilized counterweight of angry protest, Southcentral LA has been betrayed by virtually every level of government. In particular, the deafening public silence about youth unemployment and the juvenation of poverty has left many thousands of young street people with little alternative but to enlist in the crypto-Keynesian youth employment program operated by the cocaine cartels. Revisiting Watts nearly a generation after a famous pioneering study of its problems, UCLA industrial relations economist Paul Bullock discovered that the worsening conditions described by the [LA] *Times*'s 'Watts: 10 Years Later' team in 1975 had deteriorated still further, and that endemic unemployment was at the core of the community's despair. (1990: 309)

Often underplayed in reviews of *City of Quartz* is Davis's abiding concern with issues of political economy and, in particular, the way in which public funding and economic resources have been siphoned out of inner-city areas. This is regrettable, for it is on this subject that he is often at his strongest (and, in a different sense, his weakest in that it exposes the blind spots of his rigid Marxist analysis). In 'The hammer and the rock', he writes eloquently on the social problems that beset the poverty-stricken urban enclaves of Los Angeles as jobs and tax revenue 'relocated to white areas far out on the galactic spiral-arms of the LA megalopolis' (1990: 305). He argues that dramatic public spending cuts on basic social infrastructure such as education, recreational facilities and job and drug programmes have, in tandem with the erosion of legitimate employment opportunities, consigned areas like South Central to the economic and social margins (see also Reiff 1993; Bowen 1994).

Yet what does he mean, in the quote above, by 'Without the mobilized counterweight of angry protest'? In fact, Davis notoriously condemns local civil liberties groups and Black resident-activist associations for failing to offer up any real resistance to Operation HAMMER and similar 'crime-busting' initiatives (Davis 1990: 274–75). Romantically identifying gang members as true Black resistance, Davis is guilty of dramatically oversimplifying the complexities and vicissitudes of late modern race (and class) dynamics. The fact that certain sections of Los Angeles's Black community threw their weight behind the LAPD – even despite several unlawful police homicides and the debacle of Dalton Street[9] – illustrates the

---

9 The Dalton Street incident was an LAPD raid on an Exposition Park apartment complex in August 1988. During the raid, 88 officers from the controversial Southwest Division savagely beat 32 distressed residents. The resulting lawsuits yielded over $3 million in damages for the residents. Seemingly, residents preferred private litigation to more traditional public protest!

diffuse nature of coping/resistance strategies within contemporary urban space (for more on this last point, see below).

Ecology of Fear: a cautionary tale too many?

In the more recent monograph, *Ecology of Fear: Los Angeles and the Imagination of Disaster* (1998), Mike Davis seems keen to shift gears. No longer is his attention focused solely on the mean streets of urban Los Angeles. Instead he takes us far beyond the cityscapes and suburban tractlands of Los Angeles and into the desert plains and mountain ranges of Southern California in an attempt to present a history of disaster – both real and imaginary, natural and man-made – in a region that, as he puts it, is fast becoming a veritable 'Book of the Apocalypse theme park'. This is a tale inspired by the floods, fires, earthquakes and riots that beset Los Angeles in the 1990s and that, if you believe Davis's fatalistic rhetoric, made the city the disaster capital of the industrialised world.

In some circles, *Ecology of Fear* has been described – and at times dismissed – as little more than a 'green sequel' to *City of Quartz*, yet, while it is true that much of the book is given over to Davis's long-standing concern with the state of Los Angeles's fragile ecosystem,[10] he also takes time to revisit many of the themes covered so compellingly in *City of Quartz*, not least the civic injustices and vexed urban problems that remain such an enduring feature of post-industrial Los Angeles. After a typically eclectic narrative – *Ecology of Fear* covers everything from tornadoes and mountain lions to filmic and fictional representations of the destruction of Los Angeles – the final chapter, 'Beyond Bladerunner', takes us on yet another tour of the dystopian urban environment, only this time the paranoia is ratcheted up even higher.

In 'Beyond Bladerunner', Davis presents us with an 'explorative map of a future Los Angeles that is already half-born'(see Plate 13). Schematically, the map adopts that most familiar shape known to every urban sociologist and criminologist, the concentric circle model of urban development as postulated by Ernest Burgess, only this time the concentric circles are infused with the futurism of cyberpunk novelist William Gibson and the science fiction of Octavia Butler. 'My mapping,' he declares, 'takes Burgess back to the future. It preserves such "ecological" determinants as income, land values, class and race but adds a decisive new factor: fear' (1998: 363).

Thus, Davis still presents Los Angeles as a city wracked by concerns over personal safety and disproportionate fear of crime, with the affluent middle classes continuing to opt for private security initiatives rather than increase public spending to reduce crime. Now, however, his argument is tweaked to emphasise the rising demand among affluent Los Angelinos for sophisticated digital surveillance

---

10 One of Davis's major concerns is to expose the many erroneous perceptions about the recent spate of 'natural' disasters in Southern California. In Chapter 2 ('How Eden lost its garden'), for example, he documents the environmental damage visited upon Southern California's valleys, mountains and deserts by real estate speculation, the clamour for leisure facilities, and river and water redirection (see also Davis 1995b on the environmental problems facing Las Vegas).

and CCTV monitoring technology, which, he claims, will ultimately cover all well-to-do suburbs and business areas in a 'seamless scanscape': 'Inevitably, video monitoring will sooner or later be linked with home security systems in a seamless continuity of surveillance over daily routine. Indeed, up-market lifestyles may soon be defined by the ability to afford "electronic guardian angels" to watch over the owner and all significant others in her or his life' (1998: 367). We are similarly on the fringes of a world in which retinal scanners, pocket radars, face recognition monitoring software, voice keys and thermal facial imagers will become the norm. Perhaps Davis's most ominous prediction, however, concerns the fast-emerging possibilities of 'sentient buildings': intelligent, self-regulating structures reminiscent perhaps of the futuristic skyscraper 'Gridiron' in the Philip Kerr (1995) novel of the same name. Such structures have sensory systems capable of screening their inhabitants (via so-called 'active badges') and monitoring everything from smell to security.

Outside the 'scanscape', Davis turns attention to what he sees as an increasingly violent social world. Interpersonal violence is now the major currency in the schools, shops, parks and housing projects of Los Angeles's poorer neighbourhoods – areas that are now nothing less than 'free-fire zones' wherein excessive force is the norm and street gangs dictate the terms on which public space is used. Davis states that in modern-day equivalents of Burgess's 'zone of transition' – places such as MacArthur Park and the Mid-City area – the interests of the general public have been subjugated by mob rule. Whether it be the myriad of street cliques trying to establish themselves in the crack market, the violent private 'security squads' that roam the run-down projects and tenement buildings meting out slumlord justice, or indeed the increasingly militarised LAPD, law-abiding citizens, he claims, are being forced to run for cover, as this not untypical piece of hyperbole suggests:

> As in a George Romero movie, working-class families now lock themselves in every night from the zombified city outside ... In a city with the nation's worse housing shortage, project tenants, fearful of eviction, are reluctant to claim any constitutional protection against any unlawful search or seizure. Like peasants in a rebel countryside, they are routinely stopped and searched without probable cause, while their homes are broken into without court warrants. (Davis 1998: 380–82)

Social polarisation is further exacerbated by the development of a new type of urban enclave that he entitles 'social control districts'. These troubled areas of the city are the product of a combination of regressive land use policies, oppressive criminal and civil sanctions and the increasingly 'militarised' landscape. Within these spaces Davis has identified the formation of what he calls 'juridical zones', such as 'abatement districts' (areas that employ local by-laws and police-zoning restrictions to curtail all forms of 'socially unacceptable' behaviour, including prostitution, graffiti and even the establishment of liquor stores) and 'containment areas' (designed to control unwanted groups like immigrants and the homeless in police-designated 'sleeping zones').[11] Invoking Foucault (see below), Davis suggests

---

11 Davis also documents the growing importance of Neighbourhood Watch schemes in Los Angeles, characterising these proactive 'community policing' initiatives as evidence of a rise in urban vigilantism within the region (1998: 387–92).

that these 'social control districts' are simply a 'higher stage in the evolution of the "disciplinary order" of the modern city'. In other words, there have been no qualitative changes; rather, it's all a question of degree. In Davis's cityscape, things are just getting worse.

Meanwhile, in the suburbs, things have gone beyond simply 'padding the bunker' – crime, poverty and violence, he claims, are now at the doorstep. Residential and commuter suburbs have become sucked into a downward economic spiral caused by cuts in public spending and the erosion of traditional blue- and pink- (ie, female) collar employment: 'America seems to be unravelling in its traditional moral centre: the urban periphery. Indeed the 1990 census confirmed that 35% of suburban cities had experienced significant declines in median household income since 1980' (1998: 400). Davis portrays a disturbing picture of a suburban Los Angeles falling prey to the same kinds of problems – unemployment, 'white flight' and crime – that so ravaged inner-city areas in the 1980s. Likewise, racial segregation is now suburb-specific. Following the continued flight of affluent white suburbanites to mountain and beachside communities, many older suburbs like Pomona and La Puente are now almost exclusively occupied by Latino and Asian residents. Meanwhile 'edge cities' (Garreau 1991), located beyond the inner-city core, continue to prosper on the back of relocated jobs, strong tax revenues and outside investment, further exacerbating the polarity of wealth and poverty in Los Angeles.

Ecology of Fear presents a vision of the future that borders on an urban leviathan. For Davis, the Los Angeles of the not-too-distant future is likely not only to be a city characterised by suburban fortifications, sentient buildings, immense racial conflict and a network of overflowing prisons (see Plate 13), but also a place frequently ravaged by natural disasters as Southern California emerges from a period of benign seismic and climatic activity. Typically, Davis's urban reconnaissance offers little cause for optimism. Indeed, it is as if he has given up admonishing America's self-interested middle classes for their reluctance to intervene and reverse the ills of the inner-city, and has instead settled back almost in readiness to greet tomorrow's urban disasters.

Yet should we take his account as a blueprint for the future? Exactly 75 years ago Burgess's map of a continually expanding Chicago was perceived by his fellow members of the Chicago School as typifying modernising industrial cities everywhere. Only decades later, after much scholarly research by urban sociologists in both the US and Europe, was it seen for what it was – a very Chicago-specific model that had limited applicability for other cities elsewhere in the industrialised world.[12] In many ways Davis's writings on Los Angeles – especially *City of Quartz* – have had a similar impact on the social sciences, frequently held up by commentators from many diverse disciplines as the most likely scenario of the future of our cities.[13] Therefore, the question we must now ask is a rather

---

12 Eg, Abbott (1936); Alihan (1936); Robinson (1936); Morris (1958); Rex and Moore (1967).

13 See Smith (1992); Christopherson (1994); Morrison (1995: Chapter 11); Short (1996); Soja (1995); Blakely and Snyder (1997); Leo (1997); Graham and Clarke (2001: 171–86).

straightforward one: does Davis's dialectic of dystopia hold the key to our future understanding of the post-industrial city? Or will the concentric circles of his explorative map of Los Angeles – rather like its predecessor from the 1920s – again prove to be of only limited applicability?

'Davisteria': a review of recent criticisms

> The remarkable balance between grassroots reporting and prophetic tropes that Davis achieved in *City of Quartz* may be sliding, like some tectonic plate, in favour of the latter. (Schatz 1997)

> If this is hell, why is it so popular? (Bryce Nelson, quoted in Schatz 1997)

Davis's provocative interpretation of post-industrial Los Angeles as an unchecked capitalist city, in which the disparity between rich and poor has become increasingly overt, is without doubt extremely disquieting, but is it an altogether accurate representation? Is the vision of Los Angeles portrayed in *City of Quartz* a prototypical representation of the future of the ('postmodern') city? Will cities in the new millennium become spatially radically reconfigured along the lines set down in 'Beyond Bladerunner'? Or are Davis's dystopian urban predictions unlikely to unfold anywhere else but Los Angeles (if at all)? Indeed, is Davis overplaying the social problems and injustices that have always been a by-product of cities everywhere?

As Loretta Lees has commented, 'urban violence is real enough, but the rhetoric surrounding it is even more militant' (1998: 236). For some commentators, Davis's unceasing cynicism and apocalyptic semantics have proved too much. After an initial critical honeymoon period, more recently there has been a pronounced backlash against *Ecology of Fear* that has now expanded to include the Davis canon as a whole.[14] Many Los Angeles-based writers and reviewers believe that Davis's urban and ecological catastrophism is both disingenuous and inflammatory. They claim that he has dramatically overstated the social and ecological threats to the well-being of city life in Los Angeles. Certainly, there is plenty of drama in a chapter devoted exclusively to Southern California's 'killer-bees', 'plague-ridden squirrels' and marauding mountain lions, perhaps even some revelling in what Tariq Ali describes as 'millennial catastrophism' (Ali, quoted in Schatz 1997).

More relevant, the furore over *Ecology of Fear* in turn led many commentators to reappraise Davis's earlier works. The subsequent criticism has been harsh. In Los Angeles, columnist and Downtown 'booster' David Friedman (1998a) suggested that one of Davis's main themes – the fragmentation of society due to the increasing privatisation of public space in Los Angeles – had, since publication in 1990, proved 'overwhelmingly false'. Similarly, the uncompromising commentator/online media journalist Jill Stewart stated that Davis had 'falsely portrayed LA as mankind's foulest folly' and that, if one looks beyond the 'gushing reviews', one can see that

---

14 See Friedman (1998a, 1998b); Stewart (1998); Waldie (1998); de Turenne (1998); Westwater (1998); *The Economist* (1998). For objective commentary on these at times quite vitriolic reviews, see Critser (1998); Jones (1999); Ouroussoff (1999); Rohrlich (1999); Wiener (1999); Zamichow (1999).

many of the 'key anecdotes and major facts that Davis uses to build his case against Los Angeles as a mass urban disaster on the verge of collapse are fake, phony, made up, crackpot bullshit. Lies upon lies' (Stewart 1998).

Hyperbole aside, more worrying for Davis and his proponents is the factual deconstruction of *Ecology of Fear* (and parts of *City of Quartz*) undertaken by Malibu realtor 'Brady Westwater'.[15] So incensed was Westwater at what he saw as Davis's assault on Los Angeles that he fastidiously set about checking the author's facts and footnotes, posting his findings on a 22-page website (for a synopsis of Westwater's 'fact-checking', see Westwater 1998; Rohrlich 1999).[16] Westwater's obsessive digging subsequently cast doubt on a number of the 831 footnotes in *Ecology of Fear*. Just to take one example, Davis, always keen to weave conspiracies around his pet subject – the (post-Watts) redevelopment of the Downtown Bunker Hill area[17] – added in *Ecology of Fear* that the redevelopment had been initiated by a 'secretive, emergency committee of Downtown's leading corporate landowners (the so-called Committee of 25)' in an attempt to exclude the ethnic poor from the business district. However, according to Westwater, this is erroneous. The 'Committee of 25' was actually formed in 1952 (well before the Watts disturbances), was in reality never secret, and comprised Los Angeles's biggest companies and not landowners (compare Jones 1999). Moreover, as Friedman (1998a) states, 'The city couldn't condemn the area in 1965 because it already owned it'. Nor, argued Friedman, was Los Angeles's Downtown redevelopment predicated on exclusion. Far from becoming increasingly isolated, access and egress from the Downtown area actually increased following the redevelopment: 'Every Bunker Hill access that existed prior to redevelopment is still in use, supplanted with a renovated Angels Flight [hillside trolley service] and efficient escalator/elevator complexes' (1998a: see below).

Many more factual errors have been unearthed. For instance, as evidence of Los Angeles's literally conflagrationary nature, Davis submits the fact that in 1993 the immigrant district of Westlake had the 'highest urban fire incidence in the nation' (Davis 1998: 96). However, research by Westwater refuted this and proved instead that, in reality, Westlake had the least fire damage of any district in the city during 1993. Similarly controversial was Davis's unsubstantiated claim about MacArthur Park that 'in a single bad year, 30 or more corpses were found crumpled on the grass, stuffed in park trash cans, or half-buried in the muck at the bottom of the lake' (1998: 378). In fact, only five homicides took place in the park between 1990 and 1998 (Rohrlich 1999). Other notable errors (such as describing the largely white, Protestant neighbourhood of Hancock Park as a Jewish enclave) have cast some doubt on Davis's allegedly encyclopedic knowledge of the city, something not helped by an erroneous claim made on the book jacket that Davis 'was born in Los

---

15 According to various sources, Brady Westwater is a pseudonym for Ross Ernest Shockly (Jones 1999).

16 Davis is not the only high-profile social commentator to have had his work unpicked in this manner. Recently the award-winning writer/film-maker Michael Moore has also been subjected to so-called 'trial by website' (see http://moorelies.com, http://moorewatch.com and http://spinsanity.com).

17 See, more recently, Davis (2002: Chapter 8).

Angeles' (compare McAdams 1998). And so it goes on, as each 'questionable fact' is pored over in a succession of newspaper and magazine articles.

Prominent Californian academics have also entered the fray. In a monumental *volte face*, California's State Librarian, Kevin Starr, was recently quoted as saying that *Ecology of Fear* is 'a work of fantasy' and that the current criticism of Davis by Los Angeles's cognoscenti should serve as a 'wake-up call for him to smell the roses, to see LA as something other than a case study in apocalyptic meltdown' (quoted in Gumbel 1999). (Previously, Starr had been quoted on the book jacket of *Ecology of Fear*, stating: 'Mike Davis has produced another blockbuster. *Ecology of Fear* will change the way we think about Los Angeles – forever'.) Pepperdine University's Joel Kotkin similarly admonished Davis, calling him 'the poster boy for a New York left that hates Los Angeles' (see also Friedman 1998b) and suggesting that if Davis thinks things are bad in Los Angeles, he should 'go to Detroit, where he'd really have something to write about' (quoted in Schatz 1997). Ironically, Kotkin claims that much of Davis's success is due to the fact that his books play on the very middle class fears and anxieties that Davis himself claims are the root cause of Los Angeles's urban problems:[18]

> ... you have a tremendously spoiled and guilt-ridden layer of elites in Los Angeles who desperately want to believe they are up against tremendous forces in a romantic battle for survival in a desperate urban environment ... Of course the greatest worries of LA elites are really when to pick up the car from the dealer and how to get their kids into the best preschool. So Davis becomes their king of shared suffering, creator of their mass fantasy. This is how Davis can write an entire book that basically mugs Los Angeles without mentioning once that Los Angeles is booming and is enjoying its lowest crime rate since the 1960s. It's truly nauseating stuff. (Kotkin, quoted in Stewart 1998)

To what extent are such criticisms justified? In defence of Davis, Andre Gumbel (1999) suggests: 'Even where they appear to have substance – and often they do not – they hinge on a fallacious assumption that a handful of errors and questionable footnotes undermine the entire thrust of Davis's argument.'[19] This is clearly the point: surely Davis's ultimate argument is so important that the occasional exaggeration should be forgiven?

Undoubtedly, Davis is a man of rhetoric, not to mention hyperbole. Just to add two more inflammatory examples to the previous illustrations:

> In Los Angeles there are too many signs of approaching helter-skelter: everywhere in the inner-city, even in the forgotten poor-white boondocks with their zombie populations of speed freaks, gangs are multiplying at a terrific rate, cops are becoming more arrogant and trigger-happy, and a whole generation is being shunted toward some impossible Armageddon. (Davis 1990: 316)

> [A]s a result of the war on drugs every non-Anglo teenager in Southern California is now a prisoner of gang paranoia and associated demonology. (Davis 1990: 284)

---

18 One recent US survey claimed that 90% of Americans think that crime is getting worse, and 55% worry about being a victim of violent crime, despite recorded rates of violent crime dropping by on average 25% in a sample of major US cities (Hull, cited in Blakely and Snyder 1997: 100). For a more sophisticated interpretation of this point, see Furedi (1997); Glassner (2000).

19 See also Rohrlich (1999); Ouroussoff (1999); Jones (1999); Wiener (1999) for similarly sympathetic interventions.

Highly provocative – possibly even counter-productive? But one should not lose sight of the fact that Davis's main objective was clearly to try to jolt Middle America out of its apparent state of self-satisfied apathy. Indeed, *City of Quartz* was published at a time when the American liberal audience had been virtually brought to its knees by a decade of Reaganism.

That said, it is interesting to note that, in the eight years spanning publication of *City of Quartz* and *Ecology of Fear*, Davis continued to present an unswervingly negative picture of Los Angeles, consistently choosing to ignore anything positive or upbeat about the city. For example, non-Los Angelinos readers would never guess from reading *Ecology of Fear* that, during the second half of the 1990s, the city's fortunes – at least in economic terms – to some extent turned around. Since emerging from the damaging recession of 1992, the city enjoyed a fairly substantial rally in its economic position in the latter half of the decade. In 1997, for example, the area's job growth rate topped 2% (250,000 new jobs were created between 1996 and 1997), twice that of New York and a third greater than Chicago (*The Economist* 1997a). No doubt, Davis would argue that it was the affluent elite who benefited from this economic revival, thus further intensifying social polarisation.[20] The riposte, in turn, would be that such a position both ignores any trickledown effect and overlooks the fact that the majority of new jobs were created not in the high-tech industries or corporate sector, but in the blue-collar garment, toy, furniture and fabric industries (*The Economist* 1997b).

Likewise, *Ecology of Fear* has also been criticised for continuing to present a picture of rising crime in Los Angeles despite crime statistics showing dramatic falls. For instance, according to UCLA history professor and renowned expert on homicide trends Eric Monkkonen, the homicide rate in Los Angeles County declined year on year from 1992 to 1997, dropping to levels 'not seen since the mid 1970s' (Monkkonen 1997). Similar falls were also recorded in violent crime and, importantly, gang-related crime (in 1996 alone, recorded 'serious crime' in Los Angeles fell by 25% on the previous year: *The Economist* 1997c).[21] During the same period, gun sales in Los Angeles plummeted, and police clear-up rates soared (Lait 1998). None of this is acknowledged in *Ecology of Fear*, where too often hyper-violent imagery stands in for statistics.

Even so, these much stressed criticisms – especially by conservative Los Angeles 'boosters' like Kotkin and Friedman – would seem to leave *City of Quartz* unchallenged since it was written during the midst of California's worst recession for half a century. Moreover, since *Ecology of Fear* hit the bookstands in 1998, the

---

20 One could also point to the fact that, during the 1990s, Californian voters approved several taxation hikes on gasoline and (in Los Angeles County) a doubling of the local transit sales tax, moves that collectively raised massive revenues for public transport in the Los Angeles region. The result was that, by the middle of the 1990s, Los Angeles was 'pursuing the most vigorous transit capital investment program of any metropolitan area in the country, perhaps in the world' (Wachs 1996: 138). Add to this massive funding revenues raised for expenditure on the public school system, and it is clear that, despite its disparate civic structure (see below), Los Angeles at least tried to co-ordinate some sort of macro public investment.

21 Recently, however, after a nine-year decrease, homicide rates in Los Angeles have once again begun to rise, with 2000 seeing a 27.6% upturn in homicides (see Monkkonen 2000, 2002; Hale 2001).

economic fortunes of Los Angeles – and California more generally – have once again nose-dived,[22] the state's current $36 billion deficit recently putting paid to Gray Davis's tenure as Governor (on this latter subject, one can only imagine what literary brickbats Mike Davis has in store for Governor Schwarzenegger!).

What is important, of course, is not that the economic fortunes of cities rise and fall – this we all know – rather that, in both books, Davis presents Los Angeles as far more than a particular city in a particular context. His reading of Los Angeles is offered – or at least is uncritically adopted by many – as a paradigmatic expression of the future of 'postmodern' metropoles everywhere (remember that *City of Quartz* is subtitled *Excavating the Future in Los Angeles*). That's the trouble with futurology as social theory – things don't only go one way. As far as extrapolating elsewhere from the case of early 1990s Los Angeles, recently some have begun to cast doubt on the idea that Los Angeles is somehow symbolic of a 'new urban order'. For example, the urban geographer, Ed Soja – someone who rose to prominence by extolling Los Angeles's post-industrial geography as the very exemplar of postmodernity (1989) – has recently commented (in a jointly-authored article with fellow UCLA geographer, Allen Scott) that:

> It is still an open question ... whether to view Los Angeles as an exceptional case, a persistently peculiar and unreproducible type of city, or as an exemplary, if not paradigmatic, illustration of the essential and generalizable features of late-twentieth century urbanization. (Scott and Soja 1996: 1)

As Mike Featherstone has commented, surely the point is that, 'while Los Angeles may be the future of a certain type of global city, it is not relevant to think of it as the future of Amsterdam' (1998: 917).[23] To start with, in a number of ways, Los Angeles is an extremely atypical, indeed unique, metropolis. More than any other city in the world, Los Angeles is a 'freeway city'; the sprawling, decentralised nature of Los Angeles – the city extends approximately 60 miles outwards from its original settlement – being a direct consequence of a combination of affordable automotive transport and the development of the motorway (Wachs 1996). It is also unique in the extent to which it is dependent on this latticework of freeways to link together its far-flung communities. This reliance upon the freeway and the automobile has greatly contributed to Los Angeles's 'sense of placelessness' (1996: 106), engendering a feeling both of endless sprawl and of a place without a defined centre. As Dear has commented: 'The freeways ultimately created the signature landscape of modernist Los Angeles – a flat totalization, uniting a fragmented mosaic of polarized neighbourhoods segmented by race, ethnicity, gender and class' (1996: 97).

---

22 Most US economists agree that California's economy has been in recession since the second quarter of 2001.

23 Clearly European cities have not (yet?) been affected by fear of crime and social segregation to the same extent as their US equivalents (on this point, see also Taylor 1999: 111; Young 1999: 22–23; Wacquant 1996; Worpole and Greenhalgh 1996: 45). However, this is not to say that certain small 'pockets' of our towns and cities – often 'orbital' estates' found on the peripheries of cities, or in the corridors proximate to transport arteries and industrial and manufacturing sites – are not already extremely socially isolated (for more on the social dynamics at work in these areas, see Campbell 1993; Davies 1994; Hopkins 2000). Socially, historically and spatially redundant, not even the market, it seems, can reinvigorate these spaces.

Similarly, in terms of its political and municipal structure, Los Angeles is also a very atypical agglomeration, even by American standards, but especially when compared with European cities. The regional metropolis of Los Angeles encompasses over 160 separate municipalities in five counties, of which 88 are afforded city status resulting in 88 separate city halls and 88 separate police chiefs – hardly a template for citywide harmony and consistency. Indeed, the fragmented power structure that is a by-product of the disparate system of local government in Los Angeles also ensures that the city frequently experiences a broad cross-section of policing practices and vote-winning civic initiatives. Consequently, just because police powers have been extended in West Hollywood to enable the enforcement of so-called 'abatement districts' (see above), it does not follow that similar action will be taken in other separate and very differently governed and policed areas of Los Angeles. In sum, municipal fragmentation and political diffusion within Los Angeles ensure that the city can never be a unitary entity, and thus ultimately can never be completely controlled.

However, in counterpoint to these arguments, it is important to acknowledge that, as a paradigm of the postmodern city, Los Angeles in these debates is not so much an actual place but more an 'ideal type' (in the Weberian sense of the conjunction of all the elements of a paradigm). There is no place on earth exactly like Los Angeles, in just the same way that nowhere in the empirical world exactly resembled Weber's model of bureaucracy. But how is one to reconcile Los Angeles as the queen of the postmodern with Davis's brand of Marxism, which, it has to be said, is the crudest sort of Leninist conspiracy theory of class-based manipulation as practised by Los Angeles's 'invisible government' of developers and bankers (eg, Davis 1990: Chapter 2). For, as mentioned above, if the city is so fragmented, so dispersed and non-unitary, how could it ever possibly be manipulated? By the same token, Davis's version of Foucault in *Ecology of Fear* relies on just the sort of centralised, 'top-down' model of power that Foucault actually contrasts to discipline. As UCLA historian Eric Monkkonen told me: 'the plight of Los Angeles can no longer be attributed to some capitalist plot – because no one is really in charge!'[24]

Post Davis's urban reconnoitering, one thing that cannot be denied is that the urban landscape is irrevocably changing – but this process is a good deal more subtle than he portrays. Even in my own experience of Downtown Los Angeles (as a frequent visitor throughout the 1990s), the Davis image of a 'Fortress City' over-emphasises overt and physical segregation at the expense of more subtle forms of boundary. True, visitors will be struck by the desolate street life on the fringes of the business core in such places as Fifth Street's 'Skid Row' (an area described by Davis as 'the most dangerous ten square blocks in the world') or the cardboard communities east of Main Street, yet, far from being a literal fortress, Bunker Hill is in fact quite a porous space, separated neither by structural barriers or discernible signs of spatial division. Indeed, it is surprisingly easy in Downtown Los Angeles, just as it is in Baltimore, San Francisco or Chicago, to stray from the safety of the sanitised downtown area into altogether less salubrious neighbourhoods. The

---

24 Personal interview, 8 August 1998.

particular question of boundaries, exclusionary space and how to re-conceptualise them is one of the key concerns of the rest of this chapter. Then, moving even further down the route that Davis alludes to but does not develop, I shall bring into focus a more developed theoretical snapshot of the emotional and cultural aspects of the contemporary urban experience – an experience increasingly constituted around the interaction, indeed conflation, of *fear* and *desire*.

Boundaries by other means: consumer culture and the gates of self

From the moment you drive up to the gatehouse and are greeted by the friendly security guard, you sense it. The feeling that here all is safe, free from worry. (advertisement for gated community)

When you've shopped all day and it still wasn't long enough. (TV commercial for 'Next Directory' home shopping, 1998)

Los Angeles is, and to some extent always has been, a city based on conspicuous consumption, a place where the capitalist ethos prevails above all other and where urban space has traditionally been aggressively colonised by corporations and their marketing advisers and made to carry a message.[25] However, in recent years it has also come to lead the world in a new form of consumption based around the conflation of fear and desire. In an insightful passage of *City of Quartz*, Davis begins to make this important connection. Specifically, he identifies how, in affluent areas of Los Angeles, surveillance products and security initiatives are becoming increasingly commodified and commercialised:

'Security' becomes a *positional good* defined by income access to private 'protective services' and membership in some hardened residential enclave or restricted suburb. As a *prestige symbol* – and sometimes as the decisive borderline between the merely well-off and the 'truly rich' – 'security' has less to do with personal safety than with the degree of personal insulation, in residential, work, consumption and travel environments, from 'unsavory' groups and individuals, even crowds in general. (1990: 224, emphasis added)

Davis stops short of actually developing the link between consumer culture and issues of security, preferring instead to pursue William Whyte's point that 'fear proves itself' – the cyclical situation in which fear of crime leads to more security, and more security increases fear of crime. More importantly, *fear is now increasingly played on and utilised by the market*. In what follows, I intend to develop Davis's unfinished point and firmly establish the link between consumer culture and security. I will illustrate this in two ways. First, by drawing on the type of Marxist analysis of the private security industry that Davis himself might endorse but moving beyond a simplistic class-based analysis, I will highlight the way that security and surveillance services are being rendered by the market into material commodities. Secondly, I will focus on how security (in the form of the 'feel safe'

---

25 Some estimates suggest that only 4% of land is reserved for public space in Los Angeles. As Kevin Starr has pointed out, 'Everything is private in Los Angeles ... Sharing common space of any kind is not part of the Los Angeles experience' (Starr, quoted in Spiller 1993). For a more historical perspective, see Carey McWilliams' writings on Los Angeles; also Davis (1998: Chapter 2).

factor) is being used in Southern California's retail and housing sectors (and increasingly elsewhere) as a prominent marketing and advertising tool – a way of differentiating product and place in order to sell property. In this world, security and surveillance are now as desirable as floor space and acreage.

The commodification of security: 'deister strips', 'proofies' and 'bar code surveillance'

One of the very few writers to locate the material reality of selling security or surveillance at the forefront of analysis is the Canadian criminologist George S Rigakos (1999). While criminology has had much to say about the growth and intrusion of private security within society,[26] most neglect the fact that, as Rigakos says, 'private security is first and foremost a business' (1999: 1). Proceeding from a strong Marxist perspective, Rigakos suggests that 'any activity not directly producing a material commodity is a secondary, different and subsidiary activity of capitalism. It is not a productive activity' (1999: 3). Drawing on Mandel's (1975) augmentation of Marx, he outlines three logics of the service sector under conditions of 'late capitalism': first, idle capital must be converted into service capital in order to facilitate circulation; secondly, circulation itself is also largely unproductive service capital and must be transformed into productive commodities; and, thirdly, all services will invariably tend to be transformed into a material commodity. 'This process applies to all services such as the replacement of transport services with private cars, theatre film services with television sets, television programmes with videocassettes, live performances with VCRs, record players, audio cassettes and CDs' (Rigakos 1999: 5). Rigakos then marries this idea with Marx's views on commodity fetishism and Stephen Spitzer's essay on 'the fetishism of security': '[S]afety (like love, happiness, prosperity and fulfillment) is a social need that can be activated in a wide range of decisions to consume, virtually all commodities can be invested with the aura of security – that is, presented, promoted, and ultimately consumed because of their ostensible ability to free the consumer from worry, trouble, and harm' (Spitzer 1987, quoted in Rigakos 1999: 4).

Rigakos's qualitative analysis of private security firms in Toronto cleverly illustrates these commodification processes at work.[27] The Toronto private security firm the Law Enforcement Company operates a 'perpetual surveillance' system known as Intelligarde. It consists of electronic monitoring that 'wires the disordered spaces of Toronto's outsider populations, hooking these territories into the circuit of ordered and accountable society':

> Intelligarde performs this seemingly impossible task through a process of virtual mapping. The site is first visited by Intelligarde managers and an array of 'deister' strips are strategically fixed within and outside the property. The checkpoints are adhered to the inside of fire hose cabinets, door frames, roof access points, underground parking

---

26 See, eg, Johnston (1992); Corwin (1993); Platt (1995); Jones and Newburn (1996, 1998); Loader (1997).

27 Relatedly, see (Rook 1985) for a much earlier example of product differentiation in the private security industry. In a short but interesting article, Rook focuses on the design nuances of security company insignia and the display of security stickers and garden 'stake signs'.

supports, and any other spaces frequented by 'sleepers' and 'druggies' or posing any other possible risk ... Strips are even inconspicuously attached to the rear of public road signs and railings in large outdoor areas such as Toronto's harbourfront. These strips contain bar code information and numeric digits that are recorded and ascribed positional information within a 'deister' database. Each Intelligarde security officer carries a deister gun that is comparable to a Universal Price Code reader not unlike, but considerably smaller, than those found in supermarket check-out lines. As the security officer conducts patrols, he is to scan the deister strips and download this information into a computer upon returning to headquarters. Each Intelligarde mobile officer also carries a small portfolio of deister strips. These deister strips represent various happenings: from reporting on or off site to calling for PRO support (supervisor), investigating drug activity or solicitation, reporting defective lights, abandoned vehicles, and even effecting arrests ... Each incident matches a coded checkbox on Intelligarde's occurrence reports. Paperwork needs to be filed along with important electronically reported occurrences, collating the official digital incident. (1999: 6–7)

Retail techniques (ie, bar codes and the Universal Price Code reader) have woven commodity and security into everyday life:

Clients are routinely supplied deister strip read-outs along with their invoices. This billing practice is akin to providing the purchaser with an inventory of products being bought but actually represents the internal digital surveillance system of the company ... In this system surveillance is commodity ... Intelligarde helps to do two important things. First, it maintains the fetish of illusion, of safety and its aesthetic simulation as surveillance and second, it attempts to render security patrol into a material commodity. (1999: 8)

Such a system, as Rigakos suggests, could easily be offered to the public either as an adjunct to, or as a replacement for, conventional policing operations. We could soon be paying for security in a similar manner as we settle other domestic utilities like electricity, satellite TV or Internet access.

Similar tendencies are manifest in the ever-expanding slew of high-tech, often surprisingly low-price, security-related products appearing in the high street (Loader 1999: 374; Taylor 1999: 222): a list that includes mini CCTV surveillance systems (available in the UK from as little as £250); domestic drug-testing kits, or 'proofies' (£4.99 for three), used both for monitoring staff (or one's children!) and testing drinks for the presence of the 'date rape' drug Rohypnol; cut price lie-detectors (some available for as little as £50); satellite tracking devices; identity card entry mechanisms; laser security lighting; 'anti-bugging' equipment; police scanners; car immobilisers; phone-tapping (and counter phone-tapping) hardware; and Internet identity tracking software,[28] all of which are easily purchased either in specialist shops or on the Web.

The likelihood, of course, is that we have not yet scratched the surface of this burgeoning market. At the moment, security and surveillance products are still linked (albeit increasingly tangentially) to their use value, but what happens when they too become subject to the expert lifestyle marketing that currently surrounds the vast majority of high-tech or designer commodities (and security thus moves

28 For more on recent technological developments in security and surveillance, see the fascinating article 'Digital rule' by Richard Jones (2000).

from modern to postmodern)? Already there are signs that this process is well underway. As CCTV seeps into virtually every aspect of day-to-day life, a cultural transformation is taking place – surveillance has become not just acceptable or commonplace but cool, fashionable, possibly even aspirational. CCTV is now used by everyone, from artists (see, for example, the surveillance-inspired works of Julia Scher and Marko Peljhan) to advertisers (a recent strapline for a major jeans promotion read, 'You are on a video camera ten times a day. Are you dressed for it?'), restaurant and bar designers to prime-time TV shows like *Big Brother* or *Real World*. What this represents is nothing less than the dawning of a new relationship between society and surveillance, a relationship that goes far beyond the typical 'feel good' sensations (safety, comfort, reassurance) associated with established security products and consigns civil liberty anxieties to the obsolescent register of modernity. *Big Brother* is only ironic and *Real World* just unreal. This is a world where surveillance – the process of being constantly watched and scrutinised – is deemed fun, pleasurable and a potential source of entertainment and profit.

From security to segregation to 'distinction'

Los Angeles represents the apogee of the consumer age, the quintessential landscape of consumption (Baudrillard 1988; Soja 1995). In this environment, Davis, as we have seen, captures something important when he talks about security as a positional good and prestige symbol. Strange, then, that he stops short of any real engagement with *theories* of consumer culture. Obviously he is more at ease recounting tales of urban strife in crime-ridden ghettoes and spatially isolated barrios than analysing the lives of the pampered Los Angeles middle class, a group he so patently abhors. However, this does mean that his analysis of the post-industrial city (and of the urban experience therein) remains crucially incomplete. As Bauman (1987, 1991) comments, any truly inclusive representation of the 'postmodern world' must focus as much on the 'seduced' as it does on the 'repressed'. This section will therefore pick up the thread of Davis's account (and indeed the themes of the previous section) by focusing on the transformation of security into a marker of *prestige* – how the function (use) value of security is being displaced by new meanings of security bound up with status, position and identity expression.

For Lyon (following Baudrillard), because Los Angeles has no real 'origin' (or, in Ian Taylor's terms, no 'organic' base), consumption has come to serve as the primary 'reference point' for the city (Lyon 1994a: 54). Soja (1995) meanwhile believes that Los Angeles has been economically restructured in a way that exemplifies a shift (away from Fordist mass production/consumption techniques) towards more flexible systems of production associated with the pluralised, globalised consumer practices characteristic of 'post' modernity (see Chapter 2). Certainly Los Angeles bristles with the type of consumer-orientated spaces one typically associates with the processes of 21st century consumption. Indeed, if Los Angeles does provide us with a glimpse of the future of urban space, then it comes in the form of the consuming spaces of Santa Monica Boulevard. Consider, for example, the area around the 3000 block. Here one is struck immediately by the sprawl of service utilities that predominate in this area. This is a world of global products and niche service markets that provide individuals with the perfect opportunity for lifestyle creation and the construction of self. Walk around the shops and mini-plazas of this section of Santa Monica Boulevard and one sees not just one dance studio but many, each specialising in a particular style; not just one gymnasium or martial arts dojo but several – even some exclusively aimed at children; a plethora of nail, hair, make-up and stress-relief massage services, each differentiated by national style from Korean to Caribbean; and fast food emporia from virtually every corner of the globe. If there is to be such a thing as a 'postmodern' *flâneur*, then (s)he will be found in spaces like these, attempting to construct identity from the shop window of a pluralised consumer culture. But let us look beyond the literature that likens contemporary urban space to shopping malls,[29] theme parks[30] and other hyperreal landscapes of pleasure/leisure (Zukin 1991; Hannigan 1998). Instead, I now wish to focus on a less well-documented feature of consumer culture in Los Angeles.

Among affluent Los Angelinos, a reflexive concern with crime is now one of the dominant features of contemporary social life. It has created an urban landscape replete with perimeter fences, barred windows, padlocks, burglar alarms and cameras (both real and fake), as city-dwellers go to increasing lengths to fortify their homes and property against a presumed criminal 'other'. However, as James Q Wilson or George Kelling would doubtless argue, once a neighbourhood has 'tipped', there is little that can be done to stem the tide. Consequently, urban areas affected by high crime and social disorder tend next to experience a pronounced round of 'flight' to the urban fringe and semi-rural commuter zones beyond. In recent years, however, a new trend has gathered momentum. In the US and Canada it has become ever more popular for 'émigrés' from the inner city (and even, increasingly, the suburbs) to seek refuge behind the perimeter walls of so-called 'gated communities':

> Part of the explanation for the increase in gated communities is the logic of developers, for whom gated communities are a marketing device, another way to target specific submarkets ... With their often elaborate guardhouses and entrance architecture, gates also provide the crucial product differentiation – and clear identity – that is needed in crowded and competitive suburban new home markets. (Blakely and Snyder 1997: 15–16)

Emerging out of the retirement complexes and resort developments common in the Sunbelt states of Southeast and Southwest US during the 1960s and 1970s, gated communities grew in popularity during the 1980s and can now be found in metropolitan and suburban areas right across North America. A gated community is a private and secure estate, incorporating either a safeguarded perimeter or 24-hour private security (or very often both). Having recently undertaken extensive quantitative and qualitative research into this rising phenomenon, Blakely and Snyder calculate that there are now as many as 20,000 such communities in the US, with as many as 3 million units.[31] They cite one survey of home-shoppers in Southern California, which indicates that 54% of respondents currently either lived

---

29 Eg, Kowinski (1985); Shields (1989); Gardner and Sheppard (1989); Crawford (1992); Goss (1993).

30 See Sorkin (1992b); Fjellman (1992); Warren (1994, 1996).

31 Blakely and Snyder also state that the Community Associations Institute estimates that homeowner associations – described by some commentators as privatised residential governments (McKenzie 1994) – are growing at the rate of 10,000 per annum in the US.

in or wanted to move to a property within a gated or walled development – a question that 'had not even been asked a handful of years earlier' (1997: 7). Another estimate suggests that there are already as many as half a million Californians living in gated communities (Walker 1997). More worrying is Blakely and Snyder's estimation that eight out of every 10 new urban projects in the US are gated.

Although this tendency towards gated and subdivided accommodation is not as pronounced in the UK, it is clear that such developments are gaining popularity. In London, examples of secure residential complexes can be found in Docklands, Battersea, Highgate, Chelsea, Barnet and elsewhere, while a drive through the leafy suburbs of Esher and Claygate in Surrey reveals a startling number of gated residences and complexes (as a leading Surrey-based estate agent told me recently: 'In terms of professional couples with young families, security and in particular gated access, is the number one selling feature').[32] One recent investigation into the growth of gated communities in the UK put the number of such developments currently under construction in the Home Counties alone at upwards of 30 (Adams 2001). Another survey by the Royal Institute of Chartered Surveyors (2002) found that 65% of 18–24 year olds and 44% of over-65s questioned believed gated communities to be a positive social development, with RCIS Chief Executive, Lou Armstrong, ultimately warning, 'Here in the UK, we should be looking at the US scenario and asking ourselves if that is the way we want to go – because, for better or worse, that is the way we are heading' (Adams 2001). Clearly, this move towards secure residential accommodation has much to do with the ambient fear of crime that persists in urban areas. In fact, in Blakely and Snyder's survey, over 70% indicated that security was a very important issue in their decision to live within a gated community (1997: 126): 'The home is of central psychological value, and it represents most families' single largest investment, their most important source of financial security for the future. For the home to be safe, a lock on the door is not enough' (1997: 29–30).

However, precisely as a 'large investment', the family home is subject to manipulation and stylisation by the market as it strives to position gated communities and secure residential complexes as prestigious symbols of safety, status and success. For many affluent Americans, once the BMW or Mercedes-Benz has been purchased, the next status symbol on the road to perceived contentment (or what Campbell (1989: 213) would doubtless call the consumer's 'perfect image') is now very often a home within a designer gated complex, and the 'security' – or more accurately, *exclusivity* – that comes with it. Gated communities have come to symbolise a 'lifestyle choice', be it about leisure, separation or the fantasy of omnipotent security. All of this, of course, is textbook Pierre Bourdieu (1984, 1990), the French anthropologist who has written extensively on the various ways in which commodities operate as a means of expressing identity and distinguishing place and cultural 'rank' within the social hierarchy. Bourdieu's work is all about the use of consumption as a means of creating symbolic affinities with some class groupings and cultural 'distinctions' from others. On closer

---

32 Lest we forget, it was a gated community in Surrey – the Wentworth Estate in Guildford – that played host to Chilean dictator, General Pinochet, during his recent 'stay' in England.

inspection of recent developments in the design and marketing of gated communities, this is exactly what is happening here. It appears that a move is fast underway not just from security/insulation to segregation (as per Davis), but beyond to a world of 'distinction' and aesthetic elitism.[33]

While the advertisements for gated communities all tend to make the same grandiose claims (eg, 'X Gardens offers *a whole new way of life* in a new community beyond the city'), the underlying ethos is one of *product differentiation*, with each developer striving to situate the 'product' in a particular segment of the market. In their research, Blakely and Snyder, for instance, distinguish a threefold typology of gated communities. The first category, 'lifestyle' gated communities, caters for the 'New Leisure Class' and typically includes recreational and social amenities like golf courses or country clubs. Aimed squarely at the middle ground of the market, this type of secure development is designed to appeal primarily either to young retirees or second homebuyers, or to the sports- and leisure-minded white-collar middle classes. Gated communities of this ilk are homogeneous, exclusive and extremely class conscious. For example, at Leisure World in Silver Spring, Maryland, private security guards board the buses that serve the development in a bid to remove any 'undesirables', ie, non-residents (see also Davis 1990: 246). Even Girl Scouts are frequently refused entry and forced to sell their cookies from the other side of the fences. As one resident declared, the appeal '[g]oes back to when we were kids and all wanted to belong to a special club – a place where you can feel special and not everybody can come into' (Blakely and Snyder 1997: 57).

Generally speaking, the second type of gated community – the 'prestige' community – is basically a residential subdivision for the extremely affluent (over $400,000 income per household). These developments typically boast premium locations, manicured landscapes and ostentatious facades. ('In the prestige communities, image is of primary importance; their gates denote a barrier of status' (1997: 75)). They are populated by the top fifth (in terms of income) of Americans ('the ranks of a new separate – but never equal American elite') and designed around the dual concerns of exclusivity and status aspiration. Consider, for example, this quote from a resident in the moneyed Pacific Palisades area of Los Angeles: 'We knew that [the guardhouse] was going to be here, and it was a factor. It just made it that much more exciting – not only does it give you security but there's a certain amount of prestige that goes with it, too.' Similarly, a developer of custom secure complexes in St Petersburg, Florida, claimed that gated community

---

33 Such tendencies are not, of course, limited to gated communities. Increasingly, these new cultural groupings are contributing to the reorganisation of certain sections of the inner city. Take, eg, the revival in fortunes of formerly unfashionable areas such as Battersea, Clerkenwell and, more recently, Shoreditch and Borough in London; the Whiteladies Road area in Bristol; and Leith in Edinburgh. In the majority of cases the original inhabitants of these areas find it extremely difficult to continue to reside and trade in these chic new urban enclaves and are thus forced out to less glamorous areas by a combination of the destruction of affordable public or privately rented accommodation and spiralling property values. This type of urban redevelopment rarely has any substantial effect on education (gentrifiers typically send their children to private schools: Zukin 1998: 832), or on levels of long-term unemployment or homelessness (see Fainstein and Fainstein 1987; LeGates and Hartman 1986). Meanwhile local working class populations do nothing to denounce these property developments, but instead bemoan the fact that immigrant racial groups are 'stealing' their council housing.

homebuyers want property that 'makes a clear statement about themselves and their lifestyles' (1997: 82).

The third type, 'security zone' communities, have less to do with status and more to do with fundamental security and territoriality. 'Security zone' communities emerged after residents of neighbourhoods proximate to high-crime areas began to redefine local boundaries in an effort to protect their property. Typically, this process involves street barricades and rudimentary 'retrofitted' security measures in an attempt to create a buffer zone against outsiders. The resulting so-called city or suburb 'perches' are growing in popularity across the US (some states have even passed local by-laws actively encouraging the closure of streets and intersections in a bid to curb the spread of crime), as residents of all income levels endeavour to wrest back control of their neighbourhoods from the urban problems of drug dealing, gangs, traffic and poverty. Naturally, this last group, because of its emphasis on practical security initiatives, is perceived as somewhat lacking in prestige.

Intensifying this trend and taking it to a different scale is the rise of so-called 'secessionary cities'. These are more ambitious developments that attempt to offer a 'complete package'. Generally speaking, these larger-scale projects – often referred to (without irony) as 'master-planned developments' – offer prospective residents an idealised sense of 'community' within a secure (usually gated) quasi-city or themed small-town environment. Large real estate agents, like Newhall Land and Farming Company and the Irvine Company of Southern California, are already developing 'private cities', some as large as 40,000 residents, that include provision for schools, parks, refuse collection and other amenities:

> As the home has been commodified, so has the nature of community ... Green Valley, outside Las Vegas, Nevada, is a master-planned development that will have 60,000 residents by the year 2005. Walls are everywhere in Green Valley, with elaborate specifications in the master plan for their composition, height, and design. The CC&Rs [covenants, conditions and restrictions] prohibit homeowners from changing them in any way, including banning any openings in backyard walls. A marketing agent explains the appeal: 'It's safe here. And clean. The schools are good and the crime rate is low. It's what buyers are looking for'. (Blakely and Snyder 1997: 64)[34]

Extrapolating to the size of a theme park, the Disney Corporation has been quick to realise the dubious potential of these planned communities. Family ideals, traditional values, safety and hyperreal nostalgia are what Disney adds to the mix. On the outskirts of Orlando, Florida, at 'Celebration City' (a name that wonderfully exemplifies the self-aggrandisement synonymous with all things Disney), thousands of homeowners now live out the small-town American dream as imagined by Disney's architects and marketers (see Frantz 1999).

Given his concern about the demise of public space, such developments might well be the next target for a Davis broadside, but here he would need to go beyond

---

34 Despite the pervasive security, Green Valley has not been able to eradicate the problem of crime: 'In recent years the community has dealt with a serial rapist, robberies, domestic murder, drugs in schools, and a toxic cloud of chlorine gas released from a nearby chemical plant' (Blakely and Snyder 1997: 65).

the literature on urban space as a controlled environment, with its emphasis on the functionalist ordering of regulated space. (Hence, shopping malls and theme parks have always been highly controlled environments, carefully created with the dual intention of circulating customers from one purchase to another and excluding entry to those considered undesirable.) One thoughtful analysis already exists, the work of Paul Goldberger (1996) on what he calls 'urbanoid environments'. Goldberger claims that pseudo-urban spaces like CityWalk at Universal City, California, and South Street Seaport in New York are nothing less than sealed off 'private cities' masquerading as public places, a simulacrum of civic public space (see Chapter 2). In these spaces, the virtues of *civitas* and enlightenment, diversity and other notions that classically feed into the public realm have been corrupted by a kind of viral transmission of inauthenticity, a process that ultimately results in a sanitised privatised-public domain (pay on the door for a safe and fashionable public space experience; on this point see also Meštrović (1997) on the 'postemotional world' of mass simulation and 'rootless', fictitious experience).

Is this the urban future? Some trends at a seemingly more prosaic level indicate that it might be. Consider, for example, how in the UK during the 1990s many towns and cities adopted town centre management schemes. Worpole and Greenhalgh (1996: 37–38) explain:

> In 1991, there were eight town centre managers in Britain; in 1996 there are now 160. Town centre management has been one of the fastest growing partnership arrangements between local authorities and the private sector ... However, what began as an exploration of ways of facilitating use of town centres is today in danger of becoming a new orthodoxy, a formulaic approach largely overtaken by the ideology of customer care. In those town centre management schemes where the retail interest overwhelms all others, the town centre can become indistinguishable from the indoor shopping centre.[35]

In other words, it is not just that citizens as taxpayers are opting out of their civic responsibilities (in the US since the 1980s certain powerful private Homeowner Associations have attempted to create 'opt out' schemes concerning tax contributions, just as they seek to 'opt out' of urban blight).[36] Rather, it is that 'secessionary cities' also mean opting *in* to 'faux communities' – inorganic constructs that have occlusion and exclusivity at their core.[37] Whether it be in a gated city (or suburban) perch, a solipsistic mega mall in Los Angeles, or closer to home in exclusive developments like Wynard Woods in Sunderland (a gated community catering for the North East's mega-rich that boasts its own golf course, supermarket and pub)[38] or Ledborough Gate in Buckinghamshire (a private estate

---

35 Further evidence of this tendency can be seen in the way that local councils are inviting major retailers (such as Marks & Spencer) to contribute to the design and cost of town centre CCTV systems.

36 The 1990s saw a noticeable move towards so-called 'incorporated city contracts' and commercial improvement districts that enable property owners to tax themselves for certain public services (see Davis 1990: Chapter 3; McKenzie 1994; and, in relation to the UK, Minton 2002: 3).

37 See also Hughes (1996) for an interesting comparative commentary on Australian secessionary cities.

38 Minton (2002: 13) makes the point that, with a 'hairdresser and a nursery in the pipeline', Wynard Woods is now 'better supplied with facilities than many long-established rural villages'.

of 31 houses each worth in excess of £1 million currently under construction on a former school playing field in Beaconsfield),[39] living space will become increasingly artificial and any sense of community contrived (see also Smith 1987, 1996). The idea of the Bonaventure Hotel – 'a city within a city' – is now everywhere. However, while gates and cameras do add a level of satisfaction to the 'lifestyle' social environment, they alone cannot build strong, closely-knit communities or vibrant, pluralistic public spaces. The fact that CCTV cameras are often used as the first step to galvanise run-down communities shows precisely how regulation has been resituated as 'community', sanitised inclusion.[40] Unless the dual forces of private security and the market are unravelled, the result is likely to be the continued construction of 'private' or 'sequestered' city space organised along social lines corresponding to Bauman's categories of the 'seduced' and the 'repressed'.

Inside 'outsider spaces': modernist recuperation versus exclusionary separation

The term 'exclusion' is so ubiquitous that it seems self-explanatory. For Davis it is the death of public space in the dual city; in Jock's Young's *The Exclusive Society* it is social polarisation; and for Zygmunt Bauman it is as much about credit rating as spatial boundaries. This section seeks to stand back from the obviousness of exclusion in an attempt to explore some of its vagaries. In locating the multiple significances of exclusion, it will strive to introduce a little conceptual clarity, posing the simple question: what are we really talking about when we talk about exclusion?

My approach here is to begin by posing exclusion in terms of space, specifically the dramas of the unravelling or fragmentation of modernist space. Modernist space is identified with de Certeau's notion of the 'Concept-city', the planner's eye view, the rational modelling of the urban environment. It rests on a morphology of form and function ('form dictates function; function follows form'); a space that is continuous, gapless, utilitarian; a purposive and semiotically unambiguous grid that maps onto social and economic hierarchies. Nowhere is this better illustrated than in the discourse of crime prevention and administrative criminology, the smooth functionalist flows of modernist space captured in the archetypal crime prevention diagrams (see Chapter 3; and Plate 12). It is this ordered modernist space that is currently being destabilised by the shifting landscapes associated with post/late modernity. Here the picture is one of discontinuities, flows interrupted, islands and pockets of heterogeneity, spaces that are textured rather than contoured,

---

39 Ledborough Gate, as Adams (2001: 51) points out, represents the very essence of residential exclusivity and social insulation: 'As well as modem ports and comprehensive satellite communication functions these homes also come with a lifestyle package that includes valet staff for the ironing, washing and gardening, and an errand and shopping service to the West End. Unless they wish to, except for the arrival at the door of the company chauffeur, the residents of such developments need have no contact whatsoever with the world.'

40 There can be little doubt that urban space in the 21st century will continue to be watched over, monitored and policed by cameras, aerial surveillance and even satellites. *Greater surveillance, however, does not have to mean greater exclusion*. Indeed, as Jock Young suggests, it could mean quite the opposite (Young 1999: 192–93).

a realm of 'bricolage', liminality and the semiotics of ambiguity. Exclusion at this level means nothing more or less than this breakdown of modernist space – even, for some (Davis included), a return from Enlightenment ordering to mediaeval barbarism and disarray.

It will be argued here that the literature of exclusion has failed to recognise that there is more than one dynamic at play in this contemporary spatial transformation. On the one hand, there is the classical modernist attempt to recapture order, re-colonise, condition and discipline these emergent unruly zones – essentially to reintegrate the abandoned postindustrial spaces left in the wake of a superceded Fordism and repair the broken net of the modernist project. On the other hand, the literature points to the appearance of a new and distinctive mode of social control in which exclusion is precisely the crucial mechanism, *the 'solution' not the problem*. In this, the consumer society[41] – and this is crucial to both Davis and Bauman – 'social control' is no control except at the boundary. Here it is a matter of abandoned zones, guarded perimeters and secure cordons separating this world from the world of the gated community. Where the only modernist response is to de-exclude, to fill up empty spaces with the useful functional world of the productive citizen. In this new dynamic, wastelands are left to go to waste, excess to requirements. This contemporary strategy is a lockout not lock-in, a world that in some ways evokes John Carpenter's film *Escape from New York* (1981). These conceptual conflations will now be explored through two examples of contemporary social theory.

Discipline denied: Michel Foucault and modernist space

> If it is true that the grid of 'discipline' is everywhere becoming clearer and more extensive, it is all the more urgent to discover how an entire society resists being reduced to it, what popular procedures (also 'minuscule' and quotidian) manipulate the mechanisms of discipline and conform to them only in order to evade them. (de Certeau 1984: xiv)

Over the last two decades, many students of urban space have drawn attention to the way in which powerful structures of social control have been skillfully and often surreptitiously woven into the fabric of the city (eg, CCTV surveillance cameras and street lighting, face recognition software and Neighbourhood Watch schemes, etc).[42] Stressing the extent to which the 'fear factor' is now a major constitutive element of the contemporary metropolis, these practices are typically described as new and subtle strategies of disciplinary control and surveillance – which, in turn, are often glibly characterised as tools of exclusion and repression.

No doubt such practices are proliferating, but does it make sense to twin security with exclusion in this way? From the above discussion it should now be obvious that disciplinary surveillance is a classic example of the modernist attempt to recapture the dangerous spaces within our midst. The space of surveillance is

---

41 Or, in Bauman's terms, 'consumers' modernity' versus the older 'producers' modernity' (see Chapter 1).

42 Eg, S Cohen (1979); Shearing and Stenning (1981, 1983, 1985); Whyte (1988); Zukin (1991); Sorkin (1992a); Fyfe and Bannister (1996); Scheerer and Hess (1997).

precisely structured and seamless, the disciplinary grid the perfect match of form and function. In other words, in order for such controlled environments to operate, they must be spaces of *inclusion* not exclusion. For surveillance to manage its wayward subjects, to mould, shape and ultimately ensure conformity of conduct, those subjects must be *inside* the perimeter not *outside*. And, far from being covert, the entire effectiveness of surveillance rests upon its *overtness* (ie, on the subject's awareness of being (potentially) ever under scrutiny). Put bluntly, modern space is all about maximum visibility – Haussman's destruction of the old Paris, and the demolition of London's infamous rookeries provide two examples of the creation of the very conditions for disciplinary hygiene and civic surveillance. Indeed, and finally, 'disciplinary spaces' classically operate within a marked perimeter. Davis is thus quite correct to see Los Angeles's 'abatement districts' and 'containment zones' as disciplinary forms, but fails to recognise that this conflicts with his trope of exclusion. Surely the point is that *both* modernist recuperation *and* late/postmodern separation are occurring simultaneously in contemporary developments. This, however, is no excuse for conflating their fundamentally distinct dynamics.

This contrast is beautifully displayed in two treatments of what has been described as 'parafunctional' space. My starting point here is a collaborative essay by the sociologist Nikos Papastergiadis and the photographer Heather Rogers (Papastergiadis and Rogers 1996), commissioned to accompany a multi-disciplinary art exhibition on 'the paradox of the city'. Drawing on the work of de Certeau, Papastergiadis and Rogers deploy the term *parafunctional space* to refer to city spaces that appear to have 'given up' the struggle of shaping time and space, and where the discarded objects and refuse of an earlier mode of production accumulate (see Plates 14 and 15). Here even the most fundamental of modernist linkages is severed – the (functional) link between use and space as operationalised by names:

> It [parafunctional space] can be seen in all those corners which lurk at the edge of activity, or in the passages where activity occurs but the relationship between use and place remains unnamed. These are places in which names do not matter because the need for communication or the passage of time spent is already deemed to be insignificant, minimal, empty. These are places that have made no attempt to address themselves as 'a' space. (1996: 76)

Or, consider this alternative interpretation of parafunctional space, as glossed by the teaching team at The School of Architecture and Design, University of South Australia:

> Liminal spaces exist in-between – perhaps they've been abandoned or ruined, perhaps they are a set or constellation of surfaces, perhaps they are named 'waste', perhaps they are 'condemned'. These spaces do not 'function' as we might think 'function' functions – as meaning. These spaces do not do as they are told. (This is a sentence to imagine with: place an emphasis on 'do' and 'told', for example.) That is, they do not serve or operate 'the kind of action or activity proper' to their form, shape, (original) intention. While they function, the functional cannot have an exact relation to design as these spaces are marked by the yet-to-be ...[43]

---

43 http://ensemble.va.com.au/home/prjct_nts.html. I should point out that the School's particular interpretation of parafunctional space is based primarily on Papastergiadis's more recent article, 'Traces left in cities' (2002).

These functionless, evidently non-modernist, parafunctional spaces also represent the exact opposite of discipline. Not only do they lack any formal surveillance mechanisms, they are also typically devoid of any mechanical or human systematised watching. In short, parafunctional spaces represent the abandoned, anonymous and seemingly meaningless spaces within our midst – the places on the (metaphorical) edge of society.

Unsurprisingly, such paradigmatically criminogenic spaces – the run-down playground, the unsupervised car park, the troublesome block of flats, the abandoned lot or badly lit side street, etc – will be the subject of attention from within the administrative criminology discourse of situational crime prevention (SCP) (see Chapter 3). Indeed, in a statement that, in turn, is highly reminiscent of Davis's account of the micro-architecture of 'exclusion', Papastergiadis describes 'how state and council authorities try to keep specific spaces to their specificity: seating is changed in railway waiting rooms and on platforms to discourage sleeping by the homeless (UK, USA), just so they do not "sink" into a parafunctional state of ambiguity and contamination' (2002: 45). Yet, once again, the use of the term 'exclusion' is misleading, for administrative criminology/SCP essentially seeks to return space that has lost its function back *within* the ordered planner's fold of the modernist grid. To re-link 'space' and 'use' in one unequivocal functionality is thus a project of semiotic disambiguation – the attempt to close down an object/place's spatial reference so that it has only one unique meaning. Seats are *only* for sitting on, not for sleeping, skateboarding, partying or busking on. Under this rubric, controlling crime becomes as simple as mapping place, function and meaning, so that the rational utility-seeking subject no longer has to deal with any form of complexity whatsoever. However, as anyone who takes the time to walk or cycle through the city will surely tell you, city spaces are rarely, if ever, equivocal.

Equivocal non-functionalities: place, meaning, resistance

The built environment is seen as literally the terrain upon which ... cultural knowledge is created, transformed, challenged and represented. The landscape is not simply a collection of buildings, streets, parks, fire hydrants, billboards, and other elements, but also a social construction that reflects and refracts both everyday knowledge and macro structures; in other words, it is also a way of seeing ... Cultural activities form an integral component of the socially constructed landscape by acting as channels of discourse, sometimes symbolic and sometimes concrete, that mediate people's relationship with their surroundings and allow opportunities to consider, contest, and come to terms with economic, political and social aspects of place. (Warren 1996: 549)

Kids don't see the world the same way adults do. They see a beautiful marble ledge as being a great thing to jump off of! (Editor, *Transworld Skateboarding*, quoted in Ferrell 2001: 75)

Streets are always complex places, where meaning is contested and forms of cultural resistance occur (Ferrell 1997, 2001: Chapter 2; Creswell 1998; Lees 1998; Winchester and Costello 1995). This section will explore some of the ways in which street scenes challenge the assumed primacy of modernity and its adjuncts – criminology and the market among them. Recent developments in 'the new cultural geography',[44] urban sociology,[45] and certain branches of anthropology (for a criminology-specific example, see Parnell and Kane 2003) have all signposted the often hidden spatial practices and cultural differences that are such a vital component of the urban landscape. In this body of work, urban space is understood almost as if it were a living thing, a multi-layered congress of cultural, political and spatial dynamics.

Such approaches, in turn, implicitly represent a different take on the exclusionary dynamics as analysed so acutely in the work of Zygmunt Bauman, but, unlike Bauman (or, for that matter, Jock Young), this growing body of work urges us toward what one might call an appreciation rather than a denunciation of the dynamics of 'exclusionary space'. This is not to say that they reject Baumanesque concerns, but rather that they see in these spaces sparks of oppositional practices and the green shoots of future urban possibilities. Two interconnected themes link this otherwise diverse and multidisciplinary raft of work: the distinction between place and space; and the notion of cultural resistance.

As noted above, Papastergiadis implores us to shake off our standard perceptions of outsider spaces as simply abandoned, lost wastelands, for this is merely the 'view from above', from the perspective of de Certeau's 'Concept-city'. He asks us instead to consider how such spaces appear when glimpsed from street level. In answering this question, he offers us a quasi-anthropological interpretation of urban space that closely engages with the experiential realm, is about cultural, spatial and temporal nuance, strives to understand physical terrain as discourse, but above all is concerned with *specificity*. This terrain is thus to be understood in terms of distinct spatial biographies, relationships (or non-relationships) with surrounding space, intrication with different temporalities, intrinsic social role(s) – both perceived and actual – and networks of feelings and semiotic significance. These are the characteristics that many writers have mobilised in a bid to distinguish place from space.

---

44 See, eg, Cosgrove (1983, 1989); Cosgrove and Jackson (1987); Massey (1991, 1993); for a brief introduction to the 'new cultural geography', see Warren (1996: 549–53). See also Urban Geography (1996) for geography more generally.

45 Given our particular focus in this chapter on the experience of exclusion in Los Angeles, see Grannis (1998a, 1998b); the fledgling work of UCLA's NSF-REU Project; and relatedly South and Crowder (1997); Ruane (1998). In a counterpoint to Davis, Grannis considers the sociological and geographical nature of urban segregation in both Los Angeles and San Francisco, and how 'the patterning of residential streets has dramatically affected racial residential patterning in those two cities'. Specifically, he argues, the racial configuration of certain areas owes as much to 'relational connections via residential streets' as it does to geographic proximity. He claims that within these cities, certain urban 'islands' have formed – a cut-off series of streets where spatial flow is limited and neighbourly relations have been disrupted. Where Davis, taking the macro view, would take this as further evidence of social segregation/polarisation, Grannis investigates these 'street islands' as distinctive places linked not by the geographic proximity of a spatial map but the local relational connections of kith and kin support networks. Following detailed quantitative analysis, Grannis postulates that discontinuities in the residential street network (ie, the formation of exclusionary 'borders') could in effect be reconnected (and segregation reduced) simply by initiating certain 'low-cost public policy initiatives that would tend to integrate urban communities through minor modifications in the patterning of residential streets' (1998a: 1). This type of clear and practical research, that fully considers specific spatial, racial and demographic factors, while also being sensitive to local concerns, may be a way forward for research into urban spatial exclusion and the social effects of security implementation.

Buchanan goes some way towards capturing this in his account of de Certeau (cited in the Introduction to this volume), where he speaks of 'the life of the city' exceeding the 'concept of the city', the unmappability of urban lives and day-to-day experience, the 'something that always slips away' (Buchanan 2000: 110). This, alas, is merely how it looks 'from above'. More recent writings on place nuance de Certeau's duality in a potentially more sophisticated way, going further than merely filling in more of that elusive street life. Rather, place and space are seen as occupying different registers: they are simply not on the same scale. Consequently, there can be no simple reversal of top down and bottom up. There is literally no space for place in the urban cosmology. Place can only be occupied, not mapped.

Within criminology, there are signs of an emergent engagement with these themes of place and locale. In *A Tale of Two Cities: Global Change, Local Feeling and Everyday Life in the North of England* (Taylor *et al* 1996), Ian Taylor and his colleagues focus on the specific relationship between space and locality – particularly important, they argue, in what are increasingly globalised times – in two industrial cities in the North of England (Manchester and Sheffield). Taking their methodological lead from Raymond Williams (the renowned commentator on culture), and in particular his work on 'local structures of feeling' (Williams 1973),[46] Taylor *et al* utilise personal biographies, interviews, focus groups and cultural narrative (see also Taylor 1993, 1995, 1997) to produce an undeniably sensitive reading of urban space that considers in great detail place, people, ritual, history, structure, gender and age, not least in relation to strategies of coping and resistance. This reinvestment in the elements that constitute the very fabric of towns and cities is thus especially significant for areas described as 'socially excluded'. Ignoring such components of urban locales – what makes them local places and not just segments of grid space – can lead to serious policy errors. Consider, for example, how the policing practices advocated by administrative criminologists and right realists ignore local community particularities in favour of national policies of risk and resource management. Zero-tolerance policing might be readily acceptable in Teesside, but roundly rejected in Toxteth.

There is, however, one major problem, which, unfortunately, is axiomatic to the way that place has been interpreted and elaborated by Taylor and others who have adopted a similar approach (see Girling *et al* 1996, 1997, 1998). A hint of this may be found in the characterisation of Taylor's two Northern cities as 'organic' in nature. Essentially, the problem is that place here has become identified with lost tradition, even a thinly veiled nostalgia for some of the forms of 'industrial capitalism', at least as a mark of the city. In *A Tale of Two Cities*, for example, the authors' conception of city life and urban space at times reads like a paean to the demise of the industrial centres of the North of England. Certainly, there is a palpable sense of loss for the shared cultures associated with working class struggle. The

---

46 Drawing on the work of the 'sentiments school' of social history, Williams originally described structures of feeling as 'the particular quality of experience and relationship, historically distinct from other particular qualities, which gives a sense of a generation or period' (Williams 1973: 131, quoted in Taylor *et al* 1996: 312). However, Taylor *et al* extend the concept to include an implicit sense of the local social and class structures. In short, they are attempting to understand the 'impact of local place' on 'individual personality formation' and 'orientation to the world'.

significance of locality (as opposed to the national or the global), of place as opposed to space, is so heavily invested with class-orientation (encompassing class itself) that the very idea of place in this account seems to be defined in terms of the past, of history, of what has gone before – as if place could never have a future or occupy a postmodern present. (It might be an unpalatable thought for some, but the forms of identity and collective practical logics shared by those individuals who spent their lives wedded to the productivist process associated with the classic formulations of industrial capitalism are soon – at the mass level at least – to be lost forever.) This romantic and misplaced nostalgia seems rooted in the sociology of tradition, running against the tide of a 'world in transition' and the inevitable feelings of ontological insecurity that late modern society throws up. In short, what this body of work presents us with is a vision of city life that is frozen in time. It tells us much about the past but little of real value about ongoing developments.

If resistance is always resistance to change, there is no way of understanding our urban futures. Once again Papastergiadis is inspiring, for parafunctional spaces re-approached not as deficient modernist empty spaces but with all the uniqueness and specificity of place can, at the same time, be seen in terms of what de Certeau calls 'minuscule micro-cultural practices' of cultural resistance, 'zones in which creative, informal and unintended uses overtake the officially designated functions. In parafunctional spaces social life is not simply abandoned or wasted; rather it continues in ambiguous and unconventional ways' (Papastergiadis 2002: 45).

Importantly, cultural criminology is already present within these exclusionary/parafunctional spaces, describing a triumphant resistance through redeployment (Ferrell 2001: Chapter 2; see, relatedly, Dery 1993):[47]

Both skaters and [graffiti] writers view the environment different from everyone else. Staircases, handrails, curb cuts, train tunnels, truck yards, and city streets have become the new playground for the next generation. *We find value in what others deem useless.* ('Cycle', quoted in *Thrasher* 209, June 1998, quoted in Ferrell 2001: 75, emphasis added)[48]

When I was younger, I spent many nights grinding curbs, carving banks, shooting hills, and skating my city's streets aimlessly ... This mission has brought me to strange and beautiful places that average citizens will never see. Whether lying in a snowbank watching a maze of monstrous freights crash and roll or taking in the desert sky at an old drainage ditch in the middle of Nevada, I've gained a lot from this quest. I've found parts of who I am in long stretches of train tracks, in abandoned parking lots with makeshift quarterpipes on banks, under bridges, on rooftops ... alone, with the view of

---

47 See, relatedly, the compelling ethnography of Wacquant (1996, 2001) and Bourgois (1995, 1998).

48 See the work of nocturnal urban protest artists such as Krzysztof Wodiczko and Zhang Dali. According to Creswell, 'Wodiczko's aim is to ask questions of public space' by projecting huge images onto the facades of buildings, 'making the familiar (and thus unnoticed) strange and worthy of attention' (1998: 276). During the first Gulf War, eg, Wodiczko projected an image of 'skeletal arms carrying guns and petrol pumps onto the Arco de la Victoria in Madrid accompanied by the word "Cuantos?" asking both how much? (the price of petrol) and how many? (the numbers of dead)' (1998: 276). Zhnag Dali is one of a group of subversive protest artists operating in Beijing who use systematic graffiti art as a way of challenging the authority of the Chinese state.

the entire city beneath me ... ('Crisis', quoted in *Thrasher* 209, June 1998, quoted in Ferrell 2001: 78)

Like the skaters who employ parking garages and [swimming] pools, the 'useless artifacts of the technological burden [are employed] ... in a thousand ways that the original architects could never dream of'. (Ferrell 2001: 81)

This is a precursor of a new genre of criminology that approaches so-called 'criminogenic space' in the same way that the new cultural geography approaches 'postmodern space', a criminology that, like cultural geography, is infused by a strong inter-disciplinary approach and an ability to think beyond superficial interpretations – whether theoretical, structural or spatial. The era of understanding urban space from a purely rational (as in the discourse of crime prevention) or structural (as in Mike Davis's reading) perspective has past. Our complex, contradictory social world – 'a world in transition' – made more opaque by the muddiness of human action, demands more.[49] It is hoped that this chapter will help pave the way for a (culturally-inspired) criminology to focus on both sides of the exclusionary coin – those who can afford to protect themselves (*à la* Davis's 'scanscape') and those who for whatever reasons are forced onto the margins of society. That this is the current situation is not in question, but what we must strive for now are theoretical analyses that can help us work through (perhaps even with?) such a situation – analyses with the ability to look forward as well as back, while at the same time avoiding broad generalisations that fail to take into consideration the specificities of locality, culture and nation.[50]

Conclusion

My aim in this chapter was to separate out the key themes in Mike Davis's writings from some of his more sensational ideas. In a sense, I put forward the claim that, by concentrating almost exclusively on issues of structure and political economy framed in rather overblown, conspiratorial terms, Davis's reading of the post-industrial city remains one dimensional, largely underplaying many of the important cultural idiosyncrasies, lived experiences and diverse spatial practices that feed into the late modern urban experience – not just in Los Angeles, but in developed cities the world over. Los Angeles was chosen not because it represents a

---

49 Interestingly, in his recent work, *Magical Urbanism: Latinos Reinvent the US City* (2000), even Mike Davis seems finally to be engaging with such themes. In a short chapter entitled 'Tropicalizing cold urban space' (even the title suggests a more experiential, less militant approach), he makes much of the 'richness' and 'creativity' of alternative (Latino) urban cultures. There is almost a trace of de Certeau as he writes about this 'hotter more exuberant urbanism' (2000: 65), waxing lyrical about everything from the 'micro-entrepreneurship' of Barrio 'swap meets' to 'the glorious sorbet palette of Mexican and Caribbean house paint'.

50 In *The Culture of Control: Crime and Social Order in Contemporary Society* (2001), David Garland attempts a similar task in relation to the rise of penal punitiveness and social control more generally in society. Representing something of a digression from his normal mode of analysis, Garland stresses the complicit role played by new forms of late modern subjectivity. In particular 'a new pattern of mentalities, interests, and sensibilities that has altered how we think and feel about the underlying problem [of crime and punishment]' (2001: 6). Alas, despite such claims – and indeed its title – it is a work strangely devoid of culture (apart from some rather vague assertions about the changing nature of the middle classes).

paradigmatic expression of any future, generic, 'postmodern city' (to adopt such a position would be to expose my own analysis to some of the criticisms raised earlier), but rather because it exhibits to notable extremes some of the ways in which the characteristics of *fear* (or more accurately the fear of crime) and *desire* (in the form of conspicuous consumption) are contributing to the redrawing of the contours of the urban landscape. As to the applicability of my conclusions for other urban areas, that is for others to decide. In the final chapter, while the emphasis on the built environment does not go away (resurfacing as it does at various intervals in discussions about the shopping mall and the inner-city estate), the focus shifts firmly to urban crime. Once again the warped logic of a rampant consumer culture features prominently, only this time the intention is to highlight how it is bringing about change at the inner, experiential level of the subjective emotions, and how these changes are finding an outlet in certain forms of expressive criminality.

Chapter 5
Crime, Consumer Culture and the Urban Experience

[For the criminal,] thinking about crime is exciting. Committing crime is exciting. Even getting caught is exciting. Trying to figure out a way to beat the rap is exciting. (Samenow 1984)

We're living in a shop. The world is one magnificent fucking shop and if it hasn't got a price tag, it isn't worth having. (Dennis Bagly, the central character in Bruce Robinson's (1989) film, *How to Get Ahead in Advertising*)

Existentialism seeks out the meaning of things as they are in their full empirical actuality – thus, in understanding the human personality the emotions should be analyzed, not ignored as 'accidental' or inconsequential, therefore such emotions as fear and dread, boredom and passion are at the core of activity not peripheral; the results of this centrality are not always to our liking. (Morrison 1995: 352–53)

Introduction

All three of these quotes – one about excitement, one about consumption and one about the place of emotion – suggest that we have reached the point when things come together. The urban experience, both past and present, has been outlined and investigated. Criminological theories concerning urban crime have been introduced and critiqued. What follows now is my own attempt to unravel the complexities of the 'crime–city nexus'. This chapter will present what I hope is a series of insights into the myriad forms of relationships that currently exist between the categories of urban experience, consumer culture and crime, the intention being to formulate these insights into a tentative conceptual framework for thinking about the expressive aspects of crime under conditions of late modernity. Ultimately, my aim here is to contribute to the emerging inter-disciplinary enterprise of cultural criminology with its goal of constructing a bridge between, on the one hand, the existential, psychic concerns and anxieties of everyday life – the feelings, emotions and changeable moods that punctuate our day-to-day existence – and, on the inter-disciplinary other, the cultural and spatial forces that shape our role and status within society and impact on our willingness or reluctance to engage in criminal activity.

As stressed throughout this work, one of the central lacunae in the criminological tradition is the absence of any satisfactory account of the phenomenology of the criminal act. Most obviously, criminology has neglected the emotional dimension of offending. Instead, as a discipline, it has largely translated the lived reality of crime into the banal platitudes of rational discourse (Morrison 1995: 379). At best, emotions are recognised as pathology. In contrast, there stands the existential tradition associated with figures such as Nietzsche, Kierkegaard, Sartre and Bataille.[1] This

---

1 While clearly something of an over-simplification, existentialism can be seen as having its roots in two traditions. First, there is the *ethical tradition* associated with Søren Kierkegaard (broadly theological) and Friedrich Nietzsche (secular). Secondly, and in many ways strongly opposed to this ethical tradition, is the more systematic existentialism that stems from Husserl's more methodological phenomenology and on which most 20th century existential philosophy is founded (Warnock 1970: 3).

approach proposes that, if one is to fully understand transgression, one must begin with the passions, with the violent feelings which crime induces, both in offenders and victims. Something of the spirit of this existential approach can be found in perhaps the pivotal text in the postmodern reconstruction of aetiology – Jack Katz's *The Seductions of Crime: Moral and Sensual Attractions in Doing Evil* (1988). It is to Katz's work, therefore, that I now turn.

Criminology and experience: Jack Katz and the 'seductions' of transgression

As the title of his book suggests, the central contention of Katz's theory of crime is that there are 'moral and sensual attractions in doing evil' and that a truly inclusive account of 'anti-social behaviour' has to start from this premise.[2] While the subject of crime has been approached from numerous perspectives, very few (the notable exception of course being the work of David Matza and Howard Becker) have focused on the varied emotional dynamics and experiential attractions that are an integral element of much crime. Consequently, the 'lived experience of criminality' rarely features in traditional criminological and sociological explanations of crime and deviance: 'Somehow in the psychological and sociological disciplines, the lived mysticism and magic in the foreground of criminal experience became unseeable, while the abstractions hypothesized by "empirical theory" as the determining background causes, especially those conveniently quantified by state agencies, became the stuff of "scientific" thought and "rigorous" method' (1988: 311–12).

For Katz, causal explanations of criminality that stress the importance of structural, environmental, genetic or rational choice factors, over and above the emotional and interpretative qualities of crime, are often guilty of stripping away and repressing the significance of key individual emotions such as humiliation, arrogance, ridicule, cynicism, and (importantly) pleasure and excitement – emotions that, in many cases, are central to the criminal event. In doing so they 'turn the direction of inquiry' around, so that the focus of criminological attention falls on the 'background' rather then the 'foreground' of the criminal act (1988: 9). Thus, fundamentally, Katz poses a question that many criminologists either take for granted or completely ignore: 'why are people who were not determined to commit a crime one moment determined to do so the next?' (1988: 4). Only by going beyond background factors and delving deeper into the criminal act itself, he claims, can the solution be found. The various mechanisms which move actors between 'background factors and subsequent acts' have been a kind of 'black box', assumed to have some motivational force but left essentially unexamined (1988: 5). Katz proposes to retrieve and prise open the contents of this 'black box'. In short, one might say that Katz's work can be seen as an attempt to reclaim the 'unexamined spaces in criminological theory' (Henry and Milovanovic 1996: 60).

---

2   While the word 'evil' appears in the title of his book, Katz's work should not be seen as an attempt to unravel the theological and philosophical imbroglio that surrounds terms such as 'good' and 'evil'; rather, the term 'evil' is employed more in the form of a transgressive metaphor.

Using an eclectic array of sources, Katz builds up a picture of the sensual, magical and creative appeals of crime. Evoking the notion of the Nietzschean superman, Katz asserts that deviance offers the perpetrator a means of 'self transcendence', a way of overcoming the conventionality and mundanity typically associated with the banal routines and practicalities of everyday 'regular life'. At the subjective level, crime is stimulating, exciting and liberating. To think of crime either as another form of rational activity or as the result of some innate or social pathology is totally to miss the point. As I have observed elsewhere:

> It is worth noting that this argument challenges one of the central assumptions of much contemporary criminology, namely the belief that most crime is routinised and, in some way, banal. This is undoubtedly the case if one adopts the perspective of the police or other criminal justice and law enforcement agencies, however, it is not necessarily true for those participating in criminal activity, for whom the most innocuous transgression may well represent an exhilarating form of experience. (Fenwick and Hayward 2000: 36)

At the same time, Katz urges more attention to the criminal act itself, for each specific crime, he maintains, presents the criminal with a distinct set of subjective experiences and existential dilemmas, and thus has its own singular attraction. If emotions are major contingencies in the 'lived contours of crime', Katz's approach illuminates the 'sneaky thrills' of shoplifting; robbery as a spontaneous, chaotic and often hedonistic act;[3] the 'sense of superiority' involved in the act of 'stickup': and the pride robbers take in their defiant reputation as 'badmen'. Katz even examines the lived sensuality behind events of cold-blooded, 'senseless' murder, charting the role of 'defilement', 'sacrifice', 'righteous rage', 'vengeance' and 'hedonism' – emotions that are frequently at the root of most 'non-modal homicides'.[4] His account encompasses the 'sensual metaphysics', from the pleasure and 'ludic' quality of the act itself to the shame and embarrassment felt on apprehension.

Katz's work on the thrill of transgression can easily be extended to include a range of other criminal activities – especially those perpetrated by young people – and to oppose any simplistic diagnosis in terms of immediate financial or practical benefits (as I have argued elsewhere in a piece co-authored with Mark Fenwick: Fenwick and Hayward 2000: 36–39). Teenage criminal practices such as vandalism, theft and destruction of cars, fire-starting,[5] mugging, hoax emergency service call-outs, car 'cruising',[6] peer group violence and other forms of street delinquency all have much to do with youth expression and exerting control in neighbourhoods where, more often than not, traditional avenues for youthful stimulation and

---

3 A fact supported by the best empirical data on the subject (see Conklin 1972; Harin and Martin 1984; Wright and Rossi 1985; Kapardis 1989: see, relatedly, de Haan and Vos 2003).

4 By 'non-modal homicide' Katz is referring to murders that do not have an obvious explanation.

5 Interestingly, both FBI and UK Home Office statistics suggest that arson is one of the fastest growing crimes. According to UK Fire Statistics (www.homeoffice.gov.uk/rds/fire1.html), England and Wales experienced a 135% increase in 'deliberately set fires' (38,700 to 91,000) between 1989 and 1999 – compare this to the 25% decrease in accidental fires over the same period. See, relatedly, the Arson Prevention Bureau publication, *Malicious Car Fires* (1998).

6 'Cruising' is the cutting edge of *sub rosa* car culture and involves unauthorised high-speed car racing and mass car rallies at which dangerous driving practices are encouraged and lionised.

endeavour have long since evaporated.[7] Similarly, graffiti 'artists' and members of 'tag crews', in both the US and Europe, often talk at length not only about the thrill and emotional charge experienced when breaking into buildings and compounds and defacing private property, but also about how their work serves as a means of self-expression and a way in which they can make themselves heard (see Ferrell 1995, 1996; Lasley 2002). Furthermore, the phenomenon of vandalism more generally seems also to fit with Katz's thesis (compare S Cohen 1973). Arguably, if no material gain is likely to be forthcoming from this practice then it must surely centre around either the excitement of perpetrating an illegal act, or the exhilaration of wanton destruction.

A similar argument might be developed in relation to drug use – probably the most prevalent of all youthful criminal transgressions. There can be little doubt that the drug subculture is inextricably linked with emotion: from the social circumstances in which the majority of teenage drug use takes place (eg, bars, clubs and raves, etc); to the anticipation involved in the 'scoring' process; continuing with the heightened sensations experienced prior to and during ingestion of the drug; and, finally, the rollercoaster of emotions one feels following the resolution of the process and the psychopharmacological high. Lastly, football hooliganism – perhaps the original urban 'extreme sport' – seems to be the quintessential illustration of the Katzian position. Rarely, if ever, is football hooliganism (or for that matter disruptive behaviour and violence connected with other sports) concerned with rational economic gain. On the contrary, ticket prices and travel expenses ensure that following a football team home and away is a costly business. Instead, this phenomenon can be seen as stemming from the emotional charge – or 'buzz' – that is engendered from the combination of the football and the related violence.[8] For example, consider this passage from Colin Ward's book *Steaming In*, a first-hand account of football hooliganism in England in the 1970s and 1980s:

> There are certain events and experiences that make everyday, mundane existence seem tolerable and worthwhile. For thousands of football fans, myself included, it was the terraces. It became our life, for some the sole reason for existence ... Words can never fully express the emotions we experienced or recreate the heady atmosphere ... Most people are guilty of escapism and a desire to be famous. The terraces gave every participant a chance to be somebody. (Ward 1989: 5)

Moreover, one of the features of football hooliganism in the 1990s was the extent to which it became pre-arranged in a bid to counteract ever more sophisticated police

---

7 Indeed, if one reviews the literature on juvenile delinquency and street gangs from the earliest studies (see Thrasher 1927; A Cohen 1955; Yablonsky 1962) through to more contemporary work (see Hagedorn 1988; Vigil 1988), one is struck by the number of times teenagers, when interviewed, describe the gang lifestyle as being exciting, a way of relieving boredom and escaping the banal practicalities of everyday life.

8 With the exception of some excellent ethnographic work (Giulianotti 1989; Armstrong and Harris 1991; Armstrong 1993), research into football hooliganism typically tends to ignore the excitement or emotion that is a major factor in football violence. Instead, the vast majority of research in this area over the last 25 years has erroneously attempted to explain away football hooliganism as a phenomenon born out of one factor, or a combination of factors, such as working-class frustration, the class struggle or extreme right-wing politics (eg, Taylor 1982; Robins 1984; Williams 1986). This kind of analysis has largely ignored the fundamental fact that football hooliganism is very often an end in itself.

surveillance both in and around football grounds. These pre-arranged 'offs' prolong the emotional high by removing spontaneity from football violence, thus heightening and extending the anticipation and organisation periods (ie, avoiding surveillance becomes part of the pleasure).

Such examples serve to illustrate that, in many cases, individuals are seduced by the existential possibilities offered by criminal acts – by the pleasure of transgression. Hence, a key advantage of this approach is that it helps us to understand why it is that much criminality is not solely the preserve of those groups who are economically and socially disadvantaged. These groups may well be over-represented in the criminal justice system but – to make a familiar point – this may have more to do with the social construction of criminality than higher actual rates of criminal participation. Crimes as diverse as drug-taking, 'twocking',[9] mugging, peer-group fighting (see Jackson-Jacobs 2004), vandalism, computer hacking (see Stanley 1996: Chapter 7), perhaps even certain forms of terrorism (see Hamm 1995, 2004; Hayward and Morrison 2002), have a strong expressive element which (as I shall argue later) is inextricably related to excitement and the desire to exert 'control'.[10] Consequently, the motivation behind these crimes cannot be limited to any specific set of social circumstances or economic inequality. Such crimes are about the thrill of transgressing the rule and the pursuit of the limit, a point Mike Presdee has expressed well:

> It would seem that what we experience, or need to experience, in a world based on mind and rationality is the coming closer to the realms of desire and excitement, which we must deny ourselves in a civilised rather than savage society. This is what Katz has described as the 'delight of being deviant'. It is a transient, ephemeral, yet sublime experience that, like all seductions, needs to be played with and experienced again and again. In this way carnival, popular dissent, and riot become part of the fabric of fun. (Presdee 1994: 182)

Inspiring but not entirely unique,[11] Katz's work has nonetheless been criticised for failing to recognise the wider social and structural contexts within which crime, indeed all individual experience, takes place (see, eg, O'Malley and Mugford 1994; Henry and Milovanovic 1996; Van Hoorebeeck 1997). However, this seems

---

9 'Twocking' refers to the practice of taking cars without their owners' prior consent.

10 It is vitally important to recognise and acknowledge that many of these forms of crime can be seen as both a product and a reflection of 'hegemonic masculinity' (Connell 1987, 1991, 1995; Jefferson 1994, 1997). In this sense, the desire to 'exert control' becomes even more urgent when set against the backdrop of the *post*-industrial working-class urban landscape. As Steve Hall (1997: 471) succinctly points out, as the productivist economy continues to crumble, 'hard lads' are increasingly 'stripped of [traditional] functional value and cultural capital', a process that further challenges their masculinity. The result, he claims, is an over-compensation in specific cultures of emotive, 'visceral' criminality and violence: 'Yearning for a future ... those hanging on by their fingernails to the mainstream economy simulate the hostilities of the violent productivist-imperialist life in their Friday night "lager-gangs" and Saturday afternoon football "firms"' (1997: 470).

11 Importantly, Katz is not alone in his attempt to re-orientate criminology's gaze away from materialism and rationalism towards a position on crime that more fully appreciates the existential nature of the criminal act. Authors as far back as Wilson (1966) and, more recently, Lyng (1990); Salecl (1993); Morrison (1995); Ferrell (1996, 1999, 2001); Ferrell and Sanders (1995); Henry and Milovanovic (1996); Stanley (1996: Chapter 7); Presdee (1994, 2000) and myself (Hayward 2002, 2003; Fenwick and Hayward 2000) have all also contributed to this project.

circuitous, for was not Katz's starting point the failure of 'background' structural theories of crime to address the 'foreground' question why (under shared social conditions) one person rather than another commits a crime (1988: 314–16)? (Katz is not even without precedent here: witness all the 'over-prediction of crime' critiques.) At this point, we seemingly find ourselves traversing very familiar ground – the 'structure versus agency' debate. However, rather than view Katz's work simply as resurrecting one side of this binary framework, I wish to proffer a very different claim. It is my contention that Katz's analysis is not so much about agency versus structure, but rather about prioritising emotionality in such a way that it neither reduces emotions purely to the level of individual psychology (Katz should be credited for taking emotions out of the realm of pathology; see also Katz's excellent 1999 work, *How Emotions Work*), nor pre-locates the question of those emotions in the drama of state-resistance and political rebellion.

It is this line of inquiry that I wish to develop in the remainder of the chapter. In particular, I intend to highlight what it is about human experience and social conditions *today* that makes the pursuit of excitement and transgression so seductive. More specifically, it will be proposed that transgressive behaviour is becoming seductive not only because of the excitement it brings at the level of the individual experience (*à la* Katz), but also, importantly, because it offers a way of seizing control of one's destiny. This latter point is of increasing importance. For Katz, as stated above, the issue is escape from the mundane routines of everyday life (even this might not be incompatible with classic Marxism). However, the contemporary milieu is more complex. Not only do we inhabit an ever more uncertain, risk-laden world that feels increasingly out of control but, at the same time – in what is the cruellest of social ironies – late modern society responds with a series of constraining so-called rational measures that, far from creating order and stability, serve rather to bring about what I will call here the 'hyper-banalisation' of everyday life. What is more, this movement interacts with that perverse cultural as well as economic agency – the market – too often overlooked by criminologists with their relentless focus on official agencies of social control. For now, however, let us concern ourselves with the question of how best to contextualise Katz.

Contextualising Katz: the search for identity and the exertion of control

Late modern society is often characterised in terms of a pervasive sense of insecurity and disembeddedness: not just in the well-documented areas of cultural production (Featherstone 1991; Jameson 1991) and declining industrial capitalism (Bell 1976; Hall and Jacques 1990) but also, importantly, in the realms of everyday life (de Certeau 1984) and at the level of individual consciousness and awareness. Everything, it seems, is subject to change and reconstitution, as seen in the apparent 'crises' in masculinity (Jefferson 1997; Connell 1995), the family (Wilson 1985) and the demise of the nation state (Taylor 1999: 20–27). While such a set of social circumstances may, in the long term, offer society a whole new range of opportunities and possibilities, in the short term it often throws up feelings of melancholia and uncertainty as we are forced to reconsider our past, present and future, and face up to the fact that many of the teleological presuppositions we have clung on to for so long have collapsed and now cannot be reconstructed (Hayward and Morrison 2002: 146–50). Grand narratives and individual narratives rise and fall together (Lyotard 1984).

This has been the stuff of much observation. Giddens (1990), for example, colourfully equates everyday life in late modernity with trying to regain control of an out-of-control juggernaut. Mike Davis (1990, 1998) and Zygmunt Bauman (1987, 1998), meanwhile, see the future only in terms of a new dialectic of social control predicated on each individual's ability to bridge the cultural/financial gap that dictates entry into the consumer society, creating a new category of the excluded urban repressed. However, from a purely criminological perspective, perhaps the best articulation of the impact of current social and economic conditions on individual subjectivity is the one set out by Jock Young:

> We live now in a much more difficult world: we face a greater range in life choices than ever before, our lives are less firmly embedded in work and relationships, our everyday existence is experienced as a series of encounters with risk either in actuality or in the shape of fears and apprehensions. We feel both materially insecure and ontologically precarious. (Young 1999: vi)[12]

What all these commentators have in common is the belief that success in tackling the contemporary crime problem depends upon acknowledging the 'ontological insecurity' of feeling physically and psychologically at risk in an unstable and changing world. In short, we must engage with the contingencies and dilemmas/the dilemmas of the contingent brought about by the late modern condition.

So, is this simply a matter of urging criminology to engage with the 'postmodern subject'? Let us revisit one of the central themes of this book: namely, the conception of 'the subject in transition'. After lengthy reviews of the work of Harvey and Jameson, the claim was put forward in Chapter 2 that, whilst these works are of great theoretical importance (not least for the numerous insights they offer into the developing nature of human subjectivity under 'postmodern' conditions), no such thing as a fully formed 'postmodern subject' could actually be said (as yet) to exist. Rather, I agreed with Wayne Morrison's more circumspect proposal that the contemporary actor is a 'subject in transition', a strange hybrid of the modern and the postmodern. Moreover, might the common feelings of ontological insecurity that abound in late modernity be best understood as a congress of feelings that together can be described as the *dilemmas of transition* as we each attempt to reconcile our (still partly modern) selves to the fundamental changes currently being wrought by, *inter alia*, rampant consumerism, globalised (especially computer-mediated) technologies, multinational capitalism (and all its associated

---

12 The link between Young's work on ontological insecurity (eg, 1999: 97–104) and that of Georg Simmel (see Chapter 1) is extraordinary. Consider the following quote by Young: 'In such an urban existence the tendency is for attitudes to become wary and calculating, blasé and actuarial. Difficulties to be avoided, differences to be accepted yet kept at a distance, not allowed to affect one's security or composure' (1999: vii). What is interesting about Young's updated take is the way he goes on to talk about ontological precariousness as a 'fertile tool for projection and moralism' (see 1999: Chapter 4).

economic upheavals), the mapping of social relationships not just to local and national but to international class realities, 'inauthenticity', simultaneity and time-space compression?

I retrace the key features of late modernity for good reason: if one's stated aim is to '(re)contextualise Katz', then one must first accept that there is now no longer any fixed or immutable social context on which to graft Katz's analysis – in fact, quite the opposite. As illustrated above, the current social climate is one of constant change and uncertainty. In such an environment the creation of identity and the exertion of control become complex tasks. This being the case, it is essential for us to reconsider such key terms as 'identity' and 'self-actualisation' – those *prima facie* modernist concepts – and importantly their relationship to a sense of ontological control, a project that has been ongoing for some time in the intellectual debates that encompass late/postmodernity.

Inevitably, within the context of postmodern discourse the use of a term such as 'identity' is problematic, the key question being: how, in a world increasingly characterised by depthlessness, pastiche and ahistoricism – all that a modern sensibility would characterise as inauthentic – can a sense of 'authentic' individual identity be established/constructed? At this point, one could suggest that little has changed since Weber's brilliant characterisation of modern subjectivity (ie, the classical Protestant ethic/spirit of capitalism epistemological dilemma – we take it for granted that there is an individual self (soul) but, by the same token, we are never quite sure of its fate/salvation). However, to adopt such a position would be to over-simplify the current situation. Today, the notion of the individual 'interior' self has been replaced by a more dislocated and fractured conception of other possibilities such as 'identity as life project' – a never to be completed process of perpetual construction and reconstruction (Campbell 1989; Featherstone 1991; see Chapter 2). This is not to say that we should discount the concept entirely. On the contrary, a sense of identity remains of great importance (consider, for example, how central a role identity – albeit a corrupted form of identity – plays within contemporary consumer culture), only now we must accept that 'the search for authentic identity' is likely to be a far more elusive experiment, as the 'subject in transition', assailed by the 'dilemmas' of late modernity, refuses to engage with the established tropes of meaning-making. In other words, it would seem that one of the dilemmas that confronts the late modern 'subject adrift' is whether to seek a sense of authenticity, or instead to embrace the notion of multiplicity – 'today I will be X, tomorrow Y'.

My argument here is that we must approach the subject from a new perspective. We need to situate terms such as 'identity' and 'self-actualisation' within the context of a society/subject in transition.[13] In other words, we must recognise that if, within contemporary life worlds, it is becoming ever more difficult for individuals to construct a sense of identity through the 'established' norms and codes of modernity, then alternative avenues will be sought. This being the case, it is not illogical to suggest that one of the most obvious ways of retaliating against feelings

---

13 I understand the term 'self-actualisation' to mean a self-reflective consciousness linked to an individual's existential 'will'.

of ontological insecurity and diminishing identity will be to exert a sense of control – no matter how seemingly futile the gesture; if you like, to resort to the very mechanism being opposed.[14] But how best to exert control in a world increasingly out of control? It is my contention that one way of achieving a semblance of control is to engage in the marginalised activities associated with the metaphorical 'edge'. Here, a sense of self-actualisation – no matter how destructive – can be effectively realised. Here we overlap with Katz's work on the thrill of transgression, only this time we must go beyond the Katzian position that crime is seductive because of the excitement it brings at the level of individual subjective experience, and look instead at how crime represents, for many, a way of both seizing control and expressing identity. As Presdee has suggested, we need to fully appreciate how, '[I]n a powerless world, crime creates power for the individual to express their individuality ... This is the art in crime rather than the art of crime and in turn creates crime's seductive nature' (2000: 158).

It is instructive at this point to consider two previous attempts to contextualise Katz. In the interesting, if somewhat baroque, work *Constitutive Criminology* (1996: Chapter 7), Henry and Milovanovic attempt to develop the Katzian position along similar lines to those set out above by focusing on the question of diminishing control in postmodernity. They engage with three classical sociological commentaries that have all characterised the process of modernisation in terms of increased regulation – the work of Weber in relation to the 'iron cage' of bureaucracy; Foucault's analysis of disciplinary forms of social control; and Deleuze and Guattari's account of the territorialisation of desire – to suggest that, over time, capitalism gives rise to a loss of freedom and control. Despite acknowledging the value of Katz's work, Henry and Milovanovic criticise Katz, along with other non-materialistic analyses of the causes of crime (including Halleck 1971 and Salecl 1993), for what they describe as their inherent modernism and limited scope (according to Henry and Milovanovic, such purely phenomenological accounts of crime are simply 'tension-reduction models rooted in homeostasis and the modernist (order) paradigm' (1996: 156)). Moreover, they contend that Katz and other like-minded scholars have failed to consider the broader macro environment within which all individual experience occurs. Such shortcomings, they suggest, can be addressed by recourse to their own 'constitutive criminology' (1996: 158).[15]

Whilst there is much of interest in Henry and Milovanovic's 'constitutive' framework (not least its bold attempt to marry together a raft of theoretical

---

14 Once again, advertisers are already leading the way. Consider this piece of copy from a billboard advert for The Brook Street Temp Agency: 'We're all temps now. No one expects to stay in the same old job from 16–60. But what this Brave New World lacks in security it makes up for in flexibility. Forget the Euro. Attitude is the new currency. The right one will buy you the lifestyle you prefer ... Worrying about job security is a thing of the past. If you're good, you'll have job security. If you don't care, well the meter's running out.'

15 'Constitutive criminology is a postmodernist theoretical perspective that draws on several critical social theories, most notably symbolic interactionism, phenomenology, social constructionism, structural Marxism, structuration theory, semiotics, chaos theory and affirmative postmodernism. The core of the constitutive argument is that crime and its control cannot be separated from the totality of the structural and cultural contexts in which it is produced, nor can it lose sight of human agents' contribution to these contexts' (Henry and Milovanovic 2001: 50).

positions), it is my contention that, despite its various claims to the contrary, their approach is not able to free itself from the idea that there exists a fixed, and thus identifiable, social reality. One could go further and make the claim that, despite postmodernist pretensions, in certain moments their work takes on a distinctly modernist tone. For example, consider this quote from earlier in the same work:

> Our analysis of social structure begins with the strengths and limitations of recent Marxian theorizing concerning the discursive formation posited as a replacement to conceptions of the social formation and with affirmative postmodernism's insights into insatiability and plurality. *This is the transcendent position which we identify as a constitutive theory*. In this theory a central concept is the *co-production* of *reality*. This is a thesis which situates constructions of social reality in historically changing conditions. In the constitutive framework, truths are contingently and provisionally based. (1996: 65, emphasis added)

Leaving aside the reference to structural Marxism, one of the things that postmodernism (in all its various guises) is fundamentally opposed to is the search for any form of 'transcendent position'. Similarly, their use of the term 'social reality' also seems to fly in the face of much postmodern thought. Indeed, their whole stated aim of creating a vision of crime based around 'a critical postmodern phenomenology that links structure with agency' (1996: 64) seems highly commensurate with much high modernist thinking. In trying to make order out of chaos, Henry and Milovanovic are missing the point. Surely, any search for (what they describe as) 'the totality of human biography' (1996: 38) is likely to be a futile one in an era that is distinct because of the way it undoes totalities – and biographies. Sadly or happily, as outlined above, the late modern subject is, as Morrison (1995: 258) suggests, a subject adrift – a de-centred actor looking for a centre (or not!), bullied or lulled by the market and unable to exert control over future prospects. Put bluntly, the nature of postmodernity itself mitigates against the very project that Henry and Milovanovic are attempting to undertake. Consequently, Henry and Milovanovic never fully overcome the fundamental irony that haunts their account, for while they celebrate postmodernity and talk of developing an 'affirmative', 'recursive' criminology (a new 'transcendent position'?) based on new modes of 'expressive and holistic' inquiry aimed at 'contrasting prevailing modernist analyses' (Henry and Milovanovic 1996: x), in reality their work is totally reliant upon the very modernist social theory that, in many ways, they are so keen to decry.

In terms of contextualising Katz within a broader theoretical framework, a more productive way forward is set out by Pat O'Malley and Stephen Mugford in their article 'Crime, excitement and modernity' (1994). Unlike Henry and Milovanovic, it makes no bold statements about updating/augmenting Katz's framework by recourse to postmodern theorisation. It simply attempts to locate Katz's account of criminality – or, more accurately, the 'pursuit of excitement' (something central not just to Katz's analysis but also a major element of Stephen Lyng's (1990) concept of 'edgework' – of which more later) – within the context of a *fragmenting modernity* by posing the fundamental question: 'What is it about modernity that makes excitement important to the self?' (O'Malley and Mugford 1994: 197). In this sense, their account is much more in tune with the notion of the (late) modern 'subject in transition'.

Drawing on Elias's (1982) account of the 'civilizing' process as a historical and conceptual phenomenon, and echoing the Katzian argument, O'Malley and Mugford contend that the increasing need for 'moral transcendence' through excitement should be seen largely as a product of social and cultural conditions brought about by the 'emergence of rationality' ('Only in a society where there exist effective barriers to spontaneous expression of emotional extremes will a process of moral self-transcendence be called for' (O'Malley and Mugford 1994: 199)). More specifically, they put forward three (distinctly modernist) themes that they believe both account for the current crisis in ontology and help explain 'the dilemma of the modern self, and the way that excitement is relevant to that dilemma' (1994: 201) – alienation, commodification and the prevalence of 'clock time' (specifically, Eliade's 'fall into time', the artificial division of time between work and leisure). Such features create a situation in which transgression takes on a peculiar appeal:

> As commodification proceeds apace, the world becomes dominated by style, by appearance, by simulacra. In such a world, the self becomes swallowed in consumerism, but that consumerism is ultimately rather hollow and unsatisfying. The pursuit of selfhood may involve seeking liberation through consumption by indulging in more extreme forms of experience, but in so doing one risks more conformity to the consumerist perspective ... Within modern cultures there is a steady and increasing pressure towards emotionally exciting activities, as a source of transcendence and authenticity with which to offset the suffocation of an over-controlled, alienated existence within the mundane reality of modern life. (1994: 206)

Thus, O'Malley and Mugford are able to convey precisely how Katz's work on emotions is relevant to social conditions *today* and why transgressive behaviour is so 'seductive' and/or 'exciting' for the 'subject in transition'. They also provide more than a glimpse of the ratchet mechanisms in which the very processes of overcoming or escaping banality themselves become bound up in mechanisms of control and conformity.

The rest of this chapter explores the dialectic that currently exists between excitement, (self) control and crime under late modern social conditions, arguing that consumerism is engendering certain concomitant forms of subjectivity at the emotional level that are finding expression in various modes of criminal activity. Rather than being symptomatic of a lack of self-control,[16] the new cultural criminology suggests that much crime represents an attempt to take responsibility for one's own destiny.

Theorising the crime–consumerism nexus

I will now offer a series of suggestions as to how various features associated with consumer culture are creating and cultivating – especially among young people – new forms of concomitant subjectivity based around desire, simultaneity, individualism and impulsivity that, in many instances, are finding expression in certain forms of transgressive behaviour. Importantly, these suggestions should not

---

16 I should of course state at the outset that this is a very different conception of control to that normally found in criminological theory (see Gottfredson and Hirschi (1990) for the classic contemporary statement of this position).

be taken as a systematic attempt to integrate consumerism into a general theory of crime. Rather, they represent a more modest attempt to outline the striking convergence between these novel 'forms of subjectivity' and many of the characteristics identified within the criminological literature as being constitutive of 'criminality'. I should perhaps also say that it is not my intention to suggest that consumer culture is criminogenic in any simplistic sense of direct correlation/causation, nor am I offering a crude materialist reading of the criminological literature. What I am suggesting instead is that consumerism as an economic activity *and*, crucially, a cultural ethos is propagating new (and often destructive) emotional states, feelings and desires that contribute to the crime problem in a number of new and novel ways. As such, I merely intend to highlight a number of possible avenues for future research.

Transcending Merton: consumer expectation in late modernity

> The paradox of equality is that as differentials narrow differences become all the more noticeable. (Jock Young 1999: 48)

> ... desire does not desire satisfaction. To the contrary, desire desires desire. (Taylor and Saarinen, quoted in Bauman 1998: 25)

The obvious starting point for a criminological investigation into the issues surrounding consumer culture is the material analyses of Merton and, in particular, his classical strain theory (Merton 1938). Simply stated, strain theory suggests that crime and deviance occur when there is a discrepancy between what the social structure makes possible (ie, the means and opportunities for obtaining success) and what the dominant culture extols (ie, the social value of material accoutrements and the culture of consumption). Yet, despite the monumental impact of Merton's work, theorists have been somewhat reluctant to update early strain models in light of the particular cultural and economic changes associated with *late modernity* (compare A Cohen 1997; Passas 1997; and, in particular, the work of Robert Agnew, eg, 1985, 1989, 1992). One notable exception has been Wayne Morrison (1995: Chapter 13), who has argued for some time that we need more sophisticated analyses of the emotional states, the feelings and the contingencies associated with strain/anomie. He suggests we need to look more acutely at the way the self is being assailed by the various and competing cultural messages of late modern life:

> Criminology not only operates with underdeveloped models of desire, but also largely restricts itself to narrow interpretations of strain theories; wherein crime is the result of frustration by the social structure of the needs which culture identifies for the individual. Today, even in the most contemporary of mainstream criminological theory, ideas of positionality and status are underdeveloped. Instead ideas of needs and greed predominate. (1995: 317)

Whilst acknowledging the subtle differences that exist between theories of 'strain' and the concept of 'relative deprivation', there have, in recent years, been some interesting attempts to revive Stouffer's (1949) original deprivation thesis, most notably within left realist criminology (see Chapter 3). Alas, it remains the case that left realists continue to operate with a vastly under-developed concept of relative deprivation that fails to recognise the full extent to which late modern consumerism has cultivated 'new forms of consumer desire' that now extend far and beyond any simple Mertonian notion of culturally-based strain. To understand this point, it is necessary to revisit the original concept of relative deprivation.

Relative deprivation was given considerable empirical validity in the UK by Peter Townsend's various classic studies into absolute levels of poverty. A dominant theme in this body of work was what one might call the discourse of poverty: Townsend was also keen to promote the idea that 'need' was in fact *culturally determined*. Prior to his research, poverty (and therefore need) was typically defined by semi-biological standards (ie, poverty was related, *inter alia*, to starvation, disease, nutrients, etc). However, following the publication of Townsend's various findings, notions of need became entwined with (more abstract) cultural considerations (eg, in one report much was made of the British need for tea!). Accordingly, need became defined by part of the cultural consensus. In the UK, of course, the cultural consensus was highly stratified (and therefore more constrained) by class factors; however, in the US, relative deprivation was more pronounced because of a culture with a more unified set of goals that all could aspire to (what Merton (1968: 200) described as the 'cardinal American virtue, "ambition"'). This conception of relative deprivation has remained virtually undeveloped in criminology ever since. However, in his recent book, *The Exclusive Society* (1999) – a work which, in a sense, is all about the strains of late modern city life – Jock Young is keen to radically extend the concept. He argues that although relative deprivation persists in this 'era of mass unemployment and marginalization', it is being 'transformed': 'It no longer involves comparison across the serried ranks of the incorporated; it becomes comparison across the division of the labour market and between those in the market and those excluded' (Young 1999: 48). Thus, for Young, the transformation in relative deprivation stems from the fact that in contemporary society the 'inequalities have widened' and 'the prizes have also become more unequal'. It is at this point that Young augments the concept of relative deprivation in a new and novel way that goes well beyond the Townsend Report. Relative deprivation, he argues, should now be thought of not just as a 'gaze upwards', but also *as a troubled and anxious look toward the excluded of society*:

> Relative deprivation is conventionally thought of as a gaze upwards: it is the frustration of those denied equality in the market place to those of equal merit and application. But it is also a gaze downwards: *it is dismay at the relative well-being of those who although below one on the social hierarchy are perceived as unfairly advantaged*: they make too easy a living even if it is not as good as one's own. This is all the more so when rewards are accrued illicitly, particularly when the respectable citizen is also a victim of crime. It is in the way in which cities are constituted ... The regentrification which has occurred in many European cities has added a further twist to this, for 'chic' by jowl, the wealthy middle class live, in many cases, across the street from the structurally unemployed. (1999: 9, emphasis added)

This is unquestionably a very important statement that not only fits well with the overarching ethos of Young's monograph, but also goes some way to updating relative deprivation in light of the changing social formation and cultural dynamics of late modern society. However, if we set aside this important new take on relative deprivation, it appears to me that the main point of interest remains the changing nature of the 'gaze upwards' and, especially, *the expansion of need as a discourse of justification*:

[c]rime, whether street robbery or embezzlement, is rarely committed in order to reach the average median wage. The poor do not steal Beetles but Porsches, looters do not carry home a booty of baked beans but of camcorders, no one – outside of a tiny few – takes illicit drugs to feel normal. And the rich do not commit crimes in order to ensure a future retirement in comfort. That they already have; they do so in order to excel in their affluence and to exult in their edge over all comers. (1999: 53)[17]

While this insightful passage is highly important because it fully acknowledges the fact that the vast majority of crime within our cities is perpetrated not by the extreme poor, the homeless or the hungry, but by individuals whose motives are driven primarily by cultural determinants, it does not, in my opinion, fully explain what is happening to the idea of need within contemporary society. In short, the passage quoted above does not go much beyond the explanation of relative deprivation set out by Townsend. It is my contention that critical criminology must go further and develop new and more sophisticated 'deprivation' models that specifically consider the phenomenal rise of consumer culture since the 1980s (a task that Young has clearly begun by adding a 'gaze downward' to the concept of relative deprivation), for without such models, criminology will inevitably fall short of gaining a complete understanding of contemporary criminality.

Since the 1990s, within most industrialised consumer-orientated countries, the distinction between 'having' and 'being' has become somewhat confused as individuals increasingly construct identity through the commodities they consume and display (see Chapter 2). As Helga Dittmar has commented: 'In Western materialistic societies ... an individual's identity is influenced by the symbolic meaning of his or her own material possessions and the way he or she relates to those possessions ... Moreover, material possessions provide people with information about other peoples' identities' (Dittmar, quoted in Lury 1996: 8). Such a situation marks something of a break with what has gone before. Previously, a Cartesian view of identity held sway, at least in the West. Identity was conceived as unique, autonomous and uninfluenced by other people or socio-cultural surroundings, an 'interior' self behind the mask. This view has been replaced by a more dislocated and fractured conception of identity as 'life project' – a never-to-be-completed process of perpetual construction and reconstruction (Campbell 1989; Featherstone 1994). We now construct and display a self-identity chosen from the shop window of our pluralised culture. It is no longer a case of 'I think, therefore I am', but rather 'I shop, therefore I am'. Importantly, this change in the concept of identity should be seen alongside a series of other transformations, specifically the decline of the Protestant work ethic, the erosion of the savings ethos, and the undermining of the notion that purchasing an object 'represents repayment for the past and security for the future' (Baudrillard 1996: 159).[18] In the light of such a

---

17 Something similar was identified by Burney (1990: 63) in her report on street robbery, in which she stresses the importance of cultural and stylistic factors in contemporary street-crime: 'Poverty is, nevertheless, not the immediate motive for street crime, since most offenders do not lack necessities: rather they crave luxuries. The outstanding characteristic of young street offenders is their avid adherence to a group "style", which dictates a very expensive level of brand-name dressing, financed by crime' (cited in Young 1994).

18 See also S Cohen (1972) for an early version of this argument in relation to post-World War II society.

situation, the important thing to recognise is that today, *what people are now feeling deprived of is no longer simply the material product itself, but, rather, the sense of identity that products have come to bestow on the individual.*

This deprivation of identity appears to many individuals as a deprivation of a basic *right*, and thus consumption becomes not simply something that is culturally desirable, but something that is *fundamentally expected* – what one might describe as a changing rights discourse in relation to consumer practices. Consider, for example, how people in a consumer society believe they now have an implicit *right to consume*. The majority of people in Britain, for instance, now see a foreign holiday as an intrinsic right, even if its cost is prohibitive (indeed, life without such an annual break for many people would be inconceivable). Further evidence of this confusion between needs and desires is apparent in everyday modes of expression – 'I need new shoes', 'I simply must have a holiday'. This being the case, it is imperative that the wishes and the dreams of the individual are afforded greater coverage within theoretical circles, for no longer is consumer need tied in any simplistic sense to rising standards of living or expanded cultural expectations (as in Merton or Young's reading). The current situation is far more intense. In late modern society, need and desire have transmogrified, and as a consequence we now face a situation in which individual expectations are seen in terms of basic rights and are therefore no longer fettered by traditional economic or social restraints. On the contrary, a new untrammelled, straightforward form of desire prevails which bears no relation to classical notions of need whatsoever. A desire that no longer needs to be excused, an unapologetic, unrepentant sense of desire that ensures individuals are now furious at the very idea of need – 'Why should I have to justify my desire?', 'Why can't I have what I want?', 'If I want it, I need it!'

At this point it is possible to discern an important shift in explanatory frameworks in relation to the concept of relative deprivation. Specifically, one might suggest that what has been outlined above demands a move away from the *instrumentality* inherent in Merton's original strain theory towards a concept predicated more on the *expressivity* associated with new (and distinctly late modern) forms of desire. Such a situation has massive implications for our understanding of crime, for this is 'strain' on an unprecedented scale. It is interesting to evoke the psychoanalytical literature on desire (most obviously, the work of Jacques Lacan[19]) which sees desire as being attached to the lost object – or the fantasy of self-completion. In other words, what is being discussed here is the thematics of attaining something that is by definition beyond our grasp. This, in a sense, is the essence of a consumer society – *a constant sense of unfulfillment.* Morrison emphasises the tension that inevitably arises within a consumer culture when desire and fantasy become common currencies and when individual sense of identity and meaning become inextricably linked with desire and the 'lost affect':

Modernity gives us a series of expectations as to self-realization and personal growth – we are to become other than what we have been through the choosing of identities,

---

19 See also Deleuze and Guattari (1977) on the psychic structures of advanced capitalism and the important role of desire within these structures.

employment roles and seizing opportunities – but actual human beings have not fully escaped being defined by their location in situations of ennoblement and restraint. Human beings will be disappointed, they wish to take control of their selves, they wish to realise their (future) self-potential, but are located in demeaning and restraining circumstances – a crisis of action develops. (1995: 301)

In many cases, the 'crisis of action' Morrison refers to will be crime. Indeed, one might describe the situation outlined above as a recipe for criminality. This being the case, it is essential that any attempt to revamp the concept of relative deprivation takes into consideration *the concomitant forms of subjectivity* that are engendered by a fast-moving consumer culture, and attempts, when possible, to link this to criminal motivation (see below). Simply stated, emotions, sensations and consumer-orientated cognitions must now be located prominently on the criminological agenda. Interestingly, there is at least one commentator who has already recognised this fact: the American criminologist, Elliott Currie. Developing the work of Willem Bonger, Currie shares with Merton and Young the belief that market society creates crime by promoting standards of consumption which the vast majority of people can never feasibly achieve. However, he goes considerably further and points to the actual 'psychological distortions' that are engendered within individuals by a fast-paced consumer society (a theme already developed – albeit problematically – by certain Right realist criminologists: see below). Consider, for example, the following passage, which is worth quoting at some length, for all its tone of high moralism:

> One of the most chilling features of much violent street crime in America today, and also in some developing countries, is how directly it expresses the logic of immediate gratification in the pursuit of consumer goods, or of instant status and recognition ... People who study crime, perhaps especially from a 'progressive' perspective, sometimes shy away from looking hard at these less tangible 'moral' aspects ... A full analysis of these connections would need to consider, for example, the impact on crime of the specifically psychological distortions of market society, its tendencies to produce personalities less and less capable of relating to others except as consumer items or as trophies in a quest for recognition among one's peers. (Currie 1996: 348)

In the following sections I intend to develop this line of inquiry in more detail, albeit without lapsing into a simple moral critique of current social trends. Lastly, I will locate these ideas within the context of contemporary urban space, for it is within the high-tech, fast-paced contemporary city that consumer culture operates at its highest gear: fashion circulates faster; style sense is more acute; conspicuous consumption is more apparent; more sites and avenues of consumption abound; advertising and marketing are at their most pronounced; and the enhanced alienation and instantaneity associated with urban life result in a greater need for identity creation and individual differentiation.

Excitement, 'edgework' and risk: avenues for a 'controlled loss of control' in late modern life

One form of social response to the fundamental transformations and uncertainties of late modernity has been the emergence of various social agencies that attempt to deal with these changes through what has been characterised as a non-judgmental, non-reductive form of 'risk management' (Giddens 1990, 1991; Beck 1992). However, as Beck suggests in his influential text, *Risk Society*, often the very steps taken in a bid to stave off (or more accurately 'manage') risk serve only to produce new risks or exacerbate older ones. Thus, this new awareness of the consequence of our actions – what Beck describes as a heightened 'reflexivity' – can only intensify and make more anxious the sense of the 'juggernaut out of control' (see Chapter 2).

It is, however, interesting to look at the subject of risk from a somewhat different perspective, specifically, the way that many individuals are using risk (and associated practices) as a means of achieving a semblance of control – or, more accurately (following Featherstone 1994), a 'controlled sense of loss of control' – in the face of the changes and upheavals associated with late modernity. One might say that, rather than eschewing risk, the late modern subject is embracing it. Let us pause to consider this point in more detail. As alluded to above, one of the strange paradoxes of contemporary society is how, at the same moment, an individual can feel both ontologically insecure *and* – as a result of the increasing drive within everyday life towards the 'hyper-banalisation' of society – over-controlled. In other words, not only is it becoming more difficult to exert control and navigate a life pathway via the 'established' (and crumbling) norms and codes of modernity, but, at the same time, the individual is confronted by a reactive and burgeoning 'culture of control' (Garland 2001), whether in the form of state-imposed criminal legislation and other modes of rationalisation or private, decentralised, forms of surveillance and other techniques. Given such circumstances, might it not be the case, as outlined above, that many individuals will wish to escape this conflicting situation by exerting a sense of personal control and self-actualisation – to feel alive in an over-controlled *yet at the same time* highly unstable world? Moreover, might reflexive risk-calculation (such a prominent feature of our times) be the very instrumental device that enables that escape?

Indeed, within the various cultural practices associated with contemporary youth culture there is much evidence to suggest that risk-taking is becoming more pervasive. From the youthful (and now not so youthful) excesses associated with 'E' and 'rave' culture, car 'cruising' and 'binge drinking', to the rise in dangerous extreme sports (see Greenfield 1999) and hazardous adventure holidays,[20] high-risk 'day-trading'[21] and the upsurge in socially risky practices such as 'barebacking' (unprotected sex, something once again on the increase within the gay community: see M Davis 2000) and the use of hard drugs like heroin and cocaine, it seems that for many young people the greater the risk, the greater the

---

20 Adventure holidays are one of the fastest growing sectors of the tourist industry. Derek Moore, Director of extreme holiday company Explore World-wide ('which offers 200 different holidays to far-flung destinations including the uninhabited wilderness of Siberia'), estimates that over 100,000 adventure holidays are sold each year (Elliott and Woods 2001).

21 Rarely considered when discussing the phenomenal growth of high-risk day-trading is the fact that, in truth, injecting excitement into 'respectable' areas such as money making and investments is something of a novelty. Perhaps this accounts for the intense, if rather predictable, moral backlash – typically expressed in the terms 'rogue' or 'deviant capitalism' – against financial folk devils such as Nick Leeson, and the collapse of the 'dot com' and telecom bubbles.

attraction (on the way the market contributes to this situation, see below). Perhaps it should come as no surprise then that many of the forms of crime identified above also become a way of navigating a path through such uncertain times. But I am getting ahead of myself. Let us return to the question of how the conditions of late modernity are affecting everyday life, and in turn contributing to much criminality.

Stephen Lyng (1990) has explored what one would call the existential nature of voluntary risk-taking – or, as he prefers to call it, 'edgework' – in post-industrial society. According to Lyng, edgework involves:

> ... a clearly observable threat to one's physical or mental well-being or one's sense of an ordered existence. The archetypal edgework experience is one in which the individual's failure to meet the challenge at hand will result in death, or at the very least, debilitating injury. This type of edgework is best illustrated by such dangerous sports as skydiving, hang gliding, rock climbing, motor cycle racing/car racing, and downhill ski racing or by such dangerous occupations as fire fighting, test piloting, combat soldiering, movie stunt work and police work. The threat of death or injury is ever-present in such activities, although participants often claim that only those 'who don't know what they are doing' are at risk. (1990: 857)

For Lyng, edgework activities are a means of seizing control, a way of reacting against the 'unidentifiable forces that rob one of individual choice' (1990: 870).

Lyng's article raises many interesting questions about the use of risk-laden practices as a means of exerting a semblance of control. At this point an important question surfaces: is this whole discourse of risk essentially gendered (see, eg, Van Hoorebeeck 1997: 513; Howe 2000)? A growing body of feminist writing seeks to argue that risk discourse is couched in totalising narratives that ignore the particularities of gender, race and class.[22] The Canadian criminologists, Wendy Chan and George Rigakos, explain:

> A feminist analysis of women and risk seeks to expose the gendered nature of risk. To suggest that risk is gendered is to highlight how men and women are required to confront and negotiate different types of risk in their lives. For example, women's fear of crime is derived from engaging in their daily routine practices – activities which place them in situations where they are exposed to risks such as harassment, intimidation, and/or assault. For many women, this is the cost of participating in social life notwithstanding their engagement in any exceptionally risky or daring activities. Yet these risks have not been wholly recognized because what constitutes 'risky behaviour' is filtered through a masculine lens that conditions what we identify and define as 'risky'. Moreover, when women do take exceptional risks, the tendency is to conflate women's exceptional risk-taking with 'amorality' as in the case of promiscuity. (2002: 743)

It is from this position that Lyng's concept of 'edgework' is often criticised. Eleanor Miller (1991) suggests, for example, that Lyng is guilty of over-emphasising prototypically masculine, middle class (self-indulgent) pursuits while at the same time ignoring the inherent *everyday* risks faced by women simply for being female in a patriarchal society (eg, the threat of domestic violence or sexual abuse/assault; the

---

22 Eg, Stanko (1997); Walklate (1997).

risks associated with negotiating certain public spaces at certain times; 'fear of men', etc). Nowhere are these everyday strategies glamourised as 'edgework' or 'extreme sport' (Howe 2003: 279). Turning this around, by the same token Lyng's work can at least be taken as a plausible explanation for much *masculine* criminality. Developing this even further, Miller's own (1986) research allows us to be more precise about what should be called edgework and how it should be appreciated: she describes the risk-taking strategies of African American female street hustlers, an approach that indicates the value of extending the idea of edgework – or 'considered risk-taking' as a means of exerting control – to include women and other sections of society, such as the poor and the socially and racially excluded (compare with Lyng 1991), the very individuals who appear in Bauman's and Davis's accounts of the urban 'repressed'. In Miller's hands, Lyng's concept of 'edgework' is grounded in the make-or-break world of the urban street hustle, where class considerations (as well as those of race, gender and sexuality) are often the determining factor in the decision to 'play' with risk.

Miller's assertion makes perfect sense. Given my earlier arguments, the search for risk, hedonism and excitement requires an outlet – but the opportunities vary enormously, and in class/gender/neighbourhood-related ways – whether it be a certain activity, a form of experience, or indeed a specific type of space. In Lyng's account, such emotions are experienced on the cliff face, the racetrack, in the combat zone, during a sky dive, or other demarcated risk spaces. However, if one is not able to escape one's social environment to engage in licit risk-taking or edgework activities, then one has to find alternative outlets to play out these emotions. In a great many instances, the likelihood is that individuals will 'get their kicks' in spaces they know well (to use a term made famous by Brantingham and Brantingham (1984), within the 'cognitively known area'). In other words, the run-down estate or ghetto neighbourhood becomes a paradoxical space: on one hand, it symbolises the systematic powerlessness so often felt by the individuals who live in these environments; and on the other, the sink estate serves as a site of risk consumption that provides numerous illegal avenues. The ghetto becomes a 'performance zone' in which displays of risk, excitement, masculinity and even 'carnivalesque pleasure' in the form of rioting (see Presdee 2000: Chapter 3) are frequently perpetuated.

Drawing this together, we thus go beyond Katz's simple model of crime as an escape from/transcendence of the routine to present, instead, a 'control–excitement' model (understood via risk, hedonism, expressivity and the concept of edgework). Put simply, many forms of crime frequently perpetrated within urban areas should be seen for exactly what they are: attempts to achieve a semblance of control within ontologically insecure social worlds.

This idea that deviance is connected to reality construction and identity in late modern consumer society has also been explored in the fascinating book *Kamikaze Biker* by Ikuya Sato (1991). Sato's firsthand account of the motivations and phenomenology of *boso* driving culture in Japan (*boso* driving refers to the practice of illegal street-racing and high-risk, high-speed reckless driving displays undertaken by teenage – male! – Japanese car and motorcycle gangs or *bosozoku*) sheds some light on the experiential feelings of individuals involved in risk-laden, illegal activities – not least how certain feelings were common to the *bosozoku* when racing or eluding the police.[23] In particular, there is the sense that what they were doing was somehow 'bracketed off from everyday life'. Consequently, *bosozoku* self-reported that they experienced a 'loss of self-consciousness', the feeling that 'means-ends relationships were simplified', and the sense that *boso* driving involved a different temporal framework from 'ordinary life' (the work of Lyng and Sato is developed in more detail below).

Obviously, this argument applies more to crimes with a strong so-called 'expressive' element than it does to other, more utilitarian/rationalistic forms of criminality. (For example, joy-riding exemplifies these ideas in that it is both rich in excitement and may seem to offer a means of self-actualisation, while at the same time providing the participant with a physical means of traversing (and escaping) the socially deprived neighbourhood.) But one should not forget that these are the very crimes that abound within troubled inner-city neighbourhoods. Consequently, one might view such crimes as *urban edgework*, attempts to construct an enhanced sense of self by engaging in risk-laden practices on the metaphorical edge:

> On the one hand, there is the routinised alienation and boredom of everyday life – a world in which individuals find themselves over-controlled and yet without control. On the other hand, there are those activities which offer the possibility of excitement *and* control. Lyng's account focuses on extreme sports, whilst the new cultural criminology focuses on transgression. Although ostensibly dangerous, these activities offer a mode of being in which individuals take control through a calculated act of decontrol. The seductiveness of crime is not only linked to the inherent excitement of the acts involved, but also to the more general feelings of self-realisation and self-expression to which they give rise. It might be an unpalatable thought, but it is through such activities that individuals come alive. (Fenwick and Hayward 2000: 49)

The 'criminalisation of everyday life' versus the commodification of transgression

> Excitement, even ecstasy (the abandonment of reason and rationale), is the goal ... The quest for excitement is directly related to the breaking of boundaries, of confronting parameters and playing at the margins of social life in the challenging of controllers and their control mechanisms ... It is the realm of resentment and irrationality *par excellence* and also the realm of much crime. It is that part of social life that is unknowable to those in power and which therefore stands outside their consciousness and their understanding. They cannot understand it or indeed even 'read' it as real life, but only as immoral, uncivilised, obscene and unfathomable social behaviour. (Presdee 2000: 7–8)

In *Cultural Criminology and the Carnival of Crime*, Mike Presdee (2000) argues that, for many young people, the pleasure and excitement of transgression is double: not only as a direct corollary of a society currently undergoing pronounced change and reconstitution, but also as a reaction against a situation in which the only response of the state is to impose more intense forms of social control. Evoking Weber's (modernist) rubric of rationalisation, Presdee asserts that, in an effort to curb the

---

23 The considerable danger involved in *boso* driving should not be under-estimated. In 1980, 89 youths were killed and 1,097 injured in *boso*-related accidents. In 1983, a total of 6,711 *bosozoku* were arrested for 'dangerous behaviour' (Sato 1991: 20).

apparent increase in youth crime (compare Zimring 1998), Western governments have enacted a series of measures that add up to what he describes as 'the creeping criminalization of everyday life'. Ours is a world in which 'dominant and seemingly rational logics' act upon us and constrain us: 'As the individual becomes more and more trapped by applied science and the rational, so we become more and more enmeshed and oppressed within the so-called scientific measurement of our lives' (Presdee 2000: 159).

At this point it is worth reflecting on the exact nature of these 'rational logics'. On the one hand, there is the clearly punitive form (that is, prohibitive legislation, the move towards harsher punishment regimes for young offenders, banning orders and other reactionary measures); on the other hand, there are those measures based around an actuarial and calculative approach to the control and management of social problems – this latter approach being all about the creation of routines, conformity and acceptable social habits/behaviour. While traditionally these two forms of social control have been seen to have clear conceptual differences (eg, Foucault 1977 on the juridico-discursive versus disciplinary), in recent times the distinction between them has become noticeably blurred. In practice, a hybrid form of criminalisation/social control has emerged. For example, curfew orders, while seemingly punitive in essence, at the same time represent a move towards the conditioning and 'routinisation' of individual action.

Homogenising these two aspects, Presdee emphasises the paradox that the more the state imposes rationalising rubrics, the more it provokes in its citizens/subjects not compliant rationality, but rather heightened emotionality: '... we respond with irrational emotions derived from desire, pleasure and the sensualness of a postmodern commodity culture' (Presdee 2000: 29), hence a spiral in which this 'irrational response' provokes further punitive/rationalising moves from the state. Culture therefore becomes at once the site of excitement and social contestation, of experimentation and dissonance: 'It is a world full of contradictions, inequalities and struggle, yet it is a world where ... the pursuit of pleasure is potentially antagonistic to the state' (2000: 29). On this point, I am reminded of a quote from Zizek:

> On this level, power and resistance are effectively caught in a deadly embrace: there is no power without resistance (in order to function, power needs an X which eludes its grasp); there is no resistance without power (power is already formative of that very kernel on behalf of which the oppressed subject resists the hold of power). (1999: 252)

Presdee then reactivates the familiar language of moral panic (Young 1971; S Cohen 1972). Indeed, on the face of it, little has changed: the transgressive nature of youth (sub)cultural practice still provokes a general sense of fear and moral indignation; mass media coverage still serves to 'amplify deviance'; complex social phenomena continue to be reduced to simple causal relations; and politicians continue to fall over themselves in their attempts to curry favour with the 'moral majority' by vilifying and condemning the perceived 'immorality of contemporary youth'. This pervasive criminalisation process adds up to little more than a war against the young. From curfews to exclusion orders, from benefit reform to Public Disorder Acts, the government is turning the screw on the young, subjecting not only their 'oppositional forms of popular and personal pleasure' to increasing political arbitration and state agency sanction, but also their legitimate cultural practices and even, in many instances, their everyday round.[24]

In a not unfamiliar twist of this same axis, McRobbie and Thornton (1995) argue that moral panic in turn produces a response: for many young people, a decent dose of moral outrage remains the only acid test of a truly oppositional, and therefore worthwhile, cultural practice. Indeed, even this response has been, literally, incorporated. Corporations are now actively using moral panics (in the form of 'a bit of controversy – the threat of censorship, the suggestion of sexual scandal or subversive activity': 1995) for their own ends. This point is illustrated in Presdee's memorable account of the way that successive governments attempted (largely in vain) to criminalise and regulate one of the most popular forms of youth expression: contemporary club ('rave') culture (see Presdee 2000: Chapter 7). In this account we see how such intense forms of social control are always destined to fail – one need only look at the abject failure of current anti-drug legislation to recognise this to be the case. Certainly, the collective efforts of UK governments during the 1990s to regulate club culture and outlaw many of its associated *sub rosa* activities served only to train the spotlight of attention more firmly on the 'club scene' – in both its underground and its more mainstream manifestations. Once again we are forced to consider just how entwined is the relationship between the various processes that serve to vilify and ultimately criminalise the cultural practices of the young, and the very reasons why many young people actually engage in these practices in the first place:

> Being 'young' is characterised by a culture created out of the tensions that emanate between regulation and rebellion; control and care; the civilised and the savage. The result is a carnivalesque culture that forever pushes at the boundaries of transgression ... Their culture, rather than being a search for the 'authentic' as in modern culture, is an endless *search for the inauthentic*; that is, a culture that is empty of the authority and the imperatives that come with authenticity. It is this perceived 'emptiness as protest' that prompts panic from 'adult' society. (2000: 114, emphasis added)

As well as making the obvious (Foucauldian) points about repression/control proliferating rather than suppressing its object of alteration, what is interesting

---

24 Rationality is exerting its grip on the lives of young people in a number of new ways and at a much earlier age. At the governmental level, 'New' Labour's Crime and Disorder Act 1998 introduced local curfew schemes for children below the age of 10, while detention and treatment orders include provision for the imprisonment of children from the age of 12. However, more worrying is the bizarre series of rationalising practices that appear almost daily in our paranoid culture (see Furedi 2002). These range from instrumental measures, such as the recent introduction of CCTV cameras into classrooms in certain schools in Manchester in a bid to monitor the behaviour of unruly students (a council-funded measure that received the full support of staff and parents alike!), to the downright ludicrous, such as the ban imposed last winter at Fairway School, Norwich, prohibiting pupils from throwing snowballs at their classmates unless they first secured the target's written permission. Add to this the growth of drug-testing – both at the workplace (Tunnell 2004) and at places where young people go to enjoy themselves (I refer here to the introduction of drug-testing in pubs and clubs: Utley 2002) – the seemingly inexorable rise of congestion charges, and the likely future implementation of automatic speed limiters in cars, and it seems that young people's lives are likely to be subject to increasing levels of circumspection.

about Presdee's account is the notion of 'the search for the *in*authentic' – indicating a social logic considerably altered since Cohen's classic work. Certainly, this, in my opinion, can help us understand intensified social and state responses, for as Docker (1994: 117) has pointed out, while in cultural terms modernism protested against the contemporary world, the issues of young people could still be understood in terms of their search for an authentic self and the need to break free from the constraints of imposed rationality and authority. However, the 'search for the inauthentic', as Presdee seems to be suggesting, is something very different – a break with this modernist 'tradition' and a refusal to engage with established tropes of meaning-making (at this point, Presdee's argument, albeit implicitly, is highly commensurate with Morrison's conception of the 'subject in transition'). No wonder such resistance produces a greater fury.[25]

Yet it is not only as prohibition (or discipline, or indeed administrative/ actuarial criminology) that the 'wider society' engages with cultural forms that are tied in to the production of youth identity, including how images of crime are inscribed in this process (see Young 1996 for a more developed version of this argument). Let us now turn to how that other great agent of social reaction – the market – is participating in the process of promoting and marketing of transgression.

Postmodernism (as eloquently illustrated by Harvey and Jameson: see Chapter 2) celebrates heterogeneity, depthlessness, unpredictability, risk, inauthenticity and technological advances in communication, media and consumer culture (hence also a note of caution about the all too easy use of such terms as 'self-actualisation' and 'identity'). Nowhere are these cultural tendencies more in evidence than in contemporary youth culture. What is important in this context, however, is the way that, in recent years, corporate capitalism has increasingly come to rely on images of crime as a means of selling products in the youth market (Fenwick and Hayward 2000: 43–46). Certainly, crime has long sold. The compelling and sometimes salacious nature of certain criminal acts ensures a ready audience for crime, and it remained an enduring theme in popular culture throughout the 20th century (one need only look at the various songs and publications that surrounded the Whitechapel Murders in London over a century ago to recognise this to be the case: see Curtis 2002). What has changed, however, is both the force and range of the message. Crime has been seized upon: it is being packaged and marketed to young people as a romantic, exciting, cool and fashionable cultural symbol. It is in this cultural context that transgression becomes a desirable consumer choice. Within consumer culture, crime is being aestheticised and stylised, presented in the mass media on a par with a fashion aesthetic. This is not to suggest any simple deterministic link between images of violence and crime in consumer culture and contemporary youth crime; it is simply to suggest that the

---

25 It is interesting here to refer back to the quote by de Certeau in Chapter 4: 'If it is true that the grid of "discipline" is everywhere becoming clearer and more extensive, it is all the more urgent to discover how an entire society resists being reduced to it, what popular procedures (also "minuscule" and quotidian) manipulate the mechanisms of discipline and conform to them only in order to evade them' (de Certeau 1984: xiv).

distinction between representations of criminality and the pursuit of excitement, especially in the area of youth culture, is becoming extremely blurred.

One obvious example of this 're-branding' of crime is the way in which 'gangster' rap combines images of criminality with street gang iconography and designer chic to create a product that is immediately seductive to youth audiences. For instance, in recent years it has become very difficult to tell whether 'gangster rap' imagery and styling is shaping street gang culture in the US or vice versa. Since the 1980s, many cultural symbols of rap music, such as branded sports apparel and designer clothing, have been used by street gangs as a means of 'flagging' gang affiliations (J Miller 1995). Add to this the fact that several major rap artists like Tupac Shakur and the Notorious BIG have been murdered in a long-running feud between East and West Coast rap artists, and it immediately becomes apparent that, at least in the field of gangster rap, art and real life are becoming ever more intertwined.[26] Importantly, incorporating images of crime in music is not solely confined to rap. From the controversial Body Count album, *Cop Killer*, and the skate-punk group MDC (Millions of Dead Cops) to the sophisticated urban hip-hop of the Fun Lovin' Criminals, crime has become a major theme in youth-orientated commercial music. Perhaps the most explicit example is the recent video for the song *(It's Gonna Be A) Lovely Day* by clubbers' favourite Braccacio and Aisher: it depicts the theft and burning (or 'hotting' as it is known) of a stolen car. Interestingly, the narrative of the video is reversed so that the theft of the vehicle is the last thing we see – yet another example of the distortion of temporal frameworks at work in popular culture (see Chapter 2).

Stylised images of crime abound in many other areas of the mass media, sending mixed messages to a young audience who often take their lead from popular and consumer culture. In film, slick production values and carefully selected soundtracks glamorise violent crime and drug-dealing. The central characters in films such as *Pulp Fiction, New Jack City, Trainspotting, Reservoir Dogs, True Romance* and *Natural Born Killers* are then lionised as cool, popular culture icons. Likewise on television, crime is being packaged as entertainment. Shows in the US like *America's Most Wanted, Justice Files, Cops, Top Cops* and *America's Dumbest Criminals* (many of which are shown on major satellite stations in the UK), and *Police, Camera, Action, Crimewatch Files* and *Crime Report* in the UK are little more than a mixture of dramatic case re-enactments and real life crime footage, cobbled together to provide audiences with a vicarious televisual cheap thrill (Fenwick and Hayward 2000: 45–46). The most extreme example of this tendency, however, must be the prime time Russian TV show, *Intercept*, in which

---

26 Interestingly, as rap and hip-hop have become a part of the aural backdrop to urban life, the lyrical content of (now) mainstream songs, like 50 Cent's huge recent worldwide hit *PIMP* (lyrics unreproducible here!), has gone increasingly unnoticed. While only roughly two decades ago moral outrage (censure, see Sumner 1994) ensured that fairly innocuous pop songs, like Frankie Goes to Hollywood's hit *Relax*, were banned, now, it seems, any attempt to censor lyrical content is seen as evidence of authoritarianism, or at the very least a reactionary gesture that runs contrary to a culture of acceptance and the dominance of youth. Thus, in lieu of any counter protest (or indeed serious debate), levels of misogyny, homophobia and the glorification of urban violence continue to be ratcheted up.

'contestants' are required to steal a car live on air. If they successfully avoid the police for the duration of the show they win the game and a series of prizes. Not quite as socially irresponsible but almost as tasteless is UK terrestrial station Channel 5's recent (typically low brow) offering, *Swag*, in which various forms of street crime (such as car thefts and robbery) are simulated by actors in a bid to hoodwink unsuspecting members of the public for the purposes of 'comic' effect. In turn, with its compelling mix of nihilistic-hedonism, the popular MTV spin-off show (and now major feature film) *Jackass* illustrates how certain forms of extreme transgressive behaviour (including such ill-advised activities as shooting oneself in the face with pepper spray and scuba diving in municipal sewage plants!) are crossing over into mainstream entertainment (see, eg, the highly derivative MTV spin-off shows *Dirty Sanchez*, *Viva La Bam* and *The New Tom Green Show*, as well as Sky One's *Fear Factor*, ITV's *Wudja Cudja*? and Channel 4's tawdry game show *Distraction*).

It does not stop there: images of crime and transgression are now prominent themes in major advertising campaigns. In-car entertainment manufacturers Kenwood – the car stereo of choice for any discerning 'boy racer' – recently used the strapline, 'We want to be free to do what we want to do', underneath a photograph of the poll tax riots (see Plate 16), an image clearly designed to tap into many of the subjectivities associated with transgressive driving and the *sub rosa* worlds of 'hotting' and car 'cruising'. Likewise, a whole host of car manufacturers have also chosen to base recent campaigns around the theme of transgression. Nissan, for example, promote their *Shogun* model with the strapline 'Joyriding' – somewhat ironic given that throughout the 1990s the Nissan *Shogun* was often a very popular choice for 'ram raiders' and 'hoisting' firms! Another Nissan model, the *X-Trail*, was similarly marketed by playing with the idea of risk, excitement and danger, the TV commercial depicting a series of clips of dangerous sports while the voiceover proclaimed '*X-Trail* – extreme, emotion, expression'. Not to be outdone, the German manufacturer, Audi – a company who, for years, have sought to cultivate an image of Germanic refinement and efficiency – also tapped in to this transgressive sensibility in a recent commercial for their *A3* model. Against the backdrop of trance music, the central figure (a young man, obviously) sets light to a huge pyre in the desert. He then systematically burns family mementos and other such trappings of domesticity, before speeding off into the desert night and a new life of unencumbered excitement. One cannot help but wonder how the owners of these cars feel when sat in gridlock on the M25!

Even Prince Charles has got in on the act. A recent poster advertisement for the Prince's Trust Volunteers posed the question, 'How high can you get?' ('The fleur-de-lis has been manipulated to connote a marijuana leaf and the accompanying text clearly makes reference to phrases more commonly associated with drugs parlance': Issy Harvey 2000: 127). Whether it is the Scottish comedian Billy Connolly defacing a bus shelter with a marker pen in a commercial for the National Lottery, or self-styled 'hard man' Vinny Jones attaching his own particular tawdry brand of brooding violence to drinks company Bacardi, transgression is now a major weapon in the advertisers' arsenal. This point is further exemplified by the emergence of a marketing technique known as 'brandalism', a process by which marketeers use subversive means such as graffiti and illegal 'fly posters' to serve corporate ends (see also Alvelos 2004).[27] The journalist Richard Benson explains:

> Most of the surfaces in the square are currently covered with stickers and flyposters advertising, among other things, Travis, Elle Macpherson's lingerie company, and, ironically, George Monbiot's *Captive State*, a book which attacks brands' incursions into public spaces. You'll also find, tied to the railings, white ribbons with the name of a new East London art gallery written on them, and glued to the pavement, a hard-wearing ad for a website selling art. On the walls you'll see the name of several bands, in spray paint. From vandalism to brandalism. These are all examples of a phenomenon known as 'ambient advertising' (the placing of ads where people don't expect to see them) or 'guerilla marketing' (any marketing that goes through unconventional channels). (2001: 43)[28]

Nowhere, however, is the tendency more apparent than in the world of video gaming. Violent imagery has always played a major part in this pastime, most notably in role-playing and 'shoot 'em up' games. However, in recent years, game developers have begun to produce games like *Kingpin* that use criminal activities as their central theme, the two most famous examples being *Carmaggedon II* and *Grand Theft Auto III* (earlier versions of both games had their release dates put back while their content was reviewed by censors). *Carmaggedon II* celebrates reckless and aggressive driving, while in *Grand Theft Auto III* players traverse an urban landscape (the ironically named Liberty City) by hopping from one stolen car to another, gaining extra points by mugging passers-by and eluding the hapless police. *Grand Theft Auto III* was even advertised as 'The ultimate crime simulation game', with one gushing game reviewer declaring: 'This is a violent, thoroughly immoral game, but Jesus it's fun ... Steal a copy today' (Pizey 2001). These games provide their predominantly young audience with vicarious excitement from activities that are at best questionable (Fenwick and Hayward 2000: 45).[29]

Even that old family favourite, the board game, has received a crime 'makeover'. *Ghettopoly* is a MONOPOLY-style game in which 'playas' move

---

27 With this new approach, advertisers are themselves inverting the established practice of 'culture jamming' (see Dery 1993; Lasn 2000; Taylor 2004: 493), a technique in which billboards and other 'signs and significations of the mass media are hijacked and diverted to draw attention to the original message and create new messages with radically different intent ... [eg] "Tropical blend. The Savage Tan" becomes "Typical blend. Sex in adds"' (Creswell 1998: 274). This technique is far more prevalent than you might think. Even as I write this footnote, I can see from my window an 'altered' billboard. Someone has taken a spray can to a Nike advert for the RunLondon 10k fun race that reads 'I'll do it if you do it'. Underneath, they have simply inserted the word 'Revolt' and a series of anarchy signs (see Plate 17)! (On this last point, see also Ritson 2000; Williams 2000.)

28 Similar subversive practices, such as chalking symbols on the wall of a corporate office block, or 'tagging' the pavement outside a multi-media company, are often used by computer hackers as a way of pointing out buildings with computer systems that can be used for free, cable-less digital 'hook ups'.

29 Given the emphasis placed on emotionality and control in this chapter it is worth pausing to consider how the leading games console manufacturers are prioritising very similar concerns in their marketing strategies. Microsoft's *X-Box* has as its strapline, 'See more, hear more, feel more', while Sony *Playstation* runs the ancillary website www.playstationemotions.com. Indeed, a recent advertisement for *Playstation* strangely echoes one of the central themes of this chapter: 'For years I've lived a double life. In the day I go to work, roll up my sleeves with the hoi polloi. At night I live a double life of adrenaline of missed heartbeats and exhilaration – a life of dubious virtue. Though you might not think it to look at me, I've controlled armies and conquered worlds. And though I've set morality aside – at least I can say I've lived.'

around from 'Tyron's Gun Shop' to 'Ling Ling's Massage Parlour', building crack houses, 'pimping' and selling guns as they go. In *Ghettopoly* the 'chance' cards declare, 'You got your whole neighbourhood addicted to crack. Collect $75'; another says, 'You are a little short of cash so you decide to stick up a bank. Collect $75' (Harwood 2003). Perhaps the most interesting recent example of this 'genre mixing', however, was the reaction to the murder of TV presenter Jill Dando and the thought that it must be in some way linked with her role on the popular BBC show *Crimewatch*.

To conclude, while the state responds to the reconfigurations and transformations associated with the late modern condition by imposing what it believes to be more 'rational' forms of control and authority, the market takes a very different approach. Rather than attempting to curtail the excitement and emotionality that, for many individuals, is the preferred antidote to ontological precariousness, the market chooses instead to celebrate and, very importantly, commodify these same sensations. Whether via the 'vicarious televisual cheap thrill' of 'Real Crime' TV shows (Baudrillard 1983), the 'Gothic' pleasure derived from membership of one of the many serial killer 'fan clubs' that abound on the Internet,[30] or the fun experienced whilst traversing so-called 'digital crime environments' (see above), images of criminality are now firmly tied into the production of youth culture/identity and inscribed in numerous forms of related entertainment and performance. The full ramifications of such a situation are, of course, still unfolding, but, as articulated by Presdee, we must now confront a situation in which:

> ... individualism, greed, destruction, dishonesty, fear and violence are woven, through the processes of production and consumption, inevitably into all our everyday lives. Now crime, in the form of a commodity, enables us all to consume without cost as we enjoy the excitement, and the emotions of hate, rage and love that crime often contains. (2000: 58)[31]

'Neophilia': 'sensation-gatherers' and the 'pursuit of the new'[32]

> ... the work ethic has been replaced by a consumer ethic; the savings-book culture of delayed gratification has been replaced by the credit-card culture that 'takes the waiting out of wanting'. (Bauman 1997: 24)

Historically, the insatiability of desire has been regarded as a symptom of a certain moral pathology (be it sin or decadence), or as a sign of status amongst social elites. However, a unique feature of late modern consumer culture is that insatiable desire

---

30 On the 'Gothic' (and its relationship with transgression) in contemporary culture, see Davenport-Hines (1998).

31 It is also interesting to reflect on the possible de-sanitising effects of many of these forms of 'entertainment'. Presdee again (note also the emphasis on instantaneity in the following quote): 'In its consumption, violence is simplified and reduced to a trivial act of instant enjoyment; it thereby becomes no different from, say, the eating of a chocolate biscuit or the drinking of a can of coke. There is no moral debate, no constraint, no remorse, no meaning. This is disposable violence that need not concern us or delay us in our journey through the week. It is violence without responsibility' (2000: 65).

32 An earlier version of this section appeared as Fenwick and Hayward (2000).

– the constant demand for more – is now not only normal but necessary for the continuance of the socio-economic order. The 'very essence' of modern consumption is that it is 'an activity which involves an apparently endless pursuit of want':

> The modern consumer is characterised by an insatiability which arises out of a basic inexhaustibility of wants themselves, which forever arise, phoenix-like from the ashes of their predecessors. Hence no sooner is one satisfied than another is waiting in line clamouring to be satisfied, when this one is attended to, a third appears, then subsequently a fourth, and so on, apparently without end. The process is ceaseless and unbroken; rarely can an inhabitant of modern society, no matter how privileged or wealthy, declare that there is nothing that they want. That this should be so is a matter of wonder. (Campbell 1989: 37)

This insatiability of desire is not some unintended or unwanted 'side-effect' of consumerism, but is instead absolutely essential to its survival. If our desires were satiated we would stop consuming; if this were to happen on a mass scale, the current order would cease to function altogether. As Presdee puts it:

> Consumption becomes the cultural activity, which by its nature has a short shelf-life and needs to be constantly reproduced. We cannot consume only one day in twenty, we must consume, we must desire commodities, all the time. New excitements and desires become an essential part of everyday life. Excitement under these conditions becomes a commodity to be bought, sold and consumed like all other objects. (1994: 181)

One of the central tasks consumer culture therefore sets itself is the production of subjects who are constantly on the lookout for new commodities and alternative experiences – what Campbell (1989) refers to as 'neophiliacs' or lovers of novelty. Consumerism is a culture of experimentation and, perhaps paradoxically, given the perceived 'benefits' it brings, a culture of terminal dissatisfaction,[33] a world where the pursuit of the new (now combined with the ideology of 'personal growth') is valued above a more cautious satisfaction with what one has or is (see Chapter 2, and also O'Malley 1993).

Zygmunt Bauman (1997: 146) coined the phrase 'sensation-gatherers' to characterise this peculiarly postmodern form of subjectivity (again, in Bauman's use of the term 'sensation', we see an emphasis being placed on emotion). Focusing on the deregulation and privatisation of desire within contemporary culture, he describes how the 'soldier-producer' of industrial capitalism has been supplanted by a different type of subject who constantly craves new experience. Bauman describes a series of emotions that might be seen as characterising the 'sensation-gatherers': impulsivity, dissatisfaction, narcissism and spontaneity. Although

---

33 This dissatisfaction is superbly illustrated in Craig Thompson's (1994) paper on the broad disparity that often exists between the 'idealized and actual benefits' to consumers of technological and electronic consumer products. See also Barry Richards' (1994) notion of 'Neophobia', the anxiety that many people feel when confronted with new products such as digital cameras or personal computers. A recent example of this dissatisfaction would be the ongoing furore over picture-messaging phones (see Shaikh 2002). While advertisements for these expensive new phones showed pin-sharp digital photographic images being transferred from phone to phone, the reality was very different. The images are often washed out, hazy and difficult to decipher. Telephone companies later conceded that the images used to advertise these phones were actually taken by expensive, high-resolution digital cameras.

Bauman does not specify any generational distinctions, it is clear that this desire for the new will be developed most acutely within younger members of society (not least because it is this group that is exposed to the most aggressive forms of so-called 'lifestyle advertising': see Shields 1992); as we know, the vast majority of crime is perpetrated by young males between the ages of approximately 14 and 25 (eg, Gottfredson and Hirschi 1990: Chapter 6; *Bureau of Justice Statistics* 1995). It would seem clear that the kinds of activities mentioned above – joyriding, football hooliganism, drug-use, mugging and gang membership – are attractive precisely because they offer novel, unconventional and illegal forms of excitement.[34] They represent a break with the banalities of everyday life and mark an entry into a new world of possibilities and pleasures. The seductiveness of crime may thus derive, in large part, from the new kinds of *sensations* which it offers. In a culture which encourages this strange combination of perpetual dissatisfaction and a longing for the new, it is hardly surprising that so many young people (irrespective of class) are seduced by the existential possibilities offered by criminal activities, as these contrast so sharply with the routine of their everyday lives.

There is another feature of contemporary forms of desire that can help us understand why individuals tend to become separated from prevailing normative values. In addition to being insatiable, consumer culture also cultivates a desire for *immediate, rather than delayed, gratification*. Again, this represents an historical shift of some importance. Consider Baudrillard's account of Victorian concepts of ownership:

> Objects once acquired were owned in the full sense, for they were a material expression of work done. It is still not very long since buying a dinner table and chairs, or a car, represented the end-point of a sustained exercise in thrift. People worked dreaming of what they might later acquire; life was lived in accordance with the puritan notion of effort and its reward – an object finally won represented repayment for the past and security for the future. (1996: 158–59)

Today, a new 'morality' exists where consumption has precedence over accumulation, where 'forward flight, forced investment, speeded-up consumption and the absurdity of saving provide the motors of our whole present system of buying first and paying off later' (1996: 163).

The significance of this change lies not least in its implications for our experience of time.[35] Whereas in the past, personal identity was forged through a 'temporal unification of the past and the future with the present before me', the *privileging of the present* associated with consumerism cultivates 'an inability to unify the past, present and future of our own biographical experience of psychic life' (Jameson

---

34 For a recent commentary on this specific point in relation to football hooliganism, see Munday (2004).

35 One of the more striking paradoxes of the 20th century is that, whilst we initially believed that the latter decades of the 20th century would be an 'age of leisure' – a period in which technology would free up time – in fact the opposite has happened. In the offices and workplaces of the 21st century, time is more precious than ever, with individuals working longer hours under greater pressure (Schor 1992). As Thompson (1994: 107) points out: 'The products created to "save" time have ironically become implicated in a cultural time "shortage"; in a dialectical fashion, the accelerated speed of our technological equipment seems to have accelerated the pace of our lives.'

1991: 26; see Chapter 2). Thus, experience is reduced to 'a series of pure and unrelated presents', a series of 'nows'. As for the past, so for the future: the idea of saving, of any sort of postponement predicated on an expected future, becomes meaningless. This is not a moral issue (as for, say, Elliott Currie) of those who choose to 'flout' the long-term view. Rather, it is simply to suggest that, as a consequence of the bombardment of stimuli associated with today's postmodern spaces/cultures, the experience of the present (the immediate) becomes overwhelmingly vivid and intense:

> The image, the appearance, the spectacle can all be experienced with an intensity (joy or terror) made possible by their appreciation as pure and unrelated presents in time. So what does it matter 'if the world thereby momentarily loses its depth and threatens to become a glossy skin, a stereoscopic illusion, a rush of filmic images without density'. (Jameson 1991)

> The immediacy of events, the sensationalism of the spectacle (political, scientific, military, as well as those of entertainment), become the stuff of which consciousness is forged. (Harvey 1990: 54)

Bauman refers to something similar when he observes that the 'arousing of new desires' has replaced 'normative regulation' (Bauman 1997: 146). Not only are we constantly on the look out for new and ever more thrilling experiences, but we inhabit a world where old normative systems cease to matter, or at least, they are momentarily repressed during the act of transgression. With its particular emphasis on the 'new' and the 'now', consumer culture separates young people from the consequences of their actions and makes them more likely to engage in a pursuit of excitement which may well be reckless and damaging to others.

Impulsivity as a feature of late modern life: a convergence in thinking with regard to crime and consumerism

Insatiability of desire, then, is an installed feature of society. From the Lottery to *Loaded* magazine, from digitised 'sales loops'[36] to the expansion of credit facilities,[37] we are, at a societal level, increasingly encouraged to eschew long-term conservatism and pursue instead a course toward individual gratification, plotted by materialistic desires and located as sources of pleasure and identity. Such a breakdown in temporality coupled with the concomitant search for instantaneous experiences has real consequences, not least in terms of attitudes towards social

---

36 In a world increasingly reliant upon the Internet, the 'sales loop' is getting ever tighter, creating what has been described as 'the ultimate in instant gratification' (Kessler 1997: 86 see Chapter 2). One area where this practice is particularly acute is in the world of on-line gambling. In recent years, there has been an explosion in Internet casinos. For example, a year ago, there were 30 poker websites; now there are 140. The on-line gambling industry in the UK is now estimated to be worth £3.5 billion. The downside, of course, is the rising number of on-line gambling addicts, creating what Mark Griffiths of Nottingham Trent University has described as 'a subculture of secret gamblers' (cited in Barkham and Walsh 2004).

37 See Ritzer (1995); Spiers (1995); Singletary and Crenshaw (1996). Interestingly, in recent times even the credit card itself has succumbed to the processes of 'stylisation'. Consider this slice of copy from a recent credit card advertisement: 'With its cutting-edge design of a curved corner and innovative see-through middle, the revolutionary new RBS Advanta mc2 Card certainly looks great.' One can only wonder whether a see-through card will make paying the bill any easier at the end of each month!

norms. Certainly, if one thinks about the conjunction of these new forms of consciousness with the heightened sense of strain as outlined earlier, one is forced to consider serious questions about the particular relationships between expressive desires and normative regulation. Following this line of inquiry, is it possible to identify any approaches within the criminological enterprise that have begun to engage (albeit tangentially) with some of these features? In what follows, I intend to highlight a convergence in thinking currently taking place regarding notions of instant gratification (in all its various forms) within diverse branches of the social sciences. In particular, the focus will be on the concept of 'impulsivity' and its increasing currency within varied, often conflicting, theoretical perspectives.

For some time, instant gratification (at the individual level) has been recognised within psychological circles as a vital element in explaining anti-social and criminal behaviour.[38] Despite often conflicting opinions regarding the nature of the category of 'willpower', psychologists have continued to develop explanatory models and theories of delinquency and criminality that draw heavily upon the constructs of impulsivity, instant gratification and the delay of gratification paradigm. Similarly, failure to delay gratification has long been seen as a central feature of the psychopathic personality.[39] Considerable work has also been undertaken into the way in which supposed deficits in impulse control can bring about delinquent behaviour by interfering with children's ability to control their behaviour and to think of the future consequences of deviant acts.[40]

Most famously from a purely criminological perspective, Wilson and Herrnstein (1985) asserted that personality differences in traits such as impulsivity may be strongly related to the development of frequent and long-term anti-social behaviour. Central to their reading of criminality is the concept of 'present orientation': the idea that a 'rapid cognitive tempo' and 'shortened time horizons' are responsible for impulsive and disinhibited behaviour. This line of thinking is extremely apparent in right realist criminology more generally. While, typically, discussions of right realism make much of both the cognitive strategies of rational choice and the causal influence of social conditioning, less is made of the converse, the fact that impulsivity and instant gratification are also central planks of right realist thought. On the face of it, right realists might appear to be agnostic about why someone sets out to commit a crime, but buried deep within these criminologies is an implicit concern with the emotional element of criminality – namely, the conceptions of 'self-expression' and 'self-control'. Consider, for instance, Wilson's text *Thinking About Crime* (1985), perhaps the cornerstone of right realist theory. Often neglected in this work is the great store Wilson places on the emotions that act on and affect 'internalized commitment to self-control'. For example, at one point, Wilson (1985: 237–38) asserts that, as a result of the erosion of the modernist moral order, two contrasting modes of self-expression have emerged: first, rampant individualism linked to immediate gratification and greed; and, secondly, a more innovative and

---

38 Eg, Buss (1966); Maher (1966); Eysenck (1970); Robins (1978).
39 See Unikel and Blanchard (1973); Blanchard *et al* (1977); Widom (1977); Newman *et al* (1990, 1992).
40 See Farrington *et al* (1990); Moffitt (1993); White *et al* (1994).

creative sense of individualism (what Ian Taylor (1999) – proceeding, of course, from a very different ideological position – might describe as 'entrepreneurship'). Given his overarching moral position, it is the former that is of most concern to Wilson. Consider this passage from his collaboration with Richard Herrnstein (closely reminiscent of classic social control theory *à la* Travis Hirschi):

> ... broad social and cultural changes in the level and intensity of society's investment (via families, schools, churches, and the mass media) in inculcating an internalized commitment to self-control will affect the extent to which individuals at risk are willing to postpone gratification, accept as equitable the outcomes of others, and conform to rules. (Wilson and Herrnstein 1985: 437)

The problem is that Wilson's critique of immediate gratification, the rise of nouveau fully-fledged individualism and the concept of self-control (and thus his theory of crime more generally) remains one-dimensional. Wilson can only frame his analysis in terms of a perceived loss of 'traditional' (ie, modern, or, more accurately, a mix of modern and traditional) forms – the erosion of the 'Protestant work ethic' and, more importantly, the demise of community values (remember the centrepiece of Wilson's argument is that crime begets crime at a community level). By placing the concepts of impulsivity and immediate gratification so squarely within the context of a lack of social cohesion and disinvestment in society, Wilson presents us with a reading of these important aspects of criminality that is ultimately rooted in a set of conservative morals. By the same token, he chooses to ignore the fact that, in reality, these 'impulsive', 'disinvested' urbanites are simply the obvious end-products of an unmediated system of consumer capitalism. Consequently, right realists like Wilson are never able to *separate out* sociological descriptions of cultural change from their moral critique of these changes – nor, for that matter, can they rein in their moral contempt for those individuals who (for whatever reason) 'are unable to assert a sense of self control' or sufficiently delay gratification, and thus are labelled by right realists as 'lacking in moral fibre'.

The development of an (allegedly) more 'fully inclusive' concept of impulsivity is well underway elsewhere, albeit from a strictly non-criminological perspective and, not surprisingly, where one would most expect it, *the market*. In the fields of economic psychology and consumer research, traditional rational choice models of self-control and consumer decision-making are being significantly revised as researchers factor in the important visceral and emotional factors that are seen by many as a major feature of what has been described as 'hedonic consumption' (see Williams and Burns 1994).[41]

Traditionally, in the field of consumer research, consumer choices and behavioural patterns have been understood in terms of rational choice models that explain purchases in terms of consumers weighing the costs and benefits of alternatives. In these normative models (much the same as in rational choice models of crime) consumers are viewed as 'dispassionate information processors'.[42] However, such models have proved unable to answer the important question with

---

41 Colin Campbell uses the similar term 'mentalistic hedonism' (1995: 118–19).
42 Eg, Katona (1951, 1975); Bettman (1979); Peter and Olson (1994); Miller (1995: 12–19).

which this literature concerns itself: *why do consumers frequently act against their own better judgment and engage in spending they later regret?*[43] Consequently, a new school of thought has emerged that concentrates instead on the role played by short-term *emotional* factors in the consumption process.[44] This division in the field of consumer research can be conceptualised as a trade-off between 'interests' (normative rational behaviour) and 'passions' (impulsive or *akratic* action: the word *akratia* originates in Aristotelian ethics – the weak-willed person: Hoch and Lowenstein 1991: 493).[45] Interestingly, this theoretical divide closely resembles the staunch opposition that exists within contemporary criminology between, on the one hand, theories of crime predicated on classical notions of rationality and, on the other, aetiological explanations that stress instead the centrality of individual emotions and cultural concerns in the commission of the criminal act (*à la* Katz). However, rather than pulling in different directions (as has so long been the case within criminological theory), research into consumer behaviour is attempting to bridge the division between rationality and emotionality. New research is being undertaken that acknowledges the importance of *both* positions (see Belk 1995 for a general review).[46] Such an ethos is illustrated in this statement by Hoch and Lowenstein:

> Our economic-psychological model of self-control stands at the intersection of two broad currents in consumer behaviour research. One perspective views decision-making as rational and dispassionate; the other views it as visceral and emotional. Thus the desire-willpower framework provides an ideal arena for examining the interaction between rational and hedonic motives. These two types of psychological processes are normally compartmentalized into separate literatures. Although each perspective adequately describes a wide range of consumer behaviours, neither alone can provide an adequate account of the decision-making process. (1991: 504)[47]

There does, then, appear to be some mutual ground around the subjects of instant gratification and impulsivity on which very different theoretical perspectives can co-exist and indeed flourish. If conscious impulsivity is becoming a characteristic feature of late modern society, might it not be the case that further exploration of this line of inquiry could provide a possible way forward for criminology to reconcile many of its polarised theoretical positions?

---

43 Consider Daniel Miller: 'At present *"homo economicus"* is a powerful tool of ideological legitimation for academic, politician and consumer. But it remains so far from the actual practice of consumption that it is unlikely that many consumers or many economists actually believe this representation, even though they may find it expedient to defend it' (1995: 19). One could make a very similar case for rational choice theories of crime (see Chapter 3).

44 See Hirschman and Holbrook (1982); Holbrook and Hirschman (1986); Mick and DeMoss (1990); Williams and Burns (1994). In one recent survey of over 4,200 consumers, it was confirmed that over 60% of supermarket purchases and an amazing 53% of mass merchandise purchases were 'unplanned' (POP Advertising Institute 1995, cited in Wood 1998: 314).

45 *Akratic* impulse buying is defined as 'unplanned purchases, undertaken with little or no deliberation, accompanied by affectual or mood states, which furthermore are not compelled, and which, finally, are contrary to the buyer's better judgment' (Wood 1998: 299; see also Mele 1987).

46 See also the recent call for a more interdisciplinary approach to the study of consumption within psychology: eg, Dittmar (1992); Lunt and Livingston (1992); Robben and Groenland (1993); cf Lunt (1995).

47 A similar bipolar approach is also much in evidence in the psychological research into impulsivity recently undertaken by Metcalfe and Mischel (1999).

Crime, excitement and consumerism in the city spaces of late modernity

Let us now turn to some of the ways in which the developments identified above are impacting on certain forms of crime within particular urban settings. My aim here is to explore the effects of various key features of late modern life – most obviously, rampant consumerism and the concomitant forms of subjectivity it engenders, and the growing use of risk-taking strategies as a means of asserting a sense of control in increasingly ontologically uncertain life worlds – on *three* specific areas of the contemporary city. By grounding contemporary theoretical ideas concerning excitement, risk and control within particular spatio-historical contexts, this section will address perhaps the main criticism levelled at Katz and other phenomenological criminologists: that their work lacks a fundamental engagement with urban social and spatial dynamics. While it is fair to say that much contemporary criminology (including virtually all of Katz's analysis) deals with phenomena that take place within urban settings, typically it relies on an abstracted – and at times even stylised – concept of urban space that is often highly insensitive to the complex dynamics of urban life and the forms of subjectivity that constitute the late modern urban experience. If you like, Katz and others are guilty of privileging issues of agency over space – something of an irony given that, in previous chapters, we have seen how other commentators operating from very different epistemological perspectives (eg, Mike Davis and Ian Taylor) have done exactly the opposite and concentrated solely on issues of structure and space while virtually ignoring issues relating to agency and subjectivity. With an eye not just on the present but also to the future, this concluding section should also be seen as a final attempt to draw together, and thus make distinct, the main ideas of this book: namely, the various (and burgeoning) relationships that currently exist between consumerism and criminal activity within the late modern city.

Spaces of deprivation

Get Rich, or Die Tryin' (the title of US rapper 50 Cent's 2002 multi-platinum album)

In Chapter 1 we saw how capitalism and its associated processes brought about the formation of the modern industrial city. This situation clearly continues today, only now it is the economic arrangements associated with globalised capitalism that are responsible for much of the spatial and hierarchical re-organisation of our cities. The late modern city is now at the caprice of international capital flows and a new logic and geography of production and consumption. Consequently, city space in the West is undergoing a series of profound transformations in urban social structures, of which the most significant has been the onset of urban post-industrialisation (Bell 1976; Martin 1988; Lash and Urry 1987). While some cities (or more accurately, areas of cities) have prospered as centres of global communication and transnational capital flow, others have suffered massive losses in traditional working class manufacturing jobs coupled with a fall in private and public investment. In many instances this has resulted in the creation of an urban 'underclass' (Wilson 1987, 1996; Hutton 1995), the development of the inner-city ghetto (Wilson 1993) and the 'sink estate' (Davies 1994). It is to these socially and economically deprived areas that I now wish to turn in a bid to further substantiate many of the themes identified in this chapter concerning the linkages between consumerism, excitement and crime (understood in Katzian terms as a seductive form of existential choice).

Two arguments will be put forward. First, attention will be drawn to the fact that, within socially excluded urban environments, many individuals are *over-identifying* (from a normative perspective) with consumer goods in an attempt to create a sense of identity. As Carl Nightingale (1993) has specified in his ethnographic study of Black ghetto life in Philadelphia, one of the paradoxes of contemporary urban America is that members of the 'underclass' (a term disliked by Nightingale and many others) are socially and economically *excluded* yet culturally and commercially *included*. In other words, while Black youths in these areas experience tremendous feelings of alienation and exclusion from traditional employment and educational opportunities, at the same time they are also over-exposed to American mainstream culture via advertising, television, music and other forms of mass media that demand their 'participation'. Paraphrasing Bauman, one might suggest that these individuals are at once 'repressed' *and* 'seduced' (see Chapter 4). Augmenting Merton, Nightingale thus claims that the tension caused within ghetto culture by this divisive combination is resolved by a warped 'over-compensation' with many of the symbols of American consumer culture – both mainstream and subversive:

> Already at five and six, many kids in the neighborhood can recite the whole canon of adult luxury – from Gucci, Evan Piccone, and Pierre Cardin, to Mercedes and BMW ... from the age of ten, kids became thoroughly engrossed in Nike's and Reebok's cult of the sneaker ... (Nightingale 1993: 153–54, quoted in Young 1999: 84)

These social circumstances are reflected in the popular and ironic hip-hop term 'ghetto fabulous'. Indeed, rap and hip-hop culture more generally can be seen as one of the primary drivers of inner-city conspicuous consumption. Whilst brands have always been an intrinsic element of rap culture, in recent years the stakes have risen considerably. In the late 1980s and early 1990s, hardcore rappers like Ice T or Tim Dogg rapped about $60 Nike trainers or 40oz bottles of Colt 45 beer; today, the giants of corporate hip-hop like P Diddy, 50 Cent or Jay-Z extol the virtues of £200 Prada sneakers, Chanel jewellery or the new Porsche *Cayenne* sports utility vehicle. The *Newsweek* journalist, Johnnie Roberts, explains:

> This is the rich sound of hip-hop: cash registers ringing loudly for luxury brands. Though rappers have long found inspiration for lyrics in brand names like Adidas and Tanqueray, it's the prestige logos that sparkle the brightest. Stars like Busta, P Diddy, Ja Rule and Jay-Z have expensive tastes and have made themselves powerful pitchmen, lifting the aspirations of youth culture for life's finer things while spiking sales of the Cadillac Escalade, Bentley, Cristal Champagne, Burberry, Prada and Louis Vuitton ... An artist deems a product cool, sales jump, the rapper looks like a tastemaker and brands that were once the exclusive domain of bluebloods enjoy blinding exposure to a youthful crowd of new customers. (2002: 56)

This tendency is set to intensify as major hip-hop artists, fed up with promoting other people's products, now look to bring out their own range of prestige commodities. I would argue that this situation is not exclusive to the US, or indeed to Black youth; after all, hip-hop – and to a lesser degree rap – is now the biggest form of 'crossover' music (*pace* Eminen as a stalking horse for white hip-hop music).[48] Visit any inner-city 'problem' estate in this country and you cannot fail to be struck by the proliferation of brand names and designer labels (whether original or not – although as Gaines (1992) has pointed out, this distinction between the real and the fake is becoming increasingly redundant in a culture where the brand/label is the sole signifier). While logos and brands vary from culture to culture – Fila, Louis Vuitton and Hilfigger in the US; Henry Lloyd, Burberry, and Dolce and Gabbana in the UK – the value placed on these products, especially by young people, cannot be disputed. The ethos behind these overt displays of consumer product is simple: in a world of frustration and exclusion, commodities such as jewellery, sports apparel, designer watches and mobile phones act as symbolic messages of power and status (see Hayward and Presdee 2002). Identity and self-worth are reduced to simple symbolic codes (Baudrillard 1988), as interpretable as a Nike 'swoosh' or a Gucci monogram. These displays of consumer goods enable individuals to construct perceived identity (Lasch 1979; Campbell 1989; Nava 1992; Slater 1997) and exert a sense of control (Featherstone 1994; Lury 1996) in social environments that have been stripped of traditional avenues of advancement and self-expression. Inevitably, the sense of identity and control created through these displays is a delusion, a faux construction with little value outside of specific locales. Nonetheless, for many, this urgent participation in a world of blatant consumerism provides meaning, a touchstone of identity and security in an uncertain world.

Commenting on Nightingale's study, Jock Young suggests that this over-compensation on cultural identification can be understood as a development of traditional subcultural theory, only no longer should delinquency be explained in terms of a Mertonian reaction to middle class expectations inculcated in the schoolroom (as famously suggested by Albert Cohen 1955); rather, the locus of engendering expectations has shifted to a multi-mediated consumer culture, and those expectations have in turn changed beyond recognition:

> Cohen is talking about the school whilst Nightingale talks about the mass media and the consumer market ... But these differences are easily resolved if we acknowledge that the school is the chief carrier of undiluted meritocratic values of work, discipline and reward, whilst the wider commercial culture is not: it is a celebration of luck, hedonism and leisure, fun and good fortune ... Furthermore, we are speaking of a world 40 years on from *Delinquent Boys* – where the wider culture places a much greater emphasis on hedonism and expressivity than the more balanced motifs of the past. (Young 1999: 85)

This is a passage of some significance, for it crucially identifies the fact that, in today's society, both 'deviant' *and* 'mainstream' cultures now promote *the very* values that, for Merton and Cohen, comprised 'deviance as rejection of the mainstream' culture: hedonism has now become mainstream.

---

48 Consider, eg, the teeny-bop hip-hop act Big Brovaz. Promoted by their record company to appeal specifically to the pre-teen market, Big Brovaz's song lyrics lionise consumption, spending sprees and so-called 'bling bling' culture, their hit, *Favourite Things*, paying homage to everything from Bentley cars and platinum rings to Gucci dresses and convertible Mercedes *Kompressors*.

The second argument is a development of Lyng's idea that certain risk-taking strategies serve as a means of seizing control, a way of reacting against the 'unidentifiable forces that rob one of individual choice', and, more importantly, Eleanor Miller's suggestion that 'the underclass would seem to be a fertile group within which to look for evidence of edgework' (1991: 1531). Drawing on these accounts, I asserted that the run-down estate or ghetto neighbourhood could be seen as a paradoxical space: on one hand symbolising the systematic powerlessness so often felt by the individuals who live in these environments and, on the other, the sink estate serving as a site of 'risk consumption', providing numerous illegal avenues for self-actualisation. Related to this line of inquiry was the work of Ikuya Sato (1991) on the motivations and phenomenological characteristics associated with Japanese *boso* driving culture. I now wish to return to Sato's account in more detail, for it is my contention that his work sheds considerable light on the experiential feelings of individuals involved in the types of risk-laden, illegal activities that abound within troubled inner-city neighbourhoods.

Of most interest in Sato's work (at least in terms of the argument set out in this chapter) are the terms used by the *bosozoku* to describe their activities (eg, the experience of a 'loss of self-consciousness'; the sense that what they were doing was somehow 'bracketed off from everyday life'; the feeling that 'mean-ends relationships were simplified'; and the sense that *boso* driving involved a different temporal framework than 'ordinary life'). Sato believes that such feelings can best be accounted for by recourse to Csikszentmihalyi's (1975) 'flow concept'. Csikszentmihalyi identified that individuals involved in what he calls 'autotelic' activities (eg, enjoyable but highly intense pastimes that can be as diverse as chess and rock climbing) often experience 'a peculiar dynamic state', something that he calls the 'flow experience'. Put simply, this state can be described as a 'holistic sensation that people feel when they act with complete involvement':

> In the flow state, action follows action according to an internal logic that seems to need no conscious intervention by the actor. He [*sic*] experiences it as a unified flowing from one moment to the next, in which he is in control of actions, and in which there is little distinction between self and environment, between stimulus and response, or between past, present, and future. (Csikszentmihalyi, quoted in Sato 1991: 18)

Leaving aside the extent to which this notion of 'flow experience' resonates with earlier arguments about the changing nature of postmodern temporality (Jameson's 'eternal present', Wilson's 'present orientation', simultaneity, etc: see Chapter 2), the usefulness of such a framework for explaining crimes rich in excitement and risk is clear. However, might Csikszentmihalyi's framework have a broader applicability? Consider his 'six phenomenological characteristics of flow experience' (Csikszentmihalyi 1975: 38–48):

1   the merging of actions and awareness
2   the centring of attention on limited stimulus field
3   the loss of ego (or transcendence of ego)
4   feeling of competence and control
5   unambiguous goals and immediate feedback
6   autotelic nature.

Although clearly not a definitive list, it is interesting to note how many of Csikszentmihalyi's experiential characteristics overlap with features previously identified as being characteristic of the late modern 'subject in transition' – our inchoate composite of the modern and the postmodern. For example, when discussing the 'centering of attention' in relation to *boso* culture, Sato identifies how, in an effort 'to bracket themselves off from everyday life', *bosozoku* undertake practices that bear striking resemblance to the forms of 'carnivalesque' pleasure (ie, oppositional forms of popular and personal pleasure) that Mike Presdee (2000) claims are now symptomatic of the postmodern age (indeed, Sato's informants even used the terms *(o)matsuri* (festival) and *kannibal* (carnival) to describe the sensations involved in *boso* driving: Sato 1991: 19).[49] Similarly, the notion of 'feeling in control' also resonates with earlier arguments about the search for 'self-actualisation' through 'a controlled loss of control'. Sato's *boso* informants, for example, are willing to embrace the risks involved in their 'uncontrollable and unpredictable' pastime because it provides them with the feelings of competence and control that they lack in everyday situations: 'The feeling of control is derived from the recognition that one has transformed a city into one's own playground' (1991: 21), that the street has become 'their own':

> We can hear nothing but the exhaust noises. Nobody, not even the police can stop us ... The moment the engines are started, this disorderly crowd becomes a big monster. It's really overwhelming. We speed down the middle of the road. Who cares about the police cars! When I see the band from in front, it's like a tide of headlights devouring the city. (1991: 21)

Such sentiments take on an even greater urgency when one factors in Presdee's work on the creeping rationalisation/criminalisation of everyday life. Consider the following quote from one unapologetic car cruiser, which clearly illustrates how the need for control is being exacerbated by a sense of being over-controlled:

> They're trying to slow us down all the time on the roads. They've got everything. They've got bloody speed cameras that take your reg plates, your tax. They've got normal speed cameras. They've got police. They've got speed humps. When you go there [to a 'cruising meet'] no one can stop you. I'm not saying you can do what you want. But you're pretty untouchable. You can speed. You can have your music on. You can do what you want. There's no authority there. There's no police there telling you what to do. (Gary Shields, quoted on *Car Junkies*, BBC TV, 2003)

The comparison with Giddens' juggernaut metaphor is hard to resist, only in this case, thanks to the risk-laden activities associated with these transgressive forms of behaviour, the individual is firmly ensconced behind the wheel – if not in control, then at least exerting a modicum of influence. Lastly, with its emphasis on the 'transcendence of ego' and 'immediate feedback', Csikszentmihalyi's framework also echoes the themes of impulsivity and immediate gratification that, as we saw earlier, are so central to the 'subject in transition' (the lack of super ego constraint is often used by psychologists to explain impulsive and erratic behaviour: see James 1995). Without over-generalising (and gendering over) the very engaging work of

---

49 Specifically, the inhalation of paint thinner so as to 'limit the field of awareness'; the use of vehicle headlights to 'create a theatrical frame'; and the use of loud music to 'engross the youths' during *boso* driving.

Lyng, Sato and Csikszentmihalyi – remember the stated aim of this chapter was always to offer only a 'tentative conceptual framework' for thinking about certain crimes under conditions of late modernity – this line of inquiry can help us group together those illegal activities perpetrated in inner-city areas (from joyriding to street mugging to graffiti writing to crimes associated with 'binge drinking') that can be conceptualised as risk-laden, self-actualising *crimes of control*.

Centripetal spaces: the city centre and crime prevention

Such insights help to explain why situational crime prevention (SCP) has such a limited usefulness when it comes to the control and reduction of crimes that can be understood as 'urban edgework'. In situating the Katzian excitement model of crime and the 'control-excitement' model in relation to SCP, the aim here is to encourage administrative criminologists to develop what (for want of a better term) might be described as a mixed model that can be deployed in that traditional testing ground of crime prevention research, the town/city centre (Hope 1985).

Despite the fact that most urban dwellers have always recognised the town/city centre as a prodigious locus of criminality, it was not until the 1980s that crime prevention scholars, buttressed by the research into routine activity theory (Cohen and Felson 1979; Felson 1998), offender search theory (Brantingham and Brantingham 1991) and, most importantly, criminal 'hot spots' (Pierce *et al* 1986; Sherman *et al* 1989), began to advocate the deployment within specific city centre areas of focused physical measures to prevent criminal events (a technique known as 'opportunity blocking': Clarke 1995, 1997). The first thing to state about these measures is that, in many cases, such initiatives have a positive effect on the reduction of crime in specific areas.[50] However, that said, SCP is not without its problems (see Chapter 3). As John Eck (1996) states in the conclusion to perhaps the most comprehensive evaluative study of opportunity blocking initiatives yet undertaken, while the 'evidence [that blocking crime opportunities in certain places can reduce crime] may be encouraging', it must be tempered by the fact that 'there is a great deal of uncertainty about what works, at which places, [and] against which crimes'.[51] This section wishes to explore some of these problems not only in

---

50 In Eck's (1996) evaluative study of 78 crime prevention intervention projects, over 90% of the reports 'displayed evidence of crime reduction effects'.

51 After reviewing various evaluations of upgraded street lighting systems (eg, Painter 1988; Atkins *et al* 1991), Eck is forced to conclude, '[w]e can have very little confidence that improved lighting prevents crime, particularly since we do not know if offenders use lighting to their own advantage'. Flemming and Burrows (1986) even identified how offenders use lighting to help detect potential targets. Eck explains: 'Consider lighting outside ATM machines, for example. An ATM user might feel safer when the ATM and its surrounding area are well lit. However, this same lighting makes the patron more visible to passing offenders.' Secondly, consider measures aimed at controlling drinking as a means of reducing violent assaults and incivilities in city centres (eg, Ramsey 1990). Results from such studies are inconclusive, but one could just as easily make the case from available data that such policies could actually prove counterproductive. In several cases, arrests actually increased due to individuals protesting against, or deliberately flouting, drinking bans. Lastly, there has even been some speculation about the efficacy of that situational 'silver bullet', CCTV. Following concerns about crime displacement, Eck was forced to conclude, 'the level of uncertainty about CCTV effectiveness is too high to advocate its use except to test its effectiveness'. That said, it would be unreasonable not to accept the potential usefulness of CCTV in the fight against crime – both now (Brown 1995) and in the future (see Young 1999: 192).

relation to various types of 'expressive' crimes, but also in relation to the more acquisitive street crimes perpetrated by the so-called rational calculating criminal – the type of criminal on whom, as we saw in Chapter 3, SCP is very much predicated.

Let us begin the analysis with a short case study: the much-publicised case of Chowdury's newsagents in Salford, Manchester (*The Crime List*, Channel 4 TV, 2001). For the past four years, Mrs Chowdury and her four children have run a newsagents in the high-crime area of Salford. During that period the Chowdurys have been robbed seven times. After each successive attack, local police advised Mrs Chowdury to target-harden her establishment, and on each occasion she has followed their advice, fitting, *inter alia*, a panic button, a secured cash register and, ultimately, a comprehensive CCTV system. However, despite these initiatives, she continues to be robbed, latterly by three masked assailants who left Mrs Chowdury stabbed and beaten. Although the full extent of the incident was caught on camera, no arrests were forthcoming. To a certain extent, one could interpret the calculating behaviour of the robbers (eg, their decision to wear masks as a precaution against the newly-installed CCTV surveillance) as evidence to support situationists' claims that offenders exhibit a measure of rationality when undertaking their crimes (although rationality is not a word that immediately springs to mind when viewing the CCTV footage of the woefully hamfisted robbery). But by the same token, one could also argue that this case highlights the fundamental tautology inherent in simple crime prevention strategies: it is precisely because criminals are (to varying degrees) 'rational calculators', capable of reasonably complicated decision-making processes, both prior to and even during the criminal act, that rudimentary crime prevention measures (such as the installation of street lights or CCTV systems) will, over time, be circumvented or outwitted, by dint of simple force, innovative criminal practice or, that old nemesis of the situational approach, crime displacement. This much we should be able to tell simply from studying the historical development of criminal practice over the last century. In short, because SCP continues to prioritise both 'physical' and 'spatial' considerations over and above any concern with the multifarious subjective experiences of the offender (not counting the hypothetical construct of the rational actor, which, as we have seen in previous chapters, is problematic at best), it will always be severely limited by, what I wish to call here, its 'built-in obsolescence'.

Another fundamental (and related) problem inherent in the situational approach is the constant need to devise new, workable preventative strategies and, very importantly, the time it takes to develop, test and implement these initiatives. Consider, for example, the slow response of situational practitioners to the changing nature of street crime over the last few years (ie, the shift in crime targets from hard targets – or, to use the correct SCP vernacular, 'target hardened crime opportunities' – to soft targets, namely people). While this could be seen as testimony to the success of SCP measures, it also illustrates the inability of SCP scholars to predict and react expediently to changes in patterns of criminal behaviour. This last point is of considerable importance for the future of criminological research, not least because it casts real doubt on the ability of empirically-based administrative criminology to be able to actually identify, analyse and confront new modes of criminality whilst they are still current/operative. It might not be going too far to suggest that we could soon have a situation where, long before the research grant has even been approved, the proposed object of criminal activity to be studied has disappeared, or more likely morphed into a slightly different form!

A second, more minor strand of critique stems from the interaction between certain forms of transgressive behaviour and the formalised conception of 'deterrence'. Again, it is instructive to revisit Ulrich Beck's work on the growth of non-judgmental, non-reductive forms of 'risk management' and his argument that, in many instances, the very steps taken in a bid to stave off (or more accurately 'manage') risk serve only to produce new risks or exacerbate older ones. Correspondingly, certain SCP strategies aimed at reducing crime actually have the opposite effect. For example, for many urban criminals involved in expressive forms of transgression, the greater the risk, the greater the excitement. What this means in effect is that certain crime prevention measures actually add to the thrill of crime, as the 'game' takes on an even greater risk. For example, 'twockers' often view speed cameras as a challenge, while illegal 'BASE jumpers',[52] graffiti artists, skateboarders, train surfers, 'free runners'[53] and other urban-adventurer criminals all admit to being drawn to the very signs erected to deter their activities. Moreover, crime preventionists must by now be cognisant of the fact that eluding CCTV cameras or police observation actually adds to the excitement of the crime. Simply putting on a hooded jacket or balaclava can be an extremely effective precaution against CCTV surveillance – just ask any football hooligan or anti-capitalist rioter:[54]

> And so we fall into a trap. Because we ignore the sensuality of crime, we believe that law and order politics can lower crime. We oppose the interactionism of crime with the claims of rational deterrence. But how can adding to the thrill of crime – since the games take on an even greater risk (and even greater buzz of adrenaline) – reduce crime? We turn from the shady study of crime to study the offender but do not study him in his interaction ... (Morrison 1995: 378)

Spaces of consumption and pleasure

> To increase their capacity for consumption, consumers must never be given rest. They need to be constantly exposed to new temptations in order to be kept in a state of constantly seething, never wilting excitation and indeed, in a state of suspicion and disaffection. The baits commanding them to shift attention need to confirm such suspicion while offering a way out of disaffection: 'you reckon you've seen it all? You ain't seen nothing yet.' (Bauman 1998: 26)

---

52 BASE is an acronym of 'building, antenna, span (bridge) and earth (cliffs)' (see Ferrell *et al* 2001).

53 'Free running' is the high-risk practice of traversing the city without recourse to pavements or roads. Recasting the city as a playground, free runners attempt to negotiate between points of the city by roof jumping, ledge climbing and wall running. According to its founder, Sebastien Foucan, 'free running is a way of fighting one's fears and demons and then re-applying this to life'.

54 In the wake of the 2001 anti-capitalist riots in London, it was revealed that riot organisers had instructed protesters to bring with them a change of clothes in a further bid to confuse police video operators.

> A life in boundless pursuit of pleasure makes one blasé because it agitates the nerves to their strongest reactivity for such a long time that they finally cease to react at all. (Georg Simmel, quoted in Frisby and Featherstone 1997: 185)

During a brief discussion of the 'depthlessness of late-modern architecture', Wayne Morrison (1995: 258) poses a question: does a new sense of dimension or (non) control result from the flows of spectacles and images of the late modern city? His answer, although at times somewhat opaque, seems to be in the affirmative. For Morrison, such is the superficiality of the contemporary city that the late modern actor is now adrift in a cultural and communicative *mélange*, bullied by the market and unable to exert control over locality or future prospects:

> Again the individual is pushed into the dialectics of control and angst, of the feeling that he ought to know what is going on, and the impossibility of grasping meaning ... The surroundings are all artifacts; they are all creations of modernity and cannot claim any natural stability. They display the symbolism of power, but their contingency is too obvious. If stability is sought in these forms, incongruity results. Urban residents need distractions from the onset of this absurdity of contingency. (1995: 259)

In this section attention will be trained on the areas of the city that facilitate such distraction. I refer here, of course, to the parts of the city that are synonymous not with work or habitat, but with pleasure and consumption.

Whenever such evocative terms as 'cathedrals of consumption' (Presdee 1985; Gardner and Sheppard 1989), 'fantasy-scapes' (Hannigan 1998; Rojek 1993) and 'architecture of consumption' (Jencks 1977; Mullins 1991; Zukin 1991) are bandied around in theoretical circles, attention typically turns to what many commentators believe to be the symbol of postmodernism *par excellence:* the shopping mall (see Kowinski 1985; Shields 1989; Crawford 1992; Goss 1993). Two themes are traditionally espoused. First, interest is trained on the extent to which these places are at the same time generic, modular (ie, comprised of a series of familiar elements) and sterile – environments one might describe as 'socially sanitised' (Achenbach 1988). Secondly, shopping malls are said to be obsessed with security and surveillance (Shearing and Stenning 1985; Davis 1990: Chapter 4; Wilson 1991). However, simple notions of the shopping mall and other such 'theme-enhanced' environments as Foucauldian disciplinary zones (disciplinary in the sense of observation and correction), reminiscent of Cohen's 'punitive city' (S Cohen 1979), are, in my opinion, misleading (on this point, see Chapter 4). A more accurate interpretation of the shopping mall and other related urban fantasy-scapes is to think of them as an exemplar of late modern actuarial, 'risk-based' or 'post-disciplinary' society (see Simon 1987; Castel 1991). In other words, the design and organisation of such environments is characteristic of a shift underway in society more generally, whereby modern forms of disciplinary power are being supplanted by more calculative, insurance-based, risk-assessed forms of power (see Miller and Rose 1990; Defert 1991; Ewald 1991; Feeley and Simon 1994). Certainly, the emergence of so-called 'risk society' and the spread of the shopping mall within Western society seem to have occurred simultaneously (the 1980s and early 1990s). And, turning to more criminology-specific questions: what forms of criminality are taking place within such environments and, importantly, how are these forms of criminality changing, especially in relation to consumerism?

By the late 1980s, regular visits to the shopping centre or mall had become a mainstream cultural activity. However, by the middle of the 1990s, the shopping mall was serving another purpose[55] – it had also become a popular focal point for youthful delinquency. As Presdee (1994) and Taylor *et al* (1996) have identified, theme-enhanced shopping centres, with their mobility and (apparent) anonymity, were also functioning as sites of exploration, play and 'invasion' (see Fiske 1989), especially for young truants and groups of the unemployed:

> For many young people, especially the unemployed, there has been a continuing congregating within the modern shopping centers ... At the mall ... *young people push back the limits imposed upon them* ... Young people, cut off from normal consumer power, invade the space of those with consumer power. They have become the 'space invaders' of the 1990s, lost in a world of dislocation and excitement; a space where they should not be. Modern consumerism demands they look, touch, and take or appropriate. This is a culture that plays at life, where the marketplace becomes like the pleasure pier of the seaside resorts, the site of pleasure, leisure, desire and, most important, a place for pushing back the limits ... *But most of all it is a world of doing wrong.* (Presdee 1994: 182, emphasis added)

Presdee presents a picture of the shopping centre as a place of youthful transgression, thrill and 'carnival': the type of place that Katz would doubtless argue is a likely environment for 'sneaky thrills' and 'ludic activities', such as shop-lifting and other forms of illicit youthful activity (see Katz 1988: Chapter 2). However, certain important changes are taking place. To start with, because of pervasive high-tech security initiatives such as EAS (electronic article surveillance) tagging (see Bamfield 1994; DiLonardo 1996), ink tagging (see DiLonardo and Clarke 1996) and covert cameras, the contemporary shopping mall is more likely to be targeted by experienced 'professional' thieves, who have both the expertise and the technological wherewithal to circumvent such sophisticated deterrents, as opposed to the younger offender or teenage thrill-seeker. Certainly, store detectives and security contractors are more concerned with well-organised, hard-to-identify shop-lifting or 'hoisting' teams than they are with groups of teenagers who spend their time maundering around the food halls and arcades (the latter group being readily identifiable and thus easy to monitor and ultimately remove). Similarly, shopping centres are far more at risk from credit card fraud and 'kiting' (the practice of passing stolen cheques) than they are from in-house teenage incivility or disturbance (see Masuda 1993; Webb 1996). In short, the 21st century shopping centre has moved on. It no longer functions in the way it used to as a (albeit unintended) transgressive landscape for young people of the kind identified by Presdee above. The effectiveness of new methods of digital surveillance has ensured that unauthorised 'fun' is now strictly off limits within such hermetically sealed private spaces. Yes, you can still look, touch and (of course) consume (after all, this is what young people have been conditioned to do), but the role of consumer space as a 'world of dislocation and excitement' is changing. *Contra* Presdee, the shopping mall is now no longer 'a world of doing wrong', in fact quite the opposite – the shopping mall now epitomises a world of conformity and mundanity.

---

55 For examples of consumer/shopping spaces being used for purposes other than consumption, see Glennie and Thrift (1992, 1993).

Indeed, the gloss of these 'cathedrals of consumption' and other so-called fantasy-scapes is wearing thin more generally (see Miles 1998b: 1004). Pertinent here are Robins's comments on the 'postmodern city' and the way in which in recent years it has lost some of its seductive sparkle: 'there has been a kind of imaginative collapse: what was once driven by vision and energy is now drained of affect. The utopian has collapsed into the banal' (1991: 11). Certainly, the same comments could be attributed to many contemporary urban spaces of consumption and pleasure. Perhaps we should not really be surprised by this; after all, the architectural style of these modular, sanitised structures now looks increasingly dated – this despite the fact that, originally, the 'Vegas aesthetic' (see Chapter 2) was supposed to make chronology obsolete. In a world of newness and novelty, of shortened time-horizons and 'neophilia', many of these so-called 'postmodern dream-scapes' now look extremely jaded (remember, the 'Vegas aesthetic' is now nearly three decades old). Watching a film, going bowling or dining on fast food at the 'food hall' is still attractive for a great many, but for other groups – especially those seeking excitement and stimulation – the appeal has long since worn off. According to the astute urban commentator Sharon Zukin (1998), the leading 'entertainment retailers' are already well aware of this 'draining of affect'. She charts how, in a bid to counteract growing shopper apathy (something no doubt exacerbated by Internet shopping and the way this practice speeds up 'the rate at which new perceptions are brought in front of the eye': Featherstone 1998: 921), a new 'prototype entertainment store' has emerged:

> Economic factors, nonetheless, still motivate investors to create new spaces for urban consumption ... Under these conditions, developers have built elaborate, new shopping centers in both Asia and the US – from Canal City in Fukuoka, Japan, to Las Vegas, Orlando and New York City. These consumption spaces attempt to revitalize shopping by dramatizing the retail 'experience'. They try to capture shoppers' imagination by inviting them to participate in simulated forms of non-shopping entertainment, such as sports (Nike Town), interactive video installations (Viacom) or even 'wilderness' (REI trekking gear stores) and 'nature' (The Nature Experience). Although these spaces are described by the rubric 'entertainment retail', they really sell an easily recognizable 'brand name' – Disney, Nike, Sony, Viacom – in many different product variations. (Zukin 1998: 833; see also Julier 2000)

However, as Zukin confirms, even these ventures are looking economically questionable due to their 'higher prices ... eventual overexposure and inevitable reproduction of the same shops in other cities'. Ironically, such a situation is the inevitable consequence of late modern consumerism, a system that has created subjects who are now constantly on the look out not only for new commodities but also for new experiences. Thus, *safe* consumption within homogeneous, sanitised environments is no longer sufficient for those in 'pursuit of the new'.[56] Instead they seek more vibrant, *ad hoc* environments in which to consume, play with risk and

---

56 In terms of the material product itself, this tendency is already well underway in Japan, a place where many of the practices associated with postmodern consumerism have reached their zenith. Among the cutting-edge of Japan's *shinjinrui* (Japan's consumption-orientated younger generation: see Anderson and Wadkins 1992) the trend now is to eschew mainstream designer brands such as Nike or Gucci – they are simply deemed too accessible. Instead, a new subculture has emerged that places primacy on exclusivity. This is an underground world of micro labels that undertake no advertising or marketing and rely solely on word of mouth. The smaller and more discrete the logo or brand, the bigger the appeal to Japan's 'passionate specialists' or 'super consumers' as they are known.

explore the nature of transgression, a point Hannigan has touched on in his discussion of the 'future of urban themed entertainment':

> As simulation and theming become more commonplace, it will become increasingly difficult to invent new and attractive products that will jointly meet escalating expectations for novel stimulation without increasing the corresponding levels of consumer risk. (1998: 197)

The search is now on for places of excitement and 'calculating hedonism', somewhere where a 'controlled suspension of constraints' or 'controlled sense of decontrol' can be purchased, experienced and played with. What, then, might these new spaces of consumption and pleasure look like? These thoughts should not be read as a full-blown attempt at 'futurology'; rather, following the technique used by HG Wells, it is more an exercise in 'expanding the present'.

Our point of departure for this theoretical extrapolation will be the contemporary club/dance scene, perhaps the most manifest example of 'calculated hedonism' linked to consumption – a world inextricably bound up with emotionality and pleasure (Redhead 1993, 1997, 1998). Mike Presdee provides us with a window on this world of designer drugs, excess and 'ecstatic experience':

> Whereas 30 years ago leisure and pleasure stopped, like Cinderella, at midnight, now pleasure doesn't start until midnight when the fun begins and often only ends when the weekend finishes. In the same way that truants often truant for no reason other than to stand outside of the rules, regulations and regimentation of life, so the 'weekend' becomes the process of the stretching of sensation. To 'buzz' is to be beyond, untouchable, an outsider ... The whole style and process of 'clubbing' defies the rational scientific world of work which is held dream-like in the mind in contrast to the 'memories of a hedonistic consumption during the leisure hours' ... It is a celebration of irrational, ecstatic behaviour. Night becomes day and specialist clothes are worn not to work but to play. Consumption rather than production is all-important as the positive personal assessment of pleasure by the pleasured assumes the 'same qualities which were assessed negatively by their daytime controllers – eg laziness, arrogance, vanity, etc ... It is the carnival of 'otherness', of 'difference' and defiance. (Presdee 2000: 118–19)

Moreover, as Angela McRobbie points out, this is also a world capable of mixing up established modes of sexuality, gender, race and, importantly, *identity*:

> The [rave] subculture far outstrips other forms of youth entertainment because of where it takes place. Outside the regulatory space of the home or the school, the more autonomous space of the subculture contributes to the weakening of these other institutional ties. (McRobbie 1993: 424)

Importantly, club culture is no longer simply a peripheral underground phenomenon. Contemporary club culture is now 'mainstream', with the industry at best estimate worth in excess of £2 billion a year (see also Hobbs *et al* 2000: 708). Add to this the trend of extending the club experience by basing a long weekend or vacation around 'clubbing' in rave-friendly tourist locations like Ibiza and Ayia Napa, and the link between consumption and controlled hedonism becomes clear. Moreover, the type of experience engendered within the club scene is no longer limited to an elite few. It is estimated that there are currently 'over a million young people spending in excess of £35 per week on this form of pleasure' (Malbon 1998, cited in Presdee 2000: 119). More recently, club culture has also spread (in diluted form) to the high street. For example, in January 2003, the British tabloid newspaper *The Daily Star* offered coupons for a 'three day clubbing holiday for only £7.50'. The result of all this is that the sensibilities of club culture – excess, ecstasy, heightened emotion, and the feeling of being beyond control and outside of regulation – have spilled over into everyday life, or more accurately 'night life'. For a great many young people, such feelings are the default setting of the weekend experience. Visit any sizeable UK town centre on a Friday or Saturday night and the fallout is immediately apparent (albeit in its most common manifestation of so-called 'binge drinking': see Hobbs *et al* 2000 on the 'choreography' of the 'night time economy'):

> It should be no surprise that intoxication is the norm, and that unruly and violent behaviour is the central feature of an economy yet to develop a full set of codes and protocols comparable to those that dominated social relations in the industrial era. Indeed, while such high levels of prosperity and popularity mark this sector, it may be naive to suggest that such a coded device will ever evolve. (2000: 706)

In a sense all this represents little new. Young people have always sought a good time and used bars and nightclubs for fun, relaxation and 'limit experiences'. Similarly, the link between the prevalence of bars and criminal activity within the surrounding vicinity has long been established within criminological literature.[57] However, in recent times, in certain parts of certain cities, significant changes have taken place that provide us with an interesting glimpse of the future. Cities as culturally diverse as Prague, Amsterdam, Hong Kong, Hamburg, Moscow, Manchester, Berlin, Melbourne, Bangkok, Lion City (Singapore) and Tokyo (and many others) have all experienced – often alongside more established bars and social venues – the coming together of a new range of hedonistic attractions that mark out these locations as highly marketable places of excess and excitement (even Reykjavik and Tallinn, the capital of Estonia, are now thriving hen and stag night locations).[58] Indeed, local governments now very often see these previously 'marginal' spaces as a vital component in the marketing strategy of a city – what Dick Hobbs has described as 'the marketing of liminal licence' – and thus a way of maintaining 'competitiveness' (Begg 1999) in the global economy (O'Connor and Wynne 1996). From lap-dancing and strip bars to Internet-advertised brothels, rave venues to bars catering for niche market sexual fantasies,[59] these hedonistic playgrounds constitute the new 'liminal zones' as described by Arantes (1996, cited in Taylor 1999: 126; see also Hobbs *et al* 2000: 703–10), places to which the young (and the not so young) gravitate in order to temporarily suspend reality via such popular late modern pursuits as designer drug consumption, the semi-hypnotic sensation of dance/trance/rave culture, 'niche market' prostitution and sex tourism.[60]

---

57 Eg, Roneck and Bell (1981); Roneck and Meir (1991); Block and Block (1995).

58 Consider the recent re-branding of Las Vegas. After a short flirtation as a family-friendly holiday location in the 1990s, Las Vegas has recently reverted back with a vengeance to its role as the original 'Sin City' (Coman 2002).

59 See also Presdee on the growing link between the club scene and sado-masochistic pursuits (2000: 123).

60 In London, eg, today's cutting-edge urban sensation-seeker is more likely to be found in places like Shoreditch, Brick Lane or Brixton (all places where drugs and prostitution are readily available) than in Leicester Square or Piccadilly Circus under the prying eyes of the CCTV cameras that form a virtual 'scanscape' of the more established West End entertainment spots.

Ropongi, Tokyo, provides a further peek into the future of urban spaces of consumption and pleasure. Located close to the centre of globalised Tokyo, Ropongi is an extraordinary fusion of rampant Japanese consumerism, technological innovation, Western youth cultures and hedonist expression. Consequently, it has become a late modern playground – not just for the Japanese, but for 'ex-pats' and tourists from Europe, Asia, North America and Australia. Unassuming by day (Ropongi resembles any downtown commercial area during business hours), by night it comes alive as thousands of (predominantly) young people flock to the area to take part in the licentious club and bar scene,[61] indulge in the various *sub rosa* sexual services on offer, consume at the flagship premises of large chain-stores and leisure merchants, and enjoy the latest in arcade technology and hyperreal computer-mediated simulation – for Ropongi also represents the cutting edge of digital gaming and youth-orientated electronic technology.

Might the melting pot of consumerism, popular culture, hedonism and digital gaming that is turn-of-the-millennium Ropongi represent the future for urban spaces based around pleasure and entertainment? Certainly at times in Ropongi it feels that way. Look inside any one of the many high-tech computer arcades that open out onto the street (in a form of private–public 'porosity' that doubtless would have fascinated Walter Benjamin) and one is struck by an interesting scene: groups of young people of differing nationalities staring into multisonorous screens, popping strobes and virtual reality headsets, each one obsessively re-playing looped games, prior to heading out into the trance-like world of Ropongi's 'club scene' to experience yet another 'controlled loss of control', this time via a combination of digitally looped dance music and designer drugs.

That such a fusion of digital gaming/communication and the pursuit of hedonism is taking place should not surprise us. As Presdee (2000: Chapter 7), drawing on Bakhtin, suggests, youth culture is constantly on the look out for new ways and means of enhancing the 'carnivalisation' of everyday life. Rather, the question we should pose is to what extent this tendency will continue. Might the pursuit of pleasure and entertainment soon take place on-line, in liminal digital worlds reminiscent in part of William Gibson's *Neuromancer*? Will the culture of virtual reality – linked of course to credit card payment facilities – with its high-tech peripherals, intelligent pixels and 'skinning' software,[62] afford individuals the unencumbered means of self-actualisation that late modernity constantly demands but increasingly denies? In some ways such far away scenarios are already with us (see Pesce 2004). Consider the recent interactive Internet-based computer game *Majestic*, which has as its stated aim, 'the blurring of reality and fantasy'. The game sets out to become 'part of your life'; in the words of the game's creator: 'There's no CD, no joystick, and, most importantly, no "off button" – you don't play *Majestic*, it plays you.' The game reaches out to the player in real time by bombarding him or her with e-mails, faxes, and

---

61 One recent travel guide famously described a particular section of Ropongi's nightclubs as 'meat markets on steroids'.

62 'Skinning' is a digital scanning technique that allows games users to graft photographs of real people onto characters within computer/video games.

streaming audio and video (it can even crash the user's computer or ring his or her mobile phone at any time), setting tasks and leaving instructions and clues. The game thus becomes part of the player's life even when he or she is not in front of his or her computer.

The next inevitable stage of this computer-mediated reality is already well underway. According to Ray Kurzweil (1999a), a world expert on artificial intelligence, computer displays built into eyeglasses that enable the viewer to traverse the normal physical environment while at the same time generating a virtual image that masks reality are but a few years from general availability. He further claims that within two decades we will witness the arrival of 'high-resolution, three-dimensional visual and auditory virtual reality and realistic all-encompassing tactile environments [that will] enable people to do virtually anything with anybody, regardless of physical proximity' (Kurzweil 1999b). Mike Featherstone and others have already begun to explore the social theoretical implications of this new, and potentially unencumbered, world of possibilities – a world of digital or 'virtual *flâneurie*' perhaps (see Benedikt 1991; Featherstone and Burrows 1995; and Featherstone 1998: 919–23 on 'virtual *flâneurie*')?:

> Cyber-space involves a three-dimensional world, but this is not on a screen one looks at. Rather, the optical illusion created by the virtual reality interface gave a strong sense of immersion within a parallel world, where one could enjoy near full sensory involvement as well as interacting with other digital entities (avatars). (Featherstone 1998: 922)

> One of the pleasures (or threats) of cyberspace, as notions of cybersex suggest, is that it promises to 'free us' from the confines of our physical bodies and to lodge our 'disembodied' minds and emotions in computer-mediated environments and 'virtual' worlds where they are licensed to nomadically 'roam free'. Previously *being* a body stood at the forefront of who and what we were. Now, however, cyberspace simply 'brackets' these foundational claims concerning the physical appearance/co-presence of participants, omitting or 'stimulating' corporeal *immediacy* (Heim 1991). (Williams 2001: 125)

These images of 'transcendental utopianism', however, need to be counterbalanced. Set against the affirmative interpretation of virtual reality is the more dystopian version, as set out by science fiction writer Bruce Sterling in a slice of futurology that, remarkably, is now 10 years old (an aeon in futurological circles, but that doesn't matter if you're right!):

> The slums of the urban city are already matched by the red light districts of cyberspace, the porn boards, the kidporn boards, the sex chatlines. The digital underground is aswarm with electronic credit card thieves. Close on their heels will come the rest of the urban condition: gambling dives in cyberspace, offshore tax dodges, call-sell operations, bunko people and professional con artists. Intangible virtual crimes, but crimes none the less. (Sterling 1994; see also Jewkes 2003 for a more recent criminological study)

Such technology puts society at the very edge of a daunting new frontier – at least certain sections of society (see Hall 1996: Chapter 13). One question, however, still remains: will the pursuit of hedonism and the suspension of reality ultimately signal the demise of cultural difference and the idea of truly egalitarian public space? Or, paradoxically, might these new forms of youth culture and other (digital?) hedonistic pursuits offer the possibility of a new, more progressive urban experience, notwithstanding the corrosive influence of advertisers and marketers? There is of course one thing of which we can be certain: not only will the links between individual desire for self-fulfilment and self-control, excitement and criminal transgression endure, but, given the unique conditions of late modernity, they are likely to gather increased momentum.

As I have tried to illustrate throughout this work, the principal features of the late modern condition – rampant *consumer-driven* capitalism, cultural and communicative flux and disembeddedness, and the end of the unified coherent subject – have conspired to produce a 'subject adrift', an ontologically insecure actor who epitomises the destruction of the social contract of modernity. Add to this the heightened sense of dis-investment in society and community brought about by economic exclusion, the (as yet unmet) challenges of globalisation, and what Jock Young has described as 'the veritable chaos of reward' (1999: 152), and it is clear that ours is indeed a world of division and growing social and economic inequality.

One of the primary consequences of such circumstances is the tremendous 'fear of not belonging' that can well up within individuals across all levels of society. While much has been made of this at the macro level – in the UK, for example, with the welter of research into 'social exclusion', and in the US with the mass of writings on the so-called 'underclass' – it is fair to say that, at the individual subjective level, it has been afforded a good deal less attention. This work has gone some way towards addressing this lacuna by putting forward the idea that one of the ways in which the late modern subject adrift attempts to deal with the fears associated with acceptance and rejection has been to retreat into the world of unbridled consumerism; a world of unquestionable opportunities and pleasures, but also one of profound frustration and anxiety. Consumer culture, it has been argued, helps to paper over these cracks: it allays fears, dissolves insecurities and assuages doubts thrown up by a society caught in the dilemmas of transition and where seemingly everything is mutable. However, like everything else in this cultural *mélange*, it is only a 'temporary fix': 'Buy absolutely everything in all the right stores, get all the right labels, and six months later the requirements will have changed ... It just sets one on a never-ending treadmill towards goalposts that recede, chasing a carrot on a stick that, sadly, you can never reach' (Buckley 2001: 30). Add to this the fact that, in the words of Peter Mead, co-founder of Abbot Mead Vickers, one of the biggest advertising agencies in Britain, the current generation of children is 'being bombarded by more advertising messages than any other group of children in history', and that so-called 'lifestyle' advertising is being aimed at ever-younger consumer-children,[1] and it is clear that this situation looks set not just to persist but to become even more pronounced as the pace of collapse of modernist totalities is matched only by the speed at which consumer culture rushes in to fill the void.

It is vital that criminology is attuned to such social circumstances, for it is the contention of this work that the damage of consumerism ultimately outweighs its alluring pleasures and opportunities. Our goal, then, must be the creation of a criminology capable of understanding the full extent of these 'new forms of desire'

---

1 Already, Lury estimates that the average British child sees 140,000 television advertisements between the ages of 4 and 18 (1996: 205).

that have emerged as a consequence of our massively promoted consumer culture and, more importantly, of linking these subjective forces to various forms of criminality. This, of course, is a very difficult task, and one unlikely to be achieved unless much criminology reorientates its gaze. By increasingly divorcing itself from sociology (and, if I may, urban studies), too much 'conventional' criminology has lost its way. While our discipline has, in recent decades, made great strides in achieving independent academic status, and attracting research funds, too often there has been a tendency within mainstream criminology and its policy spawn to ignore fundamental questions about *social justice* (across all levels of late modern society). More specifically, given the argument set out in this book, we need to (re)focus our aim on ways of redressing the current 'chaos of rewards'. This does not mean simply re-addressing the inequity of the work-reward system (in the classical social democratic sense of creating a 'more meritocratic and diverse society which provides both fulfillment and *identity*': Young 1999: 197, emphasis added), nor even to address the important issue of social exclusion. It is rather that we must deal with the mix of inclusion *and* exclusion associated with the practices and processes of consumerism. By this I mean to stress both the floatation of identity and the way this is tied into specific *spatial loci*, something that in turn throws light on various forms of criminal behaviour. We therefore need a form of criminology that, as Jeff Ferrell suggests, does not set about 'heartlessly abstracting human experience' in the name of scientific 'rigour'. In other words, a culturally sensitive and socially inspired criminology that:

> ... continues the project of recapturing a sense of situated meaning, of human engagement, long held captive within the numeric abstractions of administrative criminology and mainstream sociology ... [C]ultural criminology has revealed time and again that the human construction of meaning around issues of crime and crime control overwhelms, in its stylish elegance and symbolic nuance, any attempted reduction of human action to independent variables, data sets, or statistical summaries. Likewise, it reveals the inadequacy and inhumanity of the sorts of reductionist models that undergird 'rational choice' and 'behaviourist' criminological approaches. In this sense the 'cultural' in 'cultural criminology' denotes an orientation that is essentially humanistic in its approach to transgression and control ... This process in turn unfolds within and between everyday social situations and larger societal dynamics. And in an increasingly multi-mediated world, it is this very interplay of images and symbols large and small that must be accounted for – and contested – in order to critically understand criminality, crime control policies, and public understandings. One of the great sociological insights of the last century – that meaning resides not in the thing itself, but in surrounding social and cultural processes – takes on even greater complexity and importance in a world where mass-produced symbols circulate amidst the situated experiences of daily life. (Ferrell 2004, forthcoming)

Such a mode of criminological understanding is useful in that it also offers up ways of developing viable oppositional voices and forms of cultural resistance strong enough to meet the challenge of an all-consuming consumer society. Moreover, it points a clear way forward for criminology to begin integrating the type of existentially-based framework set out by Jack Katz and others into the wider social context of a late modern society characterised by ontological insecurity, a material culture that propagates and feeds off unfulfilable desires and an urban experience fast being reduced to 'a series of pure and unrelated presents' – what Frederic

Jameson and others have described as 'the pursuit of the now'. Here the potential law-breaker and the potential victim are united – whichever side of the boundary they fall on – whether within the affluent gated community, or trying to cross the motorway that separates the orbital 'sink estate' from the rest of the city. As we stand upon the ledges of our late modern lives, wracked by self-doubts (and doubts about the self) and the fear of not belonging – in many cases not even knowing what to belong to – the need to fully understand the motivations, desires and existential concerns brought about by the onset of a fully-fledged consumer society becomes ever more pressing.

Bibliography

Abbott, E (1936) *The Tenements of Chicago*, Chicago, IL: University of Chicago Press

Abel, C (1986) 'Regional transformations' *Architectural Review* 180: 37

Abrahams, P (1982) *Historical Sociology*, Shepton Mallet: Open Books

Abu-Lughod, JL (1991) *Changing Cities*, New York: HarperCollins

Achenbach, J (1988) 'Creeping surrealism: does anybody really know what's real anymore?' *Utne Reader* Nov/Dec

Adams, T (2001) 'No entry ... unless you are very wealthy indeed' *The Observer Sunday Magazine*, 18 March: 46–51

Aglietta, M (1979) *A Theory of Capitalist Regulation: The United States Experience*, London: New Left Books

Agnew, R (1985) 'A revised strain theory of delinquency' *Social Forces* 64: 151–64

Agnew, R (1987) 'On testing strain theories' *Journal of Research in Crime and Delinquency* 24: 281–86

Agnew, R (1989) 'A longitudinal test on the revised strain theory' *Journal of Quantitative Criminology* 5: 373–88

Agnew, R (1992) 'Foundation for a general strain theory of crime and delinquency' *Criminology* 30: 47–86

Alihan, MA (1936) *Social Ecology: A Critical Analysis*, New York: Columbia University Press

Alloway, L, Kuspit, DB, Rosler, M and Van de Marck, J (eds) (1981) *The Idea of the Postmodern: Who is Teaching It?*, Seattle, WA: Henry Art Gallery

Alvelos, H (2004) 'The desert of imagination in the city of signs: cultural implications of sponsored trangression and branded graffiti' in Ferrell, J, Hayward, KJ, Morrison, W and Presdee, M (eds), *Cultural Criminology Unleashed*, London: GlassHouse Press (forthcoming)

Amin, A (1994) *Post-Fordism: A Reader*, Oxford: Blackwell

Amin, A and Malmberg, A (1994) 'Competing structural and institutional influences on the geography of production in Europe' in Amin, A (ed), *Post-Fordism: A Reader*, Oxford: Blackwell

Anderson, L and Wadkins, M (1992) 'The new breed in Japan: consumer culture' *Canadian Journal of Administrative Studies* 9: 146–53

Anderson, N (1975) *The Hobo: The Sociology of the Homeless Man*, Chicago, IL: University of Chicago Press

Anderson, P (1991) *The Printed Image and the Transformation of Popular Culture 1790–1860*, Oxford: Clarendon Press

Arendt, H (ed) (1973) *Walter Benjamin: Illuminations*, London: Fontana

Armstrong, G and Harris, R (1991) 'Football hooligans: theory and evidence' *Sociological Review* 39(3): 427–58

Armstrong, G (1993) 'Like that Desmond Morris?' in Hobbs, D and May, T (eds), *Interpreting the Field: Accounts of Ethnography*, Oxford: Oxford University Press

Arson Prevention Bureau (1998) *Malicious Car Fires: Research by the Arson Prevention Bureau*, London: Arson Prevention Bureau

Atkins, S, Hussain, S and Storey, A (eds) (1991) *The Influence of Street Lighting on Crime and Fear of Crime: Crime Prevention Unit Paper 28*, London: HMSO

Auslander, L (1996) 'The gendering of consumer practices in 19th-century France' in De Grazia, V (ed), *The Sex of Things: Gender and Consumption in Historical Perspective*, Berkeley, CA: University of California Press

Bachman, R, Paternoster, R and Ward, S (1992) 'The rationality of sexual offending: testing a deterrence/rational choice conception of sexual assault' *Law and Society Review* 26: 343–72

Back, L (1996) *New Ethnicities and Urban Culture*, London: UCL Press

Baigell, M (1971) *A History of American Painting*, London: Thames and Hudson

Bakhtin, M (1968) *Rabelais and His World*, Cambridge, MA: MIT Press

Baldwin, J and Bottoms, AE (1976) *The Urban Criminal*, London: Tavistock

Ballard, JG (1997) *Cocaine Nights*, London: Flamingo

Bamfield, J (1994) 'Electronic article surveillance: management and learning in curbing theft' in Gill, M (ed), *Crime at Work: Studies in Security and Crime Prevention*, Leicester: Perpetuity Press

Barbalet, J (1998) *Emotion, Social Theory and Social Structure*, Cambridge: Cambridge University Press

Barkham, P and Walsh, D (2004) 'From "The Cincinatti Kid" to www.mugsonline.com: the changing face of poker' *The Times*, 3 January

Barrett, ES and Patton, JH (1983) 'Impulsivity: cognitive, behavioural and psychophysiological correlates' in Zuckerman, M (ed), *The Biological Bases of Sensation Seeking, Impulsivity and Anxiety*, Hillsdale, NJ: Erlbaum

Battock, B (1981) *Breaking the Sound Barrier: A Critical Anthology of the New Music*, New York: EP Dutton

Baudelaire, C (1964) *The Painter of Modern Life and Other Essays*, London: Phaidon Press

Baudrillard, J (1968) *Le système des objets*, Paris: Denoel-Gonthier

Baudrillard, J (1970) *La société de consommation*, Paris: Gallimard

Baudrillard, J (1975) *The Mirror of Production*, St Louis, MO: Telos Press

Baudrillard, J (1981) *For a Critique of the Political Economy of the Sign*, St Louis, MO: Telos Press

Baudrillard, J (1983) *Simulations*, New York: Semiotext(e)

Baudrillard, J (1988) *America*, London and New York: Verso

Baudrillard, J (1990) *Fatal Strategies: Crystal Revenge*, New York: Semiotext(e)

Baudrillard, J (1994) *Simulacra and Simulation*, Ann Arbor, MI: University of Michigan Press

Baudrillard, J (1996) *The System of Objects*, London: Verso

Bauman, Z (1973) *Culture as Praxis*, London: Routledge and Kegan Paul

Bauman, Z (1983) 'Industrialism, consumerism and power' *Theory, Culture and Society* 1(3): 32–43

Bauman, Z (1987) *Legislators and Interpreters: On Modernity, Post-Modernity, and Intellectuals*, Cambridge: Polity

Bauman, Z (1991) *Modernity and Ambivalence*, Cambridge: Polity

Bauman, Z (1992) *Intimations of Postmodernity*, London: Routledge

Bauman, Z (1993) *Postmodern Ethics*, Oxford: Blackwell

Bauman, Z (1997) *Postmodernity and its Discontents*, Cambridge: Polity

Bauman, Z (1998) *Consumerism, Work and the New Poor*, Buckingham: Open University Press

Beck, U (1992) *Risk Society*, London: Sage

Becker, G (1968) 'Crime and punishment: an economic approach' *Journal of Political Economy* 76: 169–217

Begg, I (1999) 'Cities and competitiveness' *Urban Studies* 36(5–6): 795–809

Beirne, P (1987) 'Adolphe Quételet and the origins of positivist criminology' *American Journal of Sociology* 92: 1140–69

Beirne, P (1993) *Inventing Criminology: Essays on the Rise of 'Homo Criminalis'*, Albany, NY: State University of New York Press

Belk, RW (1995) 'Studies in the new consumer behaviour' in Miller, D (ed), *Acknowledging Consumption: A Review of New Studies*, London: Routledge

Bell, D (1976) *The Coming of the Post-Industrial Age: A Venture in Social Forecasting*, New York: Basic Books

Benedikt, M (ed) (1991) *Cyberspace: First Steps*, Cambridge, MA: MIT Press

Benjamin, W (1973) *Charles Baudelaire: A Lyric Poet in the Era of High Capitalism*, London: New Left Books

Benjamin, W (1979) *One Way Street*, London: Verso

Benjamin, W (1999) *The Arcades Project*, Cambridge, MA: Belknap Press

Bennett, WJ, DiIulio, JJ and Walters, JP (1996) *Body Count: Moral Poverty ... And How to Win America's War Against Crime and Drugs*, New York: Simon & Schuster

Benson, R (2001) 'It's a stick-up: tags, graffiti, fly-posters – it's an anti-establishment underworld, right?' *The London Evening Standard Magazine*, 12 October

Berger, P and Luckman, T (1979) *The Social Construction of Reality*, London: Penguin Books

Berman, M (1982) *All That Is Solid Melts Into Air: The Experience of Modernity*, London: Verso

Bettman, JR (1979) *An Information Processing Theory of Consumer Choice*, Reading, MA: Addison-Wesley

Bhasker, R (1979) *The Possibility of Naturalism: A Philosophical Critique of the Contemporary Human Sciences*, Hassocks, Sussex: Harvester Press

Blakely, EJ and Snyder, MG (1997) *'Fortress America': Gated Communities in the United States*, Washington DC: Brookings Institute Press

Blanchard, EB, Bassett, J and Koshland, E (1977) 'Psychopathy and delay of gratification' *Criminal Justice and Behaviour* 4: 265–71

Block, R and Block, C (1995) 'Space, place and crime: hot spot areas and hot places of liquor-related crime' in Eck, JE and Weisburd, D (eds), *Crime and Place*, Monsey, NJ: Criminal Justice Press

Bocock, R (1993) *Consumption*, London: Routledge

Bonger, WA (1936) *An Introduction to Criminology*, London: Methuen & Co

Booth, C (1887) 'The inhabitants of Tower Hamlets: their condition and occupations' *Journal of the Royal Statistical Society* 50: 326–91

Booth, C (1888) 'Conditions and occupations of the people in East London and Hackney, 1887' *Journal of the Royal Statistical Society* 51: 276–331

Booth, C (1892) *Life and Labour of the People in London Volume 1: East, Central and South London*, London: Macmillan

Booth, C (1901) *Improved Means of Locomotion as a First Step Towards the Cure of the Housing Difficulties of London*, London: Macmillan

Borges, JL (1970) *Labyrinths: Selected Stories and Other Writings*, London, Harmondsworth: Penguin

Bottoms, AE (1974) 'Review of "Defensible Space" by Oscar Newman' *British Journal of Criminology* 14: 203–06

Bottoms, AE (1993) 'Recent criminological and social theory and the problems of integrating knowledge about individual criminal acts and careers and areal dimensions of crime' in Farrington, DP, Sampson, RJ and Wikstrom, P-OH (eds), *Interpreting Individual and Ecological Aspects of Crime*, Stockholm: National Council for Crime Prevention

Bottoms, AE (1994) 'Environmental criminology' in Maguire, M, Morgan, R and Reiner, R (eds), *The Oxford Handbook of Criminology*, Oxford: Oxford University Press

Bottoms, AE and Xanthos, P (1981) 'Housing policy and crime in the British public sector' in Brantingham, PJ and Brantingham, PL (eds), *Environmental Criminology*, Beverly Hills, CA: Sage

Bottoms, AE and Wiles, P (1986) 'Housing tenure and residential community crime careers in Britain' in Reis, AJ and Tonry, M (eds), *Communities and Crime*, Chicago, IL: University of Chicago Press

Bottoms, AE and Wiles, P (1992) 'Explanations of crime and place' in Evans, DJ, Fyfe, NR and Herbert, DT (eds), *Crime, Policing and Place: Essays in Environmental Criminology*, London: Routledge

Bottoms, AE, Claytor, A and Wiles, P (1992) 'Housing markets and residential community crime careers: a case from Sheffield' in Evans, DJ, Fyfe, NR and Herbert, DT (eds), *Crime, Policing and Place: Essays in Environmental Criminology*, London: Routledge

Bourdieu, P (1977) *Outline of a Theory of Practice*, Cambridge: Cambridge University Press

Bourdieu, P (1984) *Distinction: A Social Critique of the Judgement of Taste*, London: Routledge and Kegan Paul

Bourdieu, P (1990) *In Other Words: Essays Towards a Reflexive Sociology*, Cambridge: Polity

Bourdieu, P and Wacquant, LJD (1992) *An Invitation to Reflexive Sociology*, Chicago, IL: Chicago University Press

Bourgois, P (1995) *In Search of Respect*, Cambridge: Cambridge University Press

Bourgois, P (1998) 'Just another night in a shooting gallery' *Theory, Culture and Society* 15(2): 37–66

Bowen, WA (1994) *Selected Statistics and Comments Concerning Poverty in California and the Nation*, Northridge, CA: California State University

Box, S (1987) *Recession, Crime and Punishment*, London: Tavistock

Boyer, C (1986) *Dreaming the Rational City*, Cambridge, MA: MIT Press

Boyer, MC (1992) 'Cities for sale: merchandising history' in Sorkin, M (ed), *Variations on a Theme Park*, New York: Noonday Press

Boyer, R (1986) *La Théorie de la Régulation: une Analyse Critique*, Paris: La Découverte

Boyle, D (2003) *Authenticity: Brands, Fakes, Spin and the Lust for Real Life*, London: Flamingo

Brantingham, PJ and Brantingham, PL (1984) *Patterns in Crime*, New York: Macmillan

Brantingham, PJ and Brantingham, PL (1991) *Environmental Criminology*, Prospect Heights, IL: Waveland

Brantingham, PJ and Brantingham, PL (1993) 'Environment, routine and situation: toward a pattern theory of crime' in Clarke, RV and Felson, M (eds), *Routine Activity and Rational Choice: Advances in Criminological Theory 5*, New Brunswick, NJ: Transaction Books

Bridge, G (1997) 'Mapping the terrain of time-space compression: power networks in everyday life' *Environment and Planning D* 15: 611–26

Bronfenbrenner, U (1979) *The Ecology of Human Development*, Cambridge, MA: Harvard University Press

Brown, B (1995) *CCTV in Town Centres: Three Case Studies: Crime Prevention and Detention Series Paper 68*, London: HMSO

Buchanan, I (2000) *Michel de Certeau: Cultural Theorist*, London: Sage

Buckley, P (2001) 'Don't shop, you might drop' *The Times*, 5 July

Buck-Morss, S (1986) 'The flâneur, the sandwichman and the whore: the politics of loitering' *New German Critique* 39: 99–140

Buck-Morss, S (1989) *The Dialectics of Seeing: Walter Benjamin and the Arcades Project*, Cambridge, MA: MIT Press

Bulmer, M (1984) *The Chicago School of Sociology: Institutionalization, Diversity, and the Rise of Sociological Research*, Chicago, IL: University of Chicago Press

Bunyan, T (1976) *The Political Police in Britain*, London: Quartet

Bureau of Justice Statistics (1995) *Sourcebook of Criminal Justice Statistics*, US Department of Justice, Washington DC: Government Printing Office

Burchell, G, Gordon, C and Miller, P (eds) (1991) *The Foucault Effect: Studies in Governmentality*, London: Harvester

Burgess, EW (1924) 'The growth of the city: an introduction to a research project' *Publications of the American Sociological Society* 18: 85–97

Burgess, EW (1925) 'The growth of the city' in Park, RE, Burgess, EW and McKenzie, RD (eds), *The City*, Chicago, IL: University of Chicago Press

Burney, E (1990) *Putting Street Crime in its Place*, London: Centre for Inner City Studies, Goldsmiths College, University of London

Burton, VS and Dunaway, RG (1994) 'Strain, relative deprivation and middle-class delinquency' in Barak, G (ed), *Varieties in Criminology: Readings from a Dynamic Discipline*, Westpoint, CT: Praeger

Buss, AH (1966) *Psychopathology*, New York: Wiley

Butler, J, Laclau, E and Zizek, S (2000) *Contingency, Hegemony, Universality: Contemporary Dialogues on the Left*, London: Verso

Campbell, B (1993) *Goliath: Britain's Dangerous Places*, London: Methuen

Campbell, C (1989) *The Romantic Ethic and the Spirit of Modern Consumerism*, London: Blackwell

Campbell, C (1995) 'The sociology of consumption' in Miller, D (ed), *Acknowledging Consumption: A Review of New Studies*, London: Routledge

Carey, JT (1975) *Sociology and Public Affairs: The Chicago School*, Beverly Hills, CA: Sage

Carlen, P (1992) 'Criminal women and criminal justice: the limits to, and potential of, feminist and left realist perspectives' in Matthews, R and Young, J (eds), *Issues in Realist Criminology*, London: Sage

Castel, R (1991) 'From dangerousness to risk' in Burchell, G, Gordon, C and Miller, P (eds), *The Foucault Effect: Studies in Governmentality*, London: Harvester

Castells, M (1976) 'Theory and ideology in urban sociology' in Pickance, C (ed), *Urban Sociology: Critical Essays*, London: Macmillan

Castells, M (1977) *The Urban Question: A Marxist Approach*, London: Edward Arnold

Castells, M (1978) *City, Class and Power*, London: Macmillan

Castells, M (1989) *The Informational City*, Oxford: Blackwell

Castells, M (1994) 'European cities, the Information Society and the global economy' *New Left Review* 204 (March–April)

Castells, M (1996) *The Rise of the Network Society*, Oxford: Blackwell

Caws, MA (1991) *City Images: Perspectives from Literature, Philosophy and Film*, New York: Gordon and Breach

Caygill, H (1998) *Walter Benjamin: The Colour of Experience*, London: Routledge

Chan, W and Rigakos, GS (2002) 'Risk, crime and gender' in *The British Journal of Criminology* 42: 743–61

Chandler, T and Fox, G (1974) *3000 Years of Urban Growth*, London: Academic Press

Chaney, D (1983) 'The department store as a cultural form' *Theory, Culture and Society* 1(3): 22–31

Chaney, D (1990) 'Subtopia in Gateshead: the MetroCentre as a cultural form' *Theory, Culture and Society* 7: 49–68

Christopherson, S (1994) '"The Fortress City": privatised spaces and consumer citizenship' in Amin, A (ed), *Post-Fordism: A Reader*, Oxford: Blackwell

Christie, N (1981) *The Limits to Pain*, Oslo: Universitetsforlaget

Cicourel, AV (1968) *The Social Organization of Juvenile Justice*, New York: Wiley

Clarke, D (1997) 'Consumption and the city: modern and postmodern' *International Journal of Urban and Regional Research* 21(2): 218–37

Clarke, DB and Bradford, MG (1998) 'Public and private consumption in the city' *Urban Studies* 35: 865–88

Clarke, RVG (1980) 'Situational crime prevention: theory and practice' *British Journal of Criminology* 20: 136–47

Clarke, RVG (1983) 'Situational crime prevention: its theoretical basis and practical scope' in Tonry, M and Morris, N (eds), *Crime and Justice: An Annual Review of Research 4*, Chicago, IL: Chicago University Press

Clarke, RVG (1995) 'Situational crime prevention' in Tonry, M and Farrington, DP (eds), *Building a Safer Society: Strategic Approaches to Crime Prevention*, Chicago, IL: Chicago University Press

Clarke, RVG (1997) *Situational Crime Prevention: Successful Case Studies*, Albany, NY: Harrow and Heston

Clarke, RVG and Cornish, DB (1983) *Crime Control in Britain: A Review of Policy Research*, Albany, NY: State University of New York Press

Clarke, RVG and Cornish, DB (1985) 'Modelling offenders' decisions: a framework for policy and research' in Tonry, M and Morris, N (eds), *Crime and Justice: An Annual Review of Research 6*, Chicago, IL: Chicago University Press

Clarke, RVG and Hough, M (1984) *Crime and Police Effectiveness*, London: HMSO

Clarke, RVG and Mayhew, P (1980) *Designing Out Crime*, London: HMSO

Cleckley, HC (1976) *The Mask of Sanity*, St Louis, MO: Mosby

Cloward, R and Ohlin, L (1960) *Delinquency and Opportunity: A Theory of Delinquent Gangs*, New York: Free Press

Cohen, A (1955) *Delinquent Boys: the Culture of the Gang*, New York: Free Press

Cohen, A (1997) 'An elaboration of anomie theory' in Passas, N and Agnew, R (eds), *The Future of Anomie Theory*, Boston, MA: Northeastern University Press

Cohen, L and Felson, M (1979) 'Social change and crime rates: a routine activity approach' *American Sociological Review* 44: 588–608

Cohen, P (1979) 'Policing the working-class city' in Fine, B, Kinsey, R, Lea, J, Picciotto, S and Young, J (eds), *Capitalism and the Rule of Law*, London: Hutchinson

Cohen, P and Ainley, P (2000) 'In the country of the blind: youth studies and cultural studies in Britain' in Pickford, J (ed), *Youth Justice: Theory and Practice*, London: Cavendish Publishing

Cohen, S (1972) *Folk Devils and Moral Panics*, London: MacGibbon and Kee

Cohen, S (1973) 'Property destruction: motives and meanings' in Ward, C (ed), *Vandalism*, New York: Van Nostrand Reinhold

Cohen, S (1979) 'The Punitive City: notes on the dispersal of social control' *Contemporary Crises* 3: 339

Cohen, S (1986) 'Community control: to demystify or to reaffirm?' in Bianchi, H and Van Swaaningen, R (eds), *Abolitionism: Towards a Non-repressive Approach to Crime*, Amsterdam: Free University Press

Cohen, S (1988) *Against Criminology*, New Brunswick, NJ: Transaction Books

Cohen, S and Taylor, I (1976) *Escape Attempts: the Theory and Practice of Resistance to Everyday Life*, London: Allen Lane

Collier, P (1985) 'Nineteenth century Paris: vision and nightmare' in Timms, E and Kelly, D (eds), *Unreal City: Urban Experience In Modern European Literature and Art*, New York: St Martin's Press

Collings, M (1999) *This is Modern Art*, London: Seven Dials

Collings, M (2001) 'Art crazy London' in *The Evening Standard Magazine*, 12 October

Coman, J (2002) 'Vegas goes back to basics (sex and gambling)' *The Sunday Telegraph*, 15 December

Conklin, JE (1972) *Robbery and the Criminal Justice System*, Philadelphia, PA: Lippincott

Connell, RW (1987) *Gender and Power Society: The Person and Sexual Politics*, Cambridge: Polity

Connell, RW (1991) 'Live fast and die young: the construction of masculinity among young working-class men on the margin of the labour market' *Australian and New Zealand Journal of Sociology* 27(2): 141–71

Connell, RW (1995) *Masculinities*, Cambridge: Polity

Cooke, P (1988) 'Modernity, postmodernity and the city' *Theory, Culture and Society* 5: 475–92

Corcoran, MP (1998) 'Commerce, culture and the New Urbanity: urban renewal strategies in the City of Dublin', Paper presented at The American Sociological Association Meeting, San Francisco

Cornish, DB and Clarke, RVG (1986a) *The Reasoning Criminal: Rational Choice Perspectives on Offending*, New York: Springer-Verlag

Cornish, DB and Clarke, RVG (1986b) 'Situational prevention, displacement of crime and rational choice theory' in Heal, K and Laycock, G (eds), *Situational Crime Prevention: From Theory Into Practice*, London: HMSO

Corrigan, C (1991) *A Cinema Without Walls: Movies and Culture After Vietnam*, London: Routledge

Corwin, M (1993) 'Guns for hire: a growing corps of private cops is the first line of defence for homes and shops – but at what a cost?' *Los Angeles Times Magazine* 24

Cosgrove, D (1983) 'Towards a radical cultural geography' *Antipode* 15: 1–11

Cosgrove, D (1989) 'Geography is everywhere: culture and symbolism in human landscapes' in Gregory, D and Walford, R (eds), *Horizons of Human Geography*, London: Macmillan

Cosgrove, D and Jackson, P (1987) 'New directions in cultural geography' *Area* 19: 95–101

Council for the Protection of Rural England (2003) *Lie of the Land*, London: Council for the Protection of Rural England

Crawford, M (1992) 'The world in a shopping mall' in Sorkin, M (ed), *Variations on a Theme Park*, New York: Noonday Press

Cressey, P (1932) *The Taxi-Dance Hall*, Chicago, IL: University of Chicago Press

Creswell, T (1998) 'Night discourse: producing/consuming meaning on the street' in Fyfe, N (ed), *Images of the Street: Planning, Identity and Control in Public Space*, London: Routledge

Critser, G (1998) 'City of self-hate' *Radical Urban Theory Web Journal* (www.rut.com)

Csikszentmihalyi, M (1975) *Beyond Boredom and Anxiety*, San Francisco, CA: Jossey-Bass

Currie, E (1993) *The Reckoning: Drugs, Cities and the American Future*, New York: Hill and Wang

Currie, E (1996) 'Social crime prevention strategies in a market society' in Muncie, J, McLaughlin, E and Langan, M (eds), *Criminological Perspectives*, London: Sage

Currie, E (1997) 'Market, crime and community: toward a mid-range theory of post-industrial violence' *Theoretical Criminology* 1(2): 147–72

Curtis, LP (2002) *Jack the Ripper and the London Press*, New Haven, CT: Yale University Press

da Costa Meyer, E (1995) *The Work of Antonio Sant'Elia*, New Haven, CT: Yale University Press

Dahrendorf, R (1985) *Law and Order*, London: Stevens and Sons

Dahrendorf, R (1987) 'The erosion of citizenship and its consequences for all of us' *New Statesman*, 12 June

Davenport-Hines, R (1998) *Gothic: Four Hundred Years of Excess, Horror and Ruin*, London: Fourth Estate

Davidson, RN (1981) *Crime and Environment*, London: Croom Helm

Davies, N (1994) 'The dark heart of Britain' in *The Guardian* (27–29, 30, 31 August, 1 September)

Davis, M (2000) 'Review of research relevant to HIV prevention for people with HIV', Paper prepared for the Terrence Higgins Trust

Davis, M (1986) *Prisoners of the American Dream*, London: Verso

Davis, M (1990) *City of Quartz: Excavating the Future in Los Angeles*, London: Vintage

Davis, M (1992a) 'Beyond Bladerunner: urban control and the ecology of fear' *Open Media Pamphlet Series* no 23

Davis, M (1992b) 'Fortress Los Angeles: the militarization of urban space' in Sorkin, M (ed), *Variations on a Theme Park*, New York: Noonday Press

Davis, M (1995a) 'Hell factories in the field: a prison-industrial complex' *The Nation* 260: 229

Davis, M (1995b) 'House of cards: too many people in the wrong place, celebrating a waste of life' *Sierra* 36–43

Davis, M (1998) *Ecology of Fear: Los Angeles and the Imagination of Disaster*, New York: Metropolitan Books

Davis, M (2000) *Magical Urbanism: Latinos Reinvent the US City*, London: Verso

Davis, M (2002) *Dead Cities*, New York: The New Press

Davison, G (1983) 'The city as a natural system: theories of urban society in early nineteenth century Britain' in Fraser, D and Sutcliffe, A (eds), *The Pursuit of Urban History*, London: Edward Arnold

Dawe, A (1979) 'Theories of social action' in Bottomore, T and Nisbet, R (eds), *A History of Sociological Analysis*, London: Heinemann

de Certeau, M (1984) *The Practice of Everyday Life*, Berkeley, CA: University of California Press

de Haan, W and Vos, J (2003) 'A crying shame: the over-rationalized conception of man in the rational choice perspective' *Theoretical Criminology* 7(1): 29–54

de Turenne, V (1998) 'Is Mike Davis's Los Angeles all in his head?' *Radical Urban Theory Web Journal* (www.rut.com)

Dear, M (1996) 'In the city, time becomes visible: intentionality and urbanism in Los Angeles' in Scott, AJ and Soja, E (eds), *The City: Los Angeles and Urban Theory at the End of the Twentieth Century*, Berkeley, CA: University of California Press

Defert, D (1991) 'Popular life and insurance technology' in Burchell, G, Gordon, C and Miller, P (eds), *The Foucault Effect: Studies in Governmentality*, London: Harvester

Deleuze, G and Guattari, F (1977) *Anti-Oedipus: Capitalism and Schizophrenia*, New York: Viking Press

Denzin, NK (1984) *On Understanding Emotion*, San Francisco, CA: Jossey-Bass

Denzin, NK (1991) *Images of Postmodern Society: Social Theory and Contemporary Society*, London: Sage

Dery, M (1993) 'Culture jamming: hacking, slashing and sniping in the empire of signs' *Open Magazine Pamphlet Series*, Westfield, NJ: Open Media

Deutsche, R (1991) 'Boys town' *Environment and Planning D: Society and Space* 9: 5–30

Dickinson, G (1997) 'Memories for sale: nostalgia and the construction of identity in Old Pasadena' *Quarterly Journal of Speech* 83: 1–27

DiLonardo, RL (1996) 'Defining and measuring the economic benefit of electronic article surveillance' *Security Journal* 7: 3–9

DiLonardo, RL and Clarke, RVG (1996) 'Reducing the rewards of shoplifting: an evaluation of ink tags' *Security Journal* 7: 11–14

Diner, SJ (1980) *A City and its Universities: Public Policy in Chicago 1892–1919*, Chapel Hill, NC: University of North Carolina Press

Dittmar, H (1992) *The Social Psychology of Material Possessions*, Hemel Hempstead: Harvester Wheatsheaf

Dixon, W (2001) *Exclusive Societies: Towards a Critical Criminology of Post-Apartheid South Africa*, Institute of Criminology, University of Cape Town

Docker, J (1994) *Postmodernism and Popular Culture: A Cultural History*, Cambridge: Cambridge University Press

Dollimore, J (1999) *Death, Desire and Loss in Western Culture*, London: Penguin

Domosh, M (1992) 'Corporate culture and the modern landscape of New York' in Anderson, K and Gale, F (eds), *Inventing Places: Studies in Cultural Geography*, Melbourne: Longman Cheshire

Donald, J (1992) 'Metropolis: the city as text' in Bocock, R and Thompson, K (eds), *Social and Cultural Forms of Modernity*, Buckingham: Open University Press

Douglas, M (1992) *Risk and Blame: Essays in Cultural Theory*, London: Routledge

Downes, D and Rock, P (1982) *Understanding Deviance*, Oxford: Oxford University Press

Duncan, MG (1996) *Romantic Outlaws, Beloved Prisons: The Unconscious Meanings of Crime and Punishment*, New York: New York University Press

Eaton, R (2002) *Ideal Cities: Utopianism and the (Un)Built Environment*, London: Thames and Hudson

Eck, J (1996) 'Preventing crime at places' in Sherman, LW, Gottfredson, D, McKenzie, D, Eck, J, Peuter, P and Bushway, S (eds), *Preventing Crime: What Works, What Doesn't, What's Promising?*, A Report to the United States Congress, prepared for the National Institute of Justice

Eco, U (1986) *Travels in Hyperreality*, San Diego, CA: Harcourt Brace Jovanovich

The Economist (1997a) 'The west is best again', 9 August

The Economist (1997b) 'How to remake a city?', 31 May

The Economist (1997c) 'A little more like angels', 12 April

The Economist (1998) 'City of frauds', 12 December

Edwards, T (2000) *Contradictions of Consumption: Concepts, Practices and Politics in Consumer Society*, Buckingham: Open University Press

Elias, N (1978) 'Civilising process revisited' *Theory and Society* 5: 243–53

Elias, N (1982) *The Civilizing Process*, Oxford: Blackwell

Elias, N (1992) *The Civilizing Process: State Formation and Civilization Vol 2*, London: Blackwell

Ellin, N (1996) *Postmodern Urbanism*, Oxford: Blackwell

Elliott, J and Woods, R (2001) 'Perils on the road to paradise' *The Sunday Times*, 26 August

Engels, F (1969 [1844]) *The Condition of the Working Class in England*, London: Granada

Eshun, E (2001) 'Spot the new Athena poster classic ... is Brit Art the new Athena?' *Evening Standard Magazine*, 19 January

Esser, J and Hirsch, J (1994) 'The crisis of Fordism and the dimensions of a "post-Fordist" regional and urban structure' in Amin, A (ed), *Post-Fordism: A Reader*, Oxford: Blackwell

Etzioni, A (1993) *The Spirit of Community: The Reinvention of American Society*, New York: Touchstone

Etzioni, A (1997) *The New Golden Rule*, London: Profile Books

Evans, D and Herbert, D (1989) *The Geography of Crime*, London: Routledge

Evans, DJ (1992) 'Left realism and the spatial study of crime' in Evans, DJ, Fyfe, NR and Herbert, DT (eds), *Crime, Policing and Place: Essays in Environmental Criminology*, London: Routledge

Evenson, N (1984) 'Paris, 1890–1940' in Sutcliffe, A (ed), *Metropolis 1890–1940*, London: Mansell

Ewald, F (1990) 'Norms, discipline and the law' *Representations* 30: 138–61

Ewald, F (1991) 'Insurance and risk' in Burchell, G, Gordon, C and Miller, P (eds), *The Foucault Effect: Studies in Governmentality*, London: Harvester

Ewen, S (1988) *All Consuming Images: The Politics of Style in Contemporary Culture*, New York: Basic Books

Ewen, S and Ewen, E (1982) *Channels of Desire*, New York: McGraw-Hill

Exum, ML (2002) 'The application and robustness of the rational choice perspective in the study of intoxicated and angry intentions to aggress' *Criminology* 40(4): 933–66

Eysenck, H (1970) *Crime and Personality*, London: Paladin

Fagan, J (1993) 'Editor's introduction' in *Journal of Research in Crime and Delinquency* 30: 381–82

Fainstein, N and Fainstein, S (1987) 'Economic restructuring and the politics of land use planning in New York City' *Journal of the American Planning Association* 53: 237–48

Farington, DP, Lober, R and Van Kammen, W (1990) 'Long-term criminal outcomes of hyperactivity-impulsivity-attention deficit and conduct problems in childhood' in Robins, LN and Rutter, M (eds), *Straight and Devious Pathways from Childhood to Adulthood*, Cambridge: Cambridge University Press

Faris, REL (1967) *Chicago Sociology 1920–1932*, Chicago, IL: University of Chicago Press

Featherstone, M (1987) 'Lifestyle and consumer culture' in Meijer, E (ed), *Everyday Life: Leisure and Culture*, Tilburg, The Netherlands: Department of Leisure Studies, University of Tilburg

Featherstone, M (1991) 'Georg Simmel: Special Edition' *Theory Culture and Society* 8(3) August

Featherstone, M (1994) *Consumer Culture and Postmodernity*, London: Sage

Featherstone, M (1998) 'The flâneur, the city and virtual public life' *Urban Studies* 35: 909–25

Featherstone, M and Burrows, R (eds) (1995) *Cyberspace/Cyberbodies/Cyberpunk: Cultures of Technological Embodiment*, London: Sage

Feeley, M and Simon, J (1992) 'The new penology: notes on the emerging strategy of corrections and its implications' *Criminology* 30(4): 449–74

Feeley, M and Simon, J (1994) 'Actuarial justice: the emerging new criminal law' in Nelken, D (ed), *The Futures of Criminology*, London: Sage

Felson, M (1998) *Crime and Everyday Life*, Thousand Oaks, CA: Pine Forge Press

Felson, RB, Ribner, S and Siegel, M (1984) 'Age and the effect of third parties during criminal violence' *Sociology and Social Research* 68: 452–62

Fenwick, M (1996) 'Emotion and criminology', unpublished PhD Thesis, Cambridge University

Fenwick, M and Hayward, KJ (2000) 'Youth crime, excitement and consumer culture: the reconstruction of aetiology in contemporary criminological theory' in Pickford, J (ed), *Youth Justice: Theory and Practice*, London: Cavendish Publishing

Ferrell, J (1995) 'Urban graffiti: crime, control and resistance' *Youth and Society* 27: 73–92

Ferrell, J (1996) *Crimes of Style: Urban Graffiti and the Politics of Criminality*, Boston, MA: Northeastern University Press

Ferrell, J (1997) 'Youth, crime and cultural space' *Social Justice*, Winter, 24(4): 21–38

Ferrell, J (1999) 'Cultural criminology' *Annual Review of Sociology* 25: 395–418

Ferrell, J (2001) *Tearing Down the Streets: Adventures in Urban Anarchy*, New York: St Martins/Palgrave

Ferrell, J (2004) 'Boredom, crime, and criminology' *Theoretical Criminology* 8(3) (forthcoming)

Ferrell, J (2005) *Empire of Scrounge*, New York: New York University Press (forthcoming)

Ferrell, J and Sanders, CR (eds) (1995) *Cultural Criminology*, Boston, MA: Northeastern University Press

Ferrell, J, Milovanovic, D and Lyng, S (2001) 'Edgework, media practices and the elongation of meaning: a theoretical ethnography of the Bridge Day Event' *Theoretical Criminology* 5(2) 177–201

Ferrell, J, Hayward, KJ, Morrison, W and Presdee, M (eds) (2004) *Cultural Criminology Unleashed*, London: GlassHouse Press (forthcoming)

Fields, F (1989) *Losing Out: The Emergence of Britain's Underclass*, Oxford: Blackwell

Figlio, FM, Hakim, S and Rengert, GF (1986) *Metropolitan Crime Patterns*, Monsey, NY: Willow Tree Press

Filion, P (1991) 'The gentrification-social structure dialectic: a Toronto case study' *International Journal of Urban and Regional Research* 15(4): 553–74

Fine, B (1995) 'From political economy to consumption' in Miller, D (ed), *Acknowledging Consumption*, London: Routledge

Fine, B and Leopold, E (1993) *The World of Consumption*, London: Routledge

Finestone, H (1976) *Victims of Change: Juvenile Delinquents in American Society*, Westport, CT: Greenwood Press

Fishman, R (1982) *Urban Utopias in the Twentieth Century: Ebeneezer Howard, Frank Lloyd Wright and Le Corbusier*, New York: Basic Books

Fiske, J (1989) *Reading the Popular*, Boston, MA: Unwin Hyman

Fjellman, SM (1992) *'Vinyl Leaves': Walt Disney World and America*, Oxford: Westview Press

Flemming, R and Burrows, J (1986) 'The case for lighting as a means of preventing crime' *Research Bulletin, Home Office Research and Planning Unit* No 22: 14–17

Fletcher, J (1848) 'Moral and educational statistics of England and Wales' *Journal Statistical Society of London* 11: 344–66

Foucault, M (1970) *The Order of Things: An Archaeology of the Human Sciences*, New York: Random House

Foucault, M (1973) *The Birth of the Clinic*, London: Tavistock

Foucault, M (1977) *Discipline and Punish: The Birth of the Prison*, London: Penguin Books

Foucault, M (1978) 'Governmentality' in Burchell, G, Gordon, C and Miller, P (eds), *The Foucault Effect: Studies in Governmentality*, Chicago, IL: Chicago University Press

Frantz, D (1999) *Celebration USA: Living in Disney's Brave New Town*, New York: Henry Holt and Company

Friedman, D (1998a) 'The ecology of Mike Davis' *Los Angeles Downtown News*, 5 March

Friedman, D (1998b) 'Taking on Armani radicals' *Los Angeles Downtown News*, 11 December

Frisby, D (1981) *Sociological Impressionism: A Reassessment of Georg Simmel's Social Theory*, London: Routledge

Frisby, D (1985) *Fragments of Modernity*, Cambridge: Polity

Frisby, D (1992) *Simmel and Since: Essays on Georg Simmel's Social Theory*, London: Routledge

Frisby, D (2001) *Cityscapes of Modernity*, Cambridge: Polity

Frisby, D and Featherstone, M (1997) *Simmel on Culture: Selected Writings*, London: Sage

Fromm, E (1976) *To Have Or To Be?*, New York: Harper and Row

Frow, J (1991) *What Was Postmodernism?*, Sydney: Local Consumption Publications

Furedi, F (1997) *Culture of Fear: Risk Taking and the Morality of Low Expectations*, London: Cassell

Furedi, F (2002) *Paranoid Parenting*, London: Penguin

Fyfe, N and Bannister, J (1996) 'City watching: CCTV in public spaces' *Area* 28(1): 37–46

Fyfe, N (ed) (1998) *Images of the Street: Planning, Identity and Control in Public Space*, London: Routledge

Gabor, T (1978) 'Crime displacement: the literature and strategies for its displacement' *Crime and Justice* 6: 100–06

Gaines, J (1992) *Contested Culture: The Image, the Voice and the Law*, London: BFI

Galbraith, JK (1992) *The Culture of Contentment*, London: Penguin

Gambino, F (1996) 'A critique of the Fordism of the Regulation School' *Wildcat-Zirkular* No 28/29, October, trans Emery, E, in *Common Sense* No 19, June 1996

Gamble, A and Walton, P (1976) *Capitalism in Crisis: Inflation and the State*, London: Macmillan

Gardner, C and Sheppard, J (1989) *Consuming Passions: The Rise of Retail Culture*, London: Unwin Hyman

Garland, D (1988) 'British criminology before 1935' in Rock, P (ed), *A History of British Criminology*, Oxford: Oxford University Press

Garland, D (1994) 'Of crimes and criminals: the development of criminology in Britain' in Maguire, M, Morgan, R and Reiner, R (eds), *The Oxford Handbook of Criminology*, Oxford: Oxford University Press

Garland, D (1997) '"Governmentality" and the problem of crime: Foucault, criminology and sociology' *Theoretical Criminology* 1(2): 173–214

Garland, D (1999) 'The commonplace and the catastrophic: interpretations of crime in late modernity' *Theoretical Criminology* 3(3): 353–64

Garland, D (2001) *The Culture of Control: Crime and Social Order in Contemporary Society*, Oxford: Oxford University Press

Garland, D and Sparks, R (2000) 'Criminology, social theory and the challenge of our times' *Special Edition: British Journal of Criminology* 40: 189–204

Garreau, J (1991) *Edge City: Life on the New Frontier*, New York: Doubleday

Gartman, D (1986) *Auto Slavery: The Labor Process in the American Automobile Industry 1897–1950*, New Brunswick, NJ: Rutgers University Press

Gartman, D (1998) 'Postmodernism: or the cultural logic of post-Fordism?' *The Sociological Quarterly* 39: 119–37

Geist, JF (1983) *Arcades: The History of a Building Type*, Cambridge, MA: MIT Press

Gibbs, J (1968) 'Crime, punishment and deterrence' *Southwestern Social Science Quarterly* 48: 515–30

Giddens, A (1979) *Central Problems in Social Theory: Action, Structure and Contradiction in Social Analysis*, London: Macmillan

Giddens, A (1981) *A Contemporary Critique of Historical Materialism*, Berkeley, CA: University of California Press

Giddens, A (1984) *The Constitution of Society*, Cambridge: Polity

Giddens, A (1990) *The Consequences of Modernity*, Cambridge: Polity

Giddens, A (1991) *Modernity and Self-Identity: Self and Society in the Late Modern Age*, Cambridge: Polity

Giedion, S (1978) *Space, Time and Architecture*, Cambridge, MA: Harvard University Press

Gilloch, G (1996) *Myth and Metropolis: Walter Benjamin and the City*, Cambridge: Polity

Girling, E, Loader, I and Sparks, R (1996) 'Crime reporting and the sense of one's place: press constructions of locality and order in late modernity', Paper presented at The American Society of Criminology Conference, Chicago

Girling, E, Loader, I and Sparks, R (1997) 'The trouble with the flats: CCTV and "visions of order" in an English middle town', Paper presented at The British Society of Criminology Conference, Belfast

Girling, E, Loader, I and Sparks, R (1998) 'Crime and the sense of one's place: globalization, restructuring and insecurity in an English town' in Ruggiero, V, South, N and Taylor, I (eds), *European Criminology: Crime and Social Order in Europe*, London: Routledge

Giulianotti, R (1989) 'A participant-observation study of Aberdeen fans at home and away' *Working Paper No 2 on Football Violence*, Aberdeen: Aberdeen University Press

Glassner, B (2000) *The Culture of Fear: Why Americans are Afraid of the Wrong Things?* New York: Basic Books

Glennie, PD (1995) 'Consumption within historical studies' in Miller, D (ed), *Acknowledging Consumption: a Review of New Studies*, London: Routledge

Glennie, PD (1998) 'Consumption, consumerism and the urban form: historical perspectives' *Urban Studies* 35(5–6): 927–51

Glennie, PD and Thrift, NJ (1992) 'Modernity, urbanism and modern consumption' *Environment and Planning D: Society and Space* 10: 423–43

Glennie, PD and Thrift, NJ (1993) 'Modern consumption: theorizing commodities *and* consumers' *Environment and Planning D: Society and Space* 11: 603–06

Glyde, J (1856) 'Localities of crime in Suffolk' *Journal Statistical Society of London* 19: 102–06

Goldberger, P (1996) 'The rise of the private city' in Vitullo, MJ (ed), *Breaking Away: The Future of Cities*, New York: The Twentieth Century Fund

Goldthorpe, JH, Lockwood, D, Bechhofer, F and Platt, J (eds) (1968) *The Affluent Worker: Industrial Attitude and Behaviour*, Cambridge: Cambridge University Press

Gordon, C (1991) 'Governmental rationality: an introduction' in Burchell, G, Gordon, C and Miller, P (eds), *The Foucault Effect: Studies in Governmentality*, London: Harvester

Goss, J (1993) 'The "Magic of the Mall": an analysis of form, function and meaning in the contemporary retail built environment' *Annals of the Association of American Geographers* 83: 18–47

Gottfredson, M and Hirschi, T (1990) *A General Theory of Crime*, London: Sage

Gould, SJ (1981) *The Mis-measure of Man*, New York: Norton

Graham, P and Clarke, J (1996) 'Dangerous places: crime and the city' in Muncie, J and McLaughlin, E (eds), *The Problem of Crime*, London: Sage

Graham, P and Clarke, J (2001) 'Dangerous places: crime and the city' in Muncie, J and McLaughlin, E (eds), *The Problem of Crime*, 2nd edn, London: Sage

Grannis, R (1998a) 'The importance of trivial streets II: residential street "islands" and urban social organization', Paper presented at The American Sociological Association Meeting, San Francisco

Grannis, R (1998b) 'The importance of trivial streets: residential streets and residential segregation' *American Journal of Sociology* 103(6): 1530–64

Greenfield, KJ (1999) 'Life on the edge: is everyday life too dull? Why else would Americans seek risk as never before?' *Time*, 6 September

Gregory, D and Urry, J (1985) *Social Relations and Spatial Structures*, London: Macmillan

Grossberg, L (1991) *We Gotta Get Out of this Place: Popular Conservatism and Postmodern Culture*, New York: Routledge

Guiton, J (1982) *The Ideas of Le Corbusier on Architecture and Urban Planning*, trans Guiton, M, New York: George Braziller

Gumbel, A (1999) 'Bad dreams in the City of Angels' *The Independent on Sunday*, 24 November

Hacking, I (1990) *The Taming of Chance*, Cambridge: Cambridge University Press

Hagedorn, J (1988) *People and Folks: Gangs, Crime and the Underclass in a Rustbelt City*, Chicago, IL: Lake View

Hakim, S and Rengert, GF (1981) *Crime Spillover*, Beverly Hills, CA: Sage

Hale, S (2001) 'Homicide rate up 276% for year in LA' *Los Angeles Times*, 3 January

Hall, P (1984) 'Metropolis 1890–1940' in Sutcliffe, A (ed), *Metropolis 1890–1940*, London: Mansell

Hall, P (1996) *Cities of Tomorrow: An Intellectual History of Urban Planning and Design in the Twentieth Century*, Oxford: Blackwell

Hall, S and Jefferson, A (eds) (1976) *Resistance Through Rituals: Youth Subcultures in Postwar Britain*, London: Hutchinson

Hall, S, Critcher, C, Jefferson, T, Clarke, J and Roberts, B (eds) (1978) *Policing the Crisis: Mugging, the State and Law 'n' Order*, London: Macmillan

Hall, S (1997) 'Visceral cultures and criminal practices' *Theoretical Criminology* 1(4): 453–78

Hall, S and Jacques, M (1990) *New Times: The Changing Face of Politics in the 1990s*, London: Lawrence and Wishart

Halleck, S (1971) *Psychiatry and the Dilemmas of Crime*, Berkeley, CA: University of California Press

Hamilton, P (1993) 'Running the motor industry' in Maidment, R and Thompson, G (eds), *Managing the United Kingdom: An Introduction to its Political Economy and Public Policy*, London: Sage

Hamm, M (1995) *American Skinheads: the Criminology and Control of Hate Crime*, Westpoint, CT: Praeger

Hamm, M (2004) 'Apocalyptic violence: the seductions of terrorist subcultures' *Special Edition: Cultural Criminology, Theoretical Criminology* 8(3) (forthcoming)

Hannigan, J (1995) 'The postmodern city: a new urbanization?' *Current Sociology* 43(1): 151–217

Hannigan, J (1998) *Fantasy City: Pleasure and Profit in the Postmodern Metropolis*, London: Routledge

Harin, J and Martin, J (1984) 'The armed urban bank robber: a profile' *Federal Probation* 48: 47–53

Harries, K (1999) *Mapping Crime: Principles and Practice*, Washington DC: National Institute of Justice

Harvey, D (1973) *Social Justice and the City*, Baltimore, MD: Johns Hopkins University Press

Harvey, D (1978) 'The urban process under capitalism' *International Journal of Urban and Regional Research* 2: 101–31

Harvey, D (1982) *The Limits to Capital*, Oxford: Blackwell

Harvey, D (1985a) *Consciousness and the Urban Experience: Studies in the History and Theory of Capitalist Urbanisation (1)*, Oxford: Blackwell

Harvey, D (1985b) *The Urbanisation of Capital: Studies in the History and Theory of Capitalist Urbanisation (2)*, Oxford: Blackwell

Harvey, D (1987) 'Flexible accumulation though urbanization: reflections on "postmodernism" in the American city' *Antipode* 19

Harvey, D (1990) *The Condition of Postmodernity*, Cambridge, MA: Blackwell

Harvey, I (2000) 'Youth culture, drugs and criminality' in Pickford, J (ed), *Youth Justice: Theory and Practice*, London: Cavendish Publishing

Harvey, L (1987) *Myths of the Chicago School of Sociology*, Aldershot: Avebury

Harwood, A (2003) 'Cards mock city crime' *Daily Mirror*, 14 October

Hassan, I (1971) *The Dismemberment of Orpheus: Towards a Postmodern Literature*, London: Oxford University Press

Hayden, D (1980) 'What would a non-sexist city be like? Speculations on housing, urban design and human work' *Signs* 5(3): 170–87

Haydon, D (1984) *Redesigning the American Dream: the Future of Housing, Work, and Family Life*, New York: WW Norton

Hayward, KJ (2001a) 'The Chicago School' in McLaughlin, E and Muncie, J (eds), *The Sage Dictionary of Criminology*, London: Sage

Hayward, KJ (2001b) '"Crime in Context" by Ian Taylor: a review' *Theoretical Criminology* 5(1): 101–05

Hayward, KJ (2002) 'The vilification and pleasures of youthful transgression' in Muncie, J, Hughes, E and McLaughlin, E (eds), *Youth Justice: Critical Readings*, London: Sage

Hayward, KJ (2003) 'Crime and consumer culture in late modern society' in Sumner, C (ed), *The Blackwell Companion to Criminology*, Oxford: Blackwell

Hayward, KJ and Morrison, W (2002) 'Locating Ground Zero: caught between the narratives of crime and war' in Strawson, J (ed), *Law After Ground Zero*, London: Cavendish Publishing

Hayward, KJ and Presdee, M (2002) 'The adult connection: Bill Sykes and the Fagin factor: adults and the criminalization of youth', 54th Annual Meeting of the American Society of Criminology Conference, Atlanta, Georgia

Hayward, KJ and Young, J (eds) (2004) *Special Edition: Cultural Criminology, Theoretical Criminology* 8(3) (forthcoming)

Hebdidge, D (1988) *Hiding in the Light: On Images and Things*, London: Routledge

Heim, M (1991) 'The erotic ontology of cyberspace' in Benedikt, M (ed), *Cyberspace: First Steps*, Cambridge, MA: MIT Press

Henry, S and Milovanovic, D (1996) *Constitutive Criminology: Beyond Postmodernism*, London: Sage

Henry, S and Milovanovic, D (2001) 'Constitutive criminology' in McLaughlin, E and Muncie, J (eds), *The Sage Dictionary of Criminology*, London: Sage

Her Majesty's Treasury Occasional Paper No 10 (1999) *Persistent Poverty and Lifetime Inequality: The Evidence*, Report Chaired by Professor John Hills, Eastbourne: Manor Park Press

Herbert, D (1982) *The Geography of Urban Crime*, London: Longman

Herrnstein, RJ and Murray, C (1994) *The Bell Curve: Intelligence and Class Structure in American Life*, New York: Free Press

Heydebrand, W and Seron, C (1990) *Rationalizing Justice*, Albany, NY: SUNY Press

Hill, DM (1995) 'Postmodernity and the city' in Lovenduski, J and Stanyer, J (eds), *Contemporary Political Studies Vol 1*, London: Political Studies Association

Hillier, B (1973) 'In defence of space' *RIBAJ* November: 539–44

Hills, P (1983) *Social Concern and Urban Realism: American Painting of the 1930s*, Boston, MA: Boston University

Hirschi, T (1969) *Causes of Delinquency*, Berkeley, CA: University of California Press

Hirschman, EC and Holbrook, MB (1982) 'Hedonic consumption: emerging concepts, methods and propositions' *Journal of Marketing* 46: 92–101

Hobbs, D, Lister, S, Hadfield, P, Winlow, S and Hall, S (2000) 'Receiving shadows: governance and liminality in the night-time economy' *British Journal of Sociology* 51(4): 701–17

Hobsbawm, E (1969) *Introduction to 'the Condition of the Working Class in England' by Frederic Engels*, London: Granada

Hoch, SJ and Lowenstein, GF (1991) 'Time-inconsistent preferences and consumer self control' *Journal of Consumer Research* 14: 492–507

Holbrook, MB and Hirschman, EC (1986) 'The experimental aspects of consumption: consumer fantasies, feelings and fun' *Journal of Consumer Research* 9: 132–40

Holston, J (1986) *The Modernist City: An Anthropological Critique of Brasilia*, Chicago, IL: Chicago University Press

Hope, T (1985) *Implementing Crime Prevention Measures*, Home Office Research Study No 86, London: HMSO

Hopkins, JSP (1990) 'West Edmonton mall: landscapes of myth and elsewhereness' *Canadian Geographer* 34: 2–17

Hopkins, N (2000) 'Crime in Britain series' *The Guardian*, 4 July

Horkheimer, M and Adorno, T (1973) *The Dialectic of Enlightenment*, New York: Continuum

Hough, JM, Clarke, RVG and Mayhew, P (1980) 'Introduction' in Clarke, RVG and Mayhew, P (eds), *Designing Out Crime*, London: HMSO

Hough, M and Mayhew, P (1983) *The British Crime Survey: First Report*, London: HMSO

Hough, M and Mayhew, P (1985) *Taking Account of Crime: Key Findings from the Second British Crime Survey*, London: HMSO

Howard, E (1898) *Tomorrow: A Peaceful Path to Real Reform*, London: Swan Sonnenschein

Howe, A (2000) 'Postmodern criminology and its feminist discontents' *Australian and New Zealand Journal of Criminology* 33(2): 221–36

Howe, A (2003) 'Managing men's violence in the criminological arena' in Sumner, C (ed), *The Blackwell Companion to Criminology*, Oxford: Blackwell

Hughes, R (1991) *The Shock of the New: Art and the Century of Change*, London: Thames and Hudson

Hughes, R (1996) *The Fatal Shore*, London: Harvill Press

Hulsman, L (1983) 'Abolire il sistema penale?' *Dei delitti e delle pene* 1: 71–90

Hutton, W (1995) *The State We're In*, London: Vintage

Huyssen, A (1990) 'Mapping the postmodern' in Nicholson, L (ed), *Feminism/Postmodernism*, London: Routledge

Jackson-Jacobs, C (2004) 'Taking a beating: narrative gratifications of fighting as an underdog' in Ferrell, J, Hayward, KJ, Morrison, W and Presdee, M (eds), *Cultural Criminology Unleashed*, London: GlassHouse Press (forthcoming)

James, O (1995) *Juvenile Violence in a Winner-Loser Culture: Socio-economic and Familial Origins of Violence Against the Person*, London: Free Association Books

Jameson, F (1984) 'Postmodernism or the cultural logic of postmodernism' *New Left Review* 146: 53–92

Jameson, F (1991) *Postmodernism, or, the Cultural Logic of Late Capitalism*, London: Verso

Jarvis, B (1998) *Postmodern Cartographies: The Geographical Imagination in Contemporary American Culture*, London: Pluto Press

Jefferson, T (1994) 'Theorizing masculine subjectivity' in Newburn, T and Stanko, E (eds), *Just Boys Doing Business?*, London: Routledge

Jefferson, T (1997) 'Masculinities and crime' in Maguire, R, Morgan, M and Reiner, R (eds), *The Oxford Handbook of Criminology*, Oxford: Oxford University Press

Jeffrey, CR (1971) *Crime Prevention through Environmental Design*, Beverly Hills, CA: Sage

Jeffrey, I (1977) 'Concerning images of the metropolis' in *Cityscape 1910–39: Urban Themes in American, German and British Art*, London: Arts Council Publication

Jencks, C (1977) *The Language of Postmodern Architecture*, London: Academy Editions

Jencks, C (1980) *Postmodern Classicism: The New Synthesis*, Architectural Design Monograph, New York: Rizzoli

Jervis, J (1998) *Exploring the Modern*, Oxford: Blackwell

Jewkes, V (2003) *Dot.cons: Crime, Deviance and Identity on the Internet*, Cullompton: Willan

Jodidio, P (1995) *Contemporary Californian Architects*, Köln: Taschen

Johnson, JH (1964) 'The suburban expansion of housing in Greater London 1918–1939' in Coppock, JT and Prince, H (eds), *Greater London*, London: Faber & Faber

Johnston, L (1992) *The Rebirth of Private Policing*, London: Routledge

Jones, RA (1999) 'The truth squad of history' *Los Angeles Times* (*Metro*), 10 January

Jones, R (2000) 'Digital rule: punishment, control and technology' *Punishment and Society* 2(1): 5–22

Jones, T, MacLean, B and Young, J (1986) *The Islington Crime Survey*, Aldershot: Gower

Jones, T and Newburn, T (1996) 'The regulation and control of the private security industry' in Saulsbury, W, Mott, J and Newburn, T (eds), *Themes in Contemporary Policing*, London: Police Foundation

Jones, T and Newburn, T (1998) *Private Security and Private Policing*, Oxford: Clarendon Press

Julier, G (2000) 'From object to experience' in Pavitt, J (ed), *Brand.New*, London: V&A Publications

Kapardis, A (1989) 'One hundred convicted armed robbers in Melbourne: myth and reality' in Challenger, D (ed), *Armed Robbery*, Canberra: Australian Institute of Criminology

Kasinitz, P (1995) *Metropolis: Centre and Symbol of Our Times*, London: Macmillan Press

Katona, G (1951) *Psychological Analysis of Economic Behaviour*, New York: McGraw-Hill

Katona, G (1975) *Psychological Economics*, New York: Elsevier

Katz, J (1988) *The Seductions of Crime: Moral and Sensual Attractions in Doing Evil*, New York: Basic Books

Katz, J (1999) *How Emotions Work*, Chicago, IL: Chicago University Press

Keating, P (1984) 'The metropolis in literature' in Sutcliffe, A (ed), *Metropolis 1890–1940*, London: Mansell

Kelling, GL and Coles, CM (1996) *Fixing Broken Windows: Restoring Order and Reducing Crime in Our Communities*, New York: Touchstone Books

Kellner, D (1989) *Jean Baudrillard: From Marxism to Postmodernism and Beyond*, Stanford, CA: Stanford University Press

Kelly, GA (1955) *The Psychology of Personal Contacts: Volumes 1 and 2*, New York: Norton

Kemper, TD (1990) *Research Agendas in the Sociology of Emotions*, New York: New York State University Press

Kerr, P (1995) *Gridiron*, London: Chatto & Windus

Kessler, AJ (1997) 'Instant gratification' *Forbes*, 25 August: 86

Kinsey, R (1984) *Merseyside Crime Survey: First Report: November 1984*, Edinburgh: Centre for Criminology, University of Edinburgh

Kinsey, R, Lea, J and Young, J (1986) *Losing the Fight Against Crime*, Oxford: Blackwell

Knorr-Cetina, K and Cicourel, AV (1981) *Advances in Social Theory: Towards an Integration of Micro- and Macro-Sociologies*, London: Routledge and Kegan Paul

Kowinski, WS (1985) *The Malling of America: An Inside Look at the Great American Paradise*, New York: William Morris and Co

Krier, R (1987) 'Tradition-modernity-modernism: some necessary explanations' *Architectural Design Profile* 65

Kurzweil, R (1999a) *The Age of Spiritual Machines*, Warriewool, NSW: Orion Business Books

Kurzweil, R (1999b) 'The future? We're virtually there' *The Guardian*, 16 January

Laermans, R (1993) 'Learning to consume: early department stores and the shaping of the modern consumer culture' *Theory, Culture and Society* 10: 79–102

Lait, M (1998) 'Homicides plunge to a 28-year low' *Los Angeles Times*, 28 December

Langham, L (1992) 'Neon cages: shopping for subjectivity' in Shields, R (ed), *Lifestyle Shopping: The Subject of Consumption*, London: Routledge

Lasch, C (1979) *The Culture of Narcissism: American Life in the Age of Diminishing Expectations*, New York: WW Norton and Co

Lash, S and Urry, J (1987) *The End of Organised Capital*, Cambridge: Polity

Lash, S and Urry, J (1994) *Economies of Signs and Space*, London: Sage

Lasley, JR (2002) 'New writing on the wall: exploring the middle class graffiti sub-culture' in Tiemann, K (ed), *Crossroads: Readings in Social Problems*, London: Longman

Lasn, K (2000) *Culture Jam: How to Reverse America's Suicidal Consumer Binge – And Why We Must*, New York: HarperCollins

Layder, D (1981) *Structure, Interaction and Social Theory*, London: Routledge and Kegan Paul

Le Corbusier (1986) [1925] *The City of Tomorrow and Its Planning*, New York: Dover

Le Corbusier (1928a) *Urbanisme*, Paris: Editions Arthaud

Le Corbusier (1928b) *Un Maison – un Palais*, Turin: Bottega d'Erasmo

Le Corbusier (1935) *La Ville Radieuse*, Paris: Vincent, Freal et Cie

Lea, J (1992) 'Left realism: a framework for the analysis of crime' in Young, J and Matthews, R (eds), *Rethinking Criminology: The Realist Debate*, London: Sage

Lea, J (1995) 'Post Fordism and criminality', article posted on *The John Lea Website* www.bunker8.pwp.blueyonder.co.uk/misc/pford.html

Lea, J (1997) 'Post-Fordism and criminality' in Jewson, N and MacGregor, S (eds), *Transforming Cities: Contested Governance and New Spatial Divisions*, London: Routledge

Lea, J and Young, J (1984) *What is to be Done about Law and Order?*, Harmondsworth: Penguin

Lechte, J (1996) '(Not) belonging in postmodern space' in Watson, S and Gibson, K (eds), *Postmodern Cities and Spaces*, Oxford: Blackwell

Lee, ML (1993) *Consumer Culture Reborn: The Cultural Politics of Consumption*, London: Routledge

Lees, L (1998) 'Urban renaissance and the street: spaces of control and contestation' in Fyfe, NR (ed), *Images of the Street: Planning, Identity and Control in Public Space*, London: Routledge

Lefebvre, H (1984) *Everyday Life in the Modern World*, Somerset, NJ: Transaction

Lefebvre, H (1991) *The Production of Space*, Oxford: Blackwell

Lefebvre, H (1995) *Introduction to Modernity: Twelve Preludes*, trans Moore, J, London: Verso

Lefebvre, H (1996) *Writings on Cities*, London: Blackwell

LeGates, RT and Hartman, C (1986) 'The anatomy of displacement in the United States' in Smith, N and Williams, P (eds), *Gentrification of the City*, Boston, MA: Allen & Unwin

Leiss, W, Kline, S and Jhally, S (1986) *Social Communication as Advertising: Persons, Products and Images of Well-being*, New York: Macmillan

Leo, C (1997) 'Urban decay: barricading our cities and our minds' *Radical Urban Theory Web Journal* (www.rut.com)

Lindstrom, FB and Hardert, RA (1988) 'Kimball Young on the founders of the Chicago School' *Sociological Perspectives* 31: 269–97

Lipietz, A (1982) 'Towards global Fordism?' *New Left Review* 132, March–April: 33–47

Lipietz, A (1987) *Mirages and Miracles: The Crisis of Global Fordism*, London: Verso

Loader, I (1997) 'Private security and the demand for protection in contemporary Britain' *Policing and Society* 7: 143–62

Loader, I (1999) 'Consumer culture and the commodification of policing and security' *Sociology* 33(2): 373–92

Lunt, P (1995) 'Psychological approaches to consumption: varieties of research – past, present and future' in Miller, D (ed), *Acknowledging Consumption: A Review of New Studies*, London: Routledge

Lunt, P and Livingstone, S (1992) *Mass Consumption and Personal Identity*, Milton Keynes: Open University Press

Lury, C (1996) *Consumer Culture*, Cambridge: Polity

Lynch, K (1960) *The Image of the City*, Cambridge, MA: MIT Press

Lyng, S (1990) 'Edgework: a social psychological analysis of voluntary risk-taking' *American Journal of Sociology* 95: 876–921

Lyng, S (1991) 'Edgework revisited: a reply to Miller' *American Journal of Sociology* 96: 1534–39

Lyon, D (1994a) *Postmodernity*, Buckingham: Open University Press

Lyon, D (1994b) *The Electronic Eye: The Rise of Surveillance Society*, Cambridge: Polity

Lyotard, JF (1984) *The Postmodern Condition: A Report on Knowledge*, Manchester: Manchester University Press

McAdams, L (1998) 'Jeremiah among the palms: the lives and dark prophecies of Mike Davis' *LA Weekly*, 29 December–3 January

McCole, J (1993) *Walter Benjamin and the Antinomies of Tradition*, New York: Cornell University Press

McCracken, G (1988) *Culture and Consumption*, Bloomington, IN: Indiana University Press

McDonald, R (1997) *Youth, the Underclass and Social Exclusion*, London: Routledge

McHale, B (1987) *Postmodernist Fiction*, London: Methuen

McIntosh, D (1969) *The Foundations of Human Society*, Chicago, IL: Chicago University Press

McKendrick, N, Brewer, J and Plumb, JH (1982) *The Birth of A Consumer Society: The Commercialization of Eighteenth Century England*, London: Europa

McKenzie, E (1994) *Privatopia: Homeowner Associations and the Rise of the Residential Private Government*, New Haven, CT: Yale University Press

McLaren, A (1990) *Our Own Master Race: Eugenics in Canada 1885–1945*, Toronto: McClelland and Stewart

McLeod, M (1985) 'Architecture' in Trachtenberg, S (ed), *The Postmodern Movement: A Handbook of Contemporary Innovation in the Arts*, Westport, CT: Greenwood Press

McRobbie, A (1993) 'Shut up and dance: youth culture and changing modes of femininity' *Cultural Studies* 7: 406–26

McRobbie, A and Thornton, S (1995) 'Rethinking "moral panic" for multi-mediated social worlds' *British Journal of Sociology* 46(4): 245–59

Maffesoli, M (1996) *The Time of Tribes: The Decline of Individualism in Mass Society*, London: Sage

Maguire, M (1994) 'Crime statistics, patterns and trends: changing perceptions and their implications' in Maguire, M, Morgan, R and Reiner, R (eds), *The Oxford Handbook of Criminology*, Oxford: Clarendon Press

Maher, BA (1966) *Principles of Psychopathology: An Experiential Approach*, New York: McGraw-Hill

Maltz, M (1994) 'Deviating from the mean: the declining significance of significance' *The Journal of Research in Crime and Delinquency* 31(4): 434–63

Mandel, E (1975) *Late Capitalism*, London: Verso

Mannheim, H (1972) *Pioneers in Criminology*, Montclair, NJ: Patterson Smith

Marcuse, H (1964) *One Dimensional Man: Studies in the Ideology of Advanced Industrial Society*, London: Routledge and Kegan Paul

Marcuse, P (1995) 'Not chaos but walls: postmodernism and the partitioned city' in Watson, S and Gibson, K (eds), *Postmodern Cities and Spaces*, Oxford: Blackwell

Martin, R (1988) 'Industrial capitalism in transition: the contemporary reorganization of the British space-economy' in Massey, D and Allen, J (eds), *Uneven Redevelopment*, London: Hodder & Stoughton

Marx, G (1995) 'Electric eye in the sky: some reflections on the new surveillance and popular culture' in Ferrell, J and Sanders, CR (eds), *Cultural Criminology*, Boston, MA: Northeastern University

Marx, K (1969) *Theories of Surplus Value*, Moscow: Foreign Languages Publishing House

Marx, K (1975) 'Economic and philosophical manuscripts of 1844' in Marx, K and Engels, F, *Collated Works Vol 3*, New York: International Publishers

Massey, D (1991) 'Flexible sexism' *Environment and Planning D: Society and Space* 9: 31–57

Massey, D (1993) 'Power geometry and a progressive sense of place' in Bird, J, Curtis, B, Putnam, T, Robertson, G and Tickner, L (eds), *Mapping the Futures*, London: Routledge

Masuda, B (1993) 'Credit card fraud prevention: a successful retail strategy' in Clarke, RVG (ed), *Crime Prevention Studies: Vol 1*, Monsey, NY: Criminal Justice Press

Matthews, FH (1977) *Quest for an American Sociology: Robert E Park and the Chicago School*, London: McGill-Queen's University Press

Matthews, R and Young, J (1992) *Issues in Realist Criminology*, London: Sage

Matza, D (1964) *Delinquency and Drift*, New York: John Wiley

Matza, D (1969) *Becoming Deviant*, Englewood Cliffs, NJ: Prentice Hall

Matzerath, H (1984) 'Berlin, 1890–1940' in Sutcliffe, A (ed), *Metropolis 1890–1940*, London: Mansell

Mayer, HM and Wade, RC (1969) *Chicago: Growth of a Metropolis*, Chicago, IL: University of Chicago Press

Mayhew, H (1968 [1862]) *London Labour and the London Poor*, New York: Dover Publications

Mazzoleni, D (1990) 'The city and the imaginary' *New Formations 11: A Journal of Culture/Theory/Politics* Vol 2 (Summer)

Mearns, A (1883) *The Bitter Cry of Outcast London: An Inquiry into the Condition of the Abject Poor*, London: James Clarke

Mele, AR (1987) *Irrationality: An Essay on Akrasia, Self-Deception and Self-Control*, New York: Oxford University Press

Mellor, R (1997) 'Cool times for a changing city' in Jewson, N and MacGregor, S (eds), *Transforming Cities: Contested Governance and New Spatial Divisions*, London: Routledge

Mellor, D and Jeffrey, I (1977) 'From order to apocalypse: the city in British art 1890–1940' in Arts Council, *Cityscape 1910–39: Urban Themes in American, German and British Art*, London: Arts Council Publications

Merleau-Ponty, M (1962) *Phenomenology of Perception*, London: Routledge and Kegan Paul

Merton, RK (1938) 'Social structure and anomie' *American Sociological Review* 3: 672–82

Merton, RK (1968) *Social Theory and Social Structure*, New York: Free Press

Meštrović, SG (1997) *Postemotional Society*, London: Sage

Metcalfe, J and Mischel, W (1999) 'A hot/cool system analysis of delay of gratification: dynamics and willpower' *Psychological Review* 106: 3–19

Mick, DG and DeMoss, M (1990) 'To me from me: a descriptive phenomenology of self gifts' *Advances in Consumer Research* 17: 677–82

Miles, MC (1997) *Art, Space and the City: Public Art and Urban Fortunes*, London: Routledge

Miles, S (1998a) *Consumerism as a Way of Life*, London: Sage

Miles, S (1998b) 'The consuming paradox: a new research agenda for urban consumption' *Urban Studies* 35: 1001–08

Miles, S and Paddison, M (1998) 'Urban consumption: an historiographical note' *Urban Studies* 35: 815–23

Miller, D (1987) *Material Culture and Mass Consumption*, Oxford: Blackwell

Miller, D (1995) 'Consumption as the vanguard of history' in Miller, D (ed), *Acknowledging Consumption*, London: Routledge

Miller, EM (1986) *Street Woman*, Philadelphia, PA: Temple University

Miller, EM (1991) 'Assessing the risk inattention to class, race/ethnicity and gender: comment on Lyng' *American Journal of Sociology* 96: 1530–34

Miller, J (1995) 'Struggles over the symbolic: gang style and the meanings of social control' in Ferrell, J and Sanders, CR (eds), *Cultural Criminology*, Boston, MA: Northeastern University Press

Miller, MB (1981) *The Bon Marché: Bourgeois Culture and the Department Store 1869–1920*, Princeton, NJ: Princeton University Press

Miller, P and Rose, N (1990) 'Governing economic life' *Economy and Society* 19: 1–31

Minden, M (1985) 'The city in early cinema: *Metropolis*, *Berlin* and *October*' in Timms, E and Kelly, D (eds), *Unreal City*, New York: St Martin's Press

Mingay, GE (1977) *Rural Life in Victorian England*, London: William Heinemann

Minton, A (2002) *Building Balanced Communities: the US and UK Compared*, London: RCIS Leading Edge Series

Mitchell, BR (1975) *European Historical Statistics 1750–1970*, London: Macmillan

Mitchell, BR (1983) *International Historical Statistics: The Americas 1750–1988*, Basingstoke: Macmillan

Moffitt, TE (1993) 'Life-course-persistent and adolescent-limited antisocial behaviour: a developmental taxonomy' *Psychological Review* 100: 674–701

Monkkonen, EH (1997) 'The violence conundrum: homicide rates across the country are falling dramatically, but no one really knows why' *Los Angeles Times*, 30 November

Monkkonen, EH (2000) 'The puzzle of murder statistics: a search for cause and effect' *Los Angeles Times*, 3 September

Monkkonen, EH (2002) *Crime, Justice, History*, Columbus, OH: Ohio State University Press

Mooney, G and Danson, M (1997) 'Beyond "Culture City": Glasgow as a "Dual City"' in Jewson, N and MacGregor, S (eds), *Transforming Cities: Contested Governance and New Spatial Divisions*, London: Routledge

Moore, C and Allen, G (1976) *Dimensions: Space, Shape and Scale in Architecture*, New York: Architectural Record Books

Morris, AEJ (1979) *History of Urban Form: Before the Industrial Revolutions*, London: George Goodwin

Morris, T (1958) *The Criminal Area: A Study In Social Ecology*, London: Routledge and Kegan Paul

Morrison, A (1894) *Tales of Mean Streets*, London: Methuen

Morrison, W (1995) *Theoretical Criminology: From Modernity to Post Modernism*, London: Cavendish Publishing

Mukerji, C (1983) *From Graven Images: Patterns of Modern Materialism*, New York: Columbia University Press

Mullins, P (1991) 'Tourism urbanization' *International Journal of Urban and Regional Research* 15: 326–42

Mumford, L (1961) *The City in History*, London: Secker & Warburg

Muncie, J and McLaughlin, E (eds) (1996) *The Problem of Crime: Crime, Order and Social Control*, London: Sage

Munday, M (2004) 'When Saturday comes' *The Times Magazine*, 31 January

Murray, C (1984) *Losing Ground*, New York: Basic Books

Murray, C (1990) *The Emerging British Underclass*, London: IEA Health and Welfare Unit

Naffine, N (1997) *Feminism and Criminology*, Cambridge: Polity

Nava, E (1992) *Changing Cultures: Feminism, Youth and Consumerism*, London: Sage

Nava, E (1997) 'Women, modernity and the city' in Falk, P and Campbell, C (eds), *The Shopping Experience*, London: Sage

Nelken, D (ed) (1994) *The Futures of Criminology*, London: Sage

New Labour's Social Exclusion Unit (1999) *Bringing Britain Together: A National Strategy for Neighbourhood Renewal*, London: The Stationery Office

Newman, G, Clarke, RVG and Shoham, SG (1997) *Rational Choice and Situational Crime Prevention: Theoretical Foundations*, Dartmouth: Ashgate

Newman, O (1972) *Defensible Space*, London: Architectural Press

Newman, O (1980) *Community of Interest*, Garden City, NY: Doubleday

Newman, JP, Patterson, CM, Howland, EW and Nichols, SL (1990) 'Passive avoidance in psychopaths: the effects of reward' *Personality and Individual Offences* 11: 1101–14

Newman, JP, Kosson, DS and Patterson, CM (1992) 'Delay of gratification in non-psychopathic offenders' *Journal of Abnormal Psychology* 101: 630–36

Newman, S and Lonsdale, S (1996) *Human Jungle*, London: Ebury Press

Nightingale, C (1993) *On the Edge*, New York: Basic Books

Nyman, N (1974) *Experimental Music: Cage and Beyond*, New York: Schrimer Books

O'Connor, J and Wynne, D (1993) *From the Margins to the Centre: Cultural Production and Consumption in the Post-Industrial City*, Manchester: Manchester Institute for Popular Culture (Working Papers in Cultural Studies No 7)

O'Connor, J and Wynne, D (eds) (1996) *From the Margins to the Centre*, Aldershot: Arena

O'Malley, P (1992) 'Risk, power, and crime prevention' *Economy and Society* 21: 252–75

O'Malley, P (1993) 'Containing in our excitement: the limits to discipline in commodity-based societies' *Studies in Law Politics and Society* 13: 159–86

O'Malley, P (1996) 'Risk and responsibility' in Osborne, T and Rose, N (eds), *Foucault and Political Reason*, Chicago, IL: Chicago University Press

O'Malley, P and Mugford, S (1994) 'Crime, excitement and modernity' in Barak, G (ed), *Varieties of Criminology: Readings From a Dynamic Discipline*, Westport, CT: Praeger

Oates, JC (1995) *Zombie*, New York: Penguin

Olsen, DJ (1986) *The City as a Work of Art: London, Paris, Vienna*, New Haven, CT: Yale University Press

Ouroussoff, N (1999) 'Time to move past the fault-finding: anger at author Mike Davis's view of LA reveals a reluctance to seriously discuss the future at a critical juncture' *Los Angeles Times* (Home Edition), 28 February

Painter, K (1988) *Lighting and Crime Prevention: The Edmonton Project*, Centre for Criminology and Police Studies: Middlesex Polytechnic

Painter, K, Lea, J, Woodhouse, T and Young, J (1989) *Hammersmith and Fulham Crime and Policing Final Report*, London: Centre for Criminology and Police Studies, Middlesex Polytechnic

Paoletti, JT (1985) 'Art' in Trachtenberg, S (ed), *The Postmodern Movement: A Handbook of Contemporary Innovation in the Arts*, Westport, CT: Greenwood Press

Papastergiadis, N (2002) 'Traces left in cities' *Architectural Design, Poetics in Architecture* No 156

Papastergiadis, N and Rogers, H (1996) 'Parafunctional spaces' in Stathatos, J (ed), *Art and the City*, London: Academy Group

Parent-Duchâtelet, A (1836) *De la prostitution dans la ville de Paris*, Paris: JB Bailliere et fils

Park, RE (1925) 'The city: suggestions for the investigation of human behaviour in the urban environment' in Park, RE, Burgess, EW and McKenzie, RD (eds), *The City*, Chicago, IL: Chicago University Press

Park, RE (1952) *Human Communities*, Glencoe, IL: The Free Press

Park, RE, Burgess, EW and McKenzie, RD (eds) (1925) *The City*, Chicago, IL: University of Chicago Press

Parnell, P and Kane, S (eds) (2003) *Crime's Power: Anthropologists and the Ethnography of Crime*, New York: Palgrave/St Martin's

Passas, N (1997) 'Anomie and relative deprivation' in Passas, N and Agnew, R (eds), *The Future of Anomie Theory*, Boston, MA: Northeastern University Press

Patton, P (1996) 'Imagining cities: images of postmodernity' in Watson, S and Gibson, K (eds) *Postmodern Cities*, Oxford: Blackwell

Pearson, G (1975) *The Deviant Imagination: Psychiatry, Social Work and Change*, London: Macmillan Press

Pesce, M (2004) *The Playful World: How Technology is Transforming our Imagination*, New York: Ballantine Publishing Group

Peter, JP and Olson, S (1994) *Understanding Consumer Behaviour*, Burr Ridge, IL: Irwin

Peters, AAG (1986) 'Main currents in criminal law theory' in Van Dijk, JPM, Haffmans, C, Ruter, F, Schutte, S and Stolwijk, S (eds), *Criminal Law in Action: An Overview of Current Issues in Western Societies*, Arnhem: Kluwer

Pfohl, S (1985) *Images of Deviance and Social Control*, New York: McGraw-Hill

Pickvance, CG (1976) *Urban Sociology: Critical Essays*, London: Tavistock

Pierce, GL, Spaar, S and Brigg, LR (1986) *The Character of Police Work: Strategic and Tactical Implications*, Boston, MA: Centre for Applied Social Research, Northeastern University

Pike, B (1981) *The Image of the City in Modern Literature*, Princeton, NJ: Princeton University Press

Piliavin, I and Briar, S (1964) 'Police encounters with juveniles' *American Journal of Sociology* 70: 206–14

Piore, MJ and Sabel, CF (1984) *The Second Industrial Divide: Possibilities for Prosperity*, New York: Basic Books

Pizey, N (2001) 'Games review' *Evening Standard Hot Tickets*, 9–15 November

Platt, A (1995) 'Crime rave: law and order demagoguery' *Monthly Review: An Independent Socialist Magazine* 47, January: 35 (also available at *Radical Urban Theory Web Journal* (www.rut.com))

Platt, J (1994) 'The Chicago School and first hand data' *History of Human Sciences* 7: 57–80

Pollock, G (1988) *Vision and Difference: Femininity, Feminism and the Histories of Art*, London: Routledge

Porter-Benson, S (1986) *Counter Cultures: Saleswomen, Managers and Customers in American Department Stores 1890–1940*, Urbana, IL: University of Illinois Press

Poster, M (1988) *Jean Baudrillard: Selected Writings*, Cambridge: Polity

Presdee, M (1985) 'Agony or ecstasy' University of South Australia Occasional Papers 1

Presdee, M (1994) 'Young people, culture and the construction of crime' in Barak, G (ed), *Varieties of Criminology: Readings From a Dynamic Discipline*, Westport, CT: Praeger

Presdee, M (2000) *Cultural Criminology and the Carnival of Crime*, London: Routledge

Pulkkinen, L (1986) 'The role of impulse control in the development of antisocial and prosocial behaviour' in Olweus, D, Block, J and Radke-Yarrow, M (eds), *Development of Antisocial and Prosocial Behaviour: Research, Theories and Issues*, San Diego, CA: Academic Press

Quételet, L-A-J (1831) 'Recherches sur la penchant au crime aux differents ages' Brussels: Royal Belgian Academy of Sciences

Raban, J (1974) *Soft City*, London: Hamilton

Rabinbach, A (1992) *The Human Motor: Energy, Fatigue and the Origins of Modernity*, Berkeley, CA: University of California Press

Radzinowicz, L (1966) *Ideology and Crime: A Study of Crime in its Social and Historical Context*, London: Heinemann Educational Books

Radzinowicz, L and Hood, R (1990) *The Emergence of Penal Policy in Victorian and Edwardian England*, Oxford: Oxford University Press

Ramsey, M (1990) *'Lagerland Lost': An Experience in Keeping Drinkers Off the Streets in Central Coventry and Elsewhere: Crime Prevention Unit Paper 22*, London: HMSO

Rawson, RW (1839) 'An inquiry into the statistics of crime in England and Wales' *Journal Statistical Society of London* 2: 316–44

Redhead, S (1993) *Rave Off: Politics and Deviance in Contemporary Youth Culture*, Aldershot: Avebury

Redhead, S (1997) *Subcultures to Club Cultures: An Introduction to Popular Cultural Studies*, London: Blackwell

Redhead, S (1998) *The Club Cultures Reader: Readings in Popular Cultural Studies*, Oxford: Blackwell

Reiff, D (1993) *Los Angeles: Capital of the Third World*, London: Phoenix

Reinarman, C and Levine, HG (1989) 'Crack in context: politics and media in the making of a drug scare' *Contemporary Drug Problems*, Winter

Reiner, R (1978) 'The Police, class and politics' *Marxism Today* 22: 69–80

Reis, AJ (1986) 'Why are communities important in understanding crime?' in Reis, AJ and Tonry, M (eds), *Community and Crime*, Chicago, IL: Chicago University Press

Relph, E (1991) 'Post-modern geography' *The Canadian Geographer* 35(1): 98–105

Rendell, J (1998) 'Displaying sexuality: gendered identities and the early nineteenth-century street' in Fyfe, NR (ed), *Images of the Street: Planning, Identity and Control in Public Space*, London: Routledge

Rengert, G and Wasilchick, J (1985) *Suburban Burglary: A Time and Place for Everything*, Springfield, IL: CC Thomas

Reppetto, TA (1976) 'Crime prevention and the displacement phenomenon' *Crime and Delinquency* 22: 166–77

Rex, J and Moore, R (1967) *Race, Community and Conflict*, Oxford: Oxford University Press

Richards, B (1994) *Disciplines of Delight: The Psychoanalysis of Popular Culture*, London: Free Association Press

Richards, B, McDury, I and Botterill, J (2000) *The Dynamics of Advertising*, London: Routledge

Richards, T (1991) *The Commodity Culture of Victorian England: Advertising and Spectacle, 1851–1914*, London: Verso

Rigakos, GS (1999) 'On securing risk markets: police as commodity in late capitalism', Paper presented at The British Society of Criminology Conference, Liverpool

Riley, T (1992) *The International Style: Exhibition 15 and The Museum of Modern Art*, New York: Rizzloi/Columbia Books of Architecture

Ritson, M (2000) 'Consumer proactivity' in Pavitt, J (ed), *Brand.New*, London: V&A Publications

Ritzer, G (1995) *Expressing America: A Critique of the Global Credit Society*, Thousand Oaks, CA: Pine Forge

Robben, HS and Groenland, EAG (1993) 'Editorial: the future of economic pyschology' *Journal of Economic Psychology* 14(3): 455–60

Roberts, R (1971) *The Classic Slum*, Manchester: Manchester University Press

Roberts, JL (2002) 'The rap of luxury' *Newsweek*, 7 October

Robins, D (1984) *We Hate Humans*, Harmondsworth: Penguin

Robins, K (1991) 'Prisoners of the city: whatever could a postmodern city be?' *New Formations*, Winter, No 15: 1–22

Robins, LN (1978) 'Sturdy predictors of adult antisocial behaviour: replications from longitudinal studies' *Psychological Medicine* 8: 611–22

Robinson, SM (1936) *Can Delinquency Be Measured?* New York: Columbia University Press

Robriquet, F (1990 [1841]) *Crimes commis dans la Corse*, Paris

Rohrlich, T (1999) 'Seer of LA or blinded by its light' *Los Angeles Times*, 13 April

Rojek, C (1993) *Ways of Escape: Modern Transformations in Leisure and Travel*, London: Macmillan

Roneck, DW and Bell, B (1981) 'Bars, blocks and crime' *Journal of Environmental Systems* 11: 35–47

Roneck, DW and Meir, PA (1991) 'Bars, blocks and crime revisited: linking the theory of routine activities to the empiricism of "hot spots"' *Criminology* 29: 725–55

Rook, DW (1985) 'Modern hex signs and symbols of security' in Umiker-Sebok, J (ed), *Marketing and Semiotics: New Directions in the Study of Signs for Sale*, Berlin: Mouton de Gruyter

Rose, G (1991) 'Review of *Postmodern Geographies* and *The Condition of Postmodernity*' *Journal of Historical Geography* 17(1): 118–21

Rose, G (1993) *Feminism and Geography*, Oxford: Polity

Rose, N and Miller, P (1992) 'Political power beyond the state: problematics of government' *British Journal of Sociology* 43: 173–205

Rosenau, PM (1992) *Postmodernism and the Social Sciences: Insights, Inroads, Intrusions*, Princeton, NJ: Princeton University Press

Roshier, B (1989) *Controlling Crime*, Milton Keynes: Open University Press

Royal Institute of Chartered Surveyors (2002) Press Release, 'The great divide: "Crime Complex" has Britain's youth on the run to "Gated Communities"' (www.rics.org)

Ruane, JW (1998) 'Whose space is it anyway', Paper presented at the 93rd Meeting of The American Sociological Association, San Francisco

Rucker, D (1969) *The Chicago Pragmatists*, Minneapolis, MN: University of Minnesota Press

Ruggiero, V (2000) *Movements in the City: Conflict in the European Metropolis*, Upper Saddle River, NJ: Prentice Hall

Salecl, R (1993) 'Crime as a mode of subjectivism: Lacan and the Law' *Law and Critique* 4(2): 3–20

Samenow, SE (1984) *Inside the Criminal Mind*, New York: Times Books

Sampson, P (1994) 'Postmodernity' in Sampson, P, Samuel, V and Sugden, C (eds), *Faith and Modernity*, Oxford: Penguin

Sarup, M (1992) *Jacques Lacan*, London: Wheatsheaf

Sassen, S (1991) *The Global City: New York, London, Tokyo*, Princeton, NJ: Princeton University Press

Sassen, S (1994) *Cities in a World Economy*, Thousand Oaks, CA: Sage

Sasson, T (1995) *Crime Talk: How Citizens Construct a Social Problem*, New York: Alidine de Gruyter

Sato, I (1991) *Kamikaze Biker: Parody and Anomy in Affluent Japan*, Chicago, IL: Chicago University Press

Savage, M, Barlow, J, Dickens, P and Fielding, T (1992) *Property, Bureaucracy and Culture: Middle Class Formation in Contemporary Britain*, London: Routledge

Schatz, A (1997) 'The American earthquake: Mike Davis and the politics of disaster' *Lingua Franca Magazine*, September

Scheerer, S and Hess, H (1997) 'Social control: a defence and reformulation' in Bergalli, R and Sumner, C (eds), *Social Control and Political Order: European Perspectives at the End of the Twentieth Century*, London: Sage

Schor, J (1992) *The Over-Worked American: The Unexpected Decline of Leisure*, New York: HarperCollins

Schutz, A (1967) *The Phenomenology of the Social World* (trans Walsh, G and Lehnert, F), Evanston/Chicago, IL: Northwestern University Press

Schwartz, MD and Friedrichs, DO (1994) 'Postmodern thought and criminological discontent: new metaphors for understanding violence' *Criminology* 32: 221–46

Schwendinger, H and Schwendinger, JR (1974) *The Sociologists of the Chair: A Radical Analysis of the Formative Years of North American Sociology*, New York: Basic Books

Scott, AJ (1988) *Metropolis: From the Division of Labour to the Urban Form*, Berkeley, CA: University of California Press

Scott, AJ (1997) 'The cultural economy of cities' *The International Journal of Urban and Regional Research* 21(2): 323–39

Scott, AJ and Soja, E (1996) *The City: Los Angeles and Urban Theory at the End of the Twentieth Century*, Berkeley, CA: University of California Press

Scraton, P (1985) *The State of the Police*, London: Pluto

Seidman, S and Wagner, D (1992) *Postmodernism and Social Theory*, Oxford: Blackwell

Sennett, R (1971) *The Uses of Disorder: Personal Identity and City Life*, Harmondsworth: Penguin

Sennett, R (1991) *The Conscience of the Eye: The Design and Social Life of Cities*, New York: Alfred A Knopf

Shaikh, T (2002) 'Say "cheesed off!": half a million picture-messaging phones are expected to sell this festive season' *The Sunday Telegraph*, 15 December

Shapiro, D (1965) *Neurotic Styles*, New York: Basic Books

Shapiro, D (1973) *Social Realism: Art as a Weapon*, New York: Frederick Ungar Publishing Co

Shapiro, T (1984) 'The metropolis in the visual arts: Paris, Berlin, New York, 1890–1940' in Sutcliffe, A (ed), *Metropolis 1890–1940*, London: Mansell

Shaw, CR (1930) *The Jackroller: A Delinquent Boy's Own Story*, Chicago, IL: University of Chicago Press

Shaw, CR and McKay, HD (1932) *Social Factors in Juvenile Delinquency*, Washington DC: Government Printing Office

Shaw, CR and McKay, HD (1942) *Juvenile Delinquency and Urban Areas*, Chicago, IL: University of Chicago Press

Shaw, CR, Zorbaugh, FM, McKay, HD and Cottrell, LS (1929) *Delinquency Areas: A Study of the Geographic Distribution of School Truants, Juvenile Delinquents, and Adult Offenders in Chicago*, Chicago, IL: University of Chicago Press

Shearing, CD and Stenning, PC (1981) 'Private security: its growth and implications' in Tonry, M and Morris, N (eds), *Crime and Justice: An Annual Review of Research Volume 3*, Chicago, IL: Chicago University Press

Shearing, CD and Stenning, PC (1983) 'Private security: implications for social control' *Social Problems* 30(5): 493

Shearing, CD and Stenning, PC (1985) 'From the panopticon to Disneyworld: the development of discipline' in Doob, A and Greenspan, E (eds), *Perspectives in Criminal Law*, Aurora, Ontario: Canada Law Books Inc

Sherman, LW, Gartin, PR and Buerger, ME (1989) 'Hot spots of predatory crime: routine activities and the criminology of place' *Criminology* 27: 27–55

Shields, R (1989) 'Social spatialization and the built environment: the West Edmonton Mall' *Environment and Planning D: Society and Space* 17: 147–64

Shields, R (1991) *Places on the Margin: Alternative Geographies of Modernity*, London: Routledge

Shields, R (ed) (1992) *Lifestyle Shopping: The Subject of Consumption*, London: Routledge

Short, JR (1996) *The Urban Order: An Introduction to Cities, Culture and Power*, Cambridge, MA: Blackwell

Sibley, D (1995) *The Geographies of Exclusion*, London: Routledge

Simmel, G (1978 [1900]) *The Philosophy of Money*, London: Routledge and Kegan Paul

Simmel, G (1995 [1903]) 'The metropolis and mental life' in Kasinitz, P (ed), *Metropolis: Centre and Symbol of Our Times*, London: Macmillan Press

Simon, HA (1983) *Reason in Human Affairs*, Stanford, CA: Stanford University Press

Simon, J (1987) 'The emergence of a risk society: insurance, law and the state' *Socialist Review* 17: 60–89

Simon, J (1988) 'The ideological effects of actuarial practices' *Law Society Review* 22: 771–800

Singletary, M and Crenshaw, AB (1996) 'Credit card flood leaves sea of debt: personal bankruptcies rising as issuers ease restrictions' *Washington Post*, 24 November

Skocpol, T and Somers, M (1980) 'The uses of comparative history in macrosocial inquiry' *Comparative Studies in Society and History* 2: 174–97

Slater, D (1997) *Consumer Culture and Modernity*, Cambridge: Polity

Smith, D (1988) *The Chicago School: A Liberal Critique of Capitalism*, New York: St Martin's Press

Smith, MP (1980) *The City and Social Theory*, Oxford: Blackwell

Smith, N (1987) 'Of yuppies and housing: gentrification, social restructuring, and the urban dream' *Environment and Planning D: Society and Space* 5: 151–72

Smith, N (1992) 'New city, new frontier: the Lower East as wild, wild, west' in Sorkin, M (ed), *Variations on a Theme Park*, New York: Hill and Wong

Smith, N (1996) *The New Urban Frontier: Gentrification and the Revanchist City*, London: Routledge

Soja, EW (1989) *Postmodern Geographies: The Reassertion of Space in Critical Social Theory*, London: Verso

Soja, EW (1995) 'Postmodern urbanization: the six restructurings of Los Angeles' in Watson, S and Gibson, K (eds), *Postmodern Cities and Spaces*, Oxford: Blackwell

Sorkin, M (ed) (1992a) *Variations of a Theme Park*, New York: Noonday Press

Sorkin, M (1992b) 'Introduction' in Sorkin, M (ed), *Variations on a Theme Park*, New York: Noonday Press

South, N (1994) 'Privatising policing in the European market: some issues for theory and policy research' *European Sociological Review* 10: 219–27

South, SJ and Crowder, K (1997) 'Escaping distressed neighborhoods: individual, community and metropolitan influences' *American Journal of Sociology* 102: 1040–84

Sparks, RF, Genn, HG and Dodd, DJ (1977) *Surveying Victims*, Chichester: Wiley

Spiers, J (1995) 'Watch out! A debt bomb is ticking' *Fortune*, 27 November: 55–62

Spiller, N (1993) 'There's no there here, either' *Mother Jones*, Jan–Feb

Spitzer, S (1987) 'Security and control in capitalist societies: the fetishism of security and the secret thereof' in Lowman, J, Menzies, RJ and Palys, TS (eds), *Transcarceration: Essays in the Sociology of Social Control*, Aldershot: Gower

Stanko, E (1997) 'Conceptualizing women's risk assessment as a "technology of the soul"' *Theoretical Criminology* 1(4): 479–99

Stanley, C (1990) 'Spaces and places of the limit: four strategies in the relationship between law and desire' *Economy and Society* 25: 36–63

Stanley, C (1996) *Urban Excess and the Law: Capital, Culture and Desire*, London: Cavendish Publishing

Stedman-Jones, GS (1971) *Outcast London*, Oxford: Oxford University Press

Stenger, N (1991) 'Mind is leaking rainbow' in Benedikt, M (ed), *Cyberspace: First Steps*, Cambridge, MA: MIT Press

Stephanson, A (1988) 'Regarding postmodernism: a conversation with Frederic Jameson' in Ross, A (ed), *Universal Abandon?: The Politics of Postmodernism*, Minneapolis, MN: University of Minnesota Press

Sterling, B (1994) 'The virtual city', speech at Rice University, Houston, TX, 2 March (www.rice.edu/projects/RDA/programs/VirtualCity/Sterling/Sterling_VirtualCity)

Stevick, P (1985) 'Literature' in Trachtenberg, S (ed), *The Postmodern Movement: A Handbook of Contemporary Innovation in the Arts*, Westport, CT: Greenwood Press

Stewart, J (1998) 'Peddling fear' *New Times Los Angeles On-Line Magazine*, 19–25 November

Stimpson, C, Dixler, E, Nelson, M and Yatrakis, K (eds) (1981) *Women and the American City*, Chicago, IL: University of Chicago Press

Storper, M (1994) 'The transition to flexible specialization in the US film industry: external economies, the division of labour and the crossing of industrial divides' in Amin, A (ed), *Post-Fordism: A Reader*, Oxford: Blackwell

Stouffer, SA (1949) *The American Soldier*, Princeton, NJ: Princeton University Press

Sudnow, D (1965) 'Normal crimes: sociological features of the penal code in a public defender office' *Social Problems* 12, Winter

Sumner, C (1990) *Censure, Politics and Criminal Justice*, Milton Keynes: Open University

Sumner, C (1994) *The Sociology of Deviance: An Obituary*, Buckingham: Open University Press

Sutcliffe, A (1984a) 'The metropolis in the cinema' in Sutcliffe, A (ed), *Metropolis 1890–1940*, London: Mansell

Sutcliffe, A (1984b) 'Metropolis 1890–1940' in Cherry, GE and Sutcliffe, A (eds), *Studies in History, Planning and the Environment*, London: Mansell

Sutherland, E (1942) *Principles of Criminology*, Philadelphia, PA: JB Lippincott

Swann, P (2000) *TV Dot Com: the Future of Interactive Television*, New York: TV Books

Taylor, I (1971) 'Social consciousness and soccer hooliganism' in Cohen, S (ed), *Images of Deviance*, Harmondsworth: Penguin

Taylor, I (1982) 'Against crime and for socialism' *Crime and Social Justice*, Winter: 14–15

Taylor, I (1993) 'Critical criminology and the free market: theoretical and practical issues in everyday social life and everyday crime', Paper presented at the British Society of Criminology Conference, University of Wales, Cardiff

Taylor, I (1995) 'Private homes and public others' *British Journal of Criminology* 35: 263–85

Taylor, I (1997) 'Crime, anxiety and locality' *Theoretical Criminology* 1(1): 53–76

Taylor, I (1999) *Crime in Context: a Critical Criminology of Market Societies*, Cambridge: Polity

Taylor, I, Evans, K and Fraser, P (1996) *A Tale of Two Cities: Global Change, Local Feeling and Everyday Life in the North of England: A Study in Manchester and Sheffield*, London: Routledge

Taylor, I, Walton, P and Young, J (1973) *New Criminology: For a Social Theory of Deviance*, London: Routledge and Kegan Paul

Taylor, I, Walton, P and Young, J (1975) *Critical Criminology*, London: Routledge and Kegan Paul

Taylor, P (2004) 'Hacktavism – resistance is fertile' in Sumner, C (ed), *The Blackwell Companion to Criminology*, Oxford: Blackwell

Tedeschi, J and Felson, RB (1993) 'Predatory and dispute-related violence: a social-interactionist approach' in Clarke, RVG and Felson, M (eds), *Routine Activity and Rational Choice: Advances in Criminological Theory*, New Brunswick, NJ: Transaction Books

Tedeschi, J and Felson, RB (1994) *Violence Aggression and Coercive Action*, Washington DC: American Psychological Association Books

Thomas, WI (1923) *The Unadjusted Girl: With Cases and Standpoint for Behaviour*, Chicago, IL: Chicago University Press

Thompson, CJ (1994) 'Unfulfilled promises: a post positivist inquiry into the idealized and experienced meanings of consumer technology' *Advances in Consumer Research* 21: 104–08

Thompson, EP (1967) 'Time, work-discipline and industrial capitalism' *Past and Present* 38: 51–68

Thompson, EP (1968) *The Making of the English Working Class*, Harmondsworth: Penguin

Thrasher, FM (1927) *The Gang: A Study of 1,313 Gangs in Chicago*, Chicago, IL: Chicago University Press

Thrift, N (1996) *Spatial Formations*, London: Sage

Timms, E and Kelly, D (1985) *Unreal City: Urban Experience in Modern European Literature and Art*, New York: St Martin's Press

Trasler, G (1986) 'Situational crime prevention and rational choice: a critique' in Heal, K and Laycock, G (eds), *Situational Crime Prevention: From Theory into Practice*, London: HMSO

Tunnell, KD (2004) *Pissing on Demand: Workplace Drug Testing and the Rise of the Detox Industry*, New York: New York University Press

Turner, JH (1988) 'The mixed legacy of the Chicago School' *Sociological Perspectives* 31: 325–38

Unikel, IP and Blanchard, EB (1973) 'Psychopathy, race and delay of gratification by adolescent delinquents' *Journal of Nervous and Mental Disease* 156: 57–60

Urban Geography (1996) *Special Issue: Public Space and the City* 17(2–3): 127–247

Urry, J (1991) 'Time and space in Giddens' social theory' in Bryant, C and Jarry, D (eds), *Giddens' Theory of Structuration*, London: Routledge

Usborne, D (1998) 'New York patents its skyline view' *The Independent*, 3 September

Utley, T (2002) 'Amateur drinkers are bad enough: now it's drug tests' *The Daily Telegraph*, 21 December

Vaaranen, H (2004) 'Notes from the field: sexuality and desire in male youth car culture' in Ferrell, J, Hayward, KJ, Morrison, W and Presdee, M (eds), *Cultural Criminology Unleashed*, London: GlassHouse Press (forthcoming)

Valier, C (2000) 'Looking daggers: a psychoanalytical reading of the scene of punishment' *Punishment and Society* 2(4): 379–94

Valier, C (2003) 'Foreigners, crime and changing mobilities' *British Journal of Criminology* 43(1): 1–21

Van Hoorebeeck, B (1997) 'Prospects of reconstructing aetiology' *Theoretical Criminology* 1(4): 501–18

Veblen, T (1925) *The Theory of the Leisure Class: An Economic Study of Institutions*, London: George Allen and Unwin

Venturi, R (1977) *Complexity and Contradiction in Architecture*, New York: Museum of Modern Art

Venturi, R, Scott Brown, D and Izenour, S (1972) *Learning From Las Vegas: The Forgotten Symbolism of Architectural Form*, Cambridge, MA: MIT Press

Viatte, G (1989) 'Commentary on the works' in *Edward Hopper: Catalogue Programme Musée Cantini*, Marseilles: Wellfleet Press

Vidal, J (2003) 'How lie of the land is belied by the bland' *The Guardian*, 21 June

Vigil, JD (1988) *Barrio Gangs: Street Life and Identity in Southern California*, Austin, TX: Texas University Press

Virilio, P (1986) *Speed and Politics*, New York: Semiotext(e)

Virilio, P (1991) *The Aesthetics of Disappearance*, New York: Semiotext(e)

Vold, GB, Bernard, TJ and Snipes, JB (2002) *Theoretical Criminology*, Oxford: Oxford University Press

Wachs, M (1996) 'The evolution of transportation policy in Los Angeles: images of past policies and future prospects' in Scott, AJ and Soja, E (eds), *The City: Los Angeles and Urban Theory at the End of the Twentieth Century*, Berkeley, CA: University of California Press

Wacquant, L (1996) 'The comparative structure and experience of urban exclusion: "race", class and space in Chicago and Paris' in McFate, K, Lawson, R and Wilson, WJ (eds), *Poverty, Inequality and the Future of Social Policy*, New York: Russell Sage Foundation

Wacquant, L (2001) 'Deadly symbiosis: when ghetto and prison meet and merge' *Punishment and Society* 3(1): 95–134

Waldie, DJ (1998) 'Pornography of despair' *Salon On Line Magazine* (www. salon.com)

Walker, M (1997) 'Behind the bars of Fortress Suburbia' *The Observer*, 6 July

Walklate, S (1997) 'Risk and criminal victimization' *British Journal of Criminology* 37(1): 35–45

Walkowitz, (1992) *City of Dreadful Delight: Narratives of Sexual Danger in Late Victorian London*, London: Virago

Ward, C (1989) *Steaming In: Journal of a Football Fan*, New York: Simon & Schuster

Warnock, M (1970) *Existentialism*, Oxford: Oxford University Press

Warren, S (1994) 'The Disneyfication of the metropolis: popular resistance in Seattle' *Journal of Urban Affairs* 16: 89–107

Warren, S (1996) 'Popular cultural practices in the "postmodern city"' *Urban Geography* 17: 545–67

Watson, S and Gibson, K (eds) (1995) *Postmodern Cities and Spaces*, Oxford: Blackwell

Webb, B (1996) 'Preventing plastic credit card fraud in the UK' *Security Journal* 7: 23–25

Weber, AF (1970 [1899]) 'The growth of cities in the nineteenth century: a study in statistics' in Cousins, AN and Nagpaul, H (eds), *Urban Man and Society: Reader in Urban Sociology*, New York: Alfred A Knopf

Weinstein, RS (1996) 'The first American city' in Scott, AJ and Soja, E (eds), *The City: Los Angeles and Urban Theory at the End of the Twentieth Century*, Berkeley, CA: University of California Press

Wekerle, G, Peterson, R and Morley, D (eds) (1980) *New Space for Women*, Boulder, CO: Westview Press

Wender, J (2001) 'The eye of the painter and the eye of the police: what criminology and law enforcement can learn from Manet', Paper presented at the Annual Conference of the American Society of Criminology, Atlanta

Westwater, B (1998) 'Research exposes Getty Fellow, McArthur recipient Mike Davis as purposefully misleading liar' *Coagula Art Journal On-Line* (www.coagula.com)

White, JL, Moffitt, TE, Avshalom, C, Bartusch, DJ, Needles, DJ and Stouthamer-Loever, TE (1994) 'Measuring impulsivity and examining its relationships to delinquency' *Journal of Abnormal Psychology* 13: 192–205

Whitford, F (1985) 'The city in painting' in Timms, E and Kelly, D (eds), *Unreal City*, New York: St Martin's Press

Whyte, W (1988) *City: Rediscovering the Centre*, New York: Doubleday

Widom, CS (1977) 'A methodology for studying non-institutional psychopaths' *Journal of Consulting and Clinical Psychology* 45: 674–83

Wiener, J (1999) 'LA Story: backlash of the boosters' *The Nation*, 4 February (www.the nation.com)

Wikstrom, P-O (1991) *Urban Crime, Criminals and Victims*, New York: Springer-Verlag

Wilde, A (1981) *Horizons of Assent: Modernism, Postmodernism and the Ironic Imagination*, Baltimore, MD: Johns Hopkins University Press

Williams, G (2000) 'The point of purchase' in Pavitt, J (ed), *Brand.New*, London: V&A Publications

Williams, J (1986) 'White riots: the English football fan abroad' in Tomlinson, A and Whannel, G (eds), *Off the Ball*, London: Pluto

Williams, LA and Burns, AC (1994) 'The halcyon days of youth: a phenomenological account of experiences and feelings accompanying spring break on the beach' *Advances in Consumer Research* 21: 98–103

Williams, R (1973) *The Country and the City*, London: Chatto & Windus

Williams, R (1974) *Television, Technology and Cultural Form*, London: Chatto & Windus

Williams, R (1981) *Culture*, Glasgow: Fontana

Williams, R (1982) *Dream Worlds: Mass Consumption in Late Nineteenth Century France*, Berkeley, CA: University of California Press

Williams, S (2001) *Emotion and Social Theory*, London: Sage

Williamson, C (2002) 'So now! So over!' *The London Evening Standard Magazine*, 25 January

Willis, P (1977) *Learning to Labour*, Aldershot: Gower

Willis, P (1990) *Common Culture*, Milton Keynes: Open University Press

Wilson, A (1991) *The Culture of Nature: North American Landscape from Disney to the Exxon Valdez*, Toronto: Between the Lines

Wilson, C (1966) *Introduction to the New Existentialism*, London: Hutchinson

Wilson, E (1996) 'The invisible flâneur' in Watson, S and Gibson, K (eds), *Postmodern Cities and Spaces*, Oxford: Blackwell

Wilson, E (2001) *The Contradictions of Culture: Cities, Culture, Women*, London: Sage

Wilson, JQ (1985) *Thinking About Crime*, New York: Vintage Books

Wilson, JQ and Herrnstein, R (1985) *Crime and Human Nature*, New York: Simon & Schuster

Wilson, JQ and Kelling, G (1982) 'Broken windows' *Atlantic Monthly*, 29–38

Wilson, S (1980) 'Vandalism and "defensible space" on London housing estates' in Clarke, RVG and Mayhew, P (eds), *Designing Out Crime*, London: HMSO

Wilson, WJ (1987) *The Truly Disadvantaged: The Inner City, the Underclass and Public Policy*, Chicago, IL: Chicago University Press

Wilson, WJ (ed) (1993) *The Ghetto Underclass: Social Science Perspectives*, Newbury Park, CA: Sage

Wilson, WJ (1996) *When Work Disappears: The World of the New Urban Poor*, New York: Vintage

Winchester, H and Costello, L (1995) 'Living on the street: social organization and gender relations of Australian street kids' *Environment and Planning D: Society and Space* 13: 329–48

Wirth, L (1995 [1938]) 'Urbanism as a way of life' in Kasinitz, P (ed), *Metropolis: Centre and Symbol of Our Times*, London: Macmillan Press

Wohl, AS (1977) *The Eternal Slum: Housing and Social Policy in Victorian England*, London: Edward Arnold

Wolff, J (1985) 'The invisible flâneuse: women and the literature of modernity' *Theory, Culture and Society* 2: 37–46

Wood, M (1998) 'Socio-economic status, delay of gratification and impulse buying' *Journal of Economic Psychology* 19: 295–320

Worpole, K and Greenhalgh, L (1996) *The Freedom of the City*, London: DEMOS

Wright, D and Rossi, P (1985) *The Armed Criminal in America*, Washington DC: United States Department of Justice

Wynne, D and O'Connor, J (1998) 'Consumption and the postmodern city' *Urban Studies* 35(5–6): 841–64

Yablonsky, L (1962) *The Violent Gang*, New York: Macmillan

Young, A (1996) *Imagining Crime*, London: Sage

Young, A and Rush, P (1994) 'The law of victimage in urbane realism: thinking through inscriptions of violence' in Nelken, D (ed), *The Futures of Criminology*, London: Sage

Young, J (1971) *The Drugtakers*, London: Paladin

Young, J (1987) 'The tasks facing a realist criminology' *Contemporary Crises* 11: 337–56

Young, J (1988) 'Radical criminology in Britain: the emergence of a competing paradigm' *British Journal of Criminology* 28: 159–83

Young, J (1989) *Criminology: A Realistic Critique*, London: Sage

Young, J (1994) 'Incessant chatter: recent paradigms in criminology' in Maguire, M, Morgan, R and Reiner, R (eds), *The Oxford Handbook of Criminology*, Oxford: Oxford University Press

Young, J (1999) *The Exclusive Society*, London: Sage

Young, J (2003) 'Merton with energy, Katz with structure: the sociology of vindictiveness and the criminology of transgression' *Theoretical Criminology* 7(3) 389–414

Young, J and Matthews, R (eds) (1992) *Rethinking Criminology: The Realist Debate*, London: Sage

Zafirovski, M (1999) 'What is really rational choice? Beyond the utilitarian conception of rationality' *Current Sociology* 47(1): 47–113

Zamichow, N (1999) 'Apocalyptic look at LA sparks literary fistfight: book supporters praise "Ecology of Fear" as brave, others condemn author's research and accuracy' *Los Angeles Times*, 6 January

Zey, M (ed), (1992) *Decision Making: Alternatives to Rational Choice Models*, Newbury Park, CA: Sage

Zimring, FE (1998) *American Youth Violence*, Oxford: Oxford University Press

Zimring, FE and Hawkins, GJ (1973) *Deterrence: The Legal Threat in Crime Control*, Chicago, IL: University of Chicago Press

Zizek, S (1999) *The Ticklish Subject: The Absent Centre of Political Ontology*, London, New York: Verso

Zorbaugh, HW (1929) *The Gold Coast and the Slum*, Chicago, IL: University of Chicago Press

Zukin, S (1988) 'The postmodern debate over urban form' *Theory, Culture and Society* 5: 431–36

Zukin, S (1991) *Landscapes of Power: From Detroit to Disneyworld*, Berkeley, CA: University of California Press

Zukin, S (1992) 'Postmodern urban landscapes: mapping culture and power' in Lash, S and Friedman, J (eds), *Modernity and Identity*, Oxford: Blackwell

Zukin, S (1995) *The Cultures of Cities*, Cambridge, MA: Blackwell Press

Zukin, S (1998) 'Urban lifestyles: diversity and standardisation in spaces of consumption' *Urban Studies* 35(5–6): 825–39

Index

Abatement districts,
Los Angeles and 120, 127, 139

Administrative criminology
crime prevention 140, 185–87
environmentalism 101, 104
exclusion 137, 140
offenders 109
situational crime prevention 140

Advertising
children 197
consumerism 5, 28
crime 171–72
emotions 11
lifestyle 175, 197
newspapers 28
transgression 171–72

Aesthetics
architecture .79–81
consumerism 5
crime 169–70
diversity, of .79, 81
inclusion, of 80
Vegas aesthetic 190
young people 169–70

Alcohol 103

Alienation, art and 37

Anderson, Nels 97

Anti-social behaviour,
impulsivity and 177

Appollinaire, Guillaume 18

Arcades in Paris 26–27, 45

Architecture
aesthetics 79–81
art, as 79
chance interaction 44
Chicago School .42
city centres, demolishing 44
collage city 79
communication, as 39
*Congrès Internationaux
d'Architecture Moderne* 45
construction techniques 42
consumerism 80, 83
density of cities .44
design 39–40, 44–45, 79,
81, 101
diversity, aesthetics of 79, 81
functionalism 45
Garden Cities 41–42
high-rise mass estates 44
inclusion, aesthetics of 80
International School 43, 79

Los Angeles,
Bonaventure Hotel. 63–64
modernity 39–45, 63, 78
Paris 40
people, of the 80
planning 39–45, 82
Pop Art 80
popular culture .80
postmodernism 78–85
Pruitt-Igoe housing blocks,
demolition of. 78–79
rational building 45, 79
recreation 81–82
regeneration .81–82
rejection, postmodernism as 78–79
skyscrapers .42, 44
social control 83–84
social utopianism 43
space .81–84, 101
street, killing the 44
tower blocks 44, 78–79
ultra modernity .43
United States 42–43, 79
urban entertainment
developments 83
urban experience 39–45
urban modelling 40
urban utopia, building an 39–45
urbanoid environment 83–84
Vegas aesthetic 190

Artists and art
abstract 37
accessibility 69
alienation 37
architecture 79
Berlin 36–37
brandalism 69
celebrity artists .69
Chicago School .36
cities 35–39
consumer culture 69
culture, contemporary 69
dehumanisation .37
Expressionist art 36–38
Germany,
Expressionist art in 36–37
graffiti 150
immediacy 68
Impressionists 35
minimalism 68
modernity 35–39, 65, 67–69
new 67–68
Paris 37
Pop Art 80
repetition/reappropriation 68–69
resistance 38–39
street 35–39

United States 36, 38
urban experience 35–39
Western art 35–36

Assembly lines 51

Average man
(*l'homme moyen*) 91–92, 103–04

Banality of everyday life 149, 152, 175

Baudelaire, Charles 20, 30, 34, 35,
40, 44

Baudrillard, Jean 6, 70–71, 74,
80, 175

Bauman, Zygmunt 3–4, 10, 59–60,
75–78, 83, 85, 131,
137–38, 141, 153,
174–76, 181

Beck, Ulrich 76, 163, 187

Beirne, Piers 89–90, 92

Benjamin, Walter 25–28, 30, 34, 38–39,
45, 49, 63–64

Benson, Richard 172

Berlin, art and .36–37

Biologism 90

Birmingham School 8–9

Blakely, Edward J 132–33

Board games,
transgression and 172–73

Bonger, Willem 162

Booth, Charles 24

***Boso* driving**
culture, Japan 165–66, 183–84

Bourdieu, Pierre 133–34

Brandalism 69, 171–72

Brands 49, 52, 69, 170–72,
181–82

Broadacre City model 42–43

Budget of crime 88–89, 92, 104

Burgess, Ernest 93–95, 119, 121

Butler, Octavia 119

Campbell, Colin 5, 72, 75, 174

Canada .49, 83, 129–30

Capetown 49

Capitalism
brand consciousness 52
changes 52–54
cocaine 118
commodification 3, 71

consumerism 3, 71
demand management
strategies 52–53
Fordism/post-Fordism 51
Internet 54
labour market disputes 52–53
Los Angeles 114, 118, 122
modernity 47
postmodernism 50–51, 58
regulation school 52
space 54, 62–64, 180
time-space 54, 62–64
urban experience 21–22, 39

Carlen, Pat 105–06

Castells, Manuel 14, 75

CCTV 99, 120, 131, 137,
186–87

de Certeau, Michel 2, 5, 6–7, 13–14, 20,
40, 61, 96–97, 137,
139, 141–43

Chan, Wendy 164

Chapman brothers .69

Chicago and the Chicago School 121
appreciative tradition 95–97
architecture 42
art 36
concept city .96–97
crime and deviance,
causes of .95, 96–97
criminology .93–98
development of 93
deviance 95, 96–97
diversity 94
ecological modelling 94–95
environment, crime and 93, 95
ethnic groups 93
offenders' lives .101
overcrowding 94
poverty 94
skyscrapers 94, 96
statistics 95
street life 95, 96–97
transition, zones in 94–95
zones 94–95

Cities
See also individual cities
(eg, Los Angeles)
art 35–39
Broadacre City model 42–43
concept city 96–97, 137
criminology .87–88
duality, city as a 2, 14
postmodernity 49
private cities, development of 135–36
secessionary 136
simulation, as
places of hyperreal 84
super-organism, as 97–98

Citizenship 107–08

Clarke, David 17, 28

Class 1
  consumerism 6, 8, 71, 73–74,
             133–34
  industrial centres 142–43
  Los Angeles................113–17, 120,
            124, 127
  Paris 40
  risk 164–65
  space 143
  underclass 180–81, 183, 197

Classical strain theory 158, 161

Club/dance culture 191–93

Cohen, Albert 182

Cohen, Stan 105, 188

Collage city 79

Collings, Matthew 68

Commercialisation of the self 30

Commodification
  capitalism 3, 71
  consumerism.....................3, 71
  gated communities 134–36
  security.........................129–31
  transgression, of 166–73

Computer arcades 193

Computer games 183–94

Concept city 96–97, 137

Constitutive criminology 155–56

Consumerism 2–3, 197
  advertising 5, 28
  aesthetics 5
  architecture 80, 83
  art 69
  benefits of 5–6, 73–74
  brands 181–82
  capitalist commodification 3, 71
  change 50, 60
  class 6, 8, 71, 73–74,
            133–34, 181
  commercial world, speed of 73
  commercialisation of the self 30
  consumption 3, 162
  contradictions of 50
  crime and 157–79
  culture 8, 57
  deprivation 160
  desire 128, 158–59, 161,
         173–75, 197–98
  duality 2, 6–7
  economics 57, 74–75
  emotions 11, 14–15, 157, 179, 181
  excitement 72–73, 77–78, 85
  exclusion from 7, 74–75
  fear 128

flâneurs 27–28
freedom resulting from 71
gated communities 134
governance 76
growth of 3
identity 4–5, 7, 70–73, 160,
         181–82
individuality 6, 71–72, 76
liberation, as 5–6
literature on 2–3
Los Angeles 128, 131–32
manipulative strategies 71
Marxism 3–4
mass urban consumption 27–30
modernity 50, 67–78,
         158–62
negative role of 6–7
neophiliacs 174
new left realism 158–59
newspapers 28
oppositional culture 3
personal style 71–72
pleasure 72–73
polarisation 75
postmodernism 5–6, 33, 49–61
prioritising 50
production 59–60
Protestant Romanticism 5
rational choice theory 178–79
right to consumer 161
security 131
segregation 75
self-expression,
  consumption as mode of 4–5
sensation-gatherers 174
social control 76, 85
social dynamics 2
social exclusion 7, 74–75
social expression 33, 71–72
social integration 74
social regulation 76
social strains, causing 7, 11
space 1, 10, 74–75
street crime 4–5
subjectivity 157–58, 174, 180, 198
transgression 169–70
underclass 181
United States,
  women's role in 29
urban experience 25–30, 70, 85–86
women, retail sector in 29
young persons 7–8, 169–70

Containment zones,
  Los Angeles and 139

Control
  See Social control

Le Corbusier 43–45, 79, 82

Creed, Martin 67, 68, 69

Crime
See also Crime prevention
administrative approach to 99, 101, 104
advertising 171–72
aesthetics 169–70
alcohol-related 103
budget of 88–89, 92, 104
causes of 95, 96–97
Chicago School 95, 96–97
consumerism 4–5, 157–79
context of 87
deviance, causes of 95, 96–97
ecologies of 88–93
economics of 102
education 89
environmentalism 88–93, 101
expressive 102–03
fear of 12, 14–15, 115, 116, 119, 132, 138, 145
Fordism/post-Fordism 52
hot spots 99–100
Los Angeles 14, 115, 116, 119, 125, 132, 145
mapping 110–11
mass media 170–71
mathematisation of 90
normal social fact, as 104
phenomenology of 147
rates, variation in crime 89
rational choice theory 102
re-branding 170
sale of 169–70
social control 167
space 87–100
statistics 88–91
street 4–5
structural theories of 150–51
stylised images of 169–71
urban experience 22
violent 102–03
young persons 149–50, 167–70
zero tolerance 117

Crime prevention
administrative criminology...............140, 185–87
CCTV 186–87
Chowdury's newsagents, Salford, Manchester...............186
deterrence 187
excitement 187
expressive crimes 186–87
opportunity blocking 185–86
rationality 186
situational crime prevention 99–102, 104, 140, 185–87

Crimewatch 173

Criminology
administrative 101, 104, 109, 140
biologism 90
Chicago School 93–98
city, view of the 87–88
classical strain theory 158, 161
constitutive 155–56
consumerism 57
cultural 8–10, 61, 147, 198
deprivation, relative 158
environmentalism 87–88
modernity 89–90
new left realism 14, 104–10
origins of 89–90
positivism 90–92, 101
rational choice theory 101–02
situational 103–04
social justice 198

Crowd 35

Csikszentmihalyi, Mihaly 183–85

Culture 85
See also Consumerism
architecture 80
art 69
club/dance 191–93
commercial world 73
consumption 162
control, of 163
deviance as part of mainstream 182
duality 2
economics 56
Fordism/post-Fordism 56
hip-hop 181–82
modernism 169
need 159–60
objective 31
oppositional 3
pastiche 64–65
popular 80
postmodernism 54–59, 169
poverty 159–60
subjective 31
youth 168–69

Currie, Elliott 162

Dance culture 191–93

Dando, murder of Jill 172–73

Davis, Mike 10, 14, 75, 84–85, 111, 113–32, 134–140, 144–45, 153

Delaunay, Robert 37

Demand management strategies 52–53

Department stores 27–28

Deprivation
consumerism 160
criminology 158

exclusion 159
identity 160–61
new left realism 158–59
poverty 159
relative 10, 158, 159–62
space 180–85

De-regulation **54**

Design
architecture 39–40, 44–45, 79,
81, 101
Garden City 41–42
Los Angeles .115–16
mass transit suburbs 41
planning 41
shopping malls 188
space 40
urban experience 21, 27, 30

Desire
consumerism 128, 158–59, 161,
173–75, 197–98
deregulation of .174
fear 15
immediate 175
insatiability of 173–77
instant gratification 176–79, 184
needs and 161
Paris 49
privatisation 174
psychopathic personalities 177
time 176–77

Deterrence **99, 187**

Deviance
average man 92
causes of 95, 96–97
Chicago School 95, 96–97
crime 95, 96–97
identity 165–66
mainstream culture,
as part of 182
rational choice theory 102
reality construction 165–66

Discipline **76–77, 138–40**

Disney Corporation **135–36**

Dittmar, Helga **160**

Diversity **79, 81, 91, 94**

Dix, Otto **37**

Douglas, Mary **1, 8**

Driving **165–66, 171, 183–84**

Drug use **117–18, 150**

Duality **2, 6–7, 14, 49**

Dublin, re-imagining **49**

Durkheim, Emile **34, 107**

Eck, John **185**

Ecologies of crime, early **88–93**

Ecological modelling **94–95**

Economics
conditions 153
consumerism 57, 74–75
crime, of 102
culture 56
Fordism/post-Fordism 54, 57, 74–75
Los Angeles .125–26
Marxism 56–57
modernity 51
night time economy 192
postmodernism .51
rational choice theory 102

Edgework **164–66, 183, 185**

Education, crime and **89**

Elevators and escalators **64**

Emin, Tracey **68–69**

Emotions
See also Fear
advertising 11
consumerism 11, 14–15, 179
desire 15, 161, 173–79, 184
downloading 11
excitement 72–73, 77–78, 85, 175–76
open space 14
pleasure 72–73, 187–95
rationality 179
sensation-gatherers 174
urban experience 31, 34

Emotions of crime **15, 148–50**
banality of everyday life 149, 152, 175
consumerism 157, 181
drug use 150
excitement of crime 149, 151–52,
155–56, 166–67,
180–81, 187
football hooliganism 150–51
graffiti artists 150
prioritising emotionality 152
risk-taking 163–65
self-transcendence 148, 152, 155, 157
sensation-gatherers 174–75
social disadvantage 151
tag crews 150
teenage crime 149–50, 163–64
vandalism 150
young persons 149–50, 163–64

Employment
Fordism/post-Fordism 53–54, 75
labour market 53–54
leisure, and division between 77
post-industrial development 53

Engels, Frederick **21–22, 93**

Entertainment
developments 83
stores 190–91

Environmentalism,
crime and .88–93, 101
  administrative criminology 101, 104
  Chicago School 93, 95
  criminology .87–88
  offenders 109
  situational crime prevention 101–02
  social environmentalism 90–91

Ethnography 22–24

Everyday life
  banality of 149, 152, 175
  criminalisation of 166–73

Excitement 15
  consumerism 72–73, 77–78, 85,
                         175–76
  crime prevention 149, 151–52,
                 155–56, 180–81, 187
  transgression 166–67
  young people 175–76

Exclusion
  administrative criminology 137, 140
  concept city 137
  consumerism 7, 74–75
  deprivation, relative 159
  inclusion 198
  Los Angeles 113–14, 116, 123
  Paris 49
  social control .138
  space 137–42
  underclass 181
  United States .197

Exclusive developments in UK 136–37

Existentialism .147–48

Experience
  See Urban experience

Expressionist art 36–38

Expressive crimes
  alcohol-related crime 103
  crime prevention 186–87
  meaning of 103
  rational choice theory 102–03

Exum, Lyn 103

Fear
  consumerism .128
  crime, of 12, 14–15, 115, 116,
                119, 132, 138, 145
  desire 15
  discipline 138
  Los Angeles 14, 115, 116, 119,
                     132, 145
  ontological insecurity 12, 15

Featherstone, Mike 5, 28, 74, 75,
                   126, 194

Felson, Marcus 103–04

Feminist writing .164

Fenwick, Mark 149–50

Ferrell, Jeff 198

Fine, Ben 57, 59

Flâneurs 20–21, 25, 27–28, 132

Fletcher, Joseph .89

Flow experience .183

Football hooliganism 150–51

Ford, Henry 51

Fordism/post-Fordism
  assembly lines .51
  capitalism 51
  consumption 51, 56–57, 59–60
  criminal justice system,
    democratic 52
  culture 56
  diversification .56
  economic changes 54, 57, 74–75
  employment 75
  flexible accumulation 53
  General Motors 56
  labour market 53–54
  postmodernity 51–56, 59–60
  production 51, 55–57
  trade unions 56
  welfare state 51–52

Foucault, Michel 138–40, 155, 188

France
  See Paris

Frankfurt 48

Frankfurt School 3

Friedman, David 122, 125

Frisby, David 32

Functionalism 45

Gambino, Ferruccio 55–56

Gangs 118, 120, 170

Gangster rap 170

Garden Cities .41–42

Garland, David 99–101, 104

Gartman, David 56, 60

Gated communities 134–36
  Disney Corporation 135–36
  exclusivity .133–34
  master-planned developments 135
  prestige 134–35
  private cities, development of 135
  secessionary cities 136
  security 132–35
  security zone communities 135
  segregation 134

status 133–35
  United Kingdom 133
  United States 132–35

Gateshead's MetroCentre 83

Gehry, Frank 79

Germany
  Berlin, art and 36–37
  Expressionist art 36–37

Ghettoisation 75

Ghettopoly 172–73

Gibson, William 119, 193

Giddens, Anthony 9–10, 12, 163, 184

Gilbert and George 68

Girling, Evi 109

Goldberger, Paul 83–84, 136

Governance 76–78

Graves, Michael 79

Great exhibitions 28

Grosz, George 37

Guerry, André-Michel 88–93, 101, 110

Gumbel, Andre 124

Hannigan, John 82–84, 191

Harries, Keith 110–11

Harvey, David 3–4, 34–35, 39,
                 50–61, 83, 153

Hedonism 191–95

Henry, Stuart 155–56

Herrnstein, Richard J 177–78

High-rise estates 44

Hill, Dilys 55

Hip-hop culture 181–82

Hirst, Damien 69

Hoch, Stephen J 179

Hollywood 84

Homme moyen 91–92, 103–04

Hong Kong 48

Hopper, Edward 38–39, 45, 67

Hot spots 99–100

Housing estates 41

Howard, Ebenezer 41–42

Hume, David 90–91

Hyperreal simulation,
  cities as places of 84

Identity
  consumerism 4–5, 7, 70–73, 160,
                 181–82
  deprivation of 160–61
  deviance 165–66
  material possessions 160
  modernity 70
  postmodernity 154
  self-actualisation 154–55, 184–85
  transition, subject in 154–55

Impressionists 35

Inclusion 80, 139, 198

Individuality 6, 12, 32–33,
                71–72, 76

Industrialisation 53, 142–43, 180–81

Instant gratification 176–79, 184

International School 43, 79

Internet
  capitalism 54
  Majestic computer game 193–94
  serial killer fan clubs 173

Jameson, Frederic 3–4, 26–27, 33, 34,
                56, 61, 63–67, 72,
                80, 153, 198–99

Jeanneret, Charles-Édouard
  (Le Corbusier) 43–45, 79, 82

Jervis, John 19, 39–40

Johnson, Philip 79

Joyriding 165–66, 171, 183–84

Katz, Jack 15, 103, 111, 148–57,
                180–81, 185,
                189, 198

Kelling, George 132

Kerr, Philip 120

Kippenberger, Martin 68

Kirchner, Ernst Ludwig 36–37

Kotkin, Joel 124, 125

Kurzweil, Ray 194

Labour market disputes 52–53

Lacan, Jacques 66, 161

Lasch, Christopher 4

Lea, John 57, 60, 74–75

Lees, Loretta 122

Lefebvre, Henri 18

Left realism
  See New left realism

Leisure and labour, division of 77

Lifestyle advertising 175, 197

Liminal zones 192

Llano del Rio 114

Logical positivism 90–91

London
  East 23
  great exhibitions .28
  housing estates, construction of 41
  London County Council 41
  overcrowding 41
  peripheral satellites 41
  poverty 23, 41
  suburbs 41

Los Angeles 113–45
  See also Los Angeles,
    Bonaventure Hotel
  abatement districts 120, 127, 139
  atypical nature of 126–27, 145
  Bantustans 75
  capitalism 114, 118, 122
  CCTV 120
  City of Quartz 113–19, 121–23,
                                  125, 128
  class 113–17, 120, 124, 127
  cocaine capitalism 118
  Committee of 25 .123
  consumer culture 128, 131–32
  containment zones 139
  crime
    fall in 125
    fear of 14, 115, 116, 119,
                              132, 145
  Davis, Mike 113–32, 134–40,
                                 144–45
  design 115–16
  downtown,
    redevelopment of 115–16, 123
  drugs, war on 117–18
  East 117–18
  economic downturn 126
  economic revival .125
  ecological threats to 119, 122
  Ecology of Fear 113, 119–27
  ecosystem 119
  edge cities 121
  exclusion 113–14, 116, 123
  fear of crime 14, 115, 116, 119,
                              132, 145
  fire 123–24
  freeway city, as 126
  gangs 118, 120
  gated communities 116, 132
  home security 120, 128
  juridical zones 120
  landscape of 126
  Llano del Rio 114
  MacArthur Park 120, 123
  mapping 119

Marxism 113
Operation HAMMER 117, 118
polarisation .114, 120
police 117–19, 127
poor, relocation of the 116
postmodernity 48, 126
privatisation of
  public space 113, 115, 128
public space 113–15, 128
race 118–19, 121
redevelopment of 115–16, 123
riots 114, 115
Santa Monica Boulevard 131–32
security 128–29
  home 120, 128
  industry, growth of
    the private 116–17
segregation .113, 115
simulation 84
social control districts 120–21
South Central 117–18
space
  consumer 131–32
  privatisation of public 113
  public 114–15, 128
suburbs 121
surveillance 119–20, 128–29
symbolic of new urban
  order, as 126–27, 145
violence 120
Westlake, fire in 123–24
zero tolerance 117

Los Angeles,
  Bonaventure Hotel 26, 82, 137
  architecture 63–64
  elevators and escalators 64
  entrances 63
  postmodernity 63–64
  public/private space 63–64
  space 63–64
  time and space 64

Lowenstein, George F 179

Lury, Celia 11

Lynch, Kevin 39

Lyng, Stephen 156, 164–66, 183, 185

Majestic computer game 193–94

Manchester 21, 142–43, 186

Mapping
  city space 61
  crime 110–11
  Los Angeles 119
  space 2

Market culture 3–4, 7
  See also Consumerism

Marxism
   Althusserian 56
   consumerism 3–4
   economic change 56–57
   Los Angeles 113
   new left realism 105
   postmodernity 61
   security 129

Mass transit suburbs 41

Massey, Doreen 59

Material possessions,
   identity and 160

Matza, David 90, 95–97

Mayhew, Henry 23–25, 93, 100

McKay, Henry 95, 108

McLeod 78–79

McRobbie, Angela 168, 191

Mead, Peter 197

Mearns, Andrew 22, 24

Mechanisation of modern life 30

Media 170–73
   See also Advertising

Meidner, Ludwig 36–37

Merton, Robert 11, 158–59, 161–62,
              181, 182

Miles, Stephen 49–50, 74

Miller, Daniel 59

Miller, Eleanor 164–65, 183

Milovanovic, Dragan 155–56

Modernity 47–50, 111
   architecture 39–45, 63, 78
   art 35–39, 65, 67–69
   capitalism, late 47
   change 47–48
   consumer expectations 158–62
   consumerism 50, 67–78,
              158–62
   criminology 89–90
   culture 169
   economics of 51
   expectations resulting from 11–12
   flâneurs, anonymity of 20
   identity 70
   individuality 12
   late 47–48, 158–64
   literature 65
   masculinity 59
   Paris 19–20, 40
   periodisation 63
   postmodernism 56, 58–59, 65, 111
   Romantics 77
   sociology of 30
   space 55, 63–64, 85,
              137–39

   surveillance 138–39
   time-space 63–64, 85
   transition, dilemma of 13, 111
   ultra 43
   uncertainty, culture of 13
   urban experience 17–19, 24–25,
              85–86

Monkkonen, Eric 125, 127

Moral panic 167–68

Morrison, Wayne 11–13, 48, 65, 67,
          70–72, 153, 158,
          161–62, 188

Moss, Eric Owen 79

Mugford, Stephen 156–57

Myazaki, Japan,
   Ocean Dome indoor beach in 83

Need 159–61

Neo-liberalism 77–78

Neophiliacs 174

Nevinson, CRW 37

New left realism
   consumerism 158–59
   criminology 14, 104–10
   criticism of 105–06
   deprivation, relative 158–59
   Marxism 105
   offenders 109–10
   social control 105
   United Kingdom 104–05
   victims and 104–09

New, shock of the 67–68

New York
   gentrified spaces in 49
   South Street Seaport 83, 136

Night time economy 192

Nightingale, Carl 181–82

Nowhereville, England 84–85

Offenders
   administrative criminology 109
   Chicago School 101
   environmentalism 109
   new left realism 109–10
   social disadvantage 150

O'Malley, Pat 76–78, 85, 156–57

Ontological insecurity 12, 15, 152–55,
          180, 197

Opportunity blocking 185–86

Opting in to faux communities 136

Orne, Richard 84

Oswestry 84–85

Overcrowding 41–42, 94

Papastergiadis, Nikos 139–41, 143

Paris
  arcades 26–27, 45
  architecture 40
  art 37
  class divisions 40
  department stores 28
  design 49
  flâneurs 20–21, 25, 27–28
    anonymity of. 20
    voyeurs, as. 20
  great exhibitions .28
  inequality in 40
  Haussmann, Georges 40
  homelessness 40
  modernity 19–20, 40
  overcrowding 41
  poverty 40, 41
  redevelopment of 27
  social exclusion .49
  street 19–20

Park, Robert 87, 93, 97–98

Phenomenology 8–9, 147, 156

Philadelphia 49

Planning
  anti-urban movement 42–43
  architecture 29–45, 82
  design 41
  deurbanism 42–43
  Garden City .41–42
  housing estates 41
  London, suburbs in 41
  mass transit suburbs 41
  overcrowding 41–42
  United States
    Broadacre City model 42–43
    railway suburbs 41

Pleasure .72–73, 187–95

Police 117–19, 127

Pop Art 80

Positivism 90–92, 101

Postindustrialisation 180–81

Postmodernity 47–61
  architecture 78–85
  capitalism .50–51, 58
  changes 50–51, 54–55, 60, 67
  consumerism 5–6, 33
  consumption .49–61
  criminology 8–9
  culture 8–9, 54–59, 169
  definition 48
  duality 49

economics of 51
flâneurs 132
flexible accumulation 53
Fordism/post-Fordism 51–56, 59–60
historicity, crisis in 64
identity 154
Los Angeles 48, 126
  Bonaventure Hotel. 63–64
Marxism 61
masculinity 59
modernity 56, 58–59, 65, 111
phenomenology .156
postmodern cities, idea of 49
present 64–65
production, restructuring of 53
rejection, as .78–79
schizophrenia 66
social control 155
space 63–66, 85, 144, 176
subject
  emergence of. 66–67
  transition, in 67, 70, 153–54, 184
superficiality 65
time-space 61, 65, 85, 176
urban experience 49, 54
youth culture 169

Poverty 1
Chicago School 94, 96
culture 159
degenerate poor 22
deprivation, relative 159
London 23, 41
Los Angeles 116
Manchester 21
need, culture and 159–60
Paris 40, 41
United Kingdom 159
United States 159
urban experience 21–24

Presdee, Mike 151, 155, 166–69, 174,
                   184, 189, 191, 193

Present
perpetual 66
postmodernity 64–65
time-space 64–65, 68, 85,
                       175–76

Privatisation 54
desire 174
public space 113, 115, 128
regulation 54

Probability, theory of 89

Production
assembly lines 51
consumerism 59–60
Fordism/post-Fordism 51, 55–57
mass 51, 56–57
restructuring of .53

Protestant Romanticism 5

Protestant work ethic 178

Pruitt-Igoe housing blocks,
    demolition of 78–79

Psychopathic personalities 177

Public services, demise of 54

Quételet, Adolphe de 88–93, 101,
                                103–04, 110

Raban, Jonathan 61

Race, Los Angeles and 118–19, 121

Railway suburbs 41

Rap and hip-hop culture 170, 181–82

Rational choice theory 101–04, 178

Rationality
    See also Rational choice theory
    building 45, 79
    crime prevention 186
    emotions 179

Rawson, Rawson W 89

Real crime shows 170–73

Realism
    See New left realism

Reality construction 165–66

Recreation, architecture and 81–82

Regeneration 81–82

Regulation 52, 54, 76, 136

Resistance 38–39, 143

Retail 28–29

Rewards, chaos of 197–98

Rigakos, George S 129–30, 164

Risk
    control 183–85
    driving 165–66, 183–84
    edgework 164–66
    emotions 163–65
    feminist writing 164
    flow experience 183
    gender, race and class 164–65
    governance 77–78
    management 76, 163–64
    ontological insecurity 180
    space 165, 183
    young persons 163–64

Roberts, Johnnie 181–82

Robins, Kevin 49, 190

Rogers, Heather 139

Romantics 5, 77

Rookeries 22–23

Ropongi, Tokyo 193

Rose, Gillian 59

Rousseau, Jean-Jacques 20

Rural areas, migration from 17–18

Sachs, Tom 69

Safe zones 10

Sampson, Philip 3

San Francisco,
    Fisherman's Wharf in 82

Sato, Ikuya 165–66, 183–85

Schizophrenia 66

Secessionary cities 136

Security
    CCTV 131
    commodification of 129–31
    consumer culture 131
    deister strips 129–30
    gated communities 132–35
    home 120, 128
    industry, growth in private 116–17
    Intelligarde 129–30
    Law Enforcement
        Company of Toronto 129–30
    Los Angeles 116–17, 120,
                                128–29
    Marxism 129
    ontological insecurity 12, 15, 152–55,
                                180, 197
    private firms 129–30
    retail products 130–31
    segregation 131–37
    shopping malls 188

Segregation
    consumerism 75
    gated communities 134
    Los Angeles 113, 115
    security 131–37

Self-actualisation 154–55, 184–85

Self-control 177–78

Self-expression,
    consumerism as 4–5

Self-transcendence 148, 152, 155, 157

Sensation-gatherers 174–75

Shaw, Clifford 95, 108

Sheffield 142–43

Shopping malls 188–89
    design 188
    security 188–89
    urban experience 26
    West Edmonton Mall, Canada 83
    young people 189

Sibley, David 75

Simmel, Georg 30–34, 44, 49, 55

Situational crime
 prevention 99–102, 104,
 185–87

Skyscrapers 42, 44, 94, 96

Snyder, Gail 132–33

Social conditions 21–24, 153

Social control
 architecture 83–84
 consumerism 76, 85
 criminalisation 167
 districts 120–21
 exclusion 138
 new left realism 105
 postmodernity 155
 rational choice theory 101–02
 space 138

Social disadvantage 150

Social expression 33, 71–72

Social Physics 88

Social theory, marginalisation of 14

Social utopianism 43

Soja, Ed 49, 126, 131

South Africa, Capetown 49

Space 8–9
 See also Time-space
 architecture 81–84, 101
 capitalism.....................54, 180
 centripetal 185–87
 class 143
 consumerism 1, 10, 74–75
 consumption 187–95
 crime 87–100
 criminogenic 10, 100, 140, 144
 deprivation 180–85
 design 40
 deterrence 99
 dynamics 141
 emotions 14
 exclusion 137–42
 experiential dimension
  of urban 2
 ghettoisation 75
 inclusion 139
 locality 142
 Los Angeles 113–15, 128,
 131–32
  Bonaventure Hotel..............63–64
 mapping 2, 61
 modernity 55, 137–39
 open 14
 parafunctional 139–40, 143
 physical environment 65
 pleasure 187–95

postmodernity 63–66, 144
 private cities in
  public space......................136
 privatisation of public 113, 115, 128
 public/private 26–29, 63–64
 regulated 136
 risk-taking 165, 183
 situational 100–02
 social control 138
 statistical analysis 100
 street 140–41
 time space 54, 61–66, 68, 85,
 175–76
 urban experience 26–29
 victims 108–09

Spitzer, Stephen 129

Starr, Kevin 124

Statistics 23–24, 88–91, 95,
 99–100, 102

Stella, Joseph 37

Sterling, Bruce 194

Stewart, Jill 122–23

Street
 architecture 44
 artists 35–39
 Chicago School 95, 96–97
 crime 4–5
 crowd 35
 interaction 44
 killing the 44
 life 95, 96–97
 Paris 19–20
 scenes 140–41
 space 140–41
 urban experience 19–20, 34–39

Structural theories of crime 150–51

Structuration theory 9–10

Suburbs
 London 41
 Los Angeles 121
 mass transit 41
 planning..........................41
 United States,
  railway suburbs in.................41

Super-organism, city as a 97–98

Surveillance
 CCTV 99, 120, 131, 137,
 186–87
 discipline 138–40
 Los Angeles 119–20, 128–29
 modernist space 138–39
 overtness of 139
 shopping malls 188–89

Sydney 48

Tag crews 150

Taylor, Frederick 51

Taylor, Ian 3, 142–43, 189

Television 170–73

Thornton, Sarah .168

Time-space
  capitalism 54, 62–64
  compression 54, 61
  desire 176–77
  frameworks 61–62
  Los Angeles,
    Bonaventure Hotel. 64
  modernity 63–64, 85
  postmodernity 61, 65, 85, 176
  present 64–66, 68, 85,
                                              175–76
  schizophrenia 66
  simultaneity 64, 66, 68
  technology 62

Tokyo 48

Tower blocks 44, 78–79

Town centre management
  schemes in UK .136

Townsend, Peter 159–60

Trade unions 56

Transgression
  advertising 171–72
  board games 172–73
  commodification of 166–73
  consumerism 169–70
  excitement of 166–67
  Ghettopoly 172–73
  instant gratification 177
  sensation-gathering 174–75
  video gaming .172

Transition
  Chicago School 94–95
  dilemmas of 13, 67, 111, 153–54
  identity 154–55
  modernity .13, 111
  postmodernity 67, 70, 153–54, 184
  subject, in 67, 70, 153–55, 184
  zones 94–95

Underclass
  consumerism 181
  edgework 183
  exclusion 181
  growth in 180–81
  postindustrialisation 180–81
  United States 181, 197

United Kingdom
  exclusive developments, in 136–37
  gated communities 133
  Gateshead's Metrocentre 83

London 23, 28, 41
  new left realism 104–05
  Nowhereville, England 84–85
  Manchester 21, 49, 142–43
  Oswestry 84–85
  poverty 159
  town centre
    management systems 159–60

United States
  See also Chicago and the
    Chicago School; Los Angeles
  architecture 42–43, 79
  art 36, 38
  Broadacre City model 42–43
  consumerism 29
  exclusion 197
  Hollywood 84
  immigration 1
  New York 49, 83, 136
  Philadelphia 49
  planning 42–43
  poverty 159
  railway suburbs .41
  underclass 181, 197
  women's role in 29

Universal City's CityWalk 85, 136

Unwin, Raymond 41

Urban entertainment
  developments 83

Urban experience 1, 11, 14
  architecture .39–45
  artists 35–39
  capitalism 21–22, 39
  changing nature of 19
  consumerism 25–30, 70, 85–86
  crime 22
  culture 31
  degenerate poor .22
  department stores 27–28
  design 21, 27, 30
  differentiation 32–34
  discontinuity 18
  effects 18
  emotions 31, 34
  ethnography 22–24
  flâneurs 20–21, 25, 27–28
  imagining the 17–45
  individuality 32–33
  junk food version of 85
  mechanisation of
    modern life 30
  metaphysical ambiguities 25–26
  modernity 17–19, 24–25,
                                              85–86
  order 33
  origin 18
  postmodernity 49, 54
  poverty 21–24
  psychic overload 31

public and private space,
blurring of 26–29
public space 28–29
rationalising city life 22–25
reading city life 22–25
recording city life 22–25
resistance 38–39
retail practices 28–29
rural areas, migration from 17–18
self-preservation .32
shopping malls 26
social conditions 21–24
social construction, product of 18
social relationships, reduction of 31
space
blurring of public
and private 26–29
inversion of 26–27
private 26–29
public 26–29
spatial ambiguities 25–26
state of mind, city as 30–33
statistical surveys 23–24
street 19–20, 34–39

Urban modelling 40

Urbanoid environment 83–84

Utopianism 39–45

Vancouver 49

Vandalism 150

Vegas aesthetic 190

Venturi, Robert .79–82

Victims
citizenship 107–08
community, notions of 107
expressive dimension
of victimisation 107
idealised 106
new left realism 104–09
rediscovery of the 106
space 108–09
surveys 108–09
types of 106

Vidal, John 84

Video gaming 172, 193–94

Violence .102–03, 120

Virilio, Paul 73

Virtual reality 194

Visual communication 110–11

Wacquant, Loic 75

Walkowitz, Abraham 37

Warren, Stacey 58

Wearing, Gillian .69

Weiner, Lawrence 69

Welfare state .51–52

Westwater, Bradley 123

Whyte, William 128

Williams, Raymond 3, 142

Williamson, Charlotte 73

Willis, Paul 8

Wilson, Elizabeth 24, 75

Wilson, James Q 132, 177–78

Wirth, Louis 17

Women .29, 164–65

Young, Alison .106–09

Young, Jock 1, 7, 10, 12, 14, 75,
137, 153, 159, 162,
182, 197–98

Young persons
advertising 197
aestheticisation and
stylisation of crime 169–70
authentic self 169
club/dance culture 191–93
consumerism 7–8, 169–70
crime 149–50, 167–68
culture 168–69
driving 165–66, 171, 183–84
emotions 149–50, 164–64
excitement 175–76
gangs 170
gangster rap 170
hedonism 191–95
hip-hop 181–82
postmodernity .169
risk 163–64
shopping malls 189

Zero tolerance 117

Zukin, Sharon 27, 81, 190–91